INSIGHT GUIDES
ENGLAND

APA PUBLICATIONS L

Part of the Langenscheidt Publishing Group

✳ INSIGHT GUIDE
ENGLAND

Editorial
Project Editor
Paula Soper
Art Director
Ian Spick
Picture Manager
Steven Lawrence
Series Manager
Rachel Fox

Distribution

UK & Ireland
GeoCenter International Ltd
Meridian House, Churchill Way West
Basingstoke, Hampshire RG21 6YR
sales@geocenter.co.uk

United States
Langenscheidt Publishers, Inc.
36–36 33rd Street 4th Floor
Long Island City, NY 11106
orders@langenscheidt.com

Australia
Universal Publishers
1 Waterloo Road
Macquarie Park, NSW 2113
sales@universalpublishers.com.au

New Zealand
Hema Maps New Zealand Ltd (HNZ)
Unit 2, 10 Cryers Road
East Tamaki, Auckland 2013
Tel: (64) 9 273 6459
sales.hema@clear.net.nz

Worldwide
Apa Publications GmbH & Co.
Verlag KG (Singapore branch)
38 Joo Koon Road, Singapore 628990
Tel: (65) 6865 1600. Fax: (65) 6861 6438

Printing

Insight Print Services (Pte) Ltd
38 Joo Koon Road, Singapore 628990
Tel: (65) 6865 1600
apasin@singnet.com.sg

CONTACTING THE EDITORS
We would appreciate it if readers
would alert us to errors or outdated information by writing to:
Insight Guides, P.O. Box 7910,
London SE1 1WE, England.
insight@apaguide.co.uk

www.insightguides.com

ABOUT THIS BOOK

The first Insight Guide pioneered the use of creative full-colour photography in travel guides in 1970. Since then, we have expanded our range to cater for our readers' need not only for reliable information about their chosen destination but also for a real understanding of the culture and workings of that destination.

Now, when the internet can supply inexhaustible facts (but not always reliable), our books marry text and pictures to provide those much more elusive qualities: knowledge and discernment.

To achieve this, they rely heavily on the authority of locally based writers and photographers.

A country with such a rich history and culture as England lends itself especially well to the approach taken by the award-winning Insight Guide series.

Insight Guide: England is carefully structured to convey an understanding of this ancient nation and its culture, as well as to guide readers through its sights and activities:

◆ The **Features** section, indicated by a pink bar at the top of each page, covers the history and culture of the country in a series of lively and informative essays.

◆ The main **Places** section, indicated by a blue bar, is a complete guide to all the sights and areas worth visiting. Places of special interest are coordinated by number with the cross-referenced maps.

◆ The **Travel Tips** listings section, with a yellow bar, provides full information on transport, hotels, restaurants, activities from culture to shopping to sports and a detailed list of outdoor activities, and an A–Z section of essential practical infor-

LEFT: poppies in a field, Wells-next-the-Sea, Norfolk.

graduate, Pam wrote the history chapters and compiled the essays on theatre and food.

Many writers brought their local knowledge to bear on the Places chapters; these contributors include: **Susie Boulton** in Cambridge, **Roland Collins** in Cornwall, **Christopher Catling** in the New Forest and the Cotswolds, **Michael Ivory** in Stratford, **W.R Mitchell** in the Lake District, **John Scott** and **Harry Mead** in Yorkshire, **Roly Smith** in Northumbria and the Peak District, **Andrew Eames** in Dorset, **Dorothy Stannard** in Bath, and **Tony Halliday** in Oxford.

Roger Williams contributed the essay on landscape painting. The feature on the English character was written by **Brian Bell**.

Such is the density of sites and attractions in England that each area of the country is worth a book in its own right. In the present guide we have concentrated on must-see sights and events, with a generous sprinkling of lesser known but rewarding destinations.

Much of the photography was taken by **Ming Tang Evans** (London), **Corrie Wingate** (East Anglia and the Thames Valley), **Steve Cutner** (South Coast), **Lydia Evans** (South and South West) and **William Shaw** (North). **Tom Smyth** picture researched the book. **Zoë Goodwin** was the book's cartography editor and was assisted by **Mike Adams**.

The index was compiled by **Helen Peters** and **Sue Pearson** proofread the text.

mation, and there are floor plans to England's top half-dozen sites. A Travel Tips index is on the back cover flap, which also serves as a handy bookmark.

The contributors

This fully updated edition was managed and edited by **Paula Soper** at Insight Guides' London office. The entire book was comprehensively updated by **Rebecca Ford**, an award-winning travel journalist who lives in London. She writes for various national newspapers and magazines, on everything from railway journeys to eco-travel. Rebecca has also added a new chapter, *Walking in England*.

The second edition builds on the earlier edition and retains much of the work of the original contributors including **Pam Barrett**, an experienced Insight Guide editor. A history

Map Legend

▬ ▬ ▬	International Boundary
▬ ▬ ▬ ▬	National Boundary
▬ ▬ ▬ ▬	County Boundary
▬ ● ▬	National Park
▬ ▬ ▬ ▬	Ferry Route
⊖	Underground
✈ ✈	Airport: International/ Regional
🚌	Bus Station
❶	Tourist Information
✝ ✝ ✝	Church/Ruins
✝	Monastery
∴	Archaeological Site
🏠	Mansion/Stately home
🏰	Castle/Ruins
☾	Mosque
✡	Synagogue
∩	Cave
⚊	Statue/Monument
★	Place of Interest

The main places of interest in the Places section are coordinated by number with a full-colour map (e.g. ❶), and a symbol at the top of every right-hand page tells you where to find the map.

Contents

LEFT: the 02 on the Greenwich Peninsula.

Maps

Travel Tips

THE BEST OF ENGLAND: TOP SIGHTS

From prehistoric sites to Gothic architecture, and sandy beaches to striking landscapes, here is a rundown of England's most spectacular attractions

△ **The Tower of London** is packed with history dating back to 1078 and housing the crown jewels. Queens were beheaded here, princes murdered and traitors tortured. Once a place to be avoided, it is now one of London's top visitor attractions. *See page 96*

△ **Cornish beaches** are where the surfers head for, especially to the north coast to ride Atlantic rollers. Towering cliffs and stretches of pristine sands bring walkers and holiday families, too. Some of the finest beaches in England are here. *See page 231*

◁ **Stratford-upon-Avon** is William Shakespeare's birthplace, situated on the river, and is a good base from which to explore the beautiful and historic Warwickshire countryside. *See page 151*

▽ **The Eden Project** is an award-winning eco-friendly extravaganza, incorporating huge geodesic biome domes. *See page 241*

△ **Stonehenge**, on Salisbury Plain, is England's most famous prehistoric monument. Stonehenge consists of an outer ring and inner horseshoe of sarsen stone brought from the Marlborough Downs. The mysterious circle's purpose is unknown, though the tumuli around the site hint at ancient funerary significance. Some scholars suggest a link with astronomy. *See page 213*

△ **Chatsworth House** is Britain's most impressive aristocratic estate. This vast Palladian mansion is set in a spacious deer park and landscaped gardens. *See page 275*

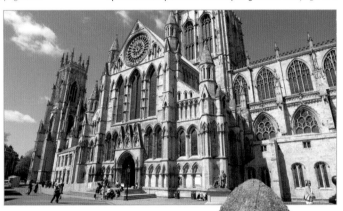

△ **York Minster** is one of the finest Gothic cathedrals in the world, with elaborate pinnacles, and a large collection of medieval stained glass. *See page 127*

△ **The Lake District** has the most striking landcape of deep lakes and steep-sided valleys. *See pages 295–305*

▷ **Oxford** has been one of Europe's most renowned places of learning since the 12th century. This fascinating city is steeped in history and culture. *See pages 127–34*

▽ **Durham Cathedral** is indisputably the finest Norman building in the country, dramatically perched above the River Wear. *See page 339*

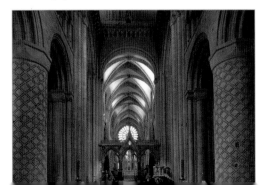

THE BEST OF ENGLAND: EDITOR'S CHOICE

Magnificent stately homes and palaces, inspiring gardens, top art galleries, unique attractions... here, at a glance, are our recommendations for making the most of your visit

THE TOP ROYAL HOMES

- **Windsor Castle**
The Queen's official residence, a day-trip from London. *See page 116.*
- **Buckingham Palace**
Her Majesty's London base, with Changing of the Guard. *See page 78.*
- **Hampton Court Palace, Surrey**
Henry VIII's magnificent Surrey palace has wonderful gardens. *See page 205.*
- **Kensington Palace**
Birthplace of Queen Victoria. *See page 104.*

- **Sandringham House**
Norfolk base for the royals at Christmas. *See page 169.*

ABOVE: tram rides on the cobbled street at Beamish.

THE FINEST STATELY HOMES

- **Alnwick Castle**
Home of the Dukes of Northumberland; Harry Potter flew around here in the movies. *See page 345.*
- **Apsley House**
"No 1, London" has been the London home of the Dukes of Wellington for 200 years. *See page 147.*

- **Blenheim Palace, Oxfordshire**
This vast, English baroque pile is the family home of the Dukes of Marlborough; Winston Churchill was born here in 1874. *See page 174.*
- **Castle Howard, Yorkshire**
One of England's grandest stately homes, with formal gardens and sandstone follies. *See page 42.*

ABOVE AND LEFT: a royal welcome from Henry VIII, and a falconry display, at Hampton Court Palace.

TOP ATTRACTIONS FOR FAMILIES

- **Alton Towers, Warwickshire**
Britain's best-known theme park has wild white-knuckle rides and other thrills. *See page 257.*
- **Beamish, County Durham**
This open-air museum in 300 acres tells the social history of the North-East, with tram rides, working farm and collier village. *See page 340.*
- **Ironbridge Gorge Museums, Telford**
Award-winning string of museums on the River Severn celebrating the "birthplace of industry". *See page 255.*
- **Jorvik Viking Centre, York**
Take an underground ride into the world of Vikings – complete with smells – in this innovative museum. *See page 315.*
- **Legoland, Windsor**
Rides, shows and multiple attractions. *See page 117.*
- **Longleat Safari Park**
The first safari park outside Africa in the grounds of a stately home. *See page 214.*
- **Maritime Museum, Greenwich**
Recalling when Britain ruled the waves. *See page 108.*
- **SS Great Britain, Bristol**
A brilliant re-enactment of life on the world's first iron-hulled ship with a screw propeller. *See page 231.*

ENTHRALLING MUSEUMS

ABOVE: appreciating fine art at the National Gallery.
LEFT: the Great Court of the British Museum.
BELOW exhibit from the National Motor Museum.

- **Merseyside Maritime Museum**
Slavery and emigration are the abiding themes in this evocative museum in Liverpool. See page 287.
- **National Media Museum, Bradford**
Covers the history of film, television and photography. See page 323.
- **National Motor Museum, Hampshire**
Beaulieu Abbey, home of the aristocratic Montagu family, puts veteran cars on show. See page 211.
- **National Railway Museum, York**
Explore over 300 years of railway history. See page 315.
- **Science Museum**
London's engrossing displays of inventions, with over 10,000 exhibits. See page 103.
- **Ashmolean, Oxford**
A peerless museum of art and archaeology collected by scholars from around the world. See page 132.
- **British Museum, London**
This world-class institution embraces the history of civilisation. See page 130.

THE BEST GARDENS

- **RHS Gardens, Wisley**
The Royal Horticultural Society's showcase with its stunning new glasshouse. See page 201.
- **Royal Botanic Gardens, Kew**
Fine day out from central London to legendary gardens first planted in 1759. See page 110.
- **Sissinghurst Castle, Kent**
Beautiful gardens designed by Vita Sackville-West. See page 185.
- **Tresco Abbey Gardens, Isles of Scilly**
Sub-tropical gardens set amid the 12th-century Priory of St Nicholas. See page 244.

THE TOP ART GALLERIES

- **Baltic Exchange, Gateshead**
The largest contemporary arts venue outside London. See page 342.
- **Barbara Hepworth, St Ives**
The sculptor's home in an attractive Cornish fishing village. See page 245.
- **Constable Country, Suffolk**
Follow the trail of Britain's great landscape painter. See page 174.
- **1853 Gallery in Salts Mill, Saltaire**
David Hockney has a permanent gallery in this splendid old mill in his native Bradford. See page 321.
- **National Gallery, London**
Treasures from the Renaissance to the Impressionists – and it's free. See page 74.
- **Tate Modern, London**
Wildly popular gallery in a former power station. See page 97.
- **The Walker, Liverpool**
Great collection of Victorian and Pre-Raphaelite paintings. See page 288.

LEFT: the Palm House at Kew Gardens.

THIS ENGLAND

Its long history has left a legacy
of contradictory images. The fun is in
finding out which of them are true

On a dull day in June 1948, a passenger on board the *Empire Windrush* looked out over the grey dock at Tilbury to the fields beyond and said to a journalist: "If this is England, I like it." He was one of the passengers arriving from the brilliant sunshine lands of Trinidad and Jamaica, lured to England by the promise of work. If his future in a multi-ethnic England turned out to be not quite as rosy as the authorities had painted, he nevertheless arrived on England's shores with great expectations that were not, at the start, disappointed.

Everybody has their own idea of England: red double-decker buses, thatched cottages and country houses, village pubs and cream teas, cheery Liverpudlians and eccentric aristocrats. Visitors will have fun finding out which of their preconceptions are true, and which false, about "this blessed plot, this earth, this realm, this England" (a quote from Shakespeare, of course). Some might be surprised to find that there is no longer smog in London, that it doesn't rain as much as they had heard, that Indian restaurants far outnumber fish-and-chip shops, and that the English cricket and football teams are constantly being beaten by the nations it taught how to play the game.

They might be delighted, too, to find that the countryside often does look remarkably green and enticing, and that in spite of motorway madness and urban sprawl, there are still corners that match up to the most fanciful idyll. For many, the essence of England is a romantic vision, though not even the most effusive brochure would attempt to match John of Gaunt's deathbed tribute in Shakespeare's *Richard II*:

This royal throne of kings, this scept'red isle,
This earth of majesty, this seat of Mars,
This other Eden, demi-paradise,
This fortress built by Nature for herself
Against infection and the hand of war,
This happy breed of men, this little world,
This precious stone set in a silver sea...'. ❑

PRECEDING PAGES: sandcastles and beach huts at Wells-next-the-Sea, Norfolk; the Red Lion pub, London; punting in Cambridge.
LEFT: walkers on Scafell Pike, the Lake District. **ABOVE:** all dressed up for the Notting Hill Carnival; relaxing in the coastal village of St Bees, Cumbria.

THE ENGLISH CHARACTER

Some see this restless island race as tolerant, charming and funny – others find them arrogant, insular and hypocritical. What are they really like?

Given the magpie-like tendency of the English to appropriate and absorb any cultural, political or linguistic invention that takes their fancy, it comes as no surprise that John Bull, the cartoon personification of the English character, was created by a Scotsman. John Arbuthnot, a mathematician and physician, invented him in 1712 as an honest cloth merchant in order to satirise the trading iniquities of the French.

Over the next century John Bull developed into a fat, jovial farmer accompanied by a no-nonsense bulldog. During World War II, when England faced the first threat of military invasion since 1066, man and dog seemed to merge eerily into the heroic figure of Winston Churchill.

But Churchill differed from the caricature in being a man of ideas as well as a man of action. John Bull had none of the war leader's imagination or eloquence: he was stolid, trustworthy and unreflective; a yeoman believing in common sense, good manners and fair play, or in other words, the epitome of a "good chap" – the ultimate accolade that an Englishman can bestow.

The view from abroad

Foreigners saw another side to John Bull's character, condemning him as arrogant and prejudiced and regarding his politeness as a cloak for hypocrisy. They still do. A French Tourist Office report once analysed the English as being "conservative and chauvinistic… profoundly independent and insular, constantly torn between America and Europe".

Historically, such judgments have an uncanny consistency. In the 16th century, a Dutch merchant, Emmanuel van Meteren, declared that the English were "bold, courageous, ardent and cruel in war, but very inconstant, rash, vainglorious, light and deceiving, and very suspicious, especially of foreigners, whom they despise." In 1800, the Prussian statesman Karl August von Hardenberg wrote: "Not only England but every Englishman is an island. He has all the qualities of a poker except its occasional warmth".

Naturally, the English simply ignored such criticisms. "The English delight in Silence more than any other European Nation," explained the essayist Joseph Addison in 1711. Breaking this silence, Cecil Rhodes, a vicar's son and an empire builder in southern Africa, posited that foreigners

LEFT: catching up with the news.
RIGHT: chatting over a pint in the pub.

were just envious: "Ask any man what nationality he would prefer to be, and 99 out of 100 will tell you they would prefer to be Englishmen."

It was the British and not the English Empire, of course, which was only fitting since many of its ablest administrators were Scots. But, as indisputably the dominant partner in the union between England, Scotland and Wales, the English have seldom made any distinction between the terms "British" and "English", using them interchangeably to the eternal annoyance of their Celtic partners. The difficulty of isolating "English" from "British" is exemplified by John Bull, who frequently sported a Union Jack waist-

coat rather than the English Cross of St George.

This imprecision – "the English never draw a line without blurring it", said Winston Churchill – is certainly a national characteristic. Perhaps it derives from their mongrel make-up. They originated as tribal hunters who arrived from Jutland and Lower Saxony and were later conquered by the Normans, a coalition of Viking pirates who, having converted to Christianity, adopted the French language. In 1867 the writer Matthew Arnold concluded: "The Germanic part, indeed, triumphs in us, we are a Germanic people; but not so wholly as to exclude hauntings of Celtism, which clash with our Germanicism, producing, as I believe, our humour, being neither Germanic nor Celtic, and so affect us that we strike people as odd and singular, not to be referred to by any known type, and like nothing but ourselves."

It was the lax aspect of the English character which most influenced the language. The anarchic, flexible nature of the English language and its ability to absorb other people's grammatical constructions and vocabulary like a sponge has helped make it the first or second language used by 650 million people around the world.

The obsession with sport

Games such as football and cricket also shook off the country that invented them, and today the English, although devoting much time to sport, mainly as spectators, routinely expect to be defeated by the countries to which they exported the games. It is, they say, playing the game rather than winning that is important, and, as the writer Vita Sackville-West put it: "The Englishman is seen at his best the moment that another man

THE ENGLISH AS SEEN BY STATISTICIANS

Although it has the highest proportion of agricultural land in Europe (71.2 percent), England has the lowest proportion of employment in farming. Most of England's 51.1 million people live in cities, yet countryside causes win widespread allegiance: the Royal Society for the Protection of Birds has over 1 million paid-up members and the National Trust has 3.5 million. National identity is fluid: 48 percent of people in England describe themselves as British, compared to only 27 percent of Scots and 35 percent of Welsh.

Women outnumber men but earn less on average (£521 a week for men, £412 for women). For a small country, there are wide discrepancies: while 74 percent of people in the South East have internet access, that figure falls to 54

percent in the North East. The highest life expectancy for men is in the prosperous South East (78.9 years) and the lowest is in the economically depressed North East (76.3); for women, the South West seems to offer the promise of the longest life (82.9).

Immigrants from the old British Empire did not distribute themselves evenly around the country, and nor have recent migrants. Almost 32 percent of Londoners were born outside the UK, a figure that rises to 39 percent in inner London. Outside London, that figure averages 9 percent, with fewest migrants gravitating to the North East (3 percent). The population of England is projected to rise by 8 percent by 2016.

starts throwing a ball at him." By this token, being a good loser is viewed as a sign of maturity – except by a minority of football hooligans – and is in many ways the essence of Englishness.

The same casual approach was brought to bear when choosing a national patron saint. St George, a 3rd-century Christian martyr, never set foot in England. Tales of his exploits – most notably, rescuing a maiden from a fire-belching dragon – must have struck a chord in medieval society when related by soldiers returning from the Crusades. St George's Day, on 23 April, has traditionally passed almost unnoticed and only recently has the English flag (a red cross on a

has been generated by the fact that Scottish and Welsh MPs can vote on matters that affect England but not their own constituents. It may be too late now to invent a national dress, and an English national anthem won't be easy to find either. (The closest anyone ever gets is a rousing rendition of William Blake's *Jerusalem*). National-

> "When two Englishmen meet, their first talk is of the weather," said the lexicographer Dr Samuel Johnson (1709–84). The reason is no doubt its great changeability.

white background) been waved at soccer matches to spur on England's hard-pressed players.

England on its own

Such old apathy may dissolve now that both Scotland and Wales have been granted by the British parliament a substantial degree of independence in the form of separate legislative assemblies in Edinburgh and Cardiff. The isolated English may for the first time need to define themselves in terms of nationalism: as yet there is no assembly for England and considerable anger

ism does not easily take root in such a land, where people lay great emphasis on their individuality ("An Englishman's home is his castle") and distrust institutions: overt, hand-on-heart patriotism of the flag-waving kind is inherently un-English.

The institutions of the European Union are not sympathetic to this philosophy – unlike the ever accommodating Church of England, which accepts, in pragmatic English style, that its social and ceremonial functions are much more important to most of its casual adherents than any spiritual enlightenment it might offer. After all, it has long been accepted that God is an Englishman, most likely educated at Eton College – and even if, by some misfortune, He isn't, He is in all probability still a jolly good chap. ❏

LEFT: cricket, a national obsession. **ABOVE LEFT:** May Day celebrations in Padstow. **ABOVE RIGHT:** blooming bargains at Columbia Road market, London.

DECISIVE DATES

PREHISTORY

500,000 BC
Boxgrove Man, from West Sussex, the first known human in England.

2000 BC
Stonehenge erected.

700 BC
Celts arrive from central Europe.

ROMAN OCCUPATION (55 BC–AD 410)

55 BC
Julius Caesar heads first Roman invasion.

AD 61
Rebellion of Boadicea, Queen of the Iceni, crushed.

ANGLO-SAXON AND DANISH KINGS (449–1066)

449–550
Arrival of Jutes, Angles and Saxons.

897
Alfred the Great, King of Wessex, defeats the Vikings.

980–1016
Viking invasions are renewed.

THE NORMANS (1066–1154)

1066
Conquest of England by William, Duke of Normandy.

1067
The Tower of London is begun.

1086
The Domesday Book, a complete inventory of England, is made.

THE PLANTAGENETS (1154–1399)

1154
Henry II becomes king.

1215
King John signs Magna Carta at Runnymede.

1348–49
The Black Death kills nearly a third to half of the population.

1381
Peasants' Revolt: rebels take London. The leader, Wat Tyler, is beheaded at Tower Hill.

1387
Geoffrey Chaucer's *Canterbury Tales* is published.

HOUSES OF LANCASTER AND YORK (1399–1485)

1455–85
Wars of the Roses between the competing Houses of York and Lancaster.

1476
William Caxton sets up England's first printing press.

THE TUDORS (1485–1603)

1485
Henry VII is crowned king after defeating Richard III.

1497
John Cabot explores the North American coast.

1509
Henry VIII succeeds to the throne. Papal authority in England is abolished; monarch becomes Supreme Head of the Church of England.

1536
Act of Union joins England and Wales.

1558
Elizabeth I begins her 45-year reign.

1580
Sir Francis Drake completes his circumnavigation of the world.

1588
The Spanish Armada is defeated.

THE STUARTS (1603–1714)
1603
James VI of Scotland is crowned James I of England.

1605
Guy Fawkes fails to blow up Parliament.

1620
The Pilgrim Fathers set sail for America.

1642–49
Civil War between Royalists and republican Roundheads. The monarchists are defeated and Charles I is beheaded.

1666
The Great Fire of London.

THE HOUSE OF HANOVER (1714–1836)
1714
George I of Hanover, Germany, takes the throne.

PRECEDING PAGES: Wat Tyler is beheaded as Richard II looks on. FAR LEFT TOP: William the Conqueror's invasion of Britain, from the 12th-century Bayeaux Tapestry. FAR LEFT MIDDLE: King John signs Magna Carta. LEFT: The Tower of London. ABOVE: Sir Walter Raleigh, Elizabethan buccaneer. RIGHT: Nancy Astor.

1721
Sir Robert Walpole becomes Britain's first prime minister.

1769
Captain Cook makes first voyage to Australia.

1775
James Watt patents the first steam engine.

1805
Admiral Lord Nelson is killed at Battle of Trafalgar.

THE VICTORIAN AGE (1837–1901)
1837
Victoria becomes Queen, at the age of 18.

1851
The Great Exhibition is held in London.

THE EDWARDIAN ERA (1901–14
1912
The *Titanic* sinks.

1914–18
World War I. More than 1 million Britons and Allies die.

HOUSE OF WINDSOR (SO NAMED FROM 1917)
1919
Nancy Astor is Britain's first woman MP.

1926
A General Strike by workers paralyses the nation.

1936
Edward VIII abdicates to marry an American divorcée, Mrs Wallis Simpson.

1939–45
World War II. Many civilians die in heavy bombing.

1946
National Health Service is established by the Labour government.

1953
Coronation of Queen Elizabeth II at Westminster Abbey.

1966
England hosts World Cup football and wins.

1973
Britain joins the European Community.

1979
Margaret Thatcher becomes Britain's first woman prime minister.

1994
First trains run through the Channel Tunnel.

1997
The Labour Party, led by Tony Blair, wins general election. Diana, Princess of Wales, dies in a car crash in Paris.

2005
Suicide bomb attacks in London, the day after the city wins 2012 Olympics.

2009
The credit crunch, and economic crisis.

CONQUEST AND CONFLICT

The Romans made their mark, Christianity was established, the Normans conquered the country, and centuries were spent in warfare

Recorded history begins with the first Roman invasion in 55 BC. The Celtic Queen (Boudicca) Boadicea led a failed rebellion in AD 61, and succeeded in destroying their capital, Londinium. In AD 122, the emperor Hadrian had a wall built across the north of England. Much of it remains, running from Carlisle to Newcastle. Roman control lasted nearly 400 years, leaving behind a series of walled towns – London, York and Bath among them – linked by a network of roads so well constructed that they survived for centuries. The remains of Roman baths, amphitheatres and villas can still be seen today. The Romans also introduced Christianity, literacy, and the use of Latin, but when they left, their influence faded surprisingly fast.

Anglo-Saxons and Vikings

The next wave of invaders – Angles and Saxons – pushed the native Celts westward into Wales and north into Scotland, and established their own kingdoms. In the mid-9th century the Danes (Vikings) gave up raiding and decided to settle. Alfred of Wessex, "Alfred the Great", agreed that they would control the north and east ("the Danelaw"), while he ruled the rest.

The Anglo-Saxons introduced their Teutonic religion and Christianity soon disappeared, except among the Celts. At Lindisfarne, in Northumberland, a monk called Aidan established a monastery where beautifully illustrated Gospels, now kept in the British Museum, were produced. At the end of the 6th century Augustine was sent on a Christian mission from Rome and became the first archbishop of Canterbury.

The Norman Conquest

After Alfred's death Canute, the Danish leader, became king and ruled well, but left no strong successor. The crown later passed to Edward "the Confessor", a pious man who built Westminster Abbey. On his death, in 1066, Harold, his nominated successor, became king. William of Normandy came to claim the throne allegedly promised him by Edward, and defeated Harold on Senlac Field, near Hastings. The Norman Conquest is the best-known event in English history.

LEFT: Henry VIII, who brought about the English Reformation. **RIGHT:** an engraving of Queen Boadicea leading an uprising of tribes against the Romans.

William was crowned in Westminster Abbey and set out to consolidate his kingdom. Faced with rebellion in the north, he took brutal action, devastating the countryside, then building a string of defensive castles. In order to collect taxes, William had a land and property record compiled: the survey was called the Domesday Book, because it seemed to the English not unlike the Book of Doom to be used by the greatest feudal lord of all on Judgement Day, and was completed in 1086.

After William's son Henry died in 1135, civil war broke out between the followers of his daughter, Matilda, and those of her cousin,

Stephen. Eventually Matilda's son by Geoffrey of Anjou, Henry, became king in 1154.

Monasteries and myths

During this period the monasteries became centres of power. Canterbury, Westminster and Winchester were the most active in the south, Fountains Abbey and Rievaulx in the north. Benedictine orders were a vital part of the feudal system, while the more spiritual Cistercians founded the wool trade, which became England's main source of wealth. Both provided hospitality to a stream of pilgrims, such as those in Chaucer's *Canterbury Tales*, written in the 14th century.

Chaucer's Knight also demonstrates the medieval courtly tradition that engendered the

Arthurian myth. Arthur probably existed, but it was Geoffrey of Monmouth, a 12th-century historian, who popularised the legends, his magical sword, Excalibur, and the wizard Merlin, and designated Tintagel Castle in Cornwall as Arthur's birthplace.

Shakespeare's kings

William Shakespeare drew on the lives of the Plantagenet and Tudor kings who ruled from 1154 to 1547, around whom he wove fanciful plots and heroic tales. But he did not tackle the first Plantagenet king, Henry II: that was left for T.S. Eliot, in *Murder in the Cathedral*. Relations between Church and State became increasingly strained during Henry's reign. Archbishop Thomas Becket resisted the king's interference in clerical matters and when Henry articulated his wish that someone would "rid me of this turbulent priest", four knights took him literally and murdered Becket on the altar steps of Canterbury Cathedral (1170).

Henry's son Richard I, known as Coeur de Lion (Lionheart), came to the throne in 1189. He spent most of his time in the Holy Land fighting Crusades. At home his prolonged absence and expensive exploits plunged the country into chaos. This period, presided over by his brother and successor John, produced the legendary Nottingham outlaw, Robin Hood, who is imagined to have preyed on the rich to give to the poor.

Magna Carta

King John is generally considered a Bad King. He quarrelled with the Pope, upset the barons and imposed high taxes. The barons presented him

THE HUNDRED YEARS' WAR

The Hundred Years' War (1337–1453) began when Edward III claimed the French throne. At the best-known battle, Crécy, more than 30,000 French troops were killed, but by 1371 the English had lost most of their French possessions. After a lull, Edward's claim was revived by his great-grandson, Henry V. With very few English casualties and the help of Welsh longbow-men, Henry defeated the French at Agincourt and made a strategic marriage to a French princess. It is said that the English "V" sign, an insulting hand gesture, comes from archers at Agincourt waving the two fingers used on their bows at the French. By the time he died in 1422, Henry controlled all northern France.

with a series of demands on behalf of the people, which became the Magna Carta (Great Charter) signed at Runnymede near Windsor in 1215. Although history sees the Charter as a milestone, it brought no immediate solution.

John's son, Henry III, proved little better, filling his court with foreign favourites and embarking on a disastrous war with France. The barons, under Simon de Montfort, rebelled and in 1265 de Montfort summoned a parliament which has been called the first House of Commons. Under Edward I, Henry's son, Wales was conquered, and Edward's newborn son became Prince of Wales, a title held by the heir to the throne ever since.

Plague and poll tax

The reign of Edward II had little to commend it. He lost Gascony, upset his barons, and was deposed by Parliament in 1327, before being brutally murdered in Berkeley Castle. His son, Edward III, spent most of his reign fighting the Hundred Years' War (*see facing page*). On the domestic front, times were hard. The Black Death, which reached England in 1348, killed nearly a third of the population. By leaving so much land untended and making labour scarce, it gave surviving peasants a better bargaining position. When a Poll Tax was introduced in 1381, the peasants of Kent and East Anglia rose in rebellion. Their revolt was brutally suppressed but it precipitated the end of the feudal system.

The Wars of the Roses

Scarcely had the Hundred Years' War ended when aristocratic rivalries for the throne led to the Wars of the Roses. This name is a convenient shorthand for the battles between the House of York, symbolised by the white rose, and that of Lancaster, symbolised by the red.

During the course of these wars the murders took place of the young Edward V and his brother Richard – although the guilt of their uncle, Richard III, has never been proved. Richard was killed during the Battle of Bosworth, in Leicestershire, where Shakespeare, portraying him as a hunchback, had him offering his kingdom for a horse.

The wars ended after Richard's defeat with the marriage of Henry VII (1485–1509) to Elizabeth of York. This united the opposing factions and put the country under the rule of the Tudors.

LEFT: King John stirred the barons to revolt.
RIGHT: the Battle of Agincourt in 1415.

The break from Rome

Henry refilled the royal coffers, but most of the money was squandered on a series of French wars by his son, Henry VIII – best remembered as the gluttonous and licentious ruler who married six times, divorced twice and beheaded two of his wives. He also brought about the Refor-

> Today, the Domesday book is kept in the National Archives, Kew and is a fascinating document of early social history. An online version is available at www.nationalarchives.gov.uk.

mation, in England for political rather than religious reasons, when the Pope refused to annul his marriage to Catherine of Aragon.

When Henry died in 1547, he was succeeded by his only male heir, Edward, a sickly 10-year-old who died six years later. His half-sister Mary then came to the throne and won the nickname "Bloody Mary". A devout Catholic, she restored the Old Religion and had some 300 Protestants burned as heretics. Mary is also remembered as the monarch who lost the French port of Calais, the last British possession on the Continent, during a renewed war with France. More remorseful about this than the loss of so many lives, she declared that when she died the word "Calais" would be found engraved on her heart. ❑

FROM ELIZABETH TO EMPIRE

Civil war, industrial revolution, the establishment
of a parliamentary system and the growth of an
Empire transformed the country

The Elizabethan Age has a swashbuckling ring to it: the Virgin Queen and her dashing courtiers, the defeat of the Spanish Armada, and the exploits of the great "sea dogs", Frobisher and Hawkins. Sir Walter Raleigh brought tobacco back from Virginia; Sir Francis Drake circumnavigated the world. Even the great poets Sir Philip Sidney and John Donne spent time before the mast – although William Shakespeare stayed at home, entertaining crowds at the Globe Theatre in London.

Elizabeth I spent much of her long reign (1558–1603) resisting Catholic attempts to dethrone or assassinate her. She had re-established Protestantism but was constantly challenged by those who wished to put the Catholic Mary, Queen of Scots, on the throne. The execution of Mary in 1587 removed the conspirators' focal point and the defeat of the Spanish Armada the year after put an end to Catholic conspiracies.

Defeating the Spanish Armada gave England naval supremacy, which laid the foundations for a future of flourishing trade, expansionism and colonisation.

Elizabeth was succeeded by Mary's son, James I (VI of Scotland), the first of the Stuarts, but his reign, too, was bedevilled by religious controversy. Puritans called for a purer form of worship and Catholics engineered a number of plots, one of which resulted in Sir Walter Raleigh's 13-year imprisonment in the Tower of London.

LEFT: English ships and the Spanish Armada.
RIGHT: Elizabeth I, the "Virgin Queen".

The most famous of the conspiracies was the Gunpowder Plot of 1605, when Guy Fawkes attempted to blow up the Houses of Parliament, an event still commemorated on 5 November, when Fawkes is burned in effigy throughout the land. Puritan protests were more peaceful, but James had little sympathy. Some left the country: a small group who became known as the Pilgrim Fathers set sail in the *Mayflower* in 1620 and founded New Plymouth in North America.

Civil War

The Stuart period was one of conflict between Crown and Parliament, and under Charles I relations with Parliament went from bad to dreadful. King and Commons were constantly at each other's throats and in 1641 discontented Irish Catholics took advantage of their disarray to attack the settlers who had taken their land during the reign of James I. Thousands were massacred and the subsequent outcry in England precipitated the Civil War.

Opposition to the royalists was led by Oliver Cromwell, whose troops' short-cropped hair led

> The English Civil War of 1642–49 has become romanticised, and today a society flourishes which re-enacts the principal battles for fun.

them to be called Roundheads. Charles's defeat in 1649 led to his execution on a scaffold erected outside Inigo Jones's Banqueting House in Whitehall. He reputedly wore two shirts, so he would not shiver in the January cold and cause people to think he was afraid.

In Scotland, Charles's son and namesake was crowned king at Scone in 1651. He marched into England where he was defeated at Worcester, and eventually escaped to France. Meanwhile, Cromwell and "the Rump" – the Parliamentary members who had voted for Charles's execution – declared England a Commonwealth. In 1653 Cromwell dissolved Parliament, formed a Protectorate with himself as Lord Protector and ruled alone until his death in 1658. Without him

republicanism faltered and in 1660 Charles II was crowned king in Westminster. In 1678 an agitator called Titus Oates disclosed a bogus "Popish Plot" to assassinate the king. Thousands of Catholics were imprisoned and no Catholic was allowed to sit in the House of Commons – a law that was not repealed for more than 150 years.

Whigs and Tories

Fear of the monarchy ever again becoming too powerful led to the emergence of the first political parties, both known by nicknames: Whigs, a derogatory name for cattle drivers; Tories, an Irish word meaning outlaws. Loosely speaking, Whigs opposed absolute monarchy and supported religious freedom, while Tories were upholders of Church and Crown.

In 1685 Charles was succeeded by his brother, James II (1685–88), who imposed illegal taxation and tried to bring back absolute monarchy and Catholicism. Rebellions were savagely put down, with hundreds hanged and many more sold into slavery. Whigs and Tories allied against him and in 1688 offered the crown to James's daughter, Mary, and her husband, the Dutch prince William of Orange. This move became known as the Glorious Revolution because Parliament had proved more powerful than the Crown – a power spelled out in a Bill of Rights, which severely limited the monarch's freedom of action.

William landed in England and James fled to France. Backed by the French, he arrived in Ireland in 1689 where Irish Catholics lent him support, but with disastrous results for both sides. At Londonderry 30,000 Protestants survived a 15-week siege but were finally defeated.

THE GREAT PRETENDERS

The Hanoverian period saw the last violent attempts to overthrow the monarchy in the shape of the two Jacobite Rebellions in support of the "Pretenders", descendants of James II. The first rebellion, in 1715, in support of his son James, the "Old Pretender", was defeated near Stirling and its leaders fled to France. Thirty years later his grandson Charles, the "Young Pretender", known as Bonnie Prince Charlie, raised a huge army in Scotland but was savagely defeated in battle at Culloden by the Duke of Cumberland. No more "Pretenders" arose. From then on power struggles would be political ones, for it was with politicians and Parliament that real power lay.

In 1690, William's troops trounced James at the Battle of the Boyne, and he fled to France, dying in 1701. Protestant victory was complete.

War with France dragged on, becoming, in Queen Anne's reign, the War of the Spanish Succession. Her commander-in-chief, John Churchill, Duke of Marlborough, won a famous victory at Blenheim in 1704, for which he was rewarded with Blenheim Palace, near Oxford. During Anne's reign the name Great Britain came into being when, in 1707, the Act of Union united England and Scotland.

Hanoverian Britain

On Anne's death, a reliable Protestant monarch was needed. George of Hanover, great-grandson of James I on his mother's side, but with a Hanoverian father, and German in language and outlook, was invited to Britain. He never learned to speak fluent English, and had no great liking for his subjects.

The Hanoverian dynasty, under the four Georges, spanned a period of nearly 115 years. It was a time of wars with France and Spain, of expanding empire, industrialisation and growing demands for political reform.

The growth of London

When George and his queen, Sophia, arrived from Hanover in 1714 the city's population stood at 550,000 despite the ravages of the Great Plague of 1665 which had killed 100,000 Londoners. This was due largely to migrants from rural areas who came in search of work.

London had been partially rebuilt after the Great Fire of 1666, which started in a baker's shop in Pudding Lane and destroyed two-thirds of the timber-built city. But the subsequent elegant buildings designed by Sir Christopher Wren (1632–1723), such as St Paul's Cathedral, were a far cry from the overcrowded and insanitary slums in which most people lived.

In the more affluent areas, some streets were widened to allow carriages to pass and rudimentary street lighting was introduced in the early 19th century. Westminster Bridge was illuminated by gaslight for the first time in 1813. Theatres, concert halls and newly fashionable coffee houses sprang up.

LEFT: John Churchill, Duke of Marlborough.
RIGHT: slums depicted by Hogarth in *Gin Lane*.

Royalty spent their time at Buckingham House, Kensington Palace and Hampton Court. George III bought Buckingham House and George IV had it redesigned by John Nash into a Palace, though Queen Victoria was the first monarch to take up residence. Parliament met at Westminster, although not in the present building, which was built after a fire destroyed its predecessor in 1834.

Colonial power

The treaty signed at the end of the Seven Years' War with France in 1763 allowed Britain to keep all its overseas colonies, making it the

leading world power. The empire had been growing since 1607 when Virginia, an English colony in America, had been established. In 1620 English Puritans had settled in Massachusetts and other settlements were made later in the century. By 1700 most were governed by a Crown official and incorporated into Britain's Atlantic Empire.

Throughout the 17th century the demand for goods – furs, silk, tobacco, sugar – led to a series of wars with the Dutch and the French from which Britain emerged in control of much of West Africa, Newfoundland and Nova Scotia and some of the Caribbean islands. French and English battled for supremacy in Canada and India during the 18th century. By 1760 England had proved the clear winner. Colonial trade, unfortunately, went hand in hand with slavery. It was not until 1807 that the tireless efforts of William Wilberforce helped make the trade illegal and another 27 years before slavery was abolished in all British colonies.

Agriculture and industry

Radical changes took place in the English countryside in the late 18th century: the narrow-strip system of farming which had prevailed since Saxon times ended when a series of Enclosure Acts empowered wealthier landowners to seize land and divide it into enclosed fields.

This explains the patchwork quality of much of Britain's countryside. Arable farming became more efficient and profitable, but for the evicted tenants it was a disaster. The dispossessed farmers left their homes to look for work in the towns, which soon became impossibly overcrowded.

The first steam engine was devised by an Englishman at the end of the 17th century but it was the Scottish inventor James Watt (1736–1819) who modified the design in the 1770s and made steam an efficient source of energy, which would power trains and ships as well as factory machinery. Steam pumps allowed speculators to drain deep coal mines, which vastly increased coal production. Abraham Darby's method of smelting iron with coke instead of charcoal hugely increased the production of iron which was used for machinery, railways and shipping. In 1779, the world's first cast-iron bridge was built in Coalbrookdale, Shropshire, and can still be seen today. Textiles had long been a vital part of Britain's economy and James Hargreaves' invention of the Spinning Jenny in the 1770s opened the way to mass production. As in agriculture, mechanisation destroyed the livelihood of many.

Goods and materials needed improved transportation to reach a market, and the 18th century saw massive outlay on canal building. By 1830 all the main industrial areas were linked by waterways, although most of these would fall into disuse when the new railways proved faster and more efficient (today, cleared out and cleaned up, they provide thousands of miles of leisure boating, with more miles of canal in Birmingham than there are in Venice). New roads were built, too. By the early 19th century, men such as Thomas Telford and John Macadam, who gave us the road surface called "tarmac", had created a road network totalling some 125,000 miles (200,000km).

Above all, this was the age of the railways, when iron and steam combined to change the face of the country, and were romanticised in such paintings as *Rain, Steam and Speed* by J.M.W. Turner. Cornishman Richard Trevithick built the first steam locomotive, and The Stockton and Darlington Line was the first railway line to open, in 1825, with George Stephenson's *Locomotion*. Isambard Kingdom Brunel, who designed the elegant Clifton Suspension Bridge across the Avon Gorge, laid down the Great Western Railway.

The fear of revolution

The two events that most alarmed the British ruling classes in the late 18th century were the American War of Independence and the French Revolution – a fear exacerbated by wars with France and Spain and the dissatisfaction provoked by heavy taxes and the loss of trade they caused. Known as the Napoleonic Wars, these hostilities began around 1799 and rumbled on until 1815, giving Britain two of its greatest heroes, Admiral Lord Nelson (1758–1805) and the Duke of Wellington (1769–1852).

However, political change in England was to come not through revolution but gradual reform. Between 1832 and 1884 three parliamentary Reform Bills were passed, extending the franchise.

The 1829 Emancipation Act, which allowed Catholics to sit in Parliament, was another measure that frightened the old school. And the Repeal of the Corn Laws – heavy taxes on imported corn which were crippling trade and starving the poor – split the ruling Conservative Party. The "Peelite" faction, followers of the pro-repeal Sir Robert Peel, joined with Whigs to form the Liberal Party.

The age of Dickens

In London, the squalor and crime that Charles Dickens (1812–70) portrayed so evocatively in his novels were all too real. But change, although slow, was on the way. After a cholera epidemic in 1832 measures were taken to provide drainage and clean water. The police force that Sir Robert Peel established in 1829, and which took the nickname "Bobbies" from him, was helping combat crime. Peel also abolished the death penalty for many petty crimes, influenced by the ideas of the utilitarian thinker Jeremy Bentham, who founded University College, London.

Working-class people, on the whole, were not attracted by revolutionary struggle and preferred to pursue their aims through trade union organisation and representation in Parliament. The first working-class member of Parliament, in 1892, was John Keir Hardie, the Scottish miners' leader, and 14 years later the British Labour Party won its first parliamentary seats. Although Karl Marx (1818–83) lived and worked in London for much of his life – his tomb can be seen in London's Highgate Cemetery – his ideas were shared only by a relatively small group of middle-class intellectuals.

Middle-class life was comfortable and pleasant. Improved transport – including the world's first underground railway, opened in London in 1863 – enabled people to work in towns but live in leafy suburbs.

Shaw and Wilde

At the theatre, audiences were being entertained by the plays of two Anglo-Irish writers:

George Bernard Shaw (1856–1950), who believed in combining education with entertainment, introduced radical politics into his work; and Oscar Wilde (1854–1900), who was to end his glittering career in a prison cell on charges of homosexuality, poked sophisticated fun at London's high society.

All in all, Britain was feeling quite pleased with itself by the time of Queen Victoria's Diamond Jubilee in 1897. The jubilee celebrated 60 years on the throne for the woman who had spent much of her reign as a black-clad widow, who had given her name to the age, and who ruled over the biggest empire in the world. ❑

THE PRE-RAPHAELITES

John Ruskin (1819–1900) was one of the founders of the Pre-Raphaelite Brotherhood of painters and writers which flourished in the final years of the 19th century. William Morris (1834–96), who devoted himself to the revival of medieval arts and crafts, shared Ruskin's ideals. Examples of his decoration and furnishings can be seen at Kelmscott Place, near Oxford, for a time the centre of the Brotherhood's activities, and also at the Red House in Bexleyheath. The latter contains fine stained glass by Edward Burne-Jones, whose work along with that of fellow Pre-Raphaelites John Millais and Dante Gabriel Rossetti is spread through galleries in London, Birmingham, Manchester and Liverpool.

LEFT: Admiral Lord Nelson, famous naval hero.
ABOVE RIGHT: four generations of royalty: Victoria with future monarchs George V, Edward VII and Edward VIII.

MODERN TIMES

Following the ravages of two world wars and the end of its imperial adventure, England was forced to redefine its relationship with the rest of Europe

World War I claimed over a million British casualties, most of them under the age of 25. But had the sacrifice been worth it? Men who had fought in France and been promised a "land fit for heroes" were disillusioned when they found unemployment and poor housing awaited them at the war's end in 1918. Women who had worked in factories while the men were away were not prepared to give up any of their independence.

There were strikes on the railways and in the mines and political unrest led to four general elections in just over five years, including one which brought the Labour Party to power for the first time. In 1926 a general strike paralysed the country but the unions' demands were not met and the men returned to work, much disgruntled and worse off than before.

The Roaring Twenties

There was another side to life, of course. For some, unaffected by gloomy financial reality,

The scale of the carnage in World War I shocked even such patriots as the writer Rudyard Kipling (1865–1936), who had been firmly committed to the aims of the war: he lost his only son.

these were the Roaring Twenties. Women with cropped hair and short dresses drank cocktails and danced to the new music, jazz, which had crossed the ocean from America. Silent films, another US import, were the wonder of the age.

The New York Stock Market crash of 1929 looked as if it would bring the party to an end. The effects soon spread throughout Europe and by 1931 England was entering the Great Depression. The principal victims of the recession were in the industrial areas of northern England, south Wales, and Clydeside in Scotland. Three million people lost their jobs and suffered real misery with only the "dole", a limited state benefit, to keep them from starvation and homelessness. British cinema thrived as people sought an escape from reality.

In the south of England and the Midlands, the depression hit less hard and recovery was faster, mainly due to the rapid growth of the motor, electrical and light engineering industries. The bold, geometric designs of Art Deco, which began in Paris in 1925, could soon be seen adorning the spanking new factories lining the main roads.

World War II

With memories of the "war to end all wars" still fresh in people's minds, there was great reluctance to enter another conflict. But by 1939 the policy of appeasement of German aggression was no longer tenable. Although Britain's island status saved it from invasion, the war involved civilians in an unprecedented way. German bombing raids tore the heart out of many ports and cities. Much of the modern building in British towns, not always blending too harmoniously, has been erected on former bomb sites.

Many London families spent their nights in the Underground stations, the safest places dur-

greatest prime minister. But when hostilities ended in 1945 the electorate declined to re-elect him and voted overwhelmingly for a Labour government: the war effort had fostered egalitarianism and many returning servicemen felt that electing a Conservative government again would simply resuscitate the old class differences.

The problems of the war-torn country proved intractable, but the Labour government laboured to keep its promises. The basis of the welfare state was laid, providing free medical care for everyone and financial help for the old, the sick and the unemployed. The Bank of England, coal mines, railways and steelworks were

ing an attack, and a lot of people from cities and industrial areas were evacuated to the countryside during the worst of the Blitz. For children, sent to live with strangers while their parents remained behind, it was both a time of great loneliness and the first glimpse many of them had ever had of green fields and woodlands. For some of the country families on whom they were billeted, it may have been their first glimpse of the effects of urban deprivation.

Sir Winston Churchill had received massive popular support as an inspirational war leader, and is still regarded by many people as Britain's

LEFT: bathing belles take to the water.
ABOVE: tube stations became wartime bomb shelters.

THE ABDICATION

In 1936, following the death of George V, the country was rocked by an unprecedented crisis. Edward VIII succeeded his father but was obliged to abdicate when family, Church and Government united in their refusal to let him marry a twice-divorced American, Mrs Wallis Simpson. The British public was kept in the dark about the matter. The couple married in France and remained in permanent exile as the Duke and Duchess of Windsor. Edward's brother came to the throne and, as George VI, became a popular monarch, not least for the solidarity which he and his Queen showed to their subjects during the Blitz, as the German bombing raids were called.

nationalised. These were hard and joyless years, however, and wartime rationing of food, clothing and fuel continued into the early 1950s.

The end of empire

One of the most far-reaching consequences of the war was that it hastened the end of Britain's empire. Starting with India's independence in 1947, the colonies one after another achieved autonomy during the next two decades. Jamaica and Trinidad did not gain independence until 1962, but they were two islands whose people were among the first black immigrants to Britain in the early 1950s, when work was plentiful

and immigrants were welcomed to fill the labour gap. Newcomers from the Caribbean settled mainly in London at first, while later immigrants from the Indian sub-continent made their homes in the Midlands, where textiles and the motor industry offered employment.

The post-war years were ones of uneasy peace. Britain joined the war against North Korea in 1950 and its troops, still a conscripted army, fought there for four years. In 1956, following Egyptian nationalisation of the Suez Canal, British and French forces conspired to attack Egypt, pleading bogus provocation. The action was widely condemned both at home and particularly in the United States, representing an ignominious end to Britain's imperial ambitions.

These were also the years of the Cold War between the Soviet Union and the West, which prompted Britain to become a nuclear power. The first British hydrogen bomb was tested in 1957, after the world's first nuclear power station had opened in Cumberland (now Cumbria). The Campaign for Nuclear Disarmament was born in response and organised large protest marches.

A new Elizabethan Age

All was not gloom and doom. In 1951 the Festival of Britain was held in the newly built Royal Festival Hall on London's South Bank – the National Theatre was added to the concrete complex in 1964.

The Festival was designed to commemorate the Great Exhibition 100 years earlier and strongly signalled the beginning of the end of postwar austerity. In 1953, a new Elizabethan Age began as Elizabeth II was crowned in Westminster Abbey. Britain's Television Age began in earnest that day too, as millions watched the coronation live on tiny flickering screens.

By the latter half of the decade things were definitely looking up. Harold Macmillan, the Conservative prime minister, declared in a famous speech that people had "never had it so good". New universities were built, with the aim of making higher education a possibility for more than just the privileged elite. Most people had two weeks' paid holiday a year and, alongside the traditional seaside resorts, holiday camps blossomed, offering cheap family vacations.

Social attitudes were changing too, reflected in the rise of a group of writers known as "angry

THE THATCHER ERA

The 1980s became known as the Thatcher decade after Britain's first female prime minister came to power in 1979. For many it was a time of increased prosperity, and bright new shopping centres sprang up over the country. For others, particularly in the north, where steelworks, shipyards and coal mines had closed, the 1980s were grim. Most nationalised industries were privatised. After 11 years of Thatcherite rule, people began to tire of the Iron Lady's uncompromising style and she was finally voted out in November 1990 – not by the electorate, but by her own party who believed she had lost touch with the country. She was replaced by a less combative leader, John Major.

young men", including John Osborne and Arnold Wesker, whose plays challenged conventional values.

The pendulum swings

The 1960s saw an explosion of new talent, much of it from the north of England. Alan Sillitoe and Stan Barstow wrote about working-class life in a way no one had done before. Northern actors, such as Albert Finney and Tom Courteney, achieved huge success and, in the cinema, directors Lindsay Anderson and Karel Reisz made British films popular box-office attractions. Pop music, as it was now called, under-

of Emergency and brought down Edward Heath's Conservative Government, that the self-confidence collapsed. In the same year, with mixed feelings, Britain finally became a full member of the Common Market (now the European Union). Rising oil prices pushed up the cost of living, high inflation took its toll, and unemployment soared.

Oil was discovered in the North Sea. But, although building oil rigs provided jobs, the oil revenues were largely soaked up in payments to the jobless. There was no economic miracle.

To deepen the gloom, English cities were again bombed. This time the perpetrators were

went a revolution when a group from Liverpool, the Beatles, became world celebrities and turned their home town into a place of pilgrimage.

The introduction of the contraceptive pill prompted a revolution in sexual attitudes, and the laws relating to abortion, homosexuality and censorship were liberalised. It was a decade of optimism and national self-confidence was infectious: in 1966 England's footballers even beat Germany to win the World Cup.

It was during the winter of 1973, when an oil embargo and a miners' strike provoked a State

the IRA, who were fighting to end British rule in Northern Ireland. By 1979, unemployment had reached 3½ million and a wave of strikes plunged the country into what was called "the winter of discontent" – the media has a tendency to quote Shakespeare in times of crisis. An election returned the Conservatives to office under their new leader, Margaret Thatcher.

The impact of the West's first woman prime minister was enormous, but her personal popularity soon began to fade as the economy remained weak. Her political stock was dramatically strengthened in 1982 by the Falklands War when an invading Argentinian force was beaten off these South Atlantic islands, remnants of the empire.

LEFT: Churchill appeals to the electorate in 1945.
ABOVE: the climax of *If...*, Lindsay Anderson's 1968 allegorical film pitting youth against the establishment.

For many, the 1980s meant increased prosperity. The most ambitious development was the renewal of London's derelict docklands area into a new industrial site, with its own small airport and light railway system and prestige housing for young urban professionals. Docklands' Canary Wharf development was dubbed Chicago-on-Thames. For many people, however, the dream of living in London faded as the strong economy pushed up the capital's house prices and rents.

The nervous '90s

As the 1990s began, the economy was no longer riding so high. A long and acrimonious miners'

strike in 1984 had weakened the unions, and coal mines, including most of those in the closely knit mining communities of South Wales, were subsequently closed. Most of Britain's nationalised industries were privatised, a move which a former Conservative prime minister, Harold Macmillan, likened to "selling the family silver".

Britain's technical status as an island was removed in 1994 when the first fare-paying passengers travelled by rail to Paris and Brussels through the long-awaited Channel Tunnel. But the big question remained: did Britain really feel European enough to be part of a full monetary union – perhaps even, one day, a political union?

That *fin de siècle* feeling

Two events in 1997 shook the nation out of its wary complacency. In a general election the Conservative Party was swept from power as the Labour Party roared in with an unassailable overall majority in the House of Commons. The Conservatives were left without a single seat in either Scotland or Wales, both of which voted in subsequent referendums for a greater degree of self-rule; devolution took effect in 1999 with the setting up of new assemblies in Edinburgh and Cardiff.

The second defining event in 1997 was the death in a car crash in Paris of Diana, Princess of Wales. The wave of grief that swept the country took everyone by surprise. Some attacked the royal family for failing to display sufficient anguish – a predicament dramatised in a 2006 movie in which Helen Mirren portrayed The Queen.

But Tony Blair's new government soon disappointed many by abandoning its socialist roots, promoting unexpectedly conservative economic policies with evangelical fervour. However in June 2001 the Labour Party won another landslide election victory, despite a great deal of voter apathy. The crucial question of whether Britain should embrace the single European currency, the euro, divided public opinion, and effectively the issue was put on the back burner.

The American connection

Europe remains an issue that can still destroy governments because it forces people to confront questions of identity and loyalties. Although Britons today are happy to holiday in a gîte in Normandy or a resort on the Costa del Sol, most still regard Europe as "foreign". Because of ancestral links and a shared language, many feel more comfortable with the United States, even though its values and attitudes are often far more "foreign" than those of, say, Germany or Italy.

Tony Blair argued that Britain was ideally placed to be a bridge between America and the European Union, but European politicians regularly accused Britain of being a less than faithful partner as it professed eternal love for its fellow Europeans while remaining reluctant to learn their languages or refusing to accept the euro as national currency.

This conflict came to a head when George W. Bush's administration determined to invade Iraq. While much of Europe opposed the war, Tony

Blair went against public opinion by making Britain a full coalition partner: more than one million people marched in protest. When a BBC reporter implied that the government had exaggerated the threat posed by Saddam Hussein, the ensuing row led to the eventual resignations of the BBC's chairman and director-general.

The failure to find the much touted weapons of mass destruction in Iraq severely dented Blair's reputation and, although Britain's economy had remained more robust than most European economies, criticism mounted that Labour had failed to deliver adequate public services and had no answers to chronic problems such as traf-

The building programme needed to accommodate the games would, it was promised, rejuvenate run-down areas of East London.

On the very next day, the jubilation ceased as suicide bombings killed 52 people and injured more than 700 on three Underground trains and a bus. Two weeks later, other bombers failed to detonate four more devices on the city's transport network. These attacks raised the question of how to make such a sprawling cosmopolitan city more secure, particularly since the bombers were not foreign terrorists who had evaded the country's border checks but British-born Muslims.

fic congestion and threats to the environment.

Yet Labour's hold on power remained secure, because not only had the Conservative Party failed to heal the splits (especially over Europe) that had forced Margaret Thatcher from power, the acrid arguments between the Thatcherite sympathisers and their opponents made them look unfit to govern.

London is targeted

In July 2005, London surprised itself by winning its bid to host the 2012 Olympic Games.

LEFT: Labour prime minister, Gordon Brown.
ABOVE: as Heathrow's Terminal 5 opens, environmental protesters have their say.

The insecure society

As in the United States after 2001, security became a major issue. Yet, curiously for such a reserved people, the British were already, per capita, the most spied-on people on the planet. In addition to a forest of speed cameras – designed, many thought, as much to raise revenue as to cut road accidents – surveillance cameras had sprung up in town centres. Britain's economy went on to crash into recession, following the "credit-crunch" of 2008. Banks were nationalised and in 2009, the extent of personal expenses claimed by MPs – everything from the cost of cleaning their moats to new lavatory seats – threatened to undermine Parliament itself when it was revealed by a national newspaper. ❑

STATELY HOMES

They reflect more than privileged
lives. They also illustrate centuries of
social history, and of great artistic
and architectural achievement

England's stately homes have a fascination that
attracts visitors in their millions every year. Many
have embraced the tourist theme enthusiastically,
with such added incentives as safari parks, transport
museums, historical re-enactments and adventure
playgrounds, but at the heart of them all lies a house
with a story. It may tell of great achievement in a
palatial mansion crammed with priceless works of
art; it may reflect centuries at the heart of a close-knit
country community in the form of a rambling old
manor house, crammed with centuries of
acquisitions; it may even show how the servants and
estate workers would go about their daily duties.

Changing times
A house that may appear to be pure 18th-century
neo-classical may well be hiding a medieval core and
perhaps a Tudor fireplace where Elizabeth I once
warmed her toes. Victorian high-flyers often confused
the issue by building convincingly fanciful medieval-
style castles, complete with every convenience that
Industrial Revolution technology provided.

The short Edwardian era saw both the carefree heyday of the country house party and the onset of World
War I, which marked the demise of stately homes in
their traditional role. Maintaining them was costly, and
an ingenious solution was provided in
1953 when the 13th Duke of Bedford,
faced with huge death duties when he
succeeded his father, was faced with
the prospect of donating Woburn
Abbey in Bedfordshire to the
National Trust. Instead, he opened
it to the public, charging them
to view the 12th-century building and its contents. He later
added a safari park to its grounds.
A golf club and antiques centre,
plus wedding and conference
facilities, were later added to the
menu Initially, many fellow
aristocrats condemned the
Duke's ideas as crass
commercialism, but soon
many followed his example.

ABOVE: Blenheim Palace is Britain's largest private house. The
exterior of the palace is an orgy of the baroque style, with Doric and
Corinthian columns. Inside is a maze of magnificent state
apartments.

BELOW: Lyme Park in Cheshire, used in the BBC's 1995 version of
Jane Austen's *Pride and Prejudice*, has Tudor origins, but was
transformed in the 18th century.

LEFT: The statues, figurines, iron benches and sundials that grace the
gardens of stately homes have not escaped the attention of
professional thieves, who have been known to peruse *Country Life*
magazine to identify opportunities.

THE POWER OF THE PAST

The National Trust, founded in 1895, is a registered charity and receives no state grant. Covering England, as well as Wales and Northern Ireland, it initially protected open spaces and threatened buildings, but soon it began preserving places of historic interest or natural beauty for the enjoyment of future generations.

It now cares for ancient monuments, historic houses and gardens, industrial sites, coastline and countryside. Many country houses and gardens were donated to it by their owners who could no longer afford to maintain them or to pay death duties. Broadening its heritage ambitions, it even acquired the childhood homes of John Lennon and Paul McCartney. The Trust is funded entirely by membership subscriptions and donations from its 3½ million members, by legacies, and by admission charges.

Another organisation, English Heritage, a quasi governmental body, cares for historic buildings and monuments such as Stonehenge. It also advises on the preservation of the historic environment. Both organisations have paid membership schemes, which allow members free access to the properties they administer.

ABOVE: Knole in Kent, birthplace of the writer Vita Sackville-West, was built by an Archbishop of Canterbury in 1456–86 and is surrounded by a 1,000-acre (400-hectare) deer park.

BELOW: The maze at Chatsworth House now stands where Joseph Paxton's Great Conservatory once stood.

BELOW: Castle Howard in Yorkshire was built between 1699 and 1712 for the 3rd Earl of Carlisle.

THEATRE

"Plays make mankind no better and no worse,"
claimed Lord Byron. But as a tourist attraction
they do wonders for England's economy

From the moment you arrive in Stratford-upon-Avon you know you are in The Birthplace of the Bard. From the Shakespeare Tour buses to the T-shirts proclaiming "Will Power", from Ann Hathaway's cottage to the site of New Place, where the great man spent his later years, this pretty little town is dedicated to the Shakespeare industry.

What it is all based on are the plays, performed by the Royal Shakespeare Company in the severe modern theatre beside the Avon, as they are in theatres throughout the world. By some rare gift this 16th-century writer was able to encapsulate emotions, to universalise petty jealousies and major tragedies, in words that still ring fresh and new, with humour that seems to work even translated into Japanese.

Shakespeare is part of the national heritage, revered even by those who rarely, if ever, visit a theatre. Lines from his plays are part of the language, most actors express a wish to play Hamlet at some time in their career, and there are few classical directors who don't itch to stage their own interpretation of the works.

Outside Stratford-upon-Avon, the best place to see Shakespeare is in London, where both commercial theatres and subsidised venues like the National Theatre regularly stage star-led productions. In summer, Shakespeare's Globe, a facsimile of the original Globe Theatre, mounts the plays in a 16th-century setting on London's Bankside. But you could probably see a Shake-

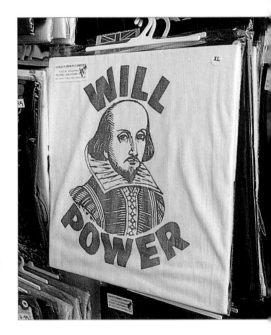

speare play, professional or amateur, somewhere in the country on most nights of the year.

More than just Shakespeare

London's theatrical history goes back to a playhouse opened at Shoreditch in 1576 by James Burbage, the son of a carpenter and travelling player, and its development encompasses a strong tradition of taking side-swipes at social issues. In the *Roaring Girl* of 1611, for example, playwright Thomas Dekker dwelt at some length on London's traffic jams.

In modern times, live theatre was supposed to succumb first to movies, then to television, yet it is still one of those essential attractions that

PRECEDING PAGES: a night performance at the Minack Theatre, Cornwall. **LEFT:** David Tennant (top) and Patrick Stewart (bottom) in the Royal Shakespeare Company's production of *Hamlet*. **RIGHT:** "Will Power" T-shirts for sale.

every visitor to London is supposed to experience. Outside the capital, there are groundbreaking repertory theatres in most major cities, and amateur dramatics fill countless church halls around the country (why the supposedly reserved English are so keen on dressing up and making fools of themselves in broad farces is worthy of a psychological dissertation).

Critics bemoan the fact that lavish musicals have come to dominate London's mainstream theatre. Once, no-one would have guessed that the West End would hijack the genre from Broadway. Yet it happened with surprising speed. First, Tim Rice and Andrew Lloyd Web-

ber demonstrated the possibilities of the cunningly crafted rock-musical form with *Jesus Christ Superstar* and *Evita*. Then, leaving Rice to indulge his passion for cricket and aptitude for writing Oscar-winning tunes for Disney cartoons, Lloyd Webber focused his fanaticism for the stage musical by composing *Cats* (a collaboration with the late T. S. Eliot), *Phantom of the*

> Unsold tickets for London theatres are sold daily at a discount at the "tkts" booth in Leicester Square. Noticeboards display what is available that day, and many tickets are half price. It is open Mon–Sat 10am–7pm, Sun noon–3pm.

Opera, Starlight Express, Sunset Boulevard and *The Lady in White*.

Traditionalists claim that the mania for musicals has squeezed out new drama productions. Yet a glance at the theatre listings in *Time Out* magazine doesn't entirely bear out this claim. Classics continue to be staged at the National Theatre and the Old Vic, new writing is still put on at the Royal Court and the Bush, experimental work and alternative comedy are mounted at the fringe theatres, and playwrights such as David Hare, Tom Stoppard and Alan Bennett do not lack an audience.

The Hollywood touch

As well as locally grown stars such as Michael Gambon, Ian McKellan, Maggie Smith, Diana Rigg and Judi Dench, American actors have never been strangers to the West End – Dustin Hoffman appeared as Shylock in *The Merchant of Venice* in 1989, for example – but recently a flood of Hollywood actors have been keen to enhance (or revive) their careers in London. Kathleen Turner, Linda Gray and Amanda Donohoe took turns to disrobe as Mrs Robinson in a stage version of *The Graduate*, and Nicole Kidman was described as "theatrical Viagra" when she briefly appeared naked in David Hare's *The Blue Room* in 1998. After Kevin Spacey scored a hit in *The Iceman Cometh* at the Old Vic, he accepted the job of part-time artistic director of the venerable theatre from its chairman, Elton John, helping to raise funds to repair its leaky roof and cracked walls and promising to appear regularly as an actor.

Fringe venues

In addition to the well known central theatres, there are many recognised fringe venues in the capital, while theatres outside the centre, in Hampstead, Richmond and Wimbledon, are used as proving grounds for West-End runs. Fringe productions range from standard Shakespeare on a low budget to the latest shows by minority groups keen to put across political or social messages, though much of the new young writing is dark and funny and well-observed.

Established fringe venues include the Young Vic (in The Cut, near the Old Vic), the Almeida (in Islington) and the Half Moon (in the East End). Lively pub theatres include the King's Head in Islington and the Gate Theatre at Notting Hill Gate.

In summer there is open-air theatre in Regent's Park (usually Shakespeare) and also in Holland Park in west London.

> In summer Shakespeare's plays can be seen on the spot where they were first performed, in a replica of the Globe Theatre on the South Bank of the River Thames.

National companies

One of the most important features of London theatre is the presence within it of two major subsidised companies: the National Theatre and the Royal Shakespeare Company.

The National, with three auditoria on the South Bank, has the advantage of a modern building, though its relentlessly concrete exterior isn't to everyone's taste, and its technology is impressive – revolving stages are only the start of it. By contrast, in 2001 the RSC gave up its London home in the Barbican Centre, to which it had brought its latest work from Stratford-upon-Avon, and began staging seasons at various theatres. This made it less visible in the capital.

The main criticisms levelled at the National have been its comparative lack of plays by European authors and the staging during Trevor Nunn's directorship of large-scale musicals such as *Oklahoma!* and *My Fair Lady* – splendidly mounted but felt by purists to be more the concern of the commercial West End theatre (to which most of them profitably transferred). The current director, Nicholas Hytner, has produced more variety and innovation and, with the help of business sponsorship, made many seats available for just £10: the stunning production of *War Horse*, with its life-sized horse puppets, is just one example of the National's work.

The National Theatre runs a back-stage tour, which mixes information and anecdote. The new Theatre and Performance Galleries at the V&A explore the whole process of performance.

Regional theatre

Although Londoners find it hard to believe, theatre is flourishing in many English cities apart from the capital, and the best regional productions regularly make their way to the West End.

Among the repertory theatres in the UK are the Royal Exchange in Manchester, the West Yorkshire Playhouse in Leeds, the Crucible in Sheffield, Nottingham Playhouse, and the Theatre Royal in Plymouth. The prolific playwright Alan Ayckbourn tried out most of his new comedies in his home town of Scarborough in Yorkshire.

Such theatres, though frequently underfunded, have been invaluable training grounds for generations of actors who have later made their names in television or movies. One star, Ian McKellen, even forsook London for Leeds for a period in the 1990s because he found the audiences there more appreciative. ❑

DRAMA FESTIVALS

Bath Fringe Festival (www.bathfringe.co.uk) mid-May to early June, coinciding with the Bath International Music Festival, tel: 01225-463 362 for both events.

Brighton Festival (www.brightonfestival.org) mid-May, drama, comedy and music staged in numerous venues, tel: 01273-709 709.

Cambridge Shakespeare Festival (www.cambridge shakespeare.com) July and August, open-air productions in college gardens, tel: 07955-218 824.

Leatherhead Drama Festival (www.leatherhead dramafestival.org) takes place in Surrey in May. Tel: 01372-365 130.

LEFT: Shakespeare's Globe Theatre.
RIGHT: Kevin Spacey, artistic director of the Old Vic.

PAINTING THE LANDSCAPE

The English countryside has inspired poets, musicians and, above all, painters. Two of them possessed genius ahead of their time

England's major contribution to European art is in landscape painting. And in landscape painting two figures – James Mallord William Turner, the son of a Covent Garden barber in London, and John Constable, whose father was a miller in Suffolk – were supreme.

England did not share Europe's earlier tradition of art based on Christianity. Church property was destroyed or seized under Henry VIII in 1535, and the puritanical Protestants who ousted the monarchy in the mid-17th century rid the church of all signs of idolatry. For longer than any Englishman can remember, paintings and icons in church have been frowned upon.

Back to nature

The English not only turned against what they saw as the vanity and pomp of Rome; they also failed to take much interest in the established Anglican Church of England. "There is no religion in England," noted the French philosopher Montesquieu in 1730. "If anyone mentions religion people begin to laugh." The great religious houses were in ruins, but Shakespeare's "ruined choirs that once so sweetly sang" inspired a piety among Romantics in the back-to-nature Age of Reason.

In England, poets such as William Wordsworth (1770–1850), bard of the Lake District and scourge of the prevailing Industrial Revolution, extolled the simple beauty of nature, an idea that soon became fashionable: walking was a habit taken up by intellectuals, and the "Eng-

lish garden" overturned the convention of formal Italianate gardens in favour of more informal plantings. The word "picturesque" entered the language, meaning a view that resembled a landscape or a view that suggested a painting.

J.M.W. Turner had no education but from time to time he was moved to write poetry, and his early paintings – *Tintern Abbey* (1794) and *Buttermere* (1798) – were also subjects of Wordsworth's poems. Turner went on the first of numerous tours of the country when he was 14, in 1789, the same year he began to study at the Royal Academy school. His tireless pens and brushes made him one of England's most pro-

LEFT: *View of Hampstead Heath, Looking Towards Harrow* (detail) by John Constable, 1821.
RIGHT: William Wordsworth, the inspirational poet of the romantic English landscape.

lific painters. He made jottings wherever he went and many parts of England can lay claim to his attention. "Turner seats" have been put up in the Yorkshire Dales to admire the scenes he painted. Around the south coast, in Hastings and elsewhere, he depicted stormy seas, influenced by Dutch maritime painting. And at Petworth House in Surrey, where he was given a studio, he painted English parklands. The Turner Gallery at the Tate Britain gallery in London holds the best part of his works.

He worked in watercolour (at the time considered merely a medium for colouring prints) and, from 1796, in oils. That same year he had his first exhibited oil painting, *Fisherman at Sea off the Needles*, depicting a small boat on a perilously stormy moonlit night. He always lived near water, never far from the Thames, and he took houses near the sea to watch the effects of the sun on the water.

He was a small, industrious figure, who wished to be left alone to get on with his work. Constable sat at the same dining table at the Royal Academy, but they were not friends and they never spoke to each other about their work. In the 1840s, living with his mistress in Chelsea, Turner was known to his neighbours as Mr Booth and was thought to be a retired admiral.

SCHOOLS AND STYLES

Medieval art Confined mainly to illuminated manuscripts, such as the Lindisfarne Gospels.

Renaissance England's Renaissance produced notable portraiture, such as the School of Miniatures.

Baroque Portraiture by Van Dyck; classical scenes, such the Banqueting House ceiling by Rubens in Whitehall.

Grand Manners and Conversation Pieces 18th-century studies of the wealthy. Principally Joshua Reynolds and Thomas Gainsborough; George Stubbs, renowned animal painter, earned more by painting portraits of horses.

Romantics Landscape paintings by John Constable and J.M.W. Turner; also paintings depicting feat at the changes of the Industrial Revolution, by artists such as John Martin.

Pre-Raphaelites Started in 1848, with Dante Gabriel Rossetti, Holman Hunt and Millais. William Morris, founder of the Arts and Crafts Movement which led to Art Nouveau in Europe, was also a Pre-Raphaelite. These idealists, including Edward Burne-Jones, harked back to a golden age of medieval craftsmanship.

Camden Town Set Walter Sickert and associates responded to the French Post-Impressionists.

St Ives Not so much a school more a 1920s West Country retreat, for Barbara Hepworth and Ben Nicholson. Now an outpost of the Tate Gallery.

Sensation! Damien Hurst, Rachael Whitehead, Tracey Emin – Tate Prize candidates bring the shock of the new.

His lack of education and rough manner may have cost him the presidency of the Royal Academy which he deserved.

Turner had been elected a full member of the Academy in 1802, the year John Constable first exhibited there. Four years later, Constable met Wordsworth in the Lake District. They had much in common: a desire for the simple rural life and no time for any luxury or grandeur their fame might have brought. Born six years after the poet, in 1776, Constable never lost sight of his Suffolk roots. Unlike Turner, Constable never strayed far from home. He never went abroad and most of his work was done in the

Constable brought a freshness of light and colour to his large canvases, such as *The Hay Wain* (1821, the National Gallery, London), which has become almost a cliché of English art, and still consistently tops popularity polls. His brush strokes were so fevered, so light and dashing that his works were called "sketches", for they were often more like impressions of what he saw. Later he might work a sketch up into a more formal, composed painting. Critics dismissed the sketches as being lesser works, and complained about his "whitewash" and "snow", the strokes of white that lightened his subjects. In 1824 *The Hay Wain* won a gold

south of England. His father owned Dedham and Flatford mills in the Stour valley which can be identified in his paintings, as can many parts of the river. Even in his day it was known as "Constable country". But pressure of work obliged him to live nearer London, at least for half the year, and he bought a house in Hampstead, which looks down over the city. The flat Suffolk landscapes had begun his obsession with skies, but it was here that he began to collect and classify them, writing down the time and date he had observed them. Clouds were, he believed, the chief organ of sentiment.

medal at the Paris Salon. Turner's work, described by Constable as "airy visions, painted with tinted steam", was also an enormous influence abroad.

Turner's impressionistic works such as *The Fighting Temeraire* or *Rain, Steam and Speed*, were as far from mainstream European art in their day as Picasso's *Les Demoiselles d'Avignon* was in his. Turner was to be emulated both in Britain and abroad. In Britain he was never surpassed. And it would be more than 50 years before a French painter, Claude Monet, exhibited in the Salon a painting of a glimpse of a sunrise on water, *Impression: Soleil Levant*, which inspired a French critic to describe him, dismissively, as an *Impressioniste*. ❑

LEFT: Turner's *Rain, Steam and Speed* (1844).
ABOVE: *The Hay Wain* (1821) painted by Constable.

FOOD AND DRINK

A growing interest in food, combined with the influences
of a multicultural society, means that eating in England
has become much more exciting

Once upon a time English food had a very
bad reputation. Charges of overcooked
vegetables and stodgy puddings were
made. Pub food consisted mainly of shepherd's
pie and sausages. Sandwiches were accused of
curling at the edges. You couldn't get a glass of
wine in many restaurants, or a cup of coffee in
many pubs. And you couldn't get a decent cup
of coffee anywhere.

Most of these criticisms were well-deserved,
although they didn't take account of the many
corners of the country where local produce
resulted in regional specialities. The joys of
freshly caught crabs in Cromer, shrimps in
Morecambe Bay or smoked fish in Craster were
often overlooked. The variety of spicy local sausages in Cumbria or new season lamb from the
Romney Marshes also went unnoticed.

But recent visitors to England have noticed
an enormous change in culinary habits.
Whether it's the plethora of television cooks

TEA – THE NATION'S FAVOURITE DRINK

On average, Britons drink five cups of tea a day, consuming
about one third of the total tea export market every year.
The finest tea is made from the bud and first two leaves of
the tea bush. They should be steeped in boiled water for
between three and five minutes. Traditionally, very strong
Indian tea, rigid with tannin and probably jaw-clenchingly
sweet, is favoured by burly men who work with their hands,
while women, children and effete males like their cuppa
watery-weak and China.

There are as many ways of making a cup of tea properly
as there are British residents and all methods involve mysterious and magical warmings and stirrings of the pot,
exact timings and individual blends.

Diarist Samuel Pepys found his first cup of China tea
such a novelty in 1660 that he gave it a special entry. In its
early days, it was so expensive that it was locked away in
caddies to stop the servants helping themselves.

A cup of tea, without sugar or milk, contains only about
four calories. Its stimulating effect is due to caffeine (weight
for weight, tea leaves contain more than twice the caffeine
of coffee beans). Its astringency and colour come from the
tannin content, its flavour from volatile oils.

The habit of afternoon tea with cakes was started
around 1840 by the Duchess of Bedford. For a traditional
afternoon tea, try a big hotel like the London Ritz, though
you have to book.

(think Gordon Ramsay, Nigella Lawson and Jamie Oliver), the renewed interest in local produce, the availability of ingredients from all over the globe, or the input of new ideas due to foreign travel, both the range and the quality of food are undeniably better.

Of course, it would not be strictly true to say that it is all English food. The lines between national cuisines have become blurred, and as new inputs have arrived, there has been a corresponding growth of interest in food which is typically English, but produced using the best and freshest ingredients.

Dietary changes have made a difference, too: venison, an old English favourite that had all but disappeared, became popular again because it is so low in fat. Ostrich didn't really catch on, and a lot of entrepreneurs lost money they had invested in the ostrich farms which seemed like the coming thing in the early 1990s. Once it was accepted that overcooking kills vitamins, crunchy vegetables came to stay; while garlic, once an English staple, but for years derided as unsociably smelly, returned to the kitchen in force once its health-giving properties were recognised.

A break with tradition

Traditional eating patterns have undergone a gradual change: few people now eat the "full English breakfast" of fried eggs, sausages, bacon and mushrooms – colloquially known as "the heart attack special". But it is still on offer in most bed-and-breakfast establishments.

The typical English tea – sandwiches, cakes and pots of tea – survives in country tea rooms, where it can be wonderfully welcoming after a long walk – but has disappeared from most households, because people usually aren't at home at "teatime".

Fish and chips are still popular, and, in seaside towns particularly can be delicious, but over-fishing has made white fish such as cod relatively scarce and expensive, so it is no longer a cheap alternative to meat. In many places fish-and-chip shops have closed down, to be replaced with restaurants selling take-away tandoori or Chinese food.

The huge increase in Chinese and Indian restaurants, ranging from the cheap take-away to the high quality establishment, reflects the influence of England's immigrant communities on the daily diet. Curry in particular is hugely popular – although much of it is an anglicised version which would be unrecognisable in India or Pakistan: think chicken tikka masala or Birmingham baltis.

Italian, food, too, has become so ubiquitous that there is a whole generation of English people who could not imagine a world where pizza or lasagne was not readily available – and may not even realise it is Italian.

The increase in vegetarianism has also been influential. Not so long ago regarded as a rather odd fad, that was probably not very good for

The rise of the "gastro pub" (pubs geared towards serving great food) have become so fashionable, they can be found even in quiet country areas.

you, it is now so acceptable that not only do specialist vegetarian restaurants thrive, but virtually every eating establishment offers vegetarian alternatives, which are frequently more adventurous and tempting than those geared towards carnivores.

The streets of London and other major cities are lined with restaurants and cafés offering a fusion of culinary styles, as might be expected,

LEFT: fine dining at L'Enclume in the Lake District.
RIGHT: chef Tom Aikens dishes it up.

but what is more surprising is that this wide choice of food has radiated to provincial towns and rural communities. Many village pubs will have menus that range from warm goat's cheese salad to roast beef, from seared sea bass to steak and kidney pie.

Culinary gains and losses

English cheeses have made a comeback in recent years. When soft cheeses from the Continent first became widely available, indigenous varieties such as Cheddar, Wensleydale and Stilton fell out of fashion. But their worth has now been recognised once more – as has that of

been bred for shape and appearance and that taste has been sacrificed.

Still more people lament the fact that, while you can buy kiwi fruit and mangoes, it can be hard to find a true scrunchy English apple, except in apple-growing areas, where you can buy them at roadside stalls and farm shops. Cob nuts and cherries from Kent are also increasingly hard to find. However farmers' markets, where fresh produce is sold direct from the growers, are making a welcome appearance. One of the most popular is Borough Market in London.

One thing the English are still traditional about is their puddings, also known as desserts.

Somerset-made varieties of soft cheeses such as Brie and Camembert, and regional cheeses like Cornish yarg and Dorset blue vinney.

Many small grocers' shops and delicatessens sell regional cheeses, and there are specialist shops where the variety is almost overwhelming. At Christmas, Stilton, recognised as the queen of English cheeses, is sold in discreetly decorated gift boxes by superior stores such as Harrods and Fortnum & Mason. It is traditionally consumed with a glass of port.

The variety of food available, together with many restrictions imposed by the European Union, has had some unfortunate side effects. Many people complain that the fruit and vegetables available in English supermarkets have

Passion fruit sorbet is all very well, and there are those who think that profiteroles represent the height of French achievement, but a strong body of opinion holds that treacle tart, syrup sponge pudding or apple pie are the only civilised way to finish a meal, with lashings of custard of course. Catering to this demand, many otherwise adventurous restaurants put such comfort foods on their menus. There is even a Pudding Club, whose members meet regularly for meals consisting only of traditional puddings, like Spotted Dick and Sussex Pond pudding (which has a whole lemon in the centre). ❑

ABOVE: a fine selection of fresh fish and cheese at London's Borough Market.

Country Pubs

The English pub is an institution, offering warm beer, good company, and a welcome to all. That's the tradition. But what's the reality?

The best pub in England is called The Moon Under Water, and it hides down a side street in an old northern industrial town. It has that indefinable richness of atmosphere that comes in part from its customers, who are mostly regulars and who attend not only for the beer but equally for the conversation, and in part from its uncompromisingly Victorian architecture and fittings, its dark-grained mahogany, ornamental mirrors and sparkling etched glass, its cast-iron fireplaces and ceiling stained yellow-brown by decades of nicotine, all combining to create the solid comfortable ugliness that often characterised the 19th century.

It has games, particularly darts, in its public bar, and good solid plain food. It has barmaids who know everyone by name, and a delightful garden where, in summer, the customers drink under the shade of plane trees.

The Moon Under Water is always quiet enough to talk, if only to praise the excellence of the fine traditional English ale.

The Moon Under Water does not exist. It was a figment of the imagination of George Orwell, the author of Nineteen Eighty-Four, who 50 years ago played a round of that perennially popular English game – dreaming of the perfect pub.

Perfection is in the eye of the beholder, of course, and just as many "Irish pubs" round the world bear only the faintest resemblance to a traditional Gaelic boozer, many an "old-worlde" English pub may not be true to pub traditions.

What, then, makes a good traditional pub? There are certain well-defined ground rules. In the English beer-drinker's Bible, the annual Good Beer Guide, author Michael Jackson wrote: "In a good pub, the greatest attention is given to the drink, and in particular to the beer. Sociability, on both sides of the bar, comes a close second… A good pub has a caring, responsive landlord…there is always one bar (and preferably two) to accommodate those people who simply want to drink and chat without the dis-

traction or inhibition induced by overbearing decor, noisy entertainment, or intrusive dining."

The word "pub" is merely a shortened form of "public house", an indication that the earliest ale houses were simply private homes where the occupant brewed beer and sold it at the front door or across a table in the living room. To indicate that the house sold ale, the owner would hang out a sign, not saying "Ale", as the average Saxon peasant never graduated to literacy, but a pole topped with a bough of evergreen.

There is no shortage of claimants to be the Oldest Pub in Britain, but one with a stronger case than most is the Trip to Jerusalem, in Nottingham – cer-

tainly in business at the time of the Crusades, hence its name. Like so much else in British life, the pub reached its zenith in Victorian times and the country is still rich in opulent pub interiors from that period, despite all the efforts of philistine pub-owning corporations to rip them out in the name of "modernisation". Pubs have been changing over the past few decades. More and more of them sell good, inexpensive food; tea and coffee are often on offer and families are being made more welcome.

A radical change came about with recent laws which allowed pubs to open not just at lunch time and in the evening, but largely to set their own opening hours. A smoking ban has also changed the character, and freshened the atmosphere, of English pubs.   ❑

ABOVE: pints ready for pulling.

WALKING IN ENGLAND

"If I could not walk far and fast, I think I should just explode and perish," said Charles Dickens, summing up the widespread English love of walking.

Walking is immensely popular throughout England and has been since Victorian times. There are paths and terrain to suit all levels of fitness, from easy family trails in country parks to long distance paths that take several days to complete. The mountains of the Lake District offer the toughest challenge, with peaks such as Scafell Pike (3210ft/978 metres) and Helvellyn (3114ft/950 metres) attracting thousands of walkers each year. The western areas of the lakes, around Buttermere and Crummock Water, are generally quieter than the eastern part, which is more accessible due to its proximity to the M6 motorway. The Derbyshire Peak District is also extremely popular, especially with weekend walkers from London and the south east.

However, if you want to escape the crowds, then Northumberland is the place to go. This is a gloriously wild landscape, where you can walk too, notably the South West Coast Path, which embraces the rugged Cornish coast and will give you a healthy blast of sea air.

> Long-distance paths are signposted and marked with an acorn symbol, public footpaths with a yellow arrow, and public bridleways (walkers and horse riders) with a blue arrow.

all day and not meet anyone – except the occasional sheep. Hadrian's Wall stretches across the lonely moors like a silent snake, while to the north lies Scotland and the once viciously contested border.

The southern parts of England offer gentler walks: you can ramble along quiet country lanes, stride out across the Downs, stroll along tracks in the flat lands of Norfolk or along canal towpaths in the Midlands. There are coastal walks

Be prepared

The best time of year for walking is April to October, when you've got a better chance of dry, sunny weather. However, this is England and you might well get sunshine in January – and snow in June. The great walker Alfred Wainwright once said that: "There is no such thing as bad weather, only unsuitable clothing", and it's important to make sure that you're well

ABOVE: walking in Wasdale, Cumbria.
RIGHT: buttercup fields in Branscombe, Devon.

equipped for your walks, especially if you're going up exposed mountains or fells. Get an up to date weather forecast before you set off, and try and let someone know where you're going. Ensure that you've got waterproof clothing (it might be sunny at the bottom of the mountain, but the weather is notoriously unpredictable here and it could be wet and misty by the time you reach the top); wear stout walking boots and layers; carry a map and compass and know how to use them; take some food and water and carry a whistle. The National Parks will have more information on safety on the hills, so do check this out before you set off.

Guided walks

If you're walking alone, then the Ordnance Survey (OS) maps are the best, at a scale of 1:25,000. You should find them at National Park Visitor Centres and outdoor shops. National Parks often run ranger-led guided walks, while the Ramblers' Association (www.ramblers.org.uk) has a full programme of guided walks across England. If you'd like to join in, just join online a month before you arrive – annual membership is £27 for one person.

You can then check the walk finder (website or 0207-339 8500) to find what walks are taking place in the area you plan to visit.   ❑

ENGLAND'S LONG DISTANCE WALKS

There are several National Trails (www.nationaltrail.co.uk) in England: long distance, waymarked walks that take you through some of the country's loveliest landscapes. You can either follow the whole route, or do short, one day sections. You can do the walks in either direction – and purchase comprehensive guides to help you follow them.

Cotswold Way 102 miles (163km), from Bath Abbey to Chipping Camden, allow 7 days.

Hadrian's Wall Path 84 miles (135km) from Wallsend in the east, to Bowness-on-Solway in the west, allow 7 days.

North Downs Way 153 miles (246km), from Farnham to Dover, allow 14 days

North Norfolk Coast Path 93 miles (150km), from Knet-

tishall Heath Country Park to Cromer Pier, allow 8 days.

Pennine Way 268 miles (429km), from Edale to Kirk Yetholm on the Scottish border, allow 16 days.

The Ridgeway 87 miles (139km), from Overton Hill, Avebury to Ivinghoe Beacon, nr Tring, allow 6 days.

South Downs Way 100 miles (160km), from Winchester to Eastbourne, allow 8 days.

South West Coast Path 630 miles (1014km), from Minehead, Somerset to Poole, Dorset, allow 56 days.

Thames Path 184 miles (294km), from the source of the Thames, nr Kemble to the Thames Barrier, allow 14 days.

Yorkshire Wolds Way – 79 miles (127km), from near the Humber Bridge to Filey Brigg, nr Scarborough, allow 5 days.

PLACES

A detailed guide to the country, with principal sites
clearly cross-referenced by number to the maps

or all the fuss it has made in history, for all the language
it has distributed about the world, England is a rather
small place. The largest of the four constituent elements
that make up the United Kingdom, it covers 50,331 sq miles
(130,357 sq km), about the same size as New York State or one
of New Zealand's islands. But its population of over 50 million is over two and a half times New York State's, and over 15
times both New Zealand's islands.

By far the greater portion of the population lives in the
south. The large northern towns, Liverpool, Manchester and
Newcastle, which grew vast on the Industrial Revolution, have struggled

to catch up with the post-industrial age, while Birmingham,
Britain's second city, has benefited from its more central
location. The country is divided into counties, the old English shires, where sheriffs transacted local business. They
have provided titles for the nation's nobility and though
their names and boundaries have been tinkered with twice
in post-war years, they are redolent of the country's past
and continue to inspire local pride.

At the start of the third millennium, England, due to post-
war migrations, is a less homogenised nation than ever before – all nations
of the world can be found in London. Local accents and dialects that not
long ago were thick on the ground, are now waning, but new cultures,
traditions and accents have been added by incoming populations.

England's ever-changing landscape provides incomparable
scenery, in the Peak District, in the Pennines, on the South
Downs, among the Yorkshire and West Country moors and
around the Lake District. The variety of architecture character-
ises every part of the country, from West Country thatch to Cotswold stone, weatherboarded Kent to half-timbered East Anglia,
black-slated Cumbria, and the sandstones, red and yellow, of
Cumbria and York. It doesn't take much effort in England, and
not many miles, to feel that you have travelled a long way. ❑

PRECEDING PAGES: Seven Sisters, Sussex; The Lowry, Manchester; Blackpool
Tower. **LEFT:** the British Museum, London. **ABOVE:** half-timbered houses,
Lavenham, Suffolk; the State Opening of Parliament; Holmfirth, Yorkshire.

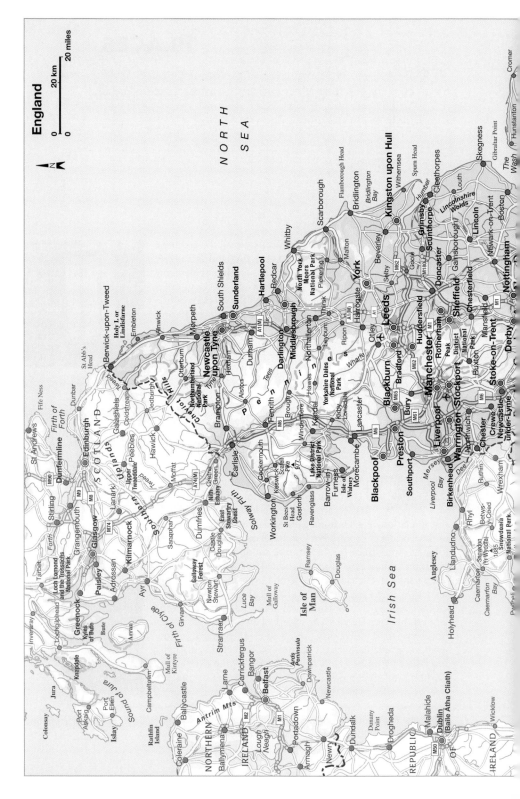

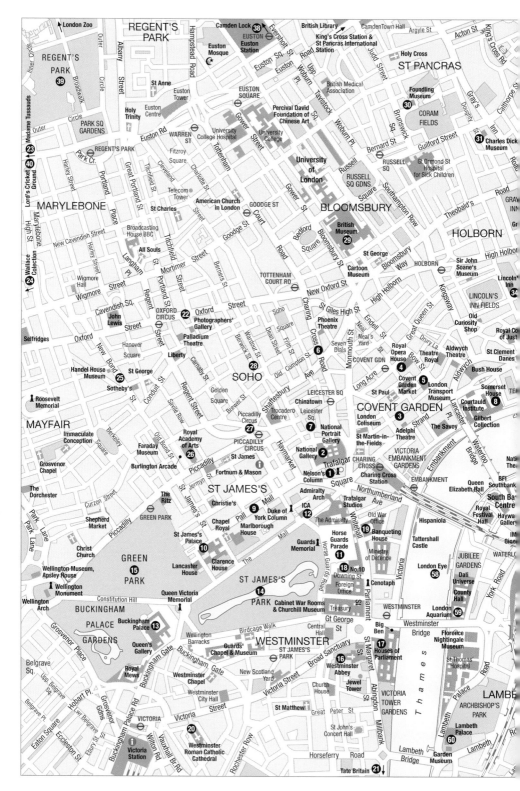

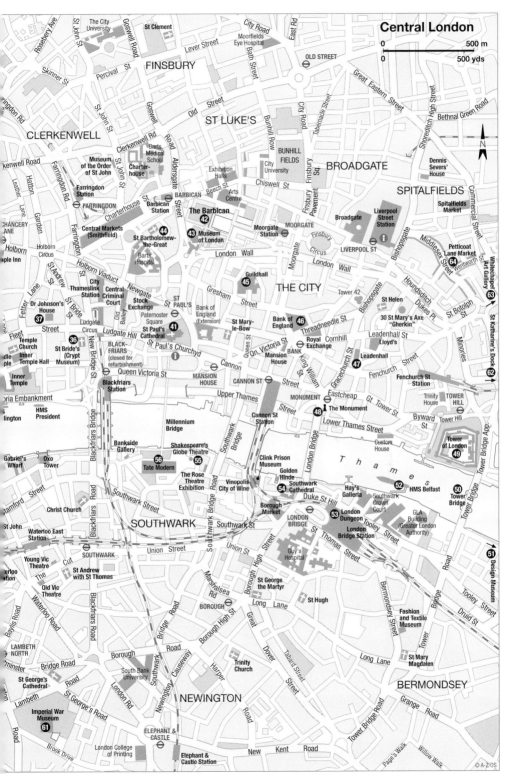

Central London

CENTRAL LONDON

Few cities offer such a variety of sites and experiences: there is something to suit every visitor. Start with the bright lights in the centre and work outwards

The centre of London is a small place. The best part of it is taken up by the West End, which includes Oxford Street, Soho and Covent Garden, as well as the elite areas of Mayfair and St James's. On its south side are the royal and political power-houses of Whitehall and Westminster, to the east Bloomsbury and the British Museum. Few cities can make a visitor so contentedly footsore from wandering the streets and discovering its secrets. As Samuel Johnson, compiler of the first English dictionary, said, "When a man is tired of London he is tired of life, for there is in London all that life can afford."

A good starting point is **Trafalgar Square ❶**, the strategic heart of London and an impressive public open space. A mayoral campaign to rid it of its traditional plague of pigeons was largely successful, and in 2003 the north side of the square was pedestrianised to give people a sporting chance of reaching the fountains without being mown down by traffic. The square, laid out in the 1830s and 1840s by Sir Charles Barry, was dedicated to the memory of Admiral Lord Nelson and his decisive victory over Napoleon's fleet off Cape Trafalgar in 1805. It is a paragon of the classical style, enclosed by graceful white facades and dominated by the 169ft (51.5-metre) **Nelson's Column** and four bronze lions. Every Christmas a 70ft (20-metre) Norwegian spruce is erected in the square, a gift from the city of Oslo in recognition of the protection given by Britain to members of the Norwegian royal family in World War II.

Trafalgar Square acts as a transportation hub, traversed by several bus and tube lines. While it is no longer the scene of London's riotous annual New Year's Eve celebrations, it is still the site of political demonstrations, as it has been for more than 100 years. Demonstrations here against Margaret Thatcher's poll tax (an unpopular local government tax) helped precipitate her downfall in 1990.

Main attractions
TRAFALGAR SQUARE
COVENT GARDEN
BUCKINGHAM PALACE
WESTMINSTER CATHEDRAL
HOUSES OF PARLIAMENT
BLOOMSBURY
HAMPSTEAD
REGENT'S PARK

LEFT: the National Gallery and Trafalgar Square.
BELOW: a traditional double-decker bus.

TIP

Look out for candlelit concerts held in St Martin-in-the-Fields – and try out the café in the crypt where the coffee is excellent.

Along the north flank of Trafalgar Square is the **National Gallery** ❷ (www.nationalgallery.org.uk; daily 10am–6pm, Fri until 9pm; free). Founded in 1824, the gallery has since grown into one of the most outstanding and comprehensive collections in the world, with a list of masters ranging from Leonardo da Vinci and Rembrandt to El Greco and Van Gogh. In 1991 the Sainsbury Wing, designed by Robert Venturi, was opened to house the rich Renaissance collection. Single pictures, or series of pictures, are often highlighted to give great detail of painters' working methods and their times. There are frequent lectures and events, and live music in the Central Hall every Friday evening.

Around the corner, established in 1856, is the superb **National Portrait Gallery** (www.npg.org.uk; daily 10am–6pm, Thur–Fri until 9pm; free). Presenting an illustrated British history, it now contains the faces of more than 10,000 famous Britons by the nation's illustrious artists and photographers, and it often stages important photographic exhibitions.

To the right of the National Gallery is **St Martin-in-the-Fields** church, the oldest surviving structure on Trafalgar Square, built along simple but elegant lines by James Gibbs in 1722–26. There has been a church on this site since 1222. The church became well known during World War II when its crypt was a refuge from the Blitz. St Martin's is still the parish church for Buckingham Palace, with royal boxes at the east end.

Covent Garden and theatreland

Northeast of Trafalgar Square begins the maze of narrow streets and tiny alleys called **Covent Garden** ❸. The name derives from the convent garden that occupied the area until Henry VIII's Dissolution. The present piazza was designed by Charles II's architect, Inigo Jones, and it was a meeting place for society until the royal palace moved from Whitehall, and a market for flowers, fruit and herbs was licensed, in 1670. At the centre of the cobblestoned piazza are the superb steel-and-glass **market pavilions** constructed in the 1830s to house market stalls.

BELOW: Claude-Oscar Monet's popular *The Thames below Westminster* (1871), on display in the National Gallery.

The market was moved to new quarters south of the river in 1974, and in the early 1980s Covent Garden was refurbished into an area of restaurants, shops and cafés. It is now a showplace for buskers (street entertainers) and a summer mecca both for office workers at lunchtime and for tourists round the clock. There is an antiques market on Mondays, and the Jubilee Market at weekends offers arts and crafts, food stalls and puppet shows. Nearby, cobblestoned **Neal Street** has some speciality shops such as The Astrology Shop and the Tea House selling more than 70 different types of teas and tisanes.

Neal's Yard, at Earlham Street, with an apothecary, bakery and natural-foods shops, is gathered around a tiny courtyard full of potted trees. Those with a taste for English tradition might imbibe at the many ancient pubs in the area such as the **Lamb and Flag** (on Rose Street, off Floral Street), a 17th-century pub once frequented by prizefighters and known as the "Bucket of Blood".

In the eastern corner of Covent Garden, helping to complete the colonnade, is the majestic **Royal Opera**

A street entertainer performs in Covent Garden.

House ❹ (box office tel: 020-7304 4000; www.roh.org.uk), home of both the Royal Opera and Royal Ballet companies. To mark the millennium, the 2,098-seat building received a £120 million facelift, giving the performers more back-stage space and the audience air conditioning.

The old flower market, in the southeastern corner of the square, is now home to the newly refurbished **London Transport Museum** ❺ (www.ltmuseum.co.uk; daily 10am–6pm; charge for adults, free for accompanied children under 16), which has a big collection of horse-drawn coaches, buses, trams, trains, rail carriages, and some working displays. It effectively traces the social history of modern London, whose growth was powered by transport, and deals intelligently with issues such as congestion and pollution. Facilities for children are especially good: there are extensive play areas, simulators to allow them to "drive" a Tube train, and actors playing early tunnellers or Victorian bus passengers who are prepared to describe yesteryear's working and living conditions.

LEFT: hand-made arts and crafts for sale in Covent Garden.

APPLE MARKET

Fact File

Situation On roughly the same latitude as Berlin and Vancouver, 40 miles (64km) from the North Sea.
Size 115 sq miles (300 sq km).
Population 7.5 million.
Transport system Underground (tube) and buses. Oyster smartcards generally offer the cheapest travel option. Paris is 2 hours, 15 minutes by Eurostar train from St Pancras International. Boat trips on the Thames from Charing Cross pier.
Tallest building 1 Canada Square, Canary Wharf.
Liveliest festival Notting Hill Carnival.
Best produce market Borough Market.
Oldest pubs Prospect of Whitby (1520), Wapping (east London); The George Inn (1676), Borough High Street, (south London). London's only galleried coaching inn.
Biggest attraction British Museum.
Newest hit attraction London Eye.
Finest building Westminster Abbey.
Best for roast beef Simpson's in the Strand, Rules in Maiden Lane.
Best view of the city Waterloo Bridge for panoramas day and night; unbeatable vistas from the London Eye.

Covent Garden, the backdrop for the musical *My Fair Lady*, is synonymous with British theatre: Drury Lane is where the **Theatre Royal** was established in 1663 and where Charles II's mistress, Nell Gwynne (1650–87), first made her name as a comedienne; while the Tuscan-style **St Paul's Church**, also designed by Inigo Jones (1633), memorialises many actors.

Books and movies

Bibliophiles hasten towards **Charing Cross Road ❻**, the western boundary of Covent Garden district with a string of bookshops ranging from old-fashioned Foyle's to giant Borders. More interesting are specialist enclaves such as Magma on Earlham Street (graphic design and photography) or the treasure trove of maps and guidebooks that is Stanford's at 12–14 Long Acre (to the north of Covent Garden Piazza).

Charing Cross Road runs up the east side of **Leicester Square ❼**, the domain of tourists, pigeons and buskers, filled with the bright lights of the capital's main cinemas. Traffic free, except for stars' limousines at premieres, it has a central square with a statue of London-born Charlie Chaplin as The Little Tramp, a Shakespeare fountain and a tendency to seediness come nightfall.

South of Covent Garden, the Strand connects Trafalgar Square with Fleet Street and the City. By Waterloo Bridge is **Somerset House ❽**, Britain's first purpose-built office block in the 1770s. For years it housed the official registry of births, marriages and deaths. It now houses the superb **Courtauld Institute of Art**, (daily 10am–6pm; charge) home to a fine collection of Impressionist and Post-Impressionist paintings, with works by Van Gogh and Gauguin, and London University's art history studies centre; notable works include Van Gogh's *Self Portrait with Bandaged Ear* and Manet's *A Bar at the Folies-Bergere*.

The Seamen's Hall gives access to the splendid River Terrace, which in summer has a café and great views. Visitors can also join free guided tours on the 1st and 3rd Sat of each month, times 12.15, 1.15, 2.15 and 3.15pm. Tickets available from 10.30am on the day, from the Information Desk at the Seamen's Waiting Room.

A service in St Paul's Church on the second Sunday in May commemorates the Punch and Judy puppet tradition.

BELOW: the Shakespeare fountain and statue, Leicester Square.

Gentlemen's clubs and royal London

Pall Mall ❾, on the west side of Trafalgar Square, is a sedate and elegant avenue that runs through the heart of St James's. This is London's "Club Land" – the exclusive gathering place of English gentlemen behind the closed doors of the Athenaeum, White's, the Carlton and a dozen other private enclaves. The street takes its name from *paille maille*, a game that originated in Italy and was a precursor to croquet. It was imported to England from France in the 17th century and played on a long green which once occupied this site: Charles II was a great fan of the game and used to play it with his mistresses.

Wedged between the wood-panelled halls of Pall Mall and the leafy landscape of Green Park are a number of stately homes. The most impressive of these is **St James's Palace ❿**, built on the site of a leper hospital by Henry VIII in the 1530s. A royal residence until the 19th century, St James's is now occupied by the Princess Royal and her staff. Neighbouring royal mansions include **Marlborough House**, and the residences of **Clarence House** (the London home of Prince Charles) and **Lancaster House** where Chopin played a royal command performance for Queen Victoria.

The Mall is London's impressive ceremonial way, a broad tree-lined avenue that runs from Admiralty Arch in Trafalgar Square to Buckingham Palace. The spectacular Trooping the Colour takes place along here each June, as Queen Elizabeth II rides down the avenue in a horse-drawn carriage with an escort of Household Cavalry as part of a 300-year-old ceremony to mark the official birthday of the monarch. The legions mass on **Horse Guards Parade ⓫**, a huge open space behind Whitehall, where a royal unit troop their regimental flags to the tune of marching music and thundering drums. The Household Cavalry can also be seen as they ride down the Mall on their way to and from the Changing the Guard at Buckingham Palace (www.changing-the-guard.com; 11.30am daily in summer, alternate days in winter).

Overlooking the Mall is the **Institute of Contemporary Arts (ICA) ⓬** (www.

In December and January, the courtyard of Somerset House is turned into a skating rink, the classical facade providing a magical backdrop.

BELOW: flags line the Mall.

Club Land

Each of London's clubs has its own character and attracts a certain type of person. It is said that bishops and Fellows of the Royal Society join the Athenaeum, the foremost academic club, while actors and publishers opt for the Garrick or Saville Club. Diplomats, politicians and spies prefer Brooks's, the Traveller's, Boodles or White's, while journalists gather at the Groucho Club in Soho. The novelist Jules Verne used the Reform Club (Pall Mall), the leading liberal club, as the setting for Phileas Fogg's wager that he could travel around the world in 80 days.

The majority of London's clubs are the near-exclusive preserve of men. Their continuing influence in the social, commercial and political life of the capital should not be underestimated.

Although St James's has not been a monarch's residence for more than 150 years, foreign ambassadors are still known as "Ambassadors to the Court of St James's".

BELOW: crowds gather outside Buckingham Palace.

ica.org.uk; daily noon–7pm, Thur until 9pm during exhibitions), the cutting edge of modern painting, sculpture and the performing arts, housed in the Georgian-style Nash House.

Buckingham Palace

Londoners have a love-hate relationship with **Buckingham Palace** ⓭. To some, the Queen's home is irredeemably ugly, but it's also held in esteem as the symbol of Britain's royalty. The palace arose within a mulberry grove in the early 18th century as a mansion for the powerful Duke of Buckingham. It was purchased in 1761 by George III for his wife Queen Charlotte (he preferred to live in St James's Palace) and he later spent £73,000 remodelling it. However, it wasn't grand enough for George IV (the Prince Regent) and soon after the building came under his control in 1820 he commissioned his favourite architect, John Nash, to rebuild it on a more magnificent scale.

Despite controversially costly alterations, which reached around half a million pounds, the palace wasn't occupied until Victoria became queen in 1837

and made it the official royal residence in London. The palace has 775 rooms, of which 19 are State Rooms. Visitors gather in front of Buckingham Palace for the Changing of the Guard and perhaps to snatch a glimpse of the Queen, who is in residence when the flag is flying. In late summer, when the Queen is not in residence, the more dedicated may pay a visit to the **State Rooms** (daily Aug–Sept 9.45am–6pm, last entry 3.45pm; ticket office at the Visitor Entrance, Buckingham Palace Road, mid-July–late Sept 9.15am–5pm). Otherwise, only two sections of the palace are open to the public: the **Royal Mews** (Apr–Oct Mon–Thur 11am–4pm), which contain royal vehicles from coaches to Rolls-Royces to horses, and the **Queen's Gallery** (daily 10am–5.30pm), which displays paintings from the priceless Royal Collection. Charges apply to all.

Bounding Buckingham Palace on the north and east are two of London's renowned green spaces – St James's Park and Green Park. **St James's Park** ⓮ in particular, has lush vegetation and a tranquil lake whose wooden foot-

bridge gives a superb view of Buckingham Palace. It provides a haven for water birds, office workers and civil servants. In contrast, **Green Park**  appears comparatively wild. There are no tidy flower beds or fountains – just expanses of grass where Charles II used to take his daily constitutional.

Westminster's grandeur

A short walk from the southeast corner of St James's Park is Westminster, the seat of English government for nearly 1,000 years. Westminster is also a holy place – the burial ground of English monarchs, the site of one of the greatest monasteries of the Middle Ages and the location of London's most inspiring Gothic architecture.

Westminster Abbey ⑯ (www.westminster-abbey.org; Mon–Fri 9.30am–4.30pm, last entry 3.30pm, Wed until 7pm, last entry 6pm, Sat 9am–2.30pm, last entry 1.30pm; charge; *floorplan at end of book*) was built by Edward the Confessor and consecrated on 28 December 1065; Edward died nine days later and was buried before the high altar. It is thought that the ill-fated Harold, his successor who later lost his throne to the Norman invaders, was crowned here the day after Edward died. On Christmas Day 1066, the Norman William the Conqueror, having taken control of England, was crowned as the new king in the abbey. Since that day, all but two English monarchs have been crowned in the church. Little remains of Edward's Saxon abbey; it was rebuilt under the Normans and then redesigned in flamboyant French-Gothic style 200 years later. The **Henry VII Chapel** is a 16th-century masterpiece of fan-vaulted ceilings in pure white stone, decked out in the colourful medieval banners of the Knights Grand Cross of the Order of the Bath. Behind lies the Royal Air Force Chapel, with a stained-glass window containing the badges of every squadron that fought in the 1940 Battle of Britain. **Poets' Corner** contains the graves of Chaucer, Tennyson, Dickens and Dryden, plus memorials to Shakespeare, Milton, Keats, Jane Austen and William Wordsworth. The abbey also houses the **English Coronation Chair**, built in 1300 for Edward I and still used for the

St James's Park, with the London Eye in the background.

LEFT: relax in the park.
BELOW: Westminster Abbey.

How Parliament Works

Widely known as the mother of parliaments, the British Parliament has been a model for democracies all over the world.

The Houses of Parliament consist of the House of Commons and the House of Lords. The Commons, the House of locally elected Members of Parliament (MPs), known as the Lower House, wields virtually all the power but inhabits only half the building. Jutting out towards Parliament Square is Westminster Hall, with the offices, dining rooms and libraries of the Commons; in the centre is the Commons' debating chamber. To the right of Westminster Hall is the domain of the Lords, whose role is to examine and sometimes block bills proposed by the Lower House, although a bill can be reintroduced. Until recently, most lords governed by birthright, as descendants of the previous ruling classes, but the voting rights of many hereditary peers have been abolished and the make-up of the Lords has changed. Most members are now life peers, ennobled for services to the nation, and their titles can't be passed to their children. Former MPs are often made peers in recognition for years of service.

There are 646 elected MPs, yet the Commons seats only about 450. This is not usually a problem since MPs attend sessions when they wish. The governing party sits on one side, facing the opposition. Cabinet ministers sit on the front bench, opposite the "Shadow Cabinet" (the leading members of the opposition). The Cabinet, consisting of up to two dozen ministers and chaired by the prime minister, meets at 10 Downing Street weekly to review major issues.

Major parties represented are the Conservatives, Labour and the Liberal Democrats. General elections are run on the basis of local rather than proportional representation. Therefore a party's presence in the house may not reflect its overall national standing. A party, however, needs an overall majority in the house to push through its bills. The procedure of lawmaking is so complex that a bill usually takes more than six months to be enacted. If it is still incomplete at the end of the parliamentary year, it is dropped. Various techniques are employed by the opposition to delay a bill.

The press can report on Parliament and the business of both houses is televised. A select group of journalists ("lobby correspondents") have daily informal "background" briefings with ministers or government officials.

Parliament meets from October to July. In November, the government's plans for the year are announced in the Queen's Speech at the State Opening of Parliament, held in the chamber of the Lords. From the Strangers' Gallery, the public can watch the House of Commons at work, though seats are limited and security precautions introduced since a flour-filled condom thrown from the gallery hit Tony Blair in 2004, have made access more difficult. The weekly Prime Minister's Question Time – an unruly affair – usually attracts a full house. Sessions are chaired by the Speaker, an MP elected by the House who resigns from their political party on taking office – as they must remain impartial. They are there to keep order and call MPs to speak. The cry of "Order, Order" is frequently heard above the parliamentary babble. ❑

ABOVE: the Commons in session.
LEFT: the opulent House of Lords.

installation of new monarchs – though the Stone of Scone, which traditionally sat underneath, has now been returned to Scotland.

Houses of Parliament

On the river side of Westminster Abbey rise the **Houses of Parliament** ⓱, an elaborate Gothic structure designed in the 1830s by Charles Barry and Augustus Pugin to replace the old Westminster Palace built by Edward the Confessor. The building is a triumph of Victorian England: 872ft (266 metres) long with 3 miles (5km) of passages, 100 staircases and 1,100 rooms. It took 30 years to build and cost over £2 million. At the south end is **Victoria Tower**, from which a Union flag flies whenever Parliament is in session, while on the north side rises the majestic Clock Tower, commonly known as **Big Ben** after the name of the massive bell, cast in 1858, that strikes the hours. Facing Big Ben is **Portcullis House**, a £250 million office block for Members of Parliament; its much criticised "chimneys" form part of the air-conditioning system.

Within Parliament are the two governing bodies of Great Britain, the House of Commons and the House of Lords, which moved into the old Palace of Westminster after Henry VIII vacated the premises in the 16th century. The Commons, comprising the elected representatives of various political parties, is the scene of both lively debate and loutish heckling. You can watch proceedings from the safety of the **Visitors' Gallery** when Parliament is in session (queue at St Stephen's Gate, expect to wait for 1–2 hours, especially for Prime Minister's Question Time; entry from 4pm Mon, 1pm Tue–Thur, and 10am Fri; UK residents should contact their MP for an advance ticket).

One relic of the old Westminster Palace to withstand a fire that all but destroyed the building in 1834 is **Westminster Hall**. At 240ft (73-metres) long, it is one of the largest medieval halls in Europe with an unsupported roof. Building started in 1097, though the present hammer-beam roof of ancient oak is 14th-century. The hall has witnessed some of the most dramatic moments in English history,

A floor plan of Westminster Abbey can be found on page 399.

BELOW: the Houses of Parliament.

The Jewel Tower, remnant of the old Westminster Palace.

BELOW: part of Boadicea's statue and Big Ben's clock tower.

including the trials of: Sir Thomas More in 1535; Guy Fawkes and his co-conspirators in the Gunpowder Plot in 1606 and that of Charles I in 1649. It also saw the investiture of Oliver Cromwell as Lord Protector in 1653. A small museum of Parliament Past and Present is housed in the **Jewel Tower** (daily Apr–Oct 10am–5pm, Nov–Mar 10am–4pm; charge), a former keep beside the abbey that held the king's jewels, clothing and furs until the reign of Henry VIII. The remains of the moat can still be seen.

Whitehall is the broad and busy avenue that runs north from the Houses of Parliament to Trafalgar Square. Once the fulcrum of British colonial power, it is still home to the Foreign and Commonwealth offices, the Treasury, Admiralty and Ministry of Defence – and the Prime Minister's 17th-century residence at **No. 10 Downing Street ⑱**, protected by gates.

At the end of King Charles Street, down Clive Steps, a small wall of sandbags identifies the **Cabinet War Rooms** (www.cwm.iwm.org.uk; daily 9.30am–6pm; charge), the underground nerve-centre from which Churchill directed Britain's war effort. Using old photographs for reference, the rooms have been meticulously restored to their 1940s state and the tour through this claustrophobic bunker is compelling enough to have attracted two US presidents, Bill Clinton and George W. Bush. A **Churchill Museum** dedicates itself to the life of the great statesman.

For a contrast to the drab architecture of modern government take a detour to **Banqueting House ⑲** (Mon–Sat 10am–5pm; charge), a relic of the old Whitehall Palace and a masterpiece of English baroque. Inigo Jones built the hall for James I in 1622. Peter Paul Rubens added the lovely allegorical ceiling commissioned by Charles I, who stepped on to the scaffold from here for his public beheading in 1649.

Westminster Cathedral

Victoria Street shoots southwest from Parliament Square as an unexpected corridor of steel and glass skyscrapers in the heart of neo-Gothic London. Almost hidden between the corporate headquarters and banking houses is the

terracotta bulk of **Westminster Cathedral** ❷⓿ England's premier Roman Catholic church. Built in the 1890s in an outlandish Italian-Byzantine style not seen elsewhere in London, it has a 330ft (100-metre) striped tower incorporating a lift for public use (daily Apr–Sept; charge). The views from the gallery at the top are superb.

Millbank follows the gentle curve of the Thames to the south of Parliament Square, first passing **Victoria Tower Gardens** (home of Rodin's *The Burghers of Calais*) before sweeping round to the grand, neoclassical mansion which is **Tate Britain** ❷❶ (www.tate.org.uk; daily 10am–5.50pm; free).

Founded in 1897 by Henry Tate, of the Tate & Lyle sugar empire, it houses British art from the past three centuries, from Constable to Gainsborough, Hogarth to Hodgkin and Stubbs to Stanley Spencer. The Clore Gallery has the extensive Turner collection. The Tate Boat runs every 40 minutes during gallery opening hours between Tate Britain and Tate Modern. For tickets tel: 020-7887 8888, Mon–Fri 9.45am–5.50pm.

Shopping and waxworks

Oxford Circus, the hub of several tube lines, is halfway down **Oxford Street** ❷❷, London's busiest shopping street *(see page 84)*. It is close enough to stroll from here to the **Photographers' Gallery** (Tue–Sat 11am–6pm, Thur–Fri until 8pm, Sun noon–6pm; free) at 16–18 Ramillies Street, where there are changing photographic exhibitions. The gallery has a café. Oxford Street marks the boundary between **Marylebone** and exclusive **Mayfair**. The Marylebone (pronounced *marry-le-bun*) district sprawls along the southern edge of Regent's Park; infamous in the 18th century for its taverns, boxing matches and cockfights, it is now a gastronomic and shopping destination with desirable housing. It is also home to the **Madame Tussaud's Wax Museum** ❷❸ (www.madamtussauds.com; Mon–Fri 9.30am–5.30pm, Sat–Sun 9am–6pm; charge) on Marylebone Road. The waxworks were founded in the early 19th century by Marie Tussaud, a tiny woman who learned her craft in post-Revolution Paris – making wax effigies of the heads of guillotine victims. In 1835 they

The bold red-and-white brickwork of Westminster Cathedral.

BELOW: the Cabinet War Rooms' Central Map Room.

Capital Shopping

London is a great place to shop, and there are retail opportunities to suit all budgets and tastes.

West End

The principal shopping streets are Oxford Street and Regent Street, which bisect at Oxford Circus. The smarter end is towards Marble Arch, and the bargain shops are to the east. As well as dozens of menswear and women's fashion shops, **Oxford Street** also has the large department stores, including Marks & Spencer, Selfridges and John Lewis. Liberty, purveyors of classic fabrics, is in a half-timbered building in **Regent Street**, near Hamley's giant toy store and Burberry's. At 235 Regent Street, the stunning flagship store of computer giant Apple is open 24 hours a day. **Tottenham Court Road** is the place to buy electronic equipment.

Bond Street and St James's

New Bond Street and Old Bond Street are the smart end of town. Designer fashion houses mingle with art galleries (including Sotheby's auction house) and nearby **Burlington Arcade** offers bijou gems for the rich. **Savile Row**, parallel to Old Bond Street,

is where shirts and suits are elegantly tailored – at a price. On the other side of Piccadilly is **St James's**, designed originally for the court hangers-on; everything here is bespoke. Old-fashioned barbers and unashamed cigarette and cigar shops make this a male preserve. Fortnum and Mason at 181 Piccadilly sells the best of British foods.

Covent Garden

One of the first, and one of the most successful, developments from old market to new, London's former fruit and vegetable traders' stalls are now bijou shops. Paul Smith, London's leading men's fashion designer, is in Floral Street. **Long Acre** has Stanford's, which claims to be the world's largest travel bookshop. The best shops for books, antiquarian, second-hand and new, are round the corner in **Charing Cross Road**. On the north side of Covent Garden are fashionable boutiques in Earlham Street, Shelton Street and Shorts Gardens.

Kensington and Chelsea

West London led the fashion stakes in the Swinging Sixties. Now rich patrons remain. In **Knightsbridge** Harvey Nichols and Harrods hold sway. Sloane Street, with a clutch of elegant fashion and jewellery designers, leads to Peter Jones department store on Sloane Square and the **King's Road**, where young fashion shops begin. **High Street Kensington**, where the famous Biba store once flourished, has a number of fashion boutiques. Adjoining it is **Kensington Church Street**, for genuine, and genuinely expensive, antiques.

Markets

London has more than 100 street markets, which carry on a tradition going back to the Middle Ages. **Berwick Street** in Soho has classic fruit and vegetable stalls every day, while **Borough Market** farmers' market offers many organic and gourmet products on Thursday, Friday and Saturday. **Petticoat Lane**'s main market, selling all kinds of items, has a genuine London heart. **Portobello Road** near Notting Hill Gate is a lively street dealing in antiques, though dedicated hunters will also head to **Bermondsey Antique Market**. Younger browsers visit **Camden Market** which has a mixture of stalls and a reputation for good-value antiques. Portobello Road and Camden Market are particularly crowded on Saturday. ❏

LEFT: the Liberty store, Great Marlborough Street.

established a permanent base in London. Today's effigies, which vary from the breathtakingly lifelike to the barely recognisable, range from pop stars and sports heroes to popes. The protective glass cases have long gone, so visitors can hob-nob with celebrities without fear of rebuff. To avoid the queues, buy timed tickets in advance.

Nearby, at a familiar address, 221b Baker Street (actually between Nos 237 and 239), is the **Sherlock Holmes Museum** (www.sherlock-holmes.co.uk; daily 9.30am–6pm; charge) where the fictitious detective's housekeeper shows visitors around his fictitious Victorian home. There are waxwork tableaux of characters, scenes from Sir Arthur Conan Doyle's famous stories – and the great detective's study complete with his deerstalker, pipe and violin.

Hereford House in Manchester Square, just off Baker Street, contains the superb **Wallace Collection** **②** (www.wallacecollection.org; daily 10am–5pm; free), a treasure chest of 17th- and 18th-century art and ornaments, among which there are Sèvres porcelain, Limoges enamels and antique French furniture. On the walls are works by Titian, Rubens, Velazquez, Holbein, Poussin and Gainsborough – as well as Hals' famous work *The Laughing Cavalier*. The panelled hall, fine carved staircase and drawing room are as they were in the 18th century.

Classy **Mayfair** is a centre of wealth in England, the home of oil barons and property giants, of landed aristocrats and self-made nabobs. Its narrow streets are abuzz by day with the flow of cash, but at night the district slides into an eerie quiet as the financial wizards and fashion models retreat into their terracotta towers. By the mid-18th century, the powerful Grosvenor family had purchased the land and developed Mayfair into an elegant Georgian housing estate. This enticed the wealthy of dreary inner London to move out and settle in one of the city's first suburbs.

Today, Mayfair is known for its stylish shops and lavish auction houses.

The names roll off the tongue as a testament to affluence: Cartier, Rolls-Royce, Floris, Gieves & Hawkes and Smythson's. **Bond Street** **②** is where you can buy something for that person who already has everything. The most venerable store is Fortnum & Mason, on Piccadilly, which dates back to 1707 and has been the holder of many Royal Warrants over the years: Queen Victoria sent consignments of beef tea from Fortnum's to soldiers in the Crimea. For a quiet walk, try one of Mayfair's elegant Victorian arcades, the tiny covered streets lined with a startling array of unique and interesting shops. The **Royal Opera Arcade** is the oldest, but the **Piccadilly**, **Prince's** and **Royal Arcades** are just as elegant. **Burlington Arcade** with its liveried guards known as Beadles is the most famous, partly due to the existence of its arcane rules which include: no singing, whistling or opening of umbrellas. They date back to 1819 when the arcade first opened. Burlington Arcade is only a few doors up from the **Royal Academy of Arts** **②** (www.royalacademy.org.uk; daily 10am–6pm, Fri until 10pm). The academy has

Savile Row, the home of traditional men's bespoke tailoring.

BELOW: shoe-shine in Burlington Arcade.

The winged statue of Eros in Piccadilly Circus.

changing exhibitions of major artists and its Summer Exhibition of amateur and professional artists provides light entertainment and perhaps the chance to pick up a bargain.

Mayfair antiques and art are world-famous. **Christie's** in King Street auctions more than 150,000 objects a year, while **Sotheby's** in New Bond Street has seen some of the most important deals in art history. Have your photograph taken between Roosevelt and Churchill in a Bond Street pavement sculpture, a reminder of Mayfair's links with Americans.

Piccadilly Circus

Piccadilly Circus ㉗ is the spiritual heart of the West End, once a roundabout and now a meeting place of black cabs, red buses and awe-struck tourists. The bronze statue of Eros stands atop a fountain on the south side of the mêlée, but is outshone by a neon curtain blasting advertising slogans to the masses. Nearby in Coventry Street is the **Trocadero** entertainment centre, a complex of shops and restaurants, whose attractions include **Funland**, a huge hi-tech

indoor entertainment theme park (Mon–Fri 10am–midnight, until 1am weekends).

On Piccadilly's north side, John Nash's **Regent Street** divides Mayfair and **Soho** as effectively as if there were an ocean between them. Soho, long known for its low-life bars and sex clubs, has returned to being a neighbourhood of cosmopolitan foodshops and restaurants, with a thriving Chinese community. The sleazy side of Soho is much less in evidence these days, though a few hole-in-the-wall dens offer "live" entertainment and relieve unwary tourists of their money.

Soho Square is a patch of green particularly lively at lunchtime and weekends. In the heart of Soho is **Berwick Street ㉘**, the site of an excellent fruit and vegetable market. Karl Marx used to live around the corner on **Dean Street** in the building now inhabited by the Quo Vadis restaurant. John Logie Baird succeeded in transmitting some of the earliest pictures via wireless from a workshop in **Frith Street** in 1926. His was a new-fangled invention soon be known as television.

BELOW: the Royal Academy of Arts.

Bloomsbury

For a change in mood, hop on the tube at Piccadilly Circus and ride four stops to Russell Square. This will deposit you in **Bloomsbury**, the intellectual and scholastic heart of the city. The area is dominated by the presence on Great Russell Street of the **British Museum** ㉙ (www.britishmuseum.org; daily 10am–5.30pm, Thur–Fri until 8.30pm; free), one of the largest and best in the world. The museum was founded in 1753 to house the vast collection of 71,000 items that the physician and naturalist Sir Hans Sloane, had amassed during his lifetime. Sloane (remembered today in place names such as Sloane Square) left his eclectic mix of antiquities, manuscripts, medals and prints to the nation. Originally housed in a 17th-century mansion, the museum opened to the public in 1759. The British Museum is both a priceless art collection and a monument to human civilisation, encompassing antiquities from almost every period and every part of the world – Egyptian, Assyrian, Greek, Roman, Indian, Chinese, Islamic and Anglo-Saxon. Among its multiple

treasures are the Rosetta Stone from Egypt (the key that unlocked the secrets of hieroglyphic script), the great 7th-century Anglo-Saxon Sutton Hoo treasures, the Nimrud friezes from Mesopotamia, the Portland Vase (a striking cameo-glass vase) and the Elgin Marbles, the remarkable figures that once graced the Parthenon in Athens. There are coins from ancient Rome, Babylonian statues, carved Native American pipes and jade from Imperial China. One of the most extraordinary sights is that of Lindow Man, the preserved body of an Iron Age man that was found in a peat bog in Cheshire. Discovered in 1984, he died a violent death – possibly a ritual killing. Scientists have established that his last meal was of unleavened bread, made from wheat and barley. More than 50,000 of the 6½ million objects owned by the museum are on display at any one time, so don't expect to see everything in one day. The museum also holds major exhibitions, housed in the Reading Room (see page 88), which can attract large crowds (charges apply to these.)

Art from the Near East in the British Museum.

LEFT:
Ronnie Scott's jazz club.

A Night on the Town

Some of the trendiest clubs are in Soho, including Ronnie Scott's jazz club in Frith Street and Madame Jo Jo's on Brewer Street. Soho entertains a real cross section of Londoners, from the casually-dressed lager drinkers packing out the more traditional pubs, to the city boys swilling champagne in their private members' bar before hitting a lap-dancing club such as Stringfellow's in Upper St Martin's Lane.

Old Compton Street is the centre of the gay scene, with pubs such as the Admiral Duncan and Comptons drawing big crowds. Around the corner on Wardour Street, Village Soho is another popular gay venue with unthreatening clientele and a sprinkling of glam.

Most of the so-called "super-clubs" in the area have now closed down but one hanger-on is Cirque at the Hippodrome (Cranbourne Street). The celebrated gay disco: G-A-Y (Villiers Street) continues to entertain, sometimes with live pop acts that have included the Spice Girls, Kylie Minogue and Madonna.

With the new late-licensing laws many bars stay open until at least 3am, which has removed much of the 11pm rush towards neighbourhood clubs. Some bars can be difficult to get into, but this tends to be because of capacity rather than the dress codes of old. Many of the cafés also stay open into the small hours.

Adults are allowed into Coram Fields only if accompanied by a child.

The **British Library** occupied the same 19th-century building until 1997, when the entire collection of more than 9 million books – including a Gutenberg Bible, the Magna Carta and original texts by Shakespeare, Dickens and Leonardo da Vinci – relocated to Euston Road. The museum glassed over the Great Court, the area surrounding the magnificent Reading Room (once the workshop of Karl Marx) to create Europe's largest covered public square. This spectacular space, which includes the majestic Lion of Knidos and an Easter Island statue, is worth a visit in itself. Treat yourself to lunch or tea in the restaurant overlooking the Reading Room.

The **Foundling Museum** ❸⓿ (www.foundlingmuseum.org.uk; Tue–Sat 10am–5pm, Sun 11am–5pm; charge) at No. 40 Brunswick Square is home of the Foundling Hospital Art Treasures and displays the works of Hogarth, Gainsborough and Reynolds. It also tells the story of the Foundling Hospital, the first purpose built home for abandoned children in Britain. Bloomsbury was the address of such intellectual figures

as John Maynard Keynes and Virginia Woolf *(see page 194)*. Adjacent is **Coram Fields**, a sheep-grazed field and play area which admits adults only if they are accompanied by children.

Of all the writers and thinkers who have lived in Bloomsbury, one stands head and shoulders above the rest: Charles Dickens. The **Charles Dickens Museum** ❸❶ (Mon–Sat 10am–5pm, Sun 11am–5pm; charge) at 48 Doughty Street is where he lived with his family from 1837 to 1839 and wrote parts of *Oliver Twist*, *Nicholas Nickleby* and *The Pickwick Papers*. The house is filled with portraits, letters, furniture and other personal effects of Victorian England's most famous novelist.

East of Bloomsbury Square is the hardworking district of **Holborn** (pronounced *ho-burn*). A pair of silver heraldic dragons on either side of Holborn High Street marks the official boundary of the City of London. Nearby is **Staple Inn** ❸❷, a timber-framed Elizabethan structure (the only one left in central London) that once served as a hostel for wool merchants. A survivor of the Great Fire of London, it shows

BELOW: the British Museum's Great Court. **RIGHT:** ivory mask from Benin on show at the museum.

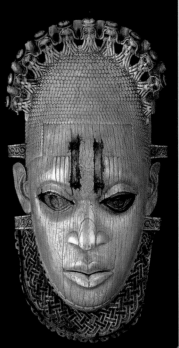

how much of the city must have looked before the 1666 fire devastated it.

Legal London

Lying between Holborn and the Thames are the prestigious **Inns of Court** – the confluence of London's legal world since the Middle Ages. There were originally 12 inns, founded in the 14th century for the lodging and education of lawyers on "neutral" ground between the merchants of the City and the monarchs of Westminster. But today only four remain. Dr Johnson called the inns "the noblest nurseries of humanity and liberty in the Kingdom". Even today, no one can enter the legal profession in London without acceptance into one of the inns – those successful in their exams are "Called to the Bar". **Gray's Inn** ⓧ has a garden designed by Francis Bacon in 1606, a haven of plane trees and smooth lawns that provides a tranquil lunchtime retreat away from the hustle of the City.

Lincoln's Inn ⓧ, north of Fleet Street, has a medieval hall and a 17th-century chapel by Inigo Jones. The leafy

expanse called **Lincoln's Inn Fields**, once a notorious venue for duels and executions, is now restricted to peaceful pursuits such as picnics, netball and summer sunbathing.

On the north side of the fields at No. 13 is **Sir John Soane's Museum** (www.soane.org; Tue–Sat 10am–5pm; free), a gloriously eccentric mansion which is a British Museum in miniature. John Soane, a celebrated 19th-century architect, lived here and built up a remarkable collection of antiquities, paintings and architectural designs. Nowhere else in London can you see such an odd assortment of artefacts under one roof. A highlight of its art gallery is Hogarth's satirical *Rake's Progress*. On the first Tuesday evening of each month (6–9pm, last entry 8.30pm) the museum is lit by candles, an atmospheric experience that attracts many people. Tickets cannot be booked in advance, so be prepared to queue.

The most fascinating of the inns is the twin complex comprising the **Inner** and **Middle Temples** ⓧ. The name derives from the Knights Templar, a mysterious medieval religious fraternity

Sir John Soane's Museum is full of paintings, drawings and models of his projects.

LEFT: Charles Dickens lived here. **BELOW:** taking a break at Lincoln's Inn Fields.

Samuel Johnson, resident of Fleet Street and compiler of the first English dictionary.

BELOW: Ye Olde Cheshire Cheese pub.
RIGHT: relaxing at lunchtime in the Temple's gardens.

that occupied this site until the early 14th century. The temple has changed little: it is still a precinct of vaulted chambers, hammer-beam roofs and lush wood panelling. In the 16th-century Middle Temple Hall, Shakespeare's own company once performed *Twelfth Night* for the Elizabethan court.

The 12th-century **Temple Church** is one of only four "round churches" left in England. It was built by the Templars and modelled on the church of the Holy Sepulchre in Jerusalem. The church became known to a wider audience when it featured in the bestselling book the Da Vinci Code. Entry is free, but opening hours vary. The lawyers and judges who now inhabit the Temple, can often be seen racing by on their way to court, often clutching their distinctive red bags of papers.

Fleet Street takes its name from the Fleet River, which once flowed from two springs on Hampstead Heath into the Thames. Until the 1980s, the street was the centre of the national newspaper industry. Then the papers adopted computers, dispensed with unionised typesetters, built new printing works in

Docklands and moved their offices to cheaper locations. **St Bride's** ❸ is the official parish church of the British Press, an impressive 17th-century church built by Christopher Wren and incorporating a distinctive "wedding cake" spire.

Dr Johnson's House ❸ (www.dr johnsonshouse.org; Mon–Sat 11am–5.30pm, Oct–Apr until 5pm; charge) is at 17 Gough Square, on the north side of Fleet Street. This is where Samuel Johnson lived from 1748 to 1759 assembling the *Complete Works of Shakespeare* and his ground-breaking dictionary. Between bouts with pen and ink, he did his drinking nearby at various local ale and coffee houses including **Ye Olde Cheshire Cheese**, a pub still open for business in Wine Office Court but now patronised by tourists rather than lexicographers.

North London attractions

To visit one of London's loveliest "villages", head north on the Underground's Northern Line. For more than 300 years **Hampstead** has attracted men of arts and letters, such as John Keats (1795–

1821). **Keats House** is open to the public (Keats Grove; Easter–end Oct Tue–Sun noon–5pm, Nov–Easter Fri–Sun 1–5pm; charge), as is the house where Sigmund Freud (1856–1939) spent his last year. The famous couch can be seen at the **Freud Museum** (www.freud.org.uk; Wed–Sun noon–5pm; charge) at 20 Maresfield Gardens.

Hampstead's elegant Georgian and Regency mansions are home to music, stage and cinema stars who help its trendy flavour, but it also has a village atmosphere, aided by the proximity of 790-acre (310-hectare) **Hampstead Heath**. Its only large structure is **Kenwood House** (daily 11am–4pm; free). This magnificent Adam building houses the Iveagh Bequest, a rich collection of English and Dutch paintings.

Highgate

Neighbouring **Highgate**, a pleasant hill-top suburb, contains London's grandest cemetery, where 300 famous people are buried. **Highgate Cemetery** (Mon–Fri 10am–5pm, Sat–Sun 11am–5pm, winter until 4pm; charge) was consecrated in 1839 and soon became fashionable. Besides its catacombs and impressive memorials, the attraction is the rather grim bust of Karl Marx, who was buried here in the eastern section in 1883. The western section, across Swain's Lane, accommodates many literary figures such as the Rossetti family and is more atmospheric but you have to take a tour. The cemetery is administered as a museum, with charges for taking photographs.

Camden

Haverstock Hill runs down from Hampstead into **Camden Town**. Camden became famous in the 1960s as a gathering place for hippies, street artists and various vagrants, who set up small shops and stalls around **Camden Lock** ❸. The market is now one of the most popular London weekend attractions, featuring antiques, crafts, vintage clothes, military surplus goods and talented buskers.

Regent's Park and London Zoo

Just west of Camden Town is **Regent's Park** ❸, a vast green space with a long and chequered history. Henry VIII established a royal hunting ground in the 16th century. **London Zoo** (daily Mar–Oct 10am–5.30pm, mid-July–early Sept until 6pm, Nov–Feb until 4pm; charge) was established here in 1826 by Sir Stamford Raffles. Today it houses a collection of over 650 species of animals. Among the zoo's features is the 1930s penguin pool.

On the north west side of the park is **Lord's Cricket Ground** ❹ (Underground: St John's Wood), belonging to the Marylebone Cricket Club, which runs the English game. To visit the ground, the portrait-packed Long Room through which players walk on their way to the field, and the **MCC Museum**, which traces cricket's 450-year-old history, you have to take the 1 hour 40 minute Tour of Lord's (tel: 020-7616 8595; www.lords.org; daily at 10am, noon, 2pm; charge). On match days, ticket holders can visit the museum only. ❑

Memorial to Karl Marx in Highgate Cemetery.

BELOW: relaxing on Hampstead Heath.

THE CITY AND SOUTHWARK

The City is the oldest part of London, where Britain's financial institutions are tightly packed. Across the river, Southwark has revived its ancient role as an entertainment centre

Fleet Street sweeps from London's theatreland into Ludgate Hill and the **City of London**, the history-packed square mile that sits on the remains of both Roman and medieval towns. The City has long been the domain of merchants and craftsmen, a powerful coalition of men who helped force democracy upon the English monarchy and then built a thriving mercantile empire. Despite wartime destruction and the encroachment of modern office blocks and computers, the City retains something of its traditional ways: the square mile is still governed separately from the rest of London, by the ancient City Corporation and its Court of Common Council – relics of the medieval trade and craft guilds. It also has its own police force and Lord Mayor.

Wren's masterpiece

Sitting at the top of Ludgate Hill is **St Paul's Cathedral ●** (www.stpauls.co.uk; Mon–Sat 8.30am–4.15pm; charge), dominating the skyline of the City like no other structure, the massive dome punching upward through the forest of high-rises that has come to surround it since World War II. After the Norman St Paul's was destroyed in the Great Fire of 1666, Charles II asked Christopher Wren to design a new cathedral to befit the status of London. Wren's first plan was rejected as too radical, but he then responded with a brilliant blend of Italian baroque and classical influences – a huge cruciform building whose stone cupola takes it to a height of 355ft (105 metres). Only St Peter's in Rome has a bigger dome.

St Paul's arose from 1675 to 1710 as the first cathedral built and dedicated to the Protestant faith, and was the crowning achievement of Wren's career. The cathedral played host to Queen Victoria's Diamond Jubilee ceremonies in 1897; Winston Churchill's funeral in 1965; and the wedding of Prince Charles and Lady Diana Spencer in 1981. The cathedral miraculously

Main attractions
ST PAUL'S CATHEDRAL
THE MONUMENT
THE TOWER OF LONDON AND THE CROWN JEWELS
TOWER BRIDGE
SOUTHWARK CATHEDRAL
THE GLOBE THEATRE
TATE MODERN
LONDON EYE

LEFT: the superb craftmanship of the interior of St Paul's Cathedral.
BELOW: the famous dome of St Paul's.

CITY OF LONDON

The Coat of Arms of the City, symbolised by a heraldic dragon, often seen in City streets.

survived the Blitz, though the neighbourhood around it was destroyed by German bombs and missiles. St Paul's is also a notable burial place; among those entombed within are Wellington, Nelson, Reynolds, Alexander Fleming and Wren himself. The cathedral's interior displays the work of the finest artists and craftsmen of the late 17th century: iron grillework by Tijou, wooden choir stalls by Grinling Gibbons, and the murals inside the dome by Sir James Thornhill.

Prior to the 300th anniversary of the "topping out" of the cathedral in 2008, centuries of soot and grime were scrubbed away as part of a £40 million restoration project.

The **Whispering Gallery** stretches around the inside of the dome; here, the voices of anyone standing on the opposite side of the void are easily heard. A winding stairway leads to the balcony outside the dome, where there is a panoramic view of London. (*A floor plan of the cathedral is printed at the back of this book.*)

On the north side of St Paul's, Paternoster Square first rose from the rubble of the Blitz. However, the much-criticised post-war office blocks were recognised as such an appalling error that the site has been developed again. Another post-war urban development, directly north, is the **Barbican Centre** ● the only residential block in the City, with a number of showcases including the **Museum of London** ● (www.museumoflondon.org; daily 10am–6pm, last entry 5.30pm; free), a superb collection devoted to the history of the city from prehistoric to modern times. There are models of old buildings, reconstructed shopfronts, audio-visual shows, a reference library, antique vehicles and a number of historic artefacts such as the Lord Mayor's State Coach. New galleries are due to open in spring 2010, with over 4,000 objects on display.

The **Barbican Arts Centre** is the City's major cultural venue, and the London base of both the Royal Shakespeare Company and the London Symphony Orchestra.

Nearby is **St Bartholomew-the-Great** ● a Norman church which, during its 1,000 year history, has also served as a stable, factory, wine cellar, coal store, and even as a printworks, where Benjamin Franklin once worked.

In the shadows of the Barbican's skyscrapers is the **Guildhall** ● (Mon–Sat 10am–4.30pm, May–end Sept also Sun 10am–4.30pm, may be closed if an event is taking place; free), one of the few buildings to survive the Great Fire and home of the government of the City. This ornate Gothic structure was built in 1411 with funds donated by livery companies, the medieval trade and craft guilds. Within the Guildhall is the famous **Great Hall**, decorated with the colourful banners of the 12 livery companies and the shields of all 92 guilds. It was here that Dick Whittington, the Lord Mayor of London recalled in nursery rhyme, once entertained Henry V. The Hall contains statues of the giants Gog and Magog, the legendary founders of London.

BELOW: Lloyd's of London.

Britain's financial heartland

A short walk east along Gresham Street brings you to the **Bank of England** ⑯, a building of powerful classical design. Though independent of the government, the bank prints and mints all English money, administers to the national debt and protects the country's gold reserves. Nearby stands the old London **Stock Exchange**, founded in 1773. The trading floor is no longer used – shares are now traded electronically from their new premises at Paternoster Square.

Once a centre of commerce, the Parthenonesque **Royal Exchange**, at Cornhill, is now occupied by a clutch of luxury retailers including Tiffany, Cartier and Bulgari.

Directly opposite the bank is **Mansion House**, the official residence of the Lord Mayor since the 1750s and the culmination of the Lord Mayor's Show which each November sets off from the Guildhall (see above). Many of the City's treasures (the 15th-century Mayoral Chain of Office, the 18th-century Great Mace and a collection of Corporation plates, tapestries and crystal) are housed within this Palladian-style palace, which is generally closed to the public. Historic churches within a short distance, some built by Wren, include the celebrated **St Stephen Walbrook**, the Lord Mayor's parish church.

The computerisation of the Stock Exchange brought demands for office buildings purpose-built for modern communications. One of the first, and most dramatic, is the 1986 **Lloyd's of London** building in Lime Street, designed by Sir Richard Rogers. Beside this modern building is the more accessible **Leadenhall Market** ⑰. Once the wholesale market for poultry and game, the magnificent Victorian structure now houses a collection of stylish restaurants, sandwich bars and shops which attract city workers at breakfast and lunchtime.

London's other steel-and-glass Victorian constructions – the railway sta-

tions – were also given facelifts during the 1980s building boom. **Liverpool Street** was completely overhauled, and Fenchurch Street acquired the 1930s' Manhattan-style **1 America Square** over its railway lines. To stand out in such an architectural playground, new buildings have to be really innovative. One recent example is the distinctive **Swiss Re building**, a 40-storey tapering glass tower designed by Lord Foster and known affectionately as "the erotic gherkin".

Gracechurch Street leads south to London Bridge and the Thames. Between the two is a tall, fluted column peering over the rooftops: the 202ft (61-metre) **Monument** ⑱ (daily 9.30am–5pm; charge), Wren's memorial to the Great Fire of 1666. The Monument stands exactly 202ft from the point in nearby Pudding Lane where the Great Fire started in a baker's shop. Climb the 311 steps to the summit for a superb panorama.

The Tower of London

Lower Thames Street traces the medieval banks of the river past the old

Miraculously, only half a dozen people died in the Great Fire of London, which destroyed most of the medieval city. Samuel Pepys, the diarist, dug a pit in his garden to save his wine and "Parmazan" cheese.

BELOW: the ornate roof structure of Leadenhall Market.

The Tower's greatest treasure is the Imperial State Crown, encrusted with 2,868 diamonds, and topped with Edward the Confessor's sapphire. It was made for George VI's coronation in 1937.

RIGHT:
the Tower of London.

Billingsgate Fish Market and the elegant Custom House. A squat stone building commands this southeast corner of the City: the medieval **Tower of London** ㊽ (www.hrp.org.uk; Tue–Sat 9am–5.30pm, Sun–Mon 10am–5.30pm, last entry 5pm; charge; *a floor plan is printed at the back of this book*). The tower has served over the centuries as fortress, palace, prison and museum, as well as arsenal, archive, menagerie and treasure chest. William the Conqueror built the inner keep, the **White Tower**, as both a military stronghold and a means of impressing his new subjects in England. Construction began in the 1070s and was completed by 1100. It was the largest building in Britain and soon symbolised royal domination. It remained a royal residence until the 16th century, when the court moved to more comfortable quarters in Westminster. The tower then became the storehouse for the Crown Jewels and the most infamous prison and execution ground in London. After 1747 the tower served as the Royal Mint, Archive and Menagerie – until the elephants, lions and bears were moved to Regent's Park Zoo. German spies were executed here in both world wars.

The White Tower contains the diminutive **St John's Chapel**, built in 1080 and now the oldest church in London. Beneath Waterloo Barracks is a vault containing the **Crown Jewels**, including the Imperial State Crown, which sparkles with over 3,000 stones, and the Royal Sceptre, which centres around a 530-carat diamond called the Star of Africa. Also worth seeing are the **Crowns and Diamonds** exhibition in the Martin Tower, the **Regimental Museum**'s permanent display of weapons from the mid-17th to mid-19th centuries, and the **New Armouries**, which is given over to temporary exhibitions. The tower is protected by the Yeoman Warders or "Beefeaters", so-called because they were founded in the 16th century as the *buffetiers* or guardians of the king's buffet (they were allowed to eat as much beef as they wanted from the king's table). One Yeoman Warder doubles up as Ravenmaster, caring for the Tower's famous ravens. Legend has it that London will fall if the ravens ever leave the

Murder in the Bloody Tower

For hundreds of years Beauchamp Tower in the Tower of London was England's most prestigious jail, reserved for enemies of the state. Henry VI and Richard II were among royal prisoners, and in 1483 Edward IV's heirs, Prince Edward, aged 12, and Prince Richard, 10, were murdered in what came to be called the Bloody Tower (they are done to death off-stage in Shakespeare's *Richard III*). The executioner's axe came down on Tower Hill behind the castle, but the privileged lost their lives on the block inside the tower's grounds, among them two wives of Henry VIII: Anne Boleyn and Catherine Howard.

The Duke of Orleans, captured at the battle of Agincourt in 1485, composed verse and contemplated his fate here for 25 years. The most eloquent prisoners were Sir Thomas More and Sir Walter Raleigh. More, author of *Utopia*, refused to recognise Henry VIII as head of the church, and before his execution he wrote *Dialogue of Comfort against Tribulation*. Raleigh, the Elizabethan buccaneer, wrote *The History of the World* during his 12-year incarceration with his family, and even managed to grow tobacco on Tower Green.

One of Shakespeare's patrons, the Earl of Southampton, kept his cat in his cell for company: legend has it that the cat climbed into the tower and down a chimney to find him.

Tower – so their wings are carefully clipped to ensure they stay.

The most widely recognised of the Thames's many spans is **Tower Bridge** ⊕, a striking Gothic edifice opened in 1894. The Tower Bridge Exhibition shows how the mechanisms work (daily Apr–Sept 10am–6.30pm, Oct–Mar 9.30am–6pm; charge). The view from the bridge's catwalk is magnificent.

Bankside

Downstream on the south side of Tower Bridge is the restaurant-lined **Butler's Wharf** and the Conran Foundation's **Design Museum** ⊕ (daily 10am–5.45pm; charge), which exhibits contemporary design in every form. Heading upstream again, the riverside walk between Tower Bridge and London Bridge passes by HMS *Belfast* ⊕. Commissioned in 1939 as the largest cruiser in the British Navy, it is now a museum (daily Mar–Oct 10am–6pm, Nov–Feb 10am–5pm, last entry 1 hour before closing; charge).

Towards London Bridge, the **London Dungeon** ⊕ (www.thedungeons.com; daily, hours vary; charge) provides a gruesome account of life in medieval London – most children love it.

Beyond London Bridge rises imposing **Southwark Cathedral** ⊕. It is the oldest cathedral church in London and there has been a church on the site since the 7th century, possibly earlier. Inside are memorial stained glass windows to celebrated literary inhabitants of Southwark: they include Oliver Goldsmith, Samuel Johnson, John Bunyan, Chaucer (whose Canterbury Tales pilgrims started their journey in Southwark) and Shakespeare. Shakespeare's brother is buried here.

Adjacent is **Borough Market**, a wholesale fruit and vegetable market whose history dates back 1,000 years, and is full of great places to eat. Nearby, is the Old Operating Theatre Museum (daily 10.30am–5pm; charge). The operating theatre, designed so that students could watch procedures, dates back to the days before anaesthetics or antiseptics. Beyond the cathedral, by the Thames in the St Mary Overie Dock, is a replica of Sir Francis Drake's galleon, the *Golden Hinde*. A few metres away, the **Clink Prison Museum** features old armour and torture instruments. Close to Southwark Bridge is a replica of the 1599 **Shakespeare's Globe** ⊕ (www.shakespeares-globe.org; performances in summer; guided tours daily every 15–30 minutes during opening hours; charge), a theatre-in-the-round which stages the Bard's plays where they were first performed.

Tate Modern ⊕ (daily 10am–6pm, Fri–Sat until 10pm; free) is the Tate's collection of international modern and contemporary art, housed in the seven-storey former Bankside Power Station which mixes the works of Picasso, Bacon, Rothko, Warhol, Ernst, Hepworth and many others. The enormous gallery also hosts major exhibitions (charges apply), showcasing the works of artists as diverse as Henri Rousseau, Frida Kahlo, Gilbert and George, Edward Hopper and Dalí. Tate Modern is linked to St Paul's across the river by

Southwark Cathedral, where Shakespeare was a parishioner.

BELOW: the Millennium Bridge leads to Tate Modern.

the **Millennium Bridge**, a slender, steel footbridge. Crossing here offers stunning views of the cathedral.

The South Bank

The **South Bank Centre** 🐱 (across Waterloo Bridge) is Europe's largest arts complex. The newly renovated **Royal Festival Hall**, a spacious arena famed for its acoustics, plays host to the London Philharmonic Orchestra. Next door, the **Queen Elizabeth Hall** and the **Purcell Room** are used for a variety of events, from chamber music to poetry readings. On the upper level of the complex is the **Hayward Gallery** (daily 10am–6pm, Fri–Sat until 10pm), which has changing exhibitions of contemporary art.

The **BFI Southbank** (formerly the National Film Theatre; booking tel: 020-7928 3232) sits in the shadow of Waterloo Bridge, presenting a repertory of vintage and foreign-language films as well as the London Film Festival each November. Close by, in the middle of a roundabout, is a huge circular glass building, the British Film Institute's **IMAX Cinema**. Large-

format film is projected onto a screen 66ft high by 85ft wide (20 by 26 metres).

The concrete bulk of the **National Theatre** encompasses three auditoria – the Olivier, Lyttelton and Cottesloe. A limited number of same-day tickets are available each morning at 9.30am, and, for a peek behind the scenes, you can take a backstage tour (www.national theatre.org.uk; tel: 020-7452 3400).

To the west, by Westminster Bridge, is the immensely popular, 450ft (135-metre) **London Eye** 🐱 (www.londoneye. com; automated telephone booking: 0870-5000 600), the world's largest observation wheel, erected for the millennium and promising views of 25 miles (40km) on a clear day. Plan ahead if you want to take one of the 30-minute rides at busy periods.

Next to it is the neoclassical **County Hall**, built between 1909 and 1922 as the seat of London's local government. It now contains two hotels; various eateries; the **London Aquarium** 🐱 (Mon–Fri 10am–6pm, last entry 5pm, Sat–Sun 10am–7pm, last entry 6pm; charge), whose exhibits range from

BELOW:
the view from the London Eye.

sharks to stingray; the **Dali Universe** (daily 10am–6pm, last entry 5pm; charge), which displays more than 500 of Salvador Dali's creations (mostly his less important works); and **Namco Station**, a neon-lit games centre.

Upriver beyond Westminster Bridge is **Lambeth Palace** ❻, the London residence of the Archbishop of Canterbury for nearly 800 years. It is seldom open to the public. The garden and deconsecrated church of St Mary nearby are home to the lovely **Garden Museum** (www.gardenmuseum.org.uk; daily 10.30am–5pm, closed 1st Mon of the month; charge); it commemorates the work of two 17th-century royal gardeners, John Tradescant, father and son, who introduced such exotic fruits as pineapple to England. The grounds contain the Tradescant family tomb, as well as the tomb of William Bligh – captain of the Bounty, whose crew so famously mutinied on their voyage to collect breadfruit.

Another great landmark south of the river is the **Imperial War Museum** ❻ (www.iwm.og.uk; daily 10am–6pm; free) on Lambeth Road. The main hall contains tanks and fighter planes. The Trench and Blitz "experiences" conjure up environments from the two world wars. On the first floor is an aeroplane fuselage that you can walk through, plus an exhibit on counter-intelligence. The second floor has a major collection of 20th-century war art. The top floors house the **Holocaust Exhibition**, a remarkable but harrowing exhibition, built around the testimonies of survivors; it is not recommended for children under 14.

The East End

Back on the north bank of the river, downstream from Tower Bridge lies **St Katharine's Dock** ❻. Built in 1828 as a shipment point for wool and wine, the docks were renovated in the early 1980s and have become a smart residential and commercial district. They are the most successful of the Docklands developments which extend east

from here to the Isle of Dogs where the **Canary Wharf** tower (Britain's tallest office block) signals their modern ambitions.

Mansell Street leads north from the Tower into the warren of narrow streets that marks the start of London's **East End**, traditionally the City's working-class district. **Whitechapel** and **Spitalfields** – both at the north end of Mansell Street – are where 19th- and early 20th-century European immigrants settled.

The **Whitechapel Art Gallery** ❻ (Tue–Sun 11am–6pm, Thur until 9pm; free) in Whitechapel High Street (by Aldgate East tube) is one of London's most exciting galleries, hosting regular exhibitions by living artists. **Spitalfields Market**, a wholesale fruit and vegetable market until 1991, is now awash with antiques and crafts stalls, and surrounded by trendy bars and boutiques. Nearby, **Petticoat Lane** ❻ is the most famous East End market. Today, the traders set up their stalls along Middlesex Street, displaying a chromatic jumble of clothes, antiques, food and much more besides. ❏

EAT

The Garden Café (daily 10.30am–4.45pm), within the Garden Museum is a great option for a bite to eat in the Lambeth Bridge area. The café serves homecooked vegetarian food, delicately spiced soups and tempting cakes.

2012 Olympics in East London

The construction of a new Olympic Park in Stratford has brought much-needed investment to the area. Situated in the Lower Lea Valley, the 500-acre (200-hectare) site will house nine purpose-built sporting venues, a media centre and an Olympic Village providing accommodation for all of the athletes. The centrepiece of the park will be an 80,000-seat athletics stadium which will also be the setting for the opening and closing ceremonies. A state-of-the-art aquatics centre is planned, as well as a hockey centre, a velopark and four multi-sports arenas for fencing, volleyball, basketball and handball.

Existing sports venues in other parts of London will also be used for the games: Horse Guards Parade, for instance, a parade ground usually reserved for royal occasions, will be transformed into a beach volleyball pitch.

The recession that began in 2008 tightened budgets, and the cost of staging the Olympics has soared way beyond initial estimates. But London's ailing transport network is being extended and improved in order to accommodate the 500,000 spectators expected to travel to the Olympic Park each day. Many of these visitors will probably travel on the Javelin, a high-speed rail shuttle which will whizz passengers from St Pancras International to the Olympic Park (Stratford International) in 7 minutes.

WEST LONDON

Home to some of Britain's best and brightest –
and wealthiest – Chelsea and Kensington offer the
visitor fine museums, lovely streets to stroll along
and superlative shopping

In the 19th century Chelsea was an avant-garde "village" just outside the sprawl of central London. Among its more famous residents were Oscar Wilde, John Singer Sargent, Thomas Carlyle, Mark Twain and T.S. Eliot. Cheyne Walk, a row of elegant Georgian terraced houses just off the river, has long been Chelsea's most prestigious residential street. George Eliot, J.M.W. Turner and Thomas Carlyle lived here in the 19th century; J. Paul Getty and Mick Jagger in the 20th. Chelsea is where England swung in the 1960s and where punk began in the 1970s.

King's Road ❶ is Chelsea's famous thoroughfare. Once a tranquil country lane, it was widened into a private carriage road from St James's Palace to Hampton Court on the order of King Charles II. It rose to fame in the 1960s when ground-breaking designers such as Mary Quant set up shop here, and it was in its boutiques that the miniskirt first made its revolutionary appearance. In the 1970s Vivienne Westwood and Malcolm McLaren took up the avant-garde baton, dominating the punk scene with their boutique "Sex".

Riverfront

Down on the riverfront is **Chelsea Royal Hospital ❷**, Sir Christopher Wren's masterpiece of the English baroque style, opened as a home for invalid and veteran soldiers in 1682 to match his hospital for sailors at Greenwich. A few hundred army pensioners

still reside there, and parade in their famous scarlet frockcoats on Oak Apple Day (29 May). Adjacent is **Ranelagh Gardens**, the site of the Chelsea Flower Show each spring; a stone's throw away is the **Saatchi Gallery** (daily 10am–6pm; free), founded by advertising mogul Charles Saatchi and exhibiting collections of top contemporary art; and near the Chelsea Royal Hospital, tracing the history of the British military from the 15th century, is the **National Army Museum** (daily 10am–5.30pm; free).

Main attractions
SAATCHI GALLERY
CHELSEA PHYSIC GARDEN
HARRODS
VICTORIA AND ALBERT MUSEUM
NATURAL HISTORY MUSEUM
SCIENCE MUSEUM
KENSINGTON PALACE

LEFT: the Royal Albert Hall.
BELOW: shopping for bargains in the King's Road.

The Victoria and Albert Museum.

On Royal Hospital Road is the beautiful little **Chelsea Physic Garden** (Apr–Oct Thur and Fri noon–5pm, Sun until 6pm; charge), a 17th-century walled garden and botanical laboratory from which cotton seeds were taken to the American South in 1732. Walk across Albert or Chelsea Bridge and enjoy the lush expanse of **Battersea Park ❸** on the south bank, with the Buddhist Peace Pagoda commemorating the 1985 Year of Peace.

Belgravia

Having crossed the Thames again and returned to King's Road, leave Chelsea by proceeding east, crossing Sloane Square and entering the elegant district of **Belgravia**. The district has an air of exclusivity, being the home of diplomats and the occasional duke or lord. Belgravia is littered with grand Regency terraces and squares, bound by cream-coloured mansions and carefully tended gardens.

North of Belgravia via Sloane Street is the bustling neighbourhood of luxury shops and hotels at **Knightsbridge**. This is the home of **Harrods ❹**, London's most famous department store. Be sure to visit the food halls for their beautiful Victorian tiling and in excess of 500 varieties of cheese, 140 different breads and 160 brands of whisky.

The Victoria and Albert Museum

South Kensington tube station (one stop after Knightsbridge) is the jumping-off point for Exhibition

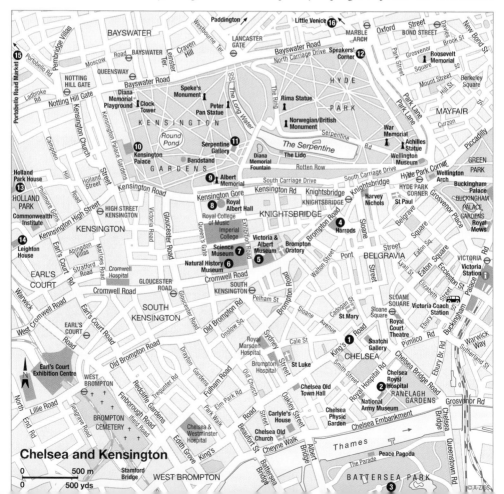

Chelsea and Kensington

Road's cluster of fine museums. The **Victoria and Albert Museum ❺** (www.vam.ac.uk; daily 10am–5.45pm, Fri until 10pm; free), popularly known as the V&A, is the most famous of these. The range of items the museum displays is astonishing. You can see everything from the **Hereford Screen** (a choir screen of cast iron and brass, studded with semi-precious stones) and Constable's studies for his famous painting *The Haywain*, to a pair of platform shoes designed by Vivienne Westwood. Its maze of rooms cover 3,000 years of history.

There are collections on: **Europe and America 1800–1900** (some extravagant Gothic Revival styles); **Sculpture** (notable British and European neoclassical works); **Raphael Cartoons** (1515–16 templates for tapestries in the Sistine Chapel); **Fashion** (history of male and female costume); **Asia** (Indian Art, Arts of the Islamic World, and China, Japan, Southest Asia and Korea); **Plaster Casts** (copies of vast monuments, tombs, pillars, friezes and effigies include Michelangelo's *David*); **Medieval and Renaissance Items** (outstanding Italian pieces); **British Galleries** (documenting British taste and containing the fabulous Great Bed of Ware, an enormous 16th-century four-poster, carved from oak and mentioned in Shakespeare's play *Twelfth Night*).

Natural History Museum

If any of London's museums encapsulates Victorians' quest for knowledge and passion for cataloguing data, it's the **Natural History Museum ❻** (Cromwell Road; www.nhm.ac.uk; daily 10am–5.50pm; free). Occupying an extravagant Gothic Romanesque building, it has one of the best dinosaur and prehistoric lizard collections anywhere. The highlights include a full-scale animatronic T-Rex that roars and twists convincingly – as well as the famous skeleton of a Diplodocus dinosaur and a 1,300 year old giant sequoia tree in the Central Hall.

The museum has colour coded zones. The **Red Zone** (entrance on Exhibition Road) explores our ever-changing planet. The **Green Zone** investigates the earth's ecology – in the Creepy Crawlies section you can watch a colony of leaf-cutter ants and see the world's longest insect. The **Blue Zone** looks at the diversity of life on earth – you can listen to what a baby experiences in the womb.

The new **Darwin Centre** is a state of the art extension to the museum where you can see scientists at work and witness the latest research. End your visit with a trip to the Wildlife Garden, a haven for British plants and insects.

Science Museum

With more than 10,000 exhibits plus attractions such as an IMAX theatre and interactive play area for children, the adjacent **Science Museum ❼** (Exhibition Road; tel: 0870-870 4868; www.sciencemuseum.co.uk; daily 10am–6pm; free) could take days to explore, so it's wise to set priorities.

The **Making the Modern World**

The skeleton and a full-size model of a blue whale, Natural History Museum.

BELOW: the Natural History Museum's Central Hall.

The Albert Memorial.

BELOW: the Royal Ceremonial Dress Collection at Kensington Palace.

Gallery includes the world's oldest surviving steam locomotive, the coal-hauling Puffing Billy (*c.*1815), Stephenson's Rocket passenger locomotive (1829), a Ford Model T (1916), a Lockheed Electra airliner hanging in silvery splendour from the ceiling (1935), a copy of Crick and Watson's model of the double helix structure of DNA (1953) and the Apollo 10 command module (1969).

The popular **Exploring Space Gallery** houses the huge Spacelab 2 x-ray telescope – the actual instrument flown on the Challenger Space Shuttle – and full-size models of the Huygens lander that landed on Saturn's largest moon, Titan, and Beagle 2 Mars Lander. There's also a replica of Galileo's telescopes.

The **Flight Gallery**'s exhibits include the 1919 Vickers Vimy in which Alcock and Brown made the first non-stop transatlantic flight and Amy Johnson's Gipsy Moth Jason 1.

The Wellcome Wing, linked to the main building, concentrating on information technology, hums with hands-on displays relating to the human experience

The Albert Hall

One of Victorian England's greatest monuments also lies within South Kensington. Queen Victoria laid the foundation stone for the **Royal Albert Hall ❽** in 1867 in memory of her late husband, Prince Albert, who was responsible for many of the South Kensington institutions. The circular 7,000-seat auditorium is still one of the largest theatres in London, and stages a varied programme from pop concerts to brass-band competitions. However, the Albert Hall is most famous for the BBC-sponsored summer Promenade Concerts – the Proms – a marvellous showcase of both classical and more modern music. The final concert (the "Last Night") is traditionally a playful combination of serious music-making and boisterous audience participation.

Across Kensington Gore the **Albert Memorial ❾**, a flamboyant Gothic monument, rises suddenly from the plane trees of Kensington Gardens and Hyde Park. Prince Albert sits under a lavish canopy, forever reading the catalogue from the 1851 Great Exhibition held in Hyde Park. Marble figures on the lower corners of the steps depict America, Asia, Africa and Europe.

Palaces and gardens

A short walk away through prolific and tranquil gardens is **Kensington Palace ❿** (daily 10am–6pm; charge). Sir Christopher Wren refurbished the mansion for William and Mary in the late 17th century, and for nearly 100 years it served as the principal private royal residence in London. Queen Victoria was born here in 1819. Today it is the London residence of some minor members of the royal family, and was, until her death, the home of Diana, Princess of Wales. Another popular spot in the park is the **Serpentine Gallery ⓫** (daily 10am–6pm; free), a tiny museum with exhibitions of cutting-edge art. Rowing boats can be taken out on the Serpentine lake and there is a lido for swimmers in summer. In the

northeast corner of Hyde Park, **Speakers' Corner ⑫** is where amateur orators can passionately defend all manner of causes and beliefs. Close by, on a central reservation in Park Lane, is a monument to **Animals in War**, with sculptures marking the role played, and suffering endured, by millions of horses and other animals on history's battlefields.

Holland Park House ⑬, just west of Kensington Palace via Kensington High Street, gives its name to leafy Holland Park, one of the more interesting green spaces in London. A lavish Jacobean manor built in 1606, the house later became the property of the Earl of Holland, who surrounded it with 55 acres (22 hectares) of exotic gardens.

At 12 Holland Park Road, a rather plain red-brick house contains one of the most extraordinary interiors in London. **Leighton House ⑭** (tel: 020-7602 3316) was the home of the Victorian artist Lord Frederic Leighton from 1866 and is a mix of lavish Orientalism and conventional Victorian comforts. The *pièce de résistance* is the Arab Hall, inspired by a Moorish palace in Palermo.

Notting Hill

North of Holland Park is **Notting Hill**, one of London's most highly sought-after residential districts with handsome white stucco Victorian terraces and villas. However, the relative calm that prevails throughout the year is shattered every August Bank Holiday when the streets explode with music and colour as the city's huge West Indian population stages Europe's largest street carnival, complete with steel bands and extravagant costumes. The district's other famous attraction is the **Portobello Road Market ⑮**. On Saturday the whole street becomes jammed with tourists in search of antique treasures, second-hand clothes and bric-a-brac. Fine *objets d'art* do exist, but at a price.

East of Notting Hill, on the north side of Hyde Park is cosmopolitan **Bayswater**, a transport hub and site of the Whiteleys Shopping Centre. The area stretches up to **Paddington Station**, the mainline terminal for trains to the west of England and Wales, and with a direct rail link to Heathrow Airport. To the north of Paddington begins a network of man-made waterways that once linked north London with Oxford and the Midlands. West of Notting Hill is Westfield, Europe's largest shopping centre with more than 265 shops.

Little Venice

The posh residential district of **Little Venice ⑯** lies at the junction of the Grand Union, Regent's and Paddington canals and residential moorings for barges here are much sought after. It is home to a number of waterside eateries. Refurbished canal barges operated by the **London Waterbus Company** (Apr–Oct daily, Nov–Mar Sat–Sun; tel: 020-7482 2660) run east from Little Venice to Regent's Park through another exclusive neighbourhood, **St John's Wood**, home of the celebrated Abbey Road recording studios. ❑

The Arab Hall at Leighton House, lavishly decorated with a priceless collection of over 1,000 Syrian tiles.

BELOW: the 1829 *Rocket* locomotive, Science Museum.

DAY TRIPS ALONG THE THAMES

Of the many day trips to be taken around London, some of the best can be made by boat along the River Thames, from Royal Greenwich downstream to Hampton Court upstream

A trip along the River Thames, the main artery around which the city grew, is an instructive and a thoroughly enjoyable way to get to know London. There is a calm, almost rural feel to the journey, which passes well-known landmarks to put history into perspective. From Greenwich to Richmond, every suburb along the river has its own personality, and each can be reached by local London transport, as well as by riverboats. Eastwards, London's Docklands have been greatly renovated, but beyond a few remaining local pubs, it will be a long time before they find any real character.

To the west, however, the river is a focus of pleasure: in the summer, oarsmen and yachtsmen pit their wits against its tides, people stroll along its towpaths and the pubs are wet with warm beer and enlivened by warm company. Regular boat services run from several piers including **Westminster** and **Embankment** (www.tfl.gov.uk).

Downstream: Royal Greenwich

Greenwich ❶ can be reached by boat from Embankment pier, by train from Cannon Street, Charing Cross or London Bridge train stations, on the Jubilee line of the Underground, or on the Docklands Light Railway (DLR). Visit at the weekend, when there are crafts and antiques markets.

There have long been settlements in Greenwich. In the 11th century Vikings pulled their longboats ashore here, killed Archbishop St Alfege and ravaged London. In 1427 Bella Court Palace was built on the riverside and it became a royal retreat, later known as Placentia Palace. Henry VI made it his favourite residence and subsequent Tudor monarchs – Henry VIII, Elizabeth I and Mary – were all born at Greenwich. It was here, too, that Sir Walter Raleigh is supposed to have laid his cloak over a pool of mud to prevent Elizabeth I getting her feet wet.

James I commissioned Inigo Jones to

Main attractions
NATIONAL MARITIME MUSEUM AND ROYAL OBSERVATORY
THAMES BARRIER
KEW GARDENS
HAMPTON COURT

LEFT: the Royal Naval College at Greenwich.
BELOW: Westminster Pier.

The Thames Barrier protects London from tidal floods.

build a new private residence for Queen Anne, nearby. The result was the **Queen's House**, completed in 1637, a masterpiece of the Palladian style and perhaps the finest piece of Stuart architecture in England. This still stands, but Placentia fell into disrepair during the Commonwealth era. Queen's House is beside the **National Maritime Museum** (www.nmm.ac.uk), an excellent seafaring collection, swelled with Millennium funds. Here the 1805 Battle of Trafalgar is relived and the glory of the nation's maritime tradition unfolds, with boats, paintings and memorabilia from heroic voyages.

A short distance up the steep hill is the **Royal Observatory**, constructed at Greenwich by Charles II in 1675 in order to perfect the arts of navigation and astronomy. Since that time, the globe's longitude and time zones have been measured from the Greenwich Meridian, which cuts right through the middle of Flamsteed House, now a museum displaying astronomical instruments including the award-winning 18th-century clocks of John Harrison, whose story was told in Dava Sobel's best-selling *Longitude*. (The Royal Observatory, Maritime Museum and Queen's House: daily 10am–5pm).

Greenwich sits on the prime Meridian: 1 January 2000 began here. The **O2 concert arena** ❷ (North Greenwich tube station; tel: 020-8463 2000; http://theo2.co.uk) was built as the Millennium Dome. It is a massive entertainments centre hosting top rock concerts and sports events. Greenwich has been associated with British sea power for 500 years (the Royal Naval Dockyards were built downstream at Chatham, *see page 181*). In the late 17th century Sir Christopher Wren built the **Royal Hospital for Seamen** at Greenwich, an elegant, baroque complex that became the **Royal Naval College**. Its chapel and Painted Hall, decorated in the early 18th century by Sir James Thornhill, are open to the public (daily 10am–5pm). On the waterfront is one of England's most famous ships. The *Cutty Sark* (closed for restoration, be aware there is no access to the ship), built in 1869, was the last of the great China tea clippers, a speedy square-rigger that once ran tea from the Orient to Europe.

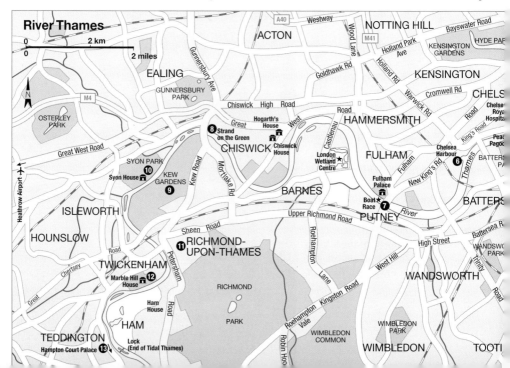

In May 2007, midway through a £25 million restoration project there was a devastating fire at the site. When the ship eventually reopens it will be suspended 3 meters (10ft) above ground, enabling visitors to pass beneath.

Take the riverboat further downstream to catch a glimpse of the **Thames Barrier ❸**. This great shining steel wall, which stretches 1,700ft (520 metres) across the width of the River Thames, protects London from flooding.

Upstream: gardens and grand houses

Riverboats go upriver from Embankment, too, past Westminster and Lambeth to Battersea and Chelsea, followed, on the north bank, by the District underground line, and on the south bank by the overground train line from Waterloo. Opposite the Peace Pagoda in **Battersea Park ❹**, erected for the 1985 Year of Peace by Japanese Buddhists, is Sir Christopher Wren's **Chelsea Royal Hospital ❺**, a home for old soldiers, and beyond, the upmarket housing and office development at **Chelsea Harbour ❻**. But the leafy riverbank does not really begin until **Putney ❼**, where the celebrated University Boat Race between Oxford and Cambridge begins each March. Putney, a residential area, can be reached by riverboat, or by taking the District Line to Putney Bridge.

The next crossing point is Hammersmith Bridge. The Piccadilly and District underground lines go to Hammersmith, the starting point of a riverside walk that leads to Chiswick and has a number of popular riverside pubs, such as the Dove on Upper Mall. This historic 18th-century tavern is where the words to the patriotic *Rule, Britannia* are supposed to have been written by the poet James Thomson. **Strand on the Green ❽**, just beyond, has lively Georgian houses and charming fishermen's cottages. After your walk, try one of the good riverside pubs, including the Bull's Head and City Barge, both nearly 400 years old.

A further diversion at Chiswick is **Hogarth's House** (tel: 020-8994 6757; re-opens after refurbishment late 2009), a 17th-century mansion now filled with engravings and personal relics of one of

The National Maritime Museum displays an unrivalled collection of maritime art and artefacts.

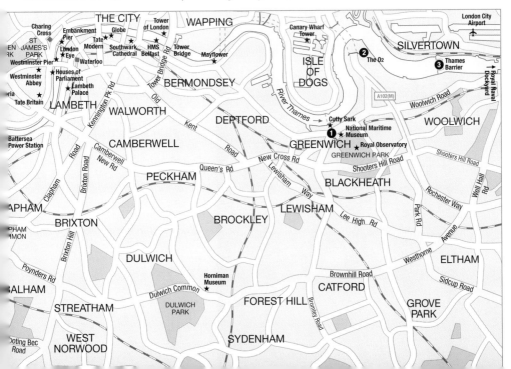

The smelliest fruit in Kew Gardens is the durian, from Indonesia. Described as: "like eating custard in a sewer", it can be found in the Palm House.

England's most famous artists. **Chiswick House**, an early 18th-century Palladian villa designed by the third Earl of Burlington, is even more delightful. (Train from Waterloo to Chiswick, or District or Piccadilly underground lines to Turnham Green; Easter–Oct Sun–Wed 10am–5pm; charge.)

Tropical house in Kew

Kew, a quiet suburb upstream and across the Thames from Chiswick, plays host to the Royal Botanic Gardens, often called simply **Kew Gardens** ❾ (tel: 020-8332 5655; www.kew.org; daily 9.30am–dusk; charge). The gardens, with 300 acres (120 hectares) of exotic plants from around the world, were first planted in 1759 under the direction of Princess Augusta. In 1772, George III put Kew in the hands of botanist Sir Joseph Banks, who had just returned from a round-the-world expedition to collect plant specimens with Captain Cook, and the collection grew. Kew Gardens was declared a Unesco World Heritage Site in 2003.

The most famous of Kew's nurseries is the **Palm House**, a vast Victorian

pavilion of steel and glass containing hundreds of tropical plants. The steamy warmth hits you as you enter this verdant tropical world. It was restored following storm damage in 1987 when many of Kew's old and rare species of trees were damaged or lost. Nearby, the **Waterlily House** (May–Oct) houses tropical, aquatic plants.

Across the Thames from Kew is another famous botanical centre – **Syon Park** ❿ (house: Apr–Sept Wed, Thur, Sun and public holidays 11am–5pm; gardens: daily 10.30am–dusk). The Dukes of Northumberland built a great mansion on the site in the 16th century, while the lush gardens were added later by the great English landscape gardener, "Capability" Brown. **Syon House** (charge) has a lavish baroque interior, magnificent state rooms and an imposing conservatory. To reach Syon Park from central London, take the underground District Line to Gunnersbury, then the 237 or 267 bus to Brent Lea Gate. From Kew, cross Kew Bridge and take the bus.

Richmond ⓫ (train from Waterloo, underground District line, or on foot along the towpath from Kew) retains its village atmosphere with a cluster of book and antiques shops, tea salons and charming riverside pubs (the White Cross is one of the most popular). The Victorian-style **Richmond Theatre** sits on the edge of the green and is an important showcase for big-name productions on their way to London's West End. **Richmond Park** was enclosed by Charles I as a hunting estate and is now the only royal park that keeps a large stock of deer. The walk to it up Richmond Hill from the centre of town leads to a magnificent view west over the Thames.

Bus 65 from Ealing Broadway or 371 from Richmond will take you to the flamboyant 17th-century **Ham House** (Mon–Wed and Sat–Sun noon–5pm; charge), which was at the heart of political intrigue during the Civil War. It has a rich collection of period paintings (notably Reynolds and Van Dyck), tap-

BELOW: the Palm House at Kew Gardens.

estries, furniture, carpets and clothing. Cavaliers and Roundheads do fierce battle each spring as part of the three-week Richmond Festival.

Richmond Bridge leads across to **Twickenham**, home of England rugby football union (international games are staged in winter at the huge Twickenham Stadium).

The 18th-century **Marble Hill House** ⑫ (Apr–end Oct Sat 10am–2pm, Sun 10am–5pm; charge) on Richmond Road is a Palladian-style dwelling that provided a retreat for secret royal love affairs: George II and George IV kept mistresses here. The kings' house contains a fine picture gallery garden. Riverside Twickenham offers such worthy pubs as the White Swan, the Eel Pie and the Barmy Arms.

King Henry's Tudor palace

Above Twickenham is Teddington and the first lock, which marks the end of the tidal Thames, and then **Hampton Court Palace** ⑬ (Mon–Sun 10am–6pm, last entry 5pm; tickets can be purchased in advance from any staffed South West trains station). Its two dis-

tinctive architectural styles make it both the paragon of the Tudor style and the self-proclaimed English version of Versailles. In the early 16th century, Hampton Court was built by Cardinal Wolsey as the finest and most flamboyant residence in the realm. When Wolsey fell from grace, he gave the palace to Henry VIII in a futile attempt to regain favour. The king fell in love with it and moved there with Anne Boleyn. He ordered the construction of the Great Hall, the Clock Court and the library, and enlarged the gardens. Elizabeth I is supposed to have used Hampton Court as an illicit love nest far from the prying eyes of London society. She also planted the gardens with exotic trees and flowers brought to England from the New World by Sir Francis Drake and Sir Walter Raleigh. In the 1690s, the sumptuous **State Apartments** were designed by Sir Christopher Wren for William and Mary, who also commissioned during their reign the famous **Maze** and the Tijou grillework atop the entrance gates. Today the 1,000 rooms are filled with paintings, tapestries and furnishings from the past 450 years. ❑

A Tudor welcome to Hampton Court.

BELOW: the Maze at Hampton Court Palace.

The Thames Path

Starting at the Thames Barrier in the east and ending at the river's source in the Cotswolds 184 miles (294km) away, the Thames Path (www.national trail.co.uk) provides some of the best views of the city and beyond. It is a trail able to be walked by people of all ages. From Putney the path takes on a rural aspect, passing the London Wetland Centre in Barnes, the grand riverside houses of Chiswick and the pretty cottages of Strand on the Green. After Kew Bridge, the path skirts round Kew Gardens, with Syon Park across the river.

At Richmond, with Petersham meadows on your left and a great sweep of the river ahead of you, it's hard to believe the city is in spitting distance. Along this stretch you'll see Marble Hill House and, a little further, Ham House.

THE THAMES VALLEY

Winding its way across the western Home Counties of Buckinghamshire, Berkshire and Oxfordshire, the Thames crosses some of the gentlest and most quintessentially English of landscapes

London

The Thames wends its way west through the so-called Home Counties, a name that encapsulates a romanticised idea of England, neat, safe and civilised. The Thames Valley is quintessentially English: lush, leafy and pretty, with half-timbered houses, stately homes and a few Roman and medieval remains, yet only a short distance from the capital and the southeast via the M25, the ever-crowded orbital motorway, or regular train services.

Start the tour by taking Exit 13 off the M25 for a visit to **Runnymede ❶** (summer 8.30am–7pm, winter 8.30am–5pm; National Trust; parking charge). This pleasant riverside meadowland is where, in 1215, King John, under pressure from his barons, signed the Magna Carta, the document that is said to contain the basis of English freedoms, although it brought little immediate benefit. According to popular tradition, the king's men camped on one side of the river, the barons on the other, and they met on the neutral ground now called Magna Carta Island, however the exact location is not really known. Above the meadows stands Cooper's Hill, which has glorious views of Windsor Castle, and which inspired the 18th-century poet Alexander Pope to garland it with "eternal wreaths". At the foot of the hill lies the not-very-impressive Magna Carta Memorial, presented by the American Bar Association in recogni-

tion of the charter's influence on the American Constitution. There is also a John F. Kennedy Memorial. Runnymede has a great diversity of flora and fauna, and parts of it have been designated a Site of Special Scientific Interest (SSSI). A well-designed programme of guided walks is available (tel: 01784-432 891 for details).

Residence of sovereigns

From Runnymede you can take the riverside road from **Staines** to **Datchet**. This is the Datchet Lane mentioned in

Main attractions
RUNNYMEDE
WINDSOR CASTLE
ETON COLLEGE
RIVER AND ROWING MUSEUM, HENLEY
STANLEY SPENCER GALLERY, COOKHAM
VERULAMIUM MUSEUM, ST ALBANS

PRECEDING PAGES: Windsor Castle.
LEFT: the Changing of the Guard.
BELOW: lazy days on the river.

Shakespeare's *The Merry Wives of Windsor*, along which Falstaff was carried in a basket of dirty linen. On a chalk cliff just across the river towers **Windsor Castle** ❷ (Mar–Oct 9.45am–5.15pm, last entry 4pm, Nov–Feb 9.45am–4.15pm, last entry 3pm; various closing days, tel: 020-7766 7304 for details). Since the reign of Henry I in the 12th century, Windsor, England's most famous castle, has been the chief residence of English and British sovereigns. William the Conqueror founded the original structure, a wooden building that probably consisted of a motte and two large baileys enclosed by palisades. The stone fortifications were built in the 12th and 13th centuries and the castle you see today incorporates additions by nearly every sovereign since. In the 19th century, George IV and Queen Victoria spent almost £1 million on improvements.

The 20th century saw great restorations of the interior, in particular of **St George's Chapel** (closed Sun except for worship), the worst casualty of a disastrous fire in 1992. The chapel, begun in 1477, is one of the finest examples of Perpendicular architecture in England (rivalled only by King's College Chapel, Cambridge and the Henry VII Chapel at Westminster). Henry VIII, his third wife Jane Seymour and Charles I are buried in the choir, while the tombs of Henry VI and VII, William IV and three of the Georges lie in the crypt.

In the Upper Ward are the **State Apartments**, accommodation for visiting foreign sovereigns, which are closed when occupied and when the Queen is in residence. Lavishly furnished, they include many important paintings from the royal collection, including works by Rubens, Van Dyck, Canaletto and Reynolds, and drawings by Holbein, Michelangelo, Leonardo and Raphael. **Queen Mary's Dolls' House** can also be seen and is one of the most popular parts in the castle.

Climb the 220 steps for the wide valley view from the Round Tower, and venture south of the castle to the **Great Park**, 4,800 acres (1,920 hectares) of lush greenery.

The **Savill Garden**, renowned for its rhododendrons, now incorporates

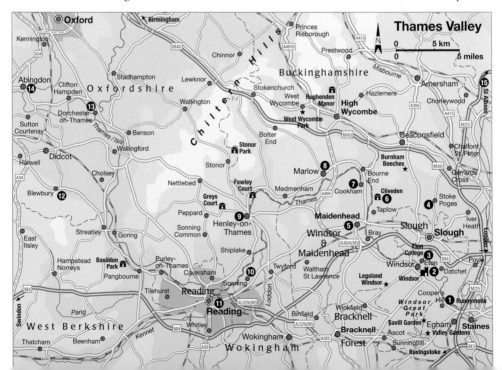

a landscape garden created to mark the Queen's Golden Jubilee in 2002.

Legoland

As a complete contrast, **Legoland Windsor**, 2 miles (3km) from the town centre on the B3022 Windsor/Ascot road, is a theme park based around the children's building blocks. Its wooded landscape includes, among other things, the lightning Jungle Coaster ride; Miniland – a miniature Europe made of millions of Lego pieces, and the new Laser Raiders Dark Ride. Lego is a contraction of two Danish words, *Leg Godt*, meaning "Play well", and the park puts a suitably worthy emphasis on learning as well as having fun (mid-Mar–end Oct variable opening days/hours, mid-July–end Aug 10am–7pm; tel: 0871-222 2001). Shuttle buses run from near Windsor station; Green Line buses run from London Victoria, tel: 0870-608 7261.

From Eton to Henley

Across the river is **Eton College ❸** (daily Apr–Sept; tel: 01753-671 177 for details, pre-booking essential), the most famous of English public schools, founded in 1440 by 18-year-old Henry VI. The original set of buildings included a collegiate church, a grammar school and an almshouse. Henry intended that the church and school should become a place of pilgrimage and devotion to the Virgin, but the Wars of the Roses intervened. He was murdered in the Tower of London and every year on the anniversary of his death an Etonian lays a wreath of lilies in the cell where he died.

Eton is a cluster of red-brick Tudor buildings with small towers and hulking chimneys. The **School Yard** (outer quadrangle), the **Long Chamber** and the **Lower School** all date from the 15th century. The chapel, in the Perpendicular style, has 15th-century wall paintings depicting miracles and legends of the Virgin. Most of the windows were damaged in World War II, but some of the modern ones are interesting. The cloisters, dating from the 1440s, are stunning.

The churchyard of St Giles, **in Stoke Poges ❹**, north of Eton and on the far side of **Slough**, is the final resting place

TIP

Weather permitting, the Changing of the Guard at Windsor takes place at 11am every day except Sunday from May–June, and on alternate days for the rest of the year. Many find it more splendid than the Buckingham Palace ceremony.

LEFT:
Windsor Castle.

Fact File

Largest town Reading.

Communications Accessible via the M25 orbital motorway; Windsor is a 50-minute train journey from London Waterloo (direct) and Paddington (change at Slough). There are also river boat services in summer between Runnymede, Windsor, Henley-on-Thames and Marlow.

Historical data Dorchester began as a Roman fortress, known as Durocina; Windsor Castle was founded in the 12th century by Henry I; Magna Carta was signed at Runnymede in 1215.

Major attractions Windsor Castle – main residence of the royal family; Cliveden – once the home of the Astor family and now a luxury hotel; Cookham – picturesque village and birthplace of eccentric artist Stanley Spencer; Henley-on-Thames – famous for the July regatta; Sonning – the prettiest of the Thames villages; Dorchester-on-Thames – an ancient Roman town.

For the children Legoland at Windsor (www.legoland.co.uk) a 150-acre (60-hectare) theme park. Direct train and/or bus connections from London.

Interesting diversions St Albans, with a medieval cathedral and the remains of the Roman city of Verulamium; the Gardens of the Rose, which grow the white rose of York and the red rose of Lancaster.

of the poet Thomas Gray and provided the inspiration for his *Elegy Written in a Country Churchyard*. A monument erected in 1799 commemorates him in somewhat maudlin fashion, but the sheer beauty of the churchyard – its old lych-gates, its rose bushes and its Garden of Remembrance – enchant most visitors.

Maidenhead

About 6 miles (10km) upriver from Eton lies **Maidenhead ❺**, the starting point for some of the most beautiful countryside in the valley. Known in medieval times as Maydenhythe, one suggested meaning being maidens' landing place, its bridges are its most interesting feature: the 128ft (38-metre) arches of Brunel's Railway Bridge are still in service today. From Maidenhead the A4130 goes 8 miles (13km) straight to Henley, but there are several picturesque villages and towns clustered on either side of the river nearby. **Bray**, nestled in a bend in the Thames just south of Maidenhead, has a lovely church that dates from 1293 though it is more famed

today for its Michelin starred restaurants. The **Jesus Hospital**, founded in 1627, is a group of almshouses that provide homes for elderly people.

Taplow is another pretty village on the north side of the Thames opposite Maidenhead. From here a road leads through Burnham to **Burnham Beeches**, a pastoral stretch of 375 wooded acres (150 hectares).

Upstream from Maidenhead, poised dramatically above cliffs, is **Cliveden ❻** (tel: 01628-605 069; main rooms and temple: Apr–Oct Thur and Sun 3–5.30pm; estate: mid-Mar–Oct daily 11am–6pm, Nov–Dec until 4pm; charge). This Italianate house was built for the Duke of Sutherland in the 1850s and was once the home of the Astor family. Before World War II Nancy Astor, the first woman to be elected to parliament, turned it into a meeting place for politicians and celebrities and in the 1960s it was the backdrop to the scandalous Profumo Affair. Today, Cliveden is owned by the National Trust but is run as a luxury hotel. The gardens are decorated in the Roman style and walks through

the stretch of woodland named **Cliveden Reach** afford spectacular views of the Thames.

Cookham

Cookham ➐ is another picturesque riverside village, but it's best known as the home of the artist Stanley Spencer (1891–1959), whose paintings claim six rooms in London's Tate Britain gallery. The newly modernised Stanley Spencer Gallery is housed in the King's Hall on Cookham High Street (Easter–Oct daily 10.30am–5.30pm, Nov–Easter Sat–Sun 11am–4.30pm; charge). A copy of his painting of the *Last Supper* hangs in Holy Trinity Church, parts of which date from the 12th century. The church tower is one of the few with both a clock and a sundial.

Marlow ➑ lies 6 miles (9km) upriver. In Saxon times it was called Merelaw, but what you see today is comparatively new: a broad high street, several pleasing 18th-century buildings, a graceful suspension bridge and **All Saints' Church** (the latter two date from the 1830s). Walks along the river below Marlow Lock or through the 25,000 acres (10,000 hectares) of **Quarry Wood** are refreshing.

Crew capital of the world

Henley-on-Thames ➒, a small market town with numerous Georgian buildings, has been known for its races since 1839, when it hosted the world's first river regatta. The four-day **Henley Royal Regatta** *(see pages 122–23)* attracts rowers from all over the globe. It also attracts a champagne-drinking crowd, some of whom are decked out in Edwardian elegance – white linen dresses, striped blazers and straw hats. A strict dress code operates in the stewards' enclosure. Less celebrated regattas are held on other summer weekends. As its name implies, the **River & Rowing Museum** in Mill Meadows (tel: 01491-415 600; www.rrm.co.uk; May–end Aug Mon–

A view of the River Thames from the gardens at Cliveden.

BELOW: the George and Dragon, a well-known watering hole at Marlow.

Taking to the water at Henley.

BELOW: racing
ahead at Henley
Royal Regatta.

Sun 10am–5.30pm, Sept–end Apr until 5pm; charge) includes historical artefacts found in the Thames, an interactive "in the cox's seat" exhibit and a re-creation of *The Wind in the Willows*, the classic children's tale.

There are several stately homes around Henley, but the most exquisite is **Greys Court**. West of Henley on the road to Peppard, this well-preserved Tudor house includes the remains of a 14th-century manor house (closed until Spring 2010; tel: 01491-755 564). There is a crenellated tower, a huge donkey wheel once used for drawing water and a maze.

Shiplake is a sprawling village notable for its church, rebuilt in 1689, but housing excellent 15th-century stained glass from the abbey church of Saint-Bertin in Saint-Omer, France.

Shiplake is best visited en route to **Sonning** ⑩, often considered the prettiest of the Thames villages. The little islands that rise here in the river make the views especially pastoral. In Saxon times, Sonning was the centre of a large diocese, with a cathedral, a bishop's palace and a deanery. Today, only parts of the Deanery garden walls remain, though the present church incorporates fragments of Saxon work. The old houses in the village are well-preserved. The 500 year old half-timbered **White Hart Inn** is now part of a large hotel, while the softly weathered, red-brick bridge is one of the oldest on the river.

Reading ⑪ is the single industrial town in the lower valley; an important traffic hub and retail centre and famous for its annual rock festival, but a somewhat dreary place, capitalising on the Thames Valley's aspiration to be Silicon Valley. The playwright Oscar Wilde (1854–1900) was a famous inmate of the gaol.

Streatley and **Goring**, 10 miles (16km) north on the A329, face each other on either side of the river. Streatley is the prettier of the two, situated at the foot of the Berkshire Downs. Five miles (8km) northwest is **Blewbury** ⑫, a lovely little town with thatched cottages, orchards, watercress beds and winding lanes.

Upriver about 8 miles (13km) is **Dorchester-on-Thames** ⑬ (backtrack to Streatley and look for signs to the A4074). This ancient town was once a Roman fort (then known as Durocina) and, during the 7th century, a cathedral city. The 12th-century abbey church was spared demolition during the Dissolution of the Monasteries (1536–40) by a local resident who bought it from the Crown for £140. The stained glass in the nave dates from the 14th century. In the chancel is a fine example of a Jesse window in which Jesse, Christ's ancestor, lies on the sill with a fruit vine springing from his belly. Dorchester's High Street, which follows the line of the

Roman road to Silchester, is lined with period timber-framed buildings.

Abbeys, roses and Romans

From Dorchester, the road leads to **Abingdon** ⓮ on the doorstep of Oxford. The town sprang up in the 7th century around a powerful Benedictine abbey. In the 14th century the townspeople led a bloody uprising against the monks, though it was not until the Dissolution that the abbey lost its power. Most of the ecclesiastical buildings were destroyed (don't be fooled by the 19th-century artificial ruins in the abbey grounds), but there are some authentic remains. These include the abbey **gateway** (though some think this was re-built from original rubble), the 13th-century **Chequer** with its idiosyncratic chimney, and the 15th-century **Long Gallery**. Dating from 1682, Abingdon **Town Hall**, of the open-ground-floor type, was built by Sir Christopher Wren's mason, responsible for the dome of St Paul's Cathedral in London. East Saint Helen's, with the church at its foot remarkable for its triple set of almshouses, is perhaps the prettiest street.

A short detour will take you to two places that should not be missed. Get back on the M25 and travel north to Exit 21A. At Chiswell Green you will find the **Gardens of the Rose** (tel: 01727-850 461 for details; June–Sept Wed–Sun 11am–5pm; charge), a glorious garden run by the Royal National Rose Society. From here it's only a few miles north-east to **St Albans** ⓯ (or take the next exit on the M25). A pleasing market town, this was once the Roman settlement of Verulamium, and remains of its walls are still visible. The **Verulamium Museum** (Mon–Sat 10am–5.30pm, Sun 2–5.30pm; charge) has a wonderful collection of mosaics and remains of a Roman bath house and theatre can also be seen. **St Alban's Cathedral** (daily 8.30am–5.45pm; donations welcomed) was founded in 793 and, while nothing of that abbey remains, there are 11th-century Norman arches and windows, as well as some magnificent Early English and Decorated arches from the 13th and 14th centuries. ❏

St Alban was the first English Christian martyr, beheaded by the Romans early in the 3rd century.

LEFT:
the remains of the Roman theatre at St Albans.

Literary Connections

For a relatively small area, the Thames Valley has a surprisingly high number of literary connections.

● Alfred, Lord Tennyson was married in Shiplake church in 1850. There are rumours that he delayed his marriage for so long because he was worried about the mental instability which ran in his family.

● Kenneth Grahame, author of the children's classic *The Wind in the Willows*, lived in the area for much of his life – at Cookham Dean as a child and in his later years in Pangbourne.

● Oscar Wilde was broken by two years' hard labour in Reading Prison, convicted of homosexual offences. On his release in 1897 he went into exile in France, where he wrote *The Ballad of Reading Gaol*.

● Eric Blair (1903–50), better known as George Orwell, author of *1984* and *Animal Farm*, is buried in the graveyard at Sutton Courtenay.

● In Marlow's West Street, also known as Poets' Row, Mary Wollstonecraft completed *Frankenstein*. In 1817 she and her husband, the poet Percy Bysshe Shelley, settled here for a short time. While here he wrote a series of pamphlets under the pseudonym of The Hermit of Marlow, and composed and published the poem *The Revolt of Islam*.

● Thomas Gray completed his *Elegy Written in a Country Churchyard* while living in Stoke Poges in 1751.

THE ENGLISH SEASON

The Season is when high society is on display. The events are mostly sporting, but a sense of style is more important than a sense of fair play

The English Season was an invention of upper-crust Londoners as a series of mid-summer amusements. This was the time when young girls "came out" at society balls, at which eligible young men would be waiting to make a suitable match.

The presence of royalty is an important ingredient, and the royal family has long taken a keen interest in the sports highlighted by the Season.

The events, cynics say, are insignificant compared to their importance as social gatherings. People who care nothing for rowing attend Henley Regatta in the first week of July; philistine amateurs flock to the Royal Academy's Summer Exhibition; the musically challenged die for a ticket to Glyndebourne's opera season and ill-informed people queueing for tickets to Wimbledon seem to think it's the only tennis tournament in the world.

ABOVE: Being a tennis umpire at Wimbledon at the end of June can take nerves of steel as the players fight it out in the game's top championship

LEFT: George Bernard Shaw's Eliza Doolittle, played here by Audrey Hepburn in *My Fair Lady*, faced her big test at Royal Ascot, held in June. Her task? To convince fashionable society that she was a lady, not a cockney flower

ABOVE: Cowes Week, held off the south coast in August, the peak of the sailing season.

THE ALTERNATIVE SEASON

Muddy fields and dripping camp sites don't dampen the spirits of those attending the "alternative" season – the annual round of music festivals. The larger ones attract the best bands from around the world and you don't have to be a hippy, crustie or a member of a youth tribe to attend. Many people take a tent to the large weekend events.

The largest rock event, the Glastonbury Festival *(above)* in Somerset, takes place at the end of June. More than 1,000 performances are given on 17 stages by more than 500 bands, and it attracts big names from Amy Winehouse to Leonard Cohen. Tickets can sell out quickly.

If you can't get to Glastonbury, try the two-day Big Chill festival which takes place in early August in the rolling Herefordshire hills. This is a family-oriented, eco-conscious event, with a wide variety of music vying with art, dance and film.

The best world music festival is WOMAD, held in Malmesbury, Wiltshire, in mid-July. The Reading Festival in late August attracts some of the best US rock groups, and the Cambridge Folk Festival takes place in July.

ABOVE: Life's a picnic at the Henley Regatta, held in the Oxfordshire town at the beginning of July. Some people even take an occasional break to watch the rowing championships.

ABOVE: The Chelsea Flower Show in May has everything you need for the garden – and a few things you probably don't.

BELOW: International Polo Day is held at the Guards Polo Club, Windsor Great Park, in July. Cartier's sponsorship sets the tone.

BELOW: Glyndebourne, a summer opera location set on the South Downs near Brighton, is renowned as much for its lavish picnic hampers as it is for the performances of its star singers.

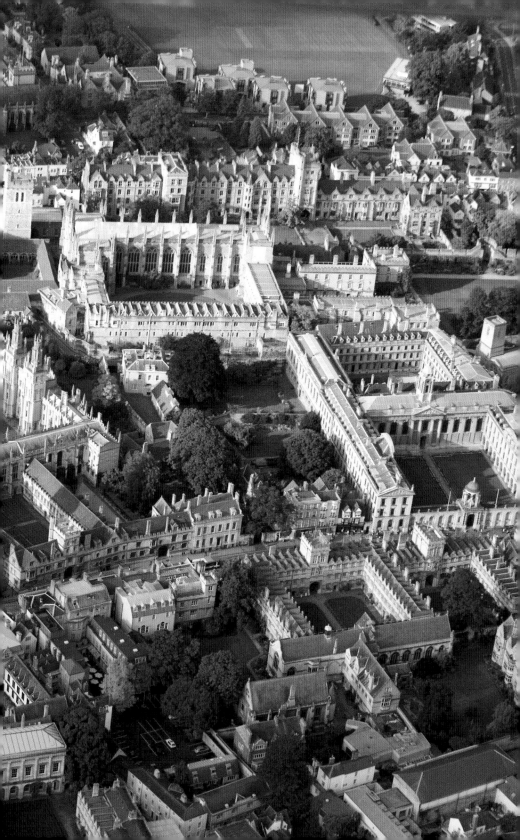

OXFORD

England's first mass-production car factory was built here but now traffic is a major headache. The town has had better luck with its university, which justifiably draws the tourists

The seat of England's oldest university, **Oxford** (www.ox.ac.uk), "the city of dreaming spires", was also the site of the first Morris Motors car factory and since World War II has been an industrial city as much as an academic one – something that is easy to forget when touring the colleges and museums. A good starting point is **Carfax** (the name derives from the Latin, quadrifurcus, "four-forked" or French *Quatre Voies*, "four ways"), where the four main streets – Cornmarket, High Street, Queen Street and St Aldate's – meet. **Carfax Tower** Ⓐ, all that remains of St Martin's Church, dates from the 14th century, and from the top you get a good view of the city (daily Apr–Oct 10am–5.30pm, Nov–Mar 10am–3.30pm; charge).

From Carfax, walk south along St Aldate's (passing the impressive, neo-Jacobite Town Hall on the left) and turn left into Blue Boar Lane and the entrance to the **Museum of Oxford** Ⓑ (Tue–Fri 10am–5pm, Sat–Sun noon–5pm). Displays inside highlight the history of the city from prehistoric times to the industrial age. The most macabre exhibit is the skeleton of Giles Covington, an Oxford Freeman who was convicted of murder and executed in 1791. Afterwards, carry on down St Aldate's to **Christ Church** Ⓒ, the grandest of the colleges (Mon–Sat 9am–5.30pm, Sun 1–5.30pm; charge), founded in 1525 by Cardinal Wolsey, Henry VIII's chancellor, on the site of

an earlier priory. **Tom Tower**, a bell tower, built by Sir Christopher Wren in 1681, looms over the main entrance (visitors enter through the **War Memorial Gardens**).

Christ Church chapel is also the city **Cathedral**; the 13th-century spire is one of the earliest in England, and the building contains some exquisite stained glass, including the St Catherine Window and other works by Pre-Raphaelite artist, Edward Burne-Jones. Lining the south side of the vast **Tom Quad** is the enormous **Hall**, with a

Main attractions
CHRIST CHURCH COLLEGE
BOTANIC GARDEN
MAGDALEN COLLEGE CHAPEL AND
    CLOISTERS
BODLEIAN LIBRARY
BRIDGE OF SIGHS
PITT-RIVERS MUSEUM
ASHMOLEAN MUSEUM
BLETCHLEY PARK

PRECEDING PAGES: the historic city of Oxford. **LEFT:** the dreaming spires. **BELOW:** the annual Encaenia parade.

It was in the pool known as Mercury in the centre of Tom Quad that Anthony Blanche was dunked in Evelyn Waugh's novel Brideshead Revisited.

magnificent hammer-beam ceiling. To the north is the neo-classical **Peckwater Quad** and the smaller Canterbury Quad, where the **Picture Gallery** (May–Sept Mon–Sat 10.30am–5pm, Sun 2–4.30pm, Oct–end Apr Mon–Sat 10.30am–1pm, Sun 2–4.30pm) has a fine collection of Renaissance paintings and drawings.

If you continue a short way down St Aldgate's you'll come to **Alice's Shop**, drawn by Sir John Tenniel as "the old sheep shop" in *Alice Through the Looking Glass*. Needless to say, it sells every imaginable Alice-related souvenir.

South of Christ Church, extending to the confluence of the Thames and Cherwell, is the glorious **Meadow** where cows graze. Along the Thames are the university boathouses and it's here, in Eights Week in late May, that the college races take place. The Broad Walk runs east–west across the Meadow, and from it a path cuts north to **Merton College ❹** (Mon–Fri 2–4pm, Sat–Sun 10am–4pm), founded in 1264. The **library** in **Mob Quad** (the oldest complete quadrangle in Oxford) was built in the 1370s (guided tours daily July–

Sept at 2, 3 and 4pm). Much of the medieval structure remains, and the 16th-century bookshelves make it the first of its kind in England, where the books were set upright instead of being kept in presses. The **Max Beerbohm Room** in the Mob Quad's west wing is devoted to drawings by the writer and caricaturist (1872–1956), one of Merton's illustrious graduates.

From botany to books

From Merton make your way to Rose Lane and the **Botanic Garden ❸** (daily 9am–5pm, winter until 4.30pm). Founded in 1621 by Henry Danvers, Earl of Danby, as a physic garden for the School of Medicine, this is the oldest Botanic Garden in Britain. From the central pond, the view through the arch to Magdalen bell tower is magnificent. A great variety of roses are grown, and there's a wide range of tropical plants in the massive **glasshouses** (daily 10am–4.30pm, winter until 4pm) next to the Cherwell. Leaving the gardens you arrive at the High Street, just opposite **Magdalen College ❺** – pronounced "maudlin" (daily

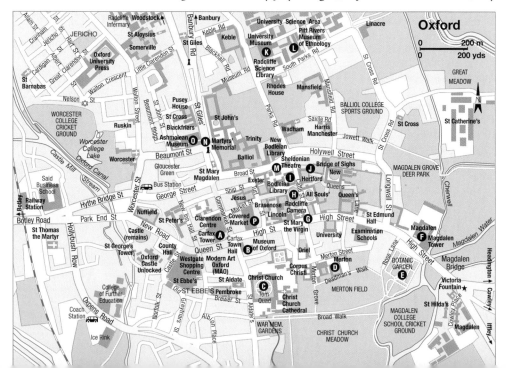

noon–6pm, winter 1pm–dusk), founded in 1458 by William of Waynflete. The chapel is a fine example of Perpendicular architecture, and the cloisters, the heart of the college, are stunning. The **bell tower** (1505) was used as a vantage point by Royalist forces during the Civil War (1642–46) and is famous for the Latin grace sung from the top by choristers on May Morning. Behind the college's New Buildings is the deer park, **Magdalen Grove**, and the lovely **Water Walks**, a maze of stream-side paths.

From Magdalen, follow the High Street to **St Mary the Virgin** , the original hub of the university, where all ceremonies were held and documents kept. The main entrance is the baroque **South Porch**: built in 1637, it was directly inspired by the canopy that Bernini had just built over the high altar of St Peter's in Rome. The 15th-century nave is a fine example of the Perpendicular style, with slender columns and large windows. It was here, in 1556, that Archbishop Thomas Cranmer faced his persecutors for the last time. Refusing to denounce the Reformation, and retracting all previous recantations, he was dragged from the church and burned at the stake in Broad Street. The **tower** (daily 9am–5pm; charge) offers a magnificent view of the city.

On the north side of Radcliffe Square stands the **Radcliffe Camera** , one of Oxford's most familiar symbols, founded as a library in 1749 and absorbed into the Bodleian as a reading room in 1860. "Camera" simply means chamber, and John Radcliffe was the physician who, despite his renowned ill temper, made a huge fortune by treating the wealthy – including the monarch, William III.

Radcliffe Camera was built after his death in 1714 to house a library devoted to the sciences. The gracious round form of the Camera was suggested by Nicholas Hawksmoor, but it was another great 18th-century architect, James Gibbs, who was asked to produce the detailed designs. The **Bodleian Library** itself dominates the scene: it is one of the world's largest libraries, founded in 1602 and now housing over 6 million volumes, including 50,000

TIP

Most of Oxford's colleges are open daily to visitors (usually in the afternoons). However, they tend to close at exam times, and at the end of term when conferences are held. Check noticeboards outside each college for opening times.

LEFT: Merton College courtyard.

Fact File

Location At the confluence of the Thames (the Isis) and the Cherwell.
By air Heathrow (40 miles/64km) connected by National Express and The Airline coach services every half-hour, journey time 1 hour 10 minutes; Gatwick (70 miles/112km) same operators run services every hour, journey time 2 hours 10 minutes; Birmingham International (65 miles/104km), trains from Birmingham International run hourly, journey time 60 minutes).
By road M40 motorway from London (Junction 8) and the Midlands (Junction 9); journey time about 90 minutes from central London except during rush hour.
By bus Oxford Tube from London Victoria 9am–8pm every 10-20 minutes (tel: 01865-772 250) and the Oxford Express (tel: 01865-785 410). Journey time approximately 1 hour 40 minutes.
By train Every hour from London Paddington, tel: 0845-748 4950, journey time approx. 1 hour.
Guided tours Walking tours start at Oxford Information Centre, Broad Street; open-top bus tours, tel: 01865-790 522.
Bike hire Tel: 01865-728 877.
Tourist information Oxford Information Centre, 15–16 Broad Street, tel: 01865-726 871; www.visitoxford.org.

Students make good tour guides.

precious manuscripts. The serene and magnificent **Old Schools Quadrangle**, in Jacobean-Gothic style, is the centrepiece, and beyond the main entrance of the library lies the old **Divinity School**.

Begun in 1426, it is regarded as one of the finest interiors in Oxford, and has an elaborate, lierne vaulted ceiling. (tel: 01865-277 178; guided tours of the library buildings, Mon–Sat 10.30 and 11.30am, 2 and 3pm; charge, university ceremonies permitting.)

Unmissable museums

Nearby, the **Bridge of Sighs** **J** marks the beginning of New College Lane and links the two parts of Hertford College. This pretty bridge is an anglicised version of the Venice original. From here you could follow the lane to **New College** (not new at all, it was founded in 1379 and has lovely original cloisters), but our tour goes north,

up Parks Road to the **Oxford University Museum** **K** (daily 10am–5pm; free), a splendid neo-Gothic structure begun in 1855, with slender iron columns and wrought-iron vaulting in the glass roof. It is a treasure house of zoological, entomological and geological exhibits, among them the skeleton of an iguanodon dominating the main hall, and a model of a dodo (plus a few remains of the real thing) brought to England in 1638.

Through the doors to the rear is the **Pitt-Rivers Museum of Ethnology** **O** (Mon noon–4.30pm, Tue–Sun 10am–4.30pm; free), an exotic collection of artefacts from all corners of the world, begun by Lt-General Pitt-Rivers (1827–1900) when serving abroad with the Grenadier Guards. A cabinet containing the shrunken heads of Ecuadorian Amerindians, along with shrinking instructions, is one of the more ghoulish exhibits in this temple to Victorian scientific curiosity.

Retrace your steps down Parks Road now to the **Sheldonian Theatre** **M** (Mon–Sat 10am–12.30pm, 2.30–4.30pm, winter until 3.30pm), the first

architectural scheme of the young Christopher Wren, which he designed in 1669 at the age of 30 while still a professor of astronomy. The bestowal of honorary degrees takes place here each June but for most of the year the Sheldonian is used for concerts and lectures. The ceiling is held up by huge wooden trusses in the roof, details of which can be seen on the climb up to the cupola.

Adjacent to the theatre is the **Museum of the History of Science** (Tue–Fri noon–5pm, Sat 10am–5pm, Sun 2–5pm), which displays the apparatus used during World War II to prepare penicillin for mass production. Opposite the Sheldonian, on the aptly named **Broad Street**, stands **Trinity College** (Mon–Fri 10am–noon, 2–4pm, Sat–Sun 2–4pm; charge), founded by monks from Durham Abbey in 1286. Unlike most Oxford colleges, the Front Quad is not closed off from the street, and its lawn almost invites visitors to enter. Apart from the baroque chapel, with its splendidly carved wooden panelling, stalls, screen and reredos, the principal attraction of Trinity is its fine gardens, entered through a wrought-

iron screen from the Garden Quad.

Next to Trinity is **Blackwell's**, one of the world's most famous academic bookshops. Opened in 1879, the original shop was tiny, and even today the initial impression is of an average-sized provincial bookstore. Downstairs, however, is the underground Norrington Room, an enormous space stacked with shelves devoted to every topic under the sun.

On the other side of Trinity is **Balliol College** (daily 1–5pm), renowned for having produced a greater number of politicians and statesmen than any other college in Oxford. They include the late Lord Jenkins of Hillhead (a former Chancellor of the University) as well as former prime ministers Harold Macmillan and Edward Heath. Together with University College and Merton, Balliol claims to be the oldest

Sir Christopher Wren's Sheldonian Theatre.

LEFT: Morris's early production line at Cowley.

The Car Capital

In 1901, young William Richard Morris, who had begun his working life in his early teens repairing bicycles, set up his own cycle shop in Oxford High Street. An ambitious and talented young man, he saw that the future lay with the horseless carriage, and by 1912 had progressed to building the prototype of the "Bullnose" Morris Oxford car in a garage in Longwall Street, a project that set Morris on the road to fame and fortune, and launched Oxford into the industrial era. Just one year later he established his automobile plant at nearby Cowley, Britain's first mass-production line for affordable cars. He sold 393 cars in his first year; by the end of the 1920s he was producing 100,000 annually, and had built a separate factory for his successful MG Super Sports model.

Knighted in 1928, Morris became Viscount Nuffield a decade later, partly through his generosity to hospitals and other medical projects. In 1937 he donated the site and funds to build Nuffield College. He had always had a prickly relationship with the university and city authorities, and was anxious that the new college should help build a bridge between the academic and non-academic worlds. He would be proud of the research developments that have taken place there in recent decades.

Balliol College has produced a great number of eminent men, in particular, statesmen and politicians.

BELOW: this aerial view centres on Christ Church's Peckwater Quad.

college in Oxford, founded in 1263. In 1361 John Wycliffe, Master of the college, spoke out against corruption and worldliness within the established church, and his teachings resonated through Europe. Little of the original college remains; what we see today is mostly Victorian.

Continuing the Oxford Story

Much of the southern side of Broad Street is distinctive for its colourful facades above shops selling art and music books and artists' materials.

Opposite Balliol a cross in the road marks the point where the Protestant Martyrs, bishops Thomas Cranmer, Hugh Latimer and Nicholas Ridley, were burnt at the stake.

Around the corner at the southern end of broad St Giles, they are further commemorated by the **Martyrs' Memorial** , which was erected in 1841. Before Latimer and Ridley were consumed by the flames in 1555 (Cranmer followed a year later) Latimer offered these words to his colleague: "Be of good comfort, Master Ridley, and play the man. We shall this day light such a candle, by God's grace, in England, as I trust shall never be put out."

Ashmole's great collection

The neoclassical building opposite the Martyrs' Memorial is the **Ashmolean Museum** (www.ashmolean.org; Tue–Sat 10am–5pm, Sun noon–5pm; free), whose main facade stretches along the north side of Beaumont Street. Built from 1841 to 1845, the Ashmolean is the oldest museum in the country. Set up by Elias Ashmole in 1683, its first home was in purpose-built premises on Broad Street (now the Museum of the History of Science). The origin of the collection goes back to Lambeth, London. There, in a pub called The Ark, the 17th-century naturalist and royal gardener John Tradescant displayed the extensive collection of rarities and curi-

osities gathered on his trips to Europe or given to him by sea captains. After his death in 1638, Tradescant's son, also called John, added numerous items from the New World. The collection was bequeathed to Ashmole, who presented it to the university. The museum is being extensively re-developed, with a new building and 39 new galleries. Displays will change but will no doubt still includes items from The Ark, which include a rhinoceros-horn cup from China, Henry VIII's stirrups and hawking gear, and, as the star attraction, **Powhattan's Mantle**. Powhattan was a Virginian Native American chief and, as any child from the USA will tell you, the father of Pocahontas.

The **Antiquities Department** has a fine Egyptian section, and extensive collections covering Ancient Greece, Rome and the Near East, as well as Dark-Age Europe and Anglo-Saxon Britain. The museum's most famous artefact is an Anglo-Saxon item, the **Alfred Jewel**. Found in Somerset in 1693, it is regarded as the finest piece of Saxon art ever discovered. It bears the inscription *Aelfred mec heht gewyr-*

can ("[King] Alfred had me made").

The other main attraction is the collection of **Western Art**, which includes drawings by Michelangelo and Raphael, as well as *The Hunt in the Forest*, painted by the Florentine artist Paolo Uccello in 1466.

Continue south down pedestrianised Cornmarket Street, and turn left into Market Street for the **Covered Market** **P**. Established by the Paving Commission in 1774 as a permanent home for the stallholders cluttering the streets, this is an Oxford institution that can't be missed. The central range is dominated by the butchers, whose fronts are hung with a variety of carcasses. There are also a high-class delicatessen and a pasta shop; shops selling sausages and meat pies; as well as tea shops and cafés – including the traditional "greasy spoon" – all vying for custom alongside smart boutiques and florists.

You can leave by an arcade via the tastefully restored **Golden Cross Yard**. Now equipped with a pizzeria, boutiques and shops selling organic products, this stands on the site of one of Oxford's oldest inns, where Shake-

Busts such as the Emperor's Heads (or Bearded Ones) put up in 1669 outside the Sheldonian Theatre were often used in antiquity to create boundaries.

BELOW: the Ashmolean Museum.

The Enigma machine.

speare's plays are said to have been performed in the cobbled yard. Leaving the yard, you'll find yourself back at Carfax, where the tour began, but if you still have any energy left you could take a right turn on to Pembroke Street to **Modern Art Oxford** (Tue–Sat 10am–5pm, Sun noon–5pm), which occupies an old brewery warehouse, is devoted to modern and contemporary art, and mounts some interesting changing exhibitions. The café in the museum is a good place to relax and rest your legs after all your exertions.

Bletchley Park

To the north east of Oxford, at Bletchley around 40 miles (70km) away, is a place that was once the best kept secret in Britain. **Bletchley Park** (www.bletchleypark.org.uk; Apr–Oct Mon–Fri 9.30am–5pm, Sat–Sun 10.30am–5pm,

Nov–end Mar daily 10.30am–4pm; charge) was a rambling country estate that became the heart of Britain's codebreaking operations in World War II. It was here that Germany's seemingly impenetrable Enigma code was broken, and here that the genius Alan Turing worked to build the Bombe, the machine that helped to break it. Today you can see the hut where Turing worked, see an operational rebuild of the Bombe (the originals were all destroyed after the war) and an operational rebuild of Colossus, the first semi-programmable electronic computer – built by Post Office engineer Tommy Flowers, to break another German cipher.

Many of the original huts are still standing and you can see displays on the vital role played by Polish codebreakers; a new Computer museum and a statue to Alan Turing.

The site was badly neglected for many years and was nearly demolished. It is now run by a charitable trust. If travelling from London you may reach Bletchley by direct train from Euston in 40 minutes. ❏

Annual Events

May Morning the choir of Magdalen College sings a Latin grace from the Magdalen bell tower at 6am – an unforgettable sound. This is followed by Morris dancing in Radcliffe Square and Broad Street, and by the unorthodox but equally traditional practice of students jumping from Magdalen Bridge into the River Cherwell.

Ascension Day the ancient ceremony of Beating the Bounds starts at St Michael's Church in Northgate, and reconfirms the limits of the parish.

Eights Week held in May, in the fifth week of the Trinity (summer) term, when eight-oared crews from all colleges compete for the distinction of "head of the river". The boat that crosses the finishing line first without being bumped is the winner.

Spring Bank Holiday Monday the Lord Mayor's Parade of splendidly decorated floats and tableaux runs from St Giles to South Park.

Encaenia in the week following the end of the summer term (in June). This is the main honorary degree ceremony, when dignitaries process to the Sheldonian Theatre.

St Giles' Fair the Monday and Tuesday following the first Sunday of September is the date of this colourful and much-loved local fair, which has been taking place since 1624.

The Great Palace of Blenheim

Blenheim Palace, near Woodstock, is a baroque masterpiece, a place of pilgrimage and a good day out for children.

Some 8 miles (13km) northwest of Oxford, its main street flanked by Georgian houses, is the attractive little town of **Woodstock** which grew prosperous through glove making. Pleasant though it is, it is overshadowed by its grand neighbour, **Blenheim Palace** (Feb–end Oct daily 10.30am–5.30pm, park: all year 9am–4.45pm; charge). In the early 18th century the great palace, designed by Sir John Vanbrugh and his assistant Nicholas Hawksmoor, was given by a grateful nation to John Churchill, 1st Duke of Marlborough, after his victory over the French at the Battle of Blenheim in 1704. Although recognised as a masterpiece of English baroque, its sheer ostentation made it an object of controversy right from the start.

The gilded **State Rooms** are the most impressive, decorated with tapestries, paintings and sculpture; and the beautiful **Long Library** contains more than 10,000 volumes. Many visitors are most interested in Blenheim as the birthplace and home of Sir Winston Churchill (1874–1965) and they will be delighted with the large collection of his manuscripts, paintings, books and letters. Visitors can also see the room in which the great man was born. The last attraction at the palace is Blenheim Palace: The Untold Story, a high-tech, interactive exhibition in which visitors can discover lesser known aspects of the history of the palace guided by a "ghostly" ladies maid. The exhibition doesn't only deal with the Marlborough family, but also sheds light on the lives of the servants.

It is quite possible to spend an enjoyable day at Blenheim without even going into the house. The huge park in which it stands, covering some 2,100 acres (800 hectares), was landscaped by "Capability" Brown (1715–83). Its centrepiece is the **lake**, spanned by Vanbrugh's Grand Bridge. The shallow side of the lake, called the Queen Pool, is home to a variety of water fowl, which makes it particularly popular with birdwatchers.

It was in the little Temple of Diana overlooking the lake that Sir Winston proposed to Clementine Hozier in August 1908. The young couple made their home in London, but spent a lot of time at Blenheim.

One of the great attractions of the grounds is the **Marlborough Maze**, the second largest in the world. It occupies the Walled Garden at the south side of the estate, an area known as the **Pleasure Gardens**, which includes putting greens, giant chess and draughts boards, and some bouncy castles for children, as well as a herb garden, butterfly house, tearoom and adventure playground. The area can be reached on a miniature railway which trundles through the grounds, but if you have the energy it's nicer to walk, admiring the ancient oak trees as you go. There are also formal gardens with terraces, cascades, roses and a tranquil Secret Garden.

The 1st Duke has a large monument in the palace chapel, but Sir Winston and his wife are buried in Bladon parish churchyard, just outside the walls of the park.   ❑

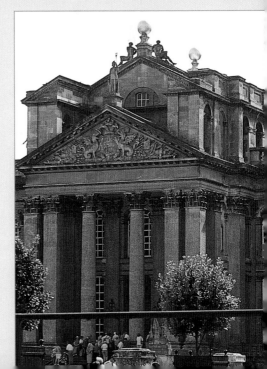

ABOVE: Sir Winston Churchill.
RIGHT: Blenheim Palace facade.

THE COTSWOLDS

To many people, this area, with its Roman remains and ancient castles, its picturesque villages and leafy lanes, its lush river valleys and riverside pubs, represents the essence of England

The creamy white limestone of the Cotswold Hills defines the boundaries of the region and gives it its character, a harmonious landscape of fields bordered by dry-stone walls, churches with majestic towers, opulent townhouses and snug cottages with roofs of limestone tiles. Most people start a visit to the Cotswolds at **Oxford ❶**, usually combined with a trip to **Blenheim Palace ❷** (*see pages 127–35*). From Oxford, go west on the A40 and make a short detour off to the right to the romantic ruins of 15th-century manor house **Minster Lovell Hall** with its interesting dovecote (daily during daylight hours; free). Then it's back on the road again to **Burford ❸**, which has one of the region's finest high streets, lined with 17th- and 18th-century cottages and descending sharply to a packhorse bridge over the River Windrush. A massive church stands beside the bridge, with a splendid Renaissance monument to Henry VIII's barber and surgeon, Edward Harman.

West of Burford the Windrush flows through a series of unspoiled villages, but we are heading a short way south on the A361 to **Lechlade**, where Percy Bysshe Shelley (1792–1822) was inspired to write *A Summer Evening Churchyard*. You can follow his footsteps on a path inevitably called Shelley's Walk, to **St John Bridge**, at the highest navigable point on the Thames. Beside the bridge is the **Trout Inn** (very pretty, but often crowded) and a minor road to **Kelmscott Manor ❹** (www.kelmscottmanor.org. uk; Apr–Sept Wed 11am–1pm and 2–5pm, Apr–Sept also 1st and 3rd Sat 11am–5pm), a Tudor farmhouse that became famous as the summer residence of the poet and craftsman William Morris (1834–96). A typical Cotswold stone-built house, the manor has a roof of split stones of which Morris said: "It gives me the same sort of pleasure in their orderly beauty as a fish's scales or a bird's feathers." There is a comprehensive account of Morris's life and the Arts and Crafts

Main attractions
CHEDWORTH ROMAN VILLA
WESTONBIRT ARBORETUM
PAINSWICK ROCOCO GARDEN
BERKELEY CASTLE
GLOUCESTER CATHEDRAL
HIDCOTE GARDEN
KIFTSGATE COURT

PRECEDING PAGES: Chipping Steps, Tetbury. **LEFT:** Chipping Campden. **BELOW:** a group of Morris dancers.

The Cotswolds towns grew prosperous through wool production.

Movement which he co-founded, and works by several members of the movement, including Burne-Jones and Rossetti. The old kitchen opened to the public in 2009, with displays of carved panels from the Society of Antiquaries London collection. William Morris and his wife, Jane, are buried beside the rustic and unspoiled village church – the kind he loved most.

A circular route: Fairford to Cirencester

Some 5 miles (8km) west in **Fairford** ❺ is the finest of Cotswold churches, St Mary the Virgin, with an extraordinary 15th-century stained-glass window which depicts the biblical story from the Creation to the Crucifixion. The Last Judgement window, with its fiery red devils with spiked teeth and yellow horns, and grim details of eternal punishment, is a masterpiece.

Continue along the A417 to Ampney Crucis – which also has a fine church – then take a right turn on the B4425 to **Barnsley** ❻ where you skirt Barnsley Park before entering the main street of a village where, until recently, overhead cables and television aerials were banned in an attempt to preserve its timeless tranquillity. The village is best known for **Barnsley House**, where the splendid 4-acre (1.6-hectare) garden created by Rosemary Verey (1918–2001) became one of the most-visited in Britain. The house is now an exclusive hotel, but the garden is open to the public on selected days (for details tel: 01285-740 000; www.barnsleyhouse.com; charge).

The B4425 joins the A40. Turn left here, then look for a right turn signposted to **Sherborne** ❼ (estate: daily; free), where 18th-century **water meadows** have been restored to working order by the National Trust. Sherborne was built as a model estate village in the mid-19th century and consists of rows of attractive identical stone cottages. Also here is Lodge Park, a beautiful 17th-century hunting lodge, created in 1634 for high living gambler John "Crump" Dutton (Mar–Oct Fri–Mon 11am–4pm).

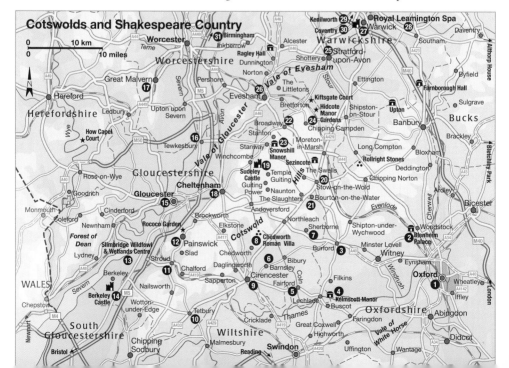

Turn left when the A429 joins the A40, and just south of Northleach you'll see signs to **Chedworth Roman Villa ❽** (Tue–Sun Apr–Oct 10am–5pm, Mar and early Nov 10am–4pm; charge), in a delightful woodland setting overlooking the Coln Valley. Chedworth is one of the largest Roman villas discovered in Britain, with two bathhouses, a latrine and a water-shrine. Mosaics here include a wonderful depiction of the seasons, with Winter personified as a peasant in a billowing hooded cloak bringing home a hare for the pot. In one corner of the site is a *nymphaeum*, a small sanctuary to the goddess of the spring who supplied the villa with water. The Romans introduced the edible snails that are found around the villa and inhabit the railway cuttings which are now a nature reserve. They used to be fed on milk to fatten them up. Chedworth village has a handsome Norman church with a fine stone-carved 15th-century pulpit, and a good pub, the Seven Tuns, in which to relax after your sightseeing. It dates back to 1610.

Capital of the Cotswolds

Whether you pronounce it "Cissiter", as purists suggest, or "Siren", as the locals say, the market town of **Cirencester ❾** used to be Corinium, the hub of a network of Roman roads, and it retains the rectilinear street plan of a Roman town. Gardeners are used to turning up pieces of mosaic and there are some spectacular examples in the excellent **Corinium Museum** (Mon–Sat 10am–5pm, Sun 2–5pm). Here, you can come face-to-face with Roman daily life through reconstructions of rooms from a townhouse and interactive displays. A new Anglo-Saxon Gallery reveals treasures from a cemetery site at Lechlade and substantial remains of the town walls are still in evidence along with a well-preserved amphitheatre.

Cirencester also has the interesting **Parish Church of St John the Baptist**, with a fine 15th-century wineglass pulpit, one of the few to survive the Reformation. If the magnificent tower is open (tel: 01285-659 317; times vary), climb to the top for a view of **Cirencester Mansion**, otherwise

A relief of William Morris carved in stone at Kelmscott.

LEFT: St John the Baptist Church, Cirencester.

Fact File

By car The M40 and M4 motorways provide easy access to the Cotswolds from London, as does the M5 from Bristol, the Midlands and the north.

By bus National Express from London Victoria to Oxford, Cheltenham, Cirencester and Gloucester, www.nationalexpress.com.

By train Regular services from London Paddington to Oxford, Cheltenham and Gloucester. National Rail Enquiries, tel: 08457-484 950; www.nationalrail.co.uk; to buy tickets online www.thetrainline.com.

Main festivals Cheltenham Festivals of Music (July) and Literature (Oct), www.cheltenhamfestivals.co.uk; International Festival of The Tree, Westonbirt Arboretum (June–Sept), tel: 01666-880 220.

Outdoor activities Guided walks, The Cotswold AONB Partnership, tel: 01451-862 000; www.cotswoldsaonb.org.uk; cycle hire, Cotswold Country Cycles, tel: 01386-438 706; horse riding, Camp Riding Centre, tel: 01285-821 219.

For children Berkeley Castle, tel: 01453-810 332; Slimbridge Wildfowl & Wetlands Centre, tel: 01453-891 900.

Tourist information Oxford, tel: 01865-252 200; Cotswolds, Stow-on-the-Wold, tel: 01451-831 082; Cheltenham, tel: 01242-522 878; Gloucester, tel: 01452-396 572.

hidden from view by what is said to be the world's tallest yew hedge. Beyond the mansion the broad tree-lined avenues of **Cirencester Park** are open to the public. An early example of English landscape gardening, it was laid out by the first Earl of Bathhurst in the 18th century, with some help from his friend, the poet Alexander Pope (1688–1744). The walk to the park takes you past handsome houses built by wealthy wool merchants.

Tetbury to Gloucester

We are going a little way south now, to **Tetbury** ⑩ off the A433, which was a quiet backwater until Prince Charles moved to nearby Highgrove. It's an attractive little place, with a 17th-century market hall, numerous antiques' shops and a wonderfully theatrical church, a rare example of Georgian Gothic built between 1777 and 1781. The Highgrove Shop in Long Street sells Prince Charles's range of organic foods as well as gifts for homes and gardens.

Just south of the town lies the **Westonbirt Arboretum** (tel: 01666-

880 220; daily 10am–8pm or dusk if earlier, Sat–Sun from 8am; charge), a glorious estate covering around 600 acres (240 hectares), its trees interplanted with camellias, azaleas, rhododendrons, cherries and maples which bring thousands of visitors during May and October for the spring and autumn colour. There are around 3,000 species of trees and shrubs, many of them rare or endangered.

Next we head north for **Stroud** ⑪, on the A46. The steep-sided valleys around the town provided it with fast-running streams, ideal conditions for woollen mills in the 18th century, when Stroud was the capital of this industry. A few of the grand old mills continue to produce high-quality cloth. The popular farmers' market is held on the first and third Saturdays in the month.

Some 3 miles (5km) north along A46 is **Painswick** ⑫, known for its elegant stone houses; a churchyard with 99 topiaried yews forming a series of avenues to the church; and some elaborately carved "table top" and "tea caddy" tombs. North of the

town is Painswick Rococo Garden (Jan–Oct daily 11am–5pm; charge), designed as an 18th-century pleasure ground for the gentry. Dotted with temples and gazebos and surrounded by woodland, the garden is magical throughout the year and is particularly impressive at snowdrop time (February) when the flowers carpet the ground.

Those interested in wildlife could make a slight detour here (take the A419 which crosses the M5, then turn left on the A38) to the **Slimbridge Wildfowl & Wetlands Centre** ⑬ (www.wwt.org.uk; daily Apr–Oct 9.30am–5pm, Nov–Mar 9.30am–4.30pm; charge), founded by artist and naturalist Sir Peter Scott in 1946 on a marshy site beside the River Severn. The ponds are home to an array of wildfowl from around the world, and viewing hides are dotted around at strategic points. It's possible to take a canoe safari, watch birds flying freely in the heated tropical house and even visit Crane School, where young cranes are being hand reared and prepared for life in the wild.

While you're on this side of the motorway, you might wish to visit a splendid castle just south of Slimbridge. At **Berkeley Castle** ⑭ (June–end Aug Sun–Thur 11am–5.30pm, Apr–May, Sept–Oct Sun only 11am–5.30pm, also open Bank Holidays, last entry 1 hour before closing; charge), with its massive Norman keep, you can see the Great Hall, where the barons met before riding to Runnymede to force King John to sign the Magna Carta in 1215; and the cell where Edward II spent his last days before he was murdered in 1327. Despite this regicide, the castle has remained in the hands of the same family from 1153 to the present – Shakespeare apparently wrote *A Midsummer Night's Dream* for a Berkeley family wedding.

Back on the A38, we are now heading north for **Gloucester** ⑮, not one of the most beautiful cities but one of great historical interest and full of unusual and fascinating museums *(see below)*.

Bagpipes at Berkeley Castle.

LEFT:
narrowboats in Gloucester docks.

Gloucester's Best Museums

The National Waterways Museum (Wed–Sun 11am–4pm and daily during school holidays; charge; www.nwm.org.uk/gloucester) is set in Gloucester's historic docks. This excellent, child-friendly museum at, Llanthony Warehouse, tells the story of England's waterways and offers cruises around the docks.

City Museum and Art Gallery (Tue–Sat 10am–5pm; free) houses a surprisingly wide collection, including dinosaur displays and fossils, local flora, 10th-century Saxon sculpture and medieval metalwork.

Gloucester Folk Museum (Tue–Sat 10am–5pm; free), a timber-framed merchant's house packed with displays on local history, an old school room and model railways.

Soldiers of Gloucester Museum (Apr–Sept daily 10am–5pm, Oct–Mar Tue–Sun 10am–5pm; charge). The history of local regiments and a section on women at war.

House of the Tailor of Gloucester (Mon–Sat 10am–4pm Sun noon–4pm) reveals the real-life tale behind the Beatrix Potter story of the mayor's magic waistcoat.

Nature in Art (Wallsworth Hall, Twigworth, 2 miles/3km north of the city on A38; Tue–Sun 10am–5pm; charge). A collection inspired by nature, including works by Picasso and David Shepherd.

Welcome to the Holst Birthplace Museum in Cheltenham.

Founded by the Romans, it became an important Saxon town, and later one of the country's busiest ports. From the renovated docklands area you can take a short cruise through the port and along the canal on the *King Arthur* (tel: 01452-318 200 for details and bookings; Apr–Oct). Gloucester's Norman **Cathedral** (daily 7.30am–Evensong; guided tours Mon–Sat 10.30am–4pm, Sun noon–2.30pm; donation requested), small by cathedral standards, has two fine tombs: that of Robert, Duke of Normandy, William the Conqueror's eldest son, and of Edward II, murdered at nearby Berkeley Castle *(see page 143)*. Today it's famous as where many scenes in the Harry Potter films were shot.

You may now decide to go north to Tewkesbury and Great Malvern, or east to Cheltenham. For **Tewkesbury** ⓰ take the A417/B4211. It's a pretty little town on the confluence of the Severn and Avon rivers, and a number of its half-timbered buildings now serve as pubs – the 17th-century Bell Inn, now an hotel, is worth a stop. **Tewkesbury Abbey** is a fine Norman church (daily)

BELOW: players at Sudeley Castle.
RIGHT: Gloucester Cathedral.

with splendid views of the Malvern Hills from the top of its square tower.

Twelve miles (20km) northwest is **Great Malvern** ⓱ once a spa town and still known for Malvern water which gushes from the spectacular surrounding hills. It's a lively cultural centre, synonymous with the composer Sir Edward Elgar (1857–1934) who lived nearby. The annual Autumn in Malvern Festival (tel: 01684-892 289, www.malvernfestival.co.uk; Oct) offers a feast of music, literature and fine-arts events.

Royal connections

If you opted for this short diversion you could now return south on the M5 to **Cheltenham** ⓲, the gracious Regency spa town which became popular as a summer resort after George II visited to "take the waters" in 1788. To get the feel of the town, stroll along the broad leafy avenue known as The Prom, where a splendid fountain is dominated by a statue of Neptune. To one end of The Prom lie the Imperial Gardens and elegant Montpellier Walk; to the other, **Cheltenham Art**

Gallery and Museum (daily Apr–Oct 10am–5pm, Nov–Mar 10am–4pm, from 11am first Thur of each month; free), which combines local history and colonial trappings with furniture made by members of the Arts and Crafts Movement. Nearby, in Clarence Road, the **Holst Birthplace Museum** (Feb–Nov Tue–Sat 10am–4pm; charge) pays homage to composer Gustav Holst (1874–1934), who spent his early years here. The house offers a delightful glimpse into the upstairs-downstairs world of the town's Victorians and Edwardians.

Cheltenham is particularly lively in March when members of the racing fraternity descend for the Cheltenham Gold Cup at the **Racecourse** (www. cheltenham.co.uk); and later in the year for the highly rated Festivals of Music (July) and Literature (Oct; for both events tel: 0844-576 8970).

North of Cheltenham on the B4632 is a place with royal connections of a different kind: **Sudeley Castle** ⓳ (end Mar–end Oct 10.30am–5pm; charge) was briefly the home of Katherine Parr (1512–48), the only one of Henry VIII's wives to survive him. Only six weeks after becoming a widow she married Lord Admiral Seymour, Sudeley's owner, but died a year later and was buried in the chapel. The castle was ruined during the Civil War which erupted in 1642, but restored during the 19th century. Among its glories are some fine furnishings, paintings by Rubens and Van Dyck, and lovely romantic gardens.

Continue north for a short way on the B4632 then turn right on the B4077 for **Stow-on-the-Wold** ⓴, the Cotswolds' highest town ("Stow-on-the-Wold where the wind blows cold", as the local rhyme has it). Here, royal connections were nothing to boast about: the church was used as a prison for Royalists during the Civil War and suffered considerable damage. The unusual north porch, with two yew trees growing out of the masonry, was added as part of the 1680 restoration. The enormous market square was in use until the 1980s, and the wooden stocks on the green were used to punish those who looked on market days as an opportunity for pilfering. Stow

KIDS

Children will love a steam-train ride on the Gloucestershire–Warwickshire Railway (days vary; check tel: 01242-621 405 or www.gwsr.com).

BELOW: Neptune's fountain, Cheltenham.

Flamingos live in natural surroundings at Birdland.

now has a reputation as an antiques centre, and you will find numerous interesting shops and galleries.

Models and manors

Around Stow are some of the Cotswolds' most attractive villages, among them **Upper** and **Lower Slaughter**, and **Bourton-on-the-Water** ㉑. The latter has far too many gift shops and cafés, but it remains a pretty little place, with elegant 18th-century bridges spanning the Windrush as it flows through the centre. The **Model Village** (in the garden of the Old New Inn) is a delightful miniature reconstruction of Bourton; and the **Model Railway** (Sept–May Sat–Sun 11am–5pm, June–Aug daily 11am–5pm; charge) will delight anyone who is nostalgic about train sets.

Close by is **Birdland** (daily Apr–Oct 10am–6pm, Nov–Mar 10am–4pm; charge) where most of the 500 or so birds were bred and can wander freely in natural surroundings. The best time to visit is at feeding time, around 2.30pm.

Backtrack now to the A424/A44 to visit **Broadway** ㉒, a manicured and mellow village, crammed with antiques shops, art galleries and tea shops. The church, about a mile away, has ancient topiaried yew trees, rustic monuments and a sense of tranquillity. In the village itself, the imposing Lygon Arms Hotel is a 16th-century building restored by members of the Arts and Crafts Movement in the early 20th century and now celebrated for its restaurant.

William Morris, co-founder of the movement, spent holidays at Broadway Tower, in nearby **Broadway Tower Country Park** (Apr–Oct daily 10.30am–5pm, Nov–Mar Sat–Sun 11am–3pm; charge). On a clear day it is possible to see 13 counties from the 18th-century tower.

Close to Morris's tower (and reached by a turning off the A44 at Broadway Green just before you enter the village) is **Snowshill Manor** ㉓ (mid-Mar–Nov Wed–Sun, Manor: noon–5pm, gardens: 11am–5.30pm; charge), an attractive Tudor manor house, restored by the eccentric Charles Paget Wade from 1919 to 1951. The Arts and

Crafts influence is evident in his work. He also assembled an eclectic range of 22,000 objects, ranging from musical instruments to toys, tools and Japanese armour. For some, Snowshill's greatest appeal is the garden, conceived as a series of outdoor rooms around the house.

Chipping Campden

Chipping Campden ❷ is an idyllic Cotswolds town, kept in a state of perfect preservation by the Campden Trust, which ensures that power cables are hidden and modern shopfronts banished. The sheer variety of buildings here is unusual, from the flamboyant Jacobean gateway of Campden House, to the Perpendicular-style church of St James, the 14th-century house of a wealthy merchant, William Grevel, and the Renaissance-style Market Hall, built in 1627.

Three miles (5km) outside town are two delights for garden lovers. **Hidcote Manor Garden** (late Mar–Oct Sat–Wed 10.30am–5pm; charge), created at the beginning of the 20th century by Lawrence "Johnnie" Johnstone, is a highly

architectural garden, known for its rare shrubs and trees and for some outstanding herbaceous borders. Laid out in a series of "rooms" it influenced Vita Sackville West when she created her garden at Sissinghurst. Even those who prefer a more naturalistic style of gardening are usually won over by Hidcote.

Just down the road is another stunning garden, **Kiftsgate Court** (Apr, Sept Sun–Mon, Wed 2–6pm, May–July Sat–Wed noon–6pm, Aug Sat–Wed 2–6pm), an informal terraced garden famous for its roses, especially the *rosa filipes* (Kiftsgate Rose) which grows at will and flowers profusely in June.

If you are visiting at this time, it makes a lovely last stop on your tour of the Cotswolds. ❏

The ancient Market Hall at Chipping Campden.

LEFT: a mellow corner in Chipping Campden.

Conserving the Cotswolds

The Cotswolds has been an Area of Outstanding Natural Beauty (AONB) since 1966: a designation that covers 790 sq miles (2,038 sq km) of land. Development is restricted within the AONB, while government funds are provided to encourage traditional low-intensity farming. Almost every town and village centre is now a Conservation Area, which means that development is kept to a minimum. Where new buildings are permitted they have to conform to strict criteria, using recycled Cotswolds stone.

As in many other parts of the country, local authorities tread a tightrope: they must maintain the life of the area and provide employment and housing, but also try to preserve the essential character of the region, which attracts vital tourism and makes the area such a desirable place to live. Above all, they must avoid making museum pieces out of the villages; while preserving their beauty is important, they are living communities and must be allowed some degree of change.

The Cotswolds AONB Partnership works with local councils, the Forestry Commission, English Nature and the National Trust, among others, to care for the region as a whole. Conservation projects within the AONB have focused on everything from trying to reverse the decline in numbers of farmland birds to supporting apprenticeships in dry stone walling. For details, tel: 01451-862 000 or see www.cotswoldsaonb.org.uk.

SHAKESPEARE COUNTRY

You may go to Warwickshire to see Stratford, Shakespeare's town, but it has many other treasures – great castles, cathedrals, and the art galleries of Birmingham, England's second city

he novelist Henry James (1843–1916) described his much-loved county of Warwickshire as "midmost England, unmitigated England…" and this is the region we shall cover in this tour. It is a land of patchwork fields, mellow brick houses and country lanes, with the River Avon running through it. But this area of the West Midlands also contains Birmingham, England's second-largest city, and Coventry, which was once synonymous with the British car industry.

A tour of Shakespeare Country must begin in **Stratford-upon-Avon** ㉕, where the Bard was born on 23 April 1564. Stratford is a pleasant town, set on an attractive stretch of the Avon where it is joined by the Stratford Canal. Start your tour at the point where the two bridges over the Avon funnel pedestrians and traffic into town, and where there is a large car park and the ever-busy Tourist Information Centre. Beyond the traffic, in **Bancroft Gardens**, overlooking the canal basin, is the **Gower Memorial** Ⓐ, on which Shakespeare sits, surrounded by characters from his plays: Hamlet, Prince Hal, Falstaff and Lady Macbeth.

Follow Bridge Street now to Henley Street where the informative **Shakespeare Centre** (tel: 01789-204 016; www.shakespeare.org.uk) stands next door to **Shakespeare's Birthplace** Ⓑ (daily summer 9am–5pm, winter 10am–4pm; charge). This timber-framed building

was the Shakespeare family home and business premises – his father was a glove maker, wool merchant and moneylender, and became mayor in 1568. The building has been authentically restored and furnished (it served as a pub before it was bought for the nation in 1847).

In the nearby High Street is a building not associated with Shakespeare: **Harvard House** Ⓒ (for hours tel: 01789-204 016), covered with ornate carved heads and friezes. This was the childhood home of Katherine Rogers,

PRECEDING PAGES: celebrating Shakespeare's birthday. **LEFT:** Anne Hathaway's Cottage. **BELOW:** William Shakespeare.

TIP

Save money and buy a ticket that covers entry to all five historic Shakespeare houses. To book tickets tel: 01789-204 016, www. shakespeare.org.uk.

who married Robert Harvard and whose son John emigrated to America in the 17th century before becoming principal benefactor of the university that bears his name.

Continue to Chapel Street, where **Nash's House** **D** (daily summer 10am–5pm, winter 11am–4pm; charge), home of Shakespeare's granddaughter Elizabeth, is a fine building stocked with 17th-century tapestries, ceramics and furnishings, and which now houses a small history museum. It adjoins the site of **New Place**, which Shakespeare bought as a retreat from London. All that remains of New Place are a well and some foundations but beyond lies a lovely Tudor-style **knot garden** and the **Great Garden** where two mulberry trees stand; one supposedly a cutting from the original planted by Shakespeare, the other planted by the actress Peggy Ashcroft; her ashes were scattered there after her death in 1991. It was at New Place that Shakespeare died, in 1616 – on his birthday.

Opposite the site of New Place stands the **Guild Chapel**, mostly 15th-century but originally founded in 1269.

Over the chancel arch are the remains of what must have been a spectacular wall painting of the Last Judgement. Continue along Church Street, past the wonderfully intact **Almshouses**, and turn into the street appropriately named Old Town where stands Hall's Croft, home of Shakespeare's daughter, Susanna. At the bottom, go right into Trinity Street to **Holy Trinity Church** **E** (Apr–Sept Mon–Sat 8.30am–6pm, Sun 12.30–5pm, Nov–Feb Mon–Sat 9am–4pm, Sun 12.30–5pm, Mar and Oct Mon–Sat 9am–5pm, Sun 12.30–5pm), dating mostly from the 14th century. It is worth a visit for its own sake, but most people come to pay homage at **Shakespeare's grave** beneath a simple stone in the chancel.

The riverside park can be entered through Old Town. Dominating the far end is the **Royal Shakespeare Theatre** **F**, adjacent to the Elizabethan-style **Swan Theatre** (for backstage tours, tel: 0844-800 1114). Built in the early 1930s, after the previous building was destroyed by fire, the theatre, which has some marvellous Art Deco interior fittings, is home to the Royal Shakespeare

BELOW: the Knot Garden on the site of New Place.

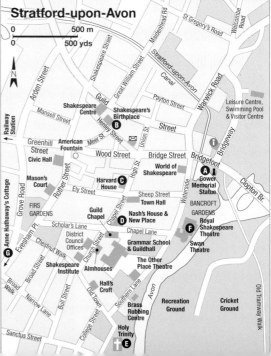

Company (RSC). The theatre is being redeveloped with a scheduled completion for 2010. Performances have transferred to the temporary Courtyard Theatre in Southern Lane.

We are now back at Bancroft Gardens and the nine-arched bridge where we began, but there is one more pilgrimage to make: **Anne Hathaway's Cottage G** (daily summer 9am–5pm, winter 10am–4pm; charge) is in **Shottery**, about 1 mile (2km) west of town. It's a delightful timber-framed thatched cottage, with an idyllic cottage garden (not the working farmyard it would have been in Anne's day). The house remained in the Hathaway family until 1892, when it was bought by the Birthplace Trust. Beyond the house is the **Shakespeare Tree Garden**, planted with most of the trees mentioned in the plays.

The Vale of Evesham

Follow the River Avon now for a bit of a detour, crossing into Worcestershire to the Vale of Evesham, with its orchards and market gardens. The river swings in a great bend around the town of **Evesham 26**, once the site of one of the most important abbeys in the Midlands, founded in 701. The abbey's wealth funded the great Perpendicular **Bell Tower**, still the town's most important landmark. Attractive parkland, popular with picnickers, drops gently towards the river.

In the town museum housed in the **Almonry** (Mon–Sat 10am–5pm, Sun 2–5pm) you can learn about the great Battle of Evesham in 1265, which ended the rebellion of Simon de Montfort against Henry III. De Montfort's mutilated remains were buried in the abbey church, but such was the veneration shown them by pilgrims that they were removed to a secret resting place.

Warwick and Royal Leamington Spa

We head north again, past Stratford to **Warwick 27**, the county town, built on a rise above the Avon, and dominated by the majestic tower of **St Mary's Church**, which can be climbed for a splendid view over the town and surrounding countryside. The tower and nave were rebuilt after a great fire in

Evesham Abbey was demolished during the Dissolution of the Monasteries, and only the Bell Tower remains.

LEFT:
Harvard House.

Fact File

By car The area is fringed with motorways: the M5 to the west, and the M1 and M6 to the north and east; the M42 orbits Birmingham from the south; the M40 from London and Oxford gives direct access to Stratford, Warwick and Leamington Spa.

By coach There are National Express services from London Victoria Coach Station as well as between major towns in the area; www.national express.com.

By rail Direct services run from London Paddington to Evesham, with other services to Stratford and Leamington; from London Marylebone to Warwick; and from London Euston to Birmingham and Coventry; tel: 08457-484 950, www.nationalrail.co.uk.

By air From Birmingham International there are flights to and from New York (Newark), plus internal flights and scheduled and charter flights to more than 40 European cities; tel: 0844-576 6000, www.bhx.co.uk.

Tourist information Birmingham, tel: 0844-576 6000; Coventry, tel: 024-7622 5616; Evesham, tel: 01386-446 944; Leamington, tel: 01926-742 762; Stratford, tel: 0870-160 7930, www.shakespeare-country. co.uk.

Guided tours Stratford Town Walks, tel: 01789-292 478, daily; City Sightseeing, open-top bus tours to Shakespeare sites, tel: 01789-299 123.

Althorp Park (July–Aug only 11am–5pm; booking advised; tel: 01604 770107) lies off the A428 north-west of Northampton. This is the family estate of the Earl of Spencer and the burial place of his sister Diana, Princess of Wales.

1694, but the 15th-century **Beauchamp Chapel** was spared the flames. The gilded brass effigy of Richard Beauchamp, Earl of Warwick, is splendid.

Warwick is a delightful town, with a wealth of Georgian buildings and a few medieval ones which survived the fire. Chief among these is the timbered and gabled **Lord Leycester Hospital** (Tue–Sun summer 10am–5pm, winter 10am–4pm; charge). It has been a home for old soldiers ever since Robert Dudley, favourite of Queen Elizabeth I, renovated the old guildhall as almshouses in 1571.

Most people come here, however, to see **Warwick Castle** (www.warwick-castle.co.uk; daily summer 10am–6pm, winter 10am–5pm; charge), described as "the most perfect piece of castellated antiquity in the kingdom". It has everything you expect of a castle: a wonderful site, great towers and walls, grim dungeons, sumptuous state rooms and glorious grounds, re-landscaped during the 18th century by "Capability" Brown. There are also convincing historical tableaux, recreated sieges, and a new – rather gruesome – Castle Dungeon experience. The entrance charge is quite steep, but it makes a wonderful day's outing. The castle also hosts classical concerts with fireworks, and events such as medieval banquets.

Royal Leamington Spa ㉘, close by, has been declared the most favoured place to live in Britain. It began as a spa town in the late 18th century, and the focal point is still the **Royal Pump Rooms** by the bridge over the River Leam. These now shelter a museum and gallery, but a sample of the spa water is available to those visitors intrepid enough to ask – it flows from a fountain and cups are available from the museum information desk. To the east are the showpiece Jephson Gardens, named after the 19th-century physician and philanthropist who contributed so much to the town. They are just part of the Grade II-listed sequence of parks that unfolds along the river. Some of the finest buildings are to be found along Newbold Terrace opposite the Pump Room; in The Parade, an elegant thoroughfare running northwards; and in the superb curve of Lansdowne Crescent.

BELOW: guarding Warwick Castle.

Kenilworth and Coventry

Some 4 miles (7km) north is another splendid castle, **Kenilworth** ㉙ (daily Mar–Oct 10am–5pm, Nov–Feb 10am–4pm; charge, English Heritage).

Despite years of neglect and deliberate destruction after the Civil War (1642–49), the extensive ruins remain an evocative setting, full of the echoes of history which are brought to life during the summer months by a lively programme of events. The 14th-century Great Hall is one of the many additions made by John of Gaunt (1340–99), which turned the grim Norman stronghold into a fine palace. In 1563 Elizabeth I granted the castle to her favourite, Robert Dudley, who added the gatehouse and apartments. When the queen came to visit she was entertained by a "lady of the lake" floating with her nymphs on a torchlit vessel, firework displays and lavish feasts. A recreated Elizabethan garden was opened in 2009, with a magnificent fountain and carved arbours.

Coventry ㉚ is known principally for three things: for the destruction it suffered during World War II and the cathedral which sprang phoenix-like from the ashes; for the story of 11th-century Lady Godiva, a noblewoman, who rode naked through the streets, protected only by her long hair, in protest against her husband's imposition of taxes; and as the birthplace of the British car industry.

All three are celebrated in the city: the first *(see below)* is the reason many come to Coventry. The second is commemorated more light-heartedly every July at the costumed **Godiva Procession**, and by the **Herbert Art Gallery and Museum** (Mon–Sat 10am–5.30pm, Sun noon–5pm; free), which aims to spotlight the city's heritage with the creation of a History Centre. And the third, which began with Daimler in 1896, can be explored in the **Coventry Transport Museum** (daily 10am–5pm; free), where the largest collection of British road transport in the world evokes Coventry's special contribution to the industry.

Much of Coventry was, necessarily, redeveloped after the war, culminating in the radical redesign of the city centre which garnered high praise in 2004.

Among Warwick Castle's most famous lords were Richard Neville, known as "The Kingmaker" for his role in the Wars of the Roses; and the Duke of Clarence, accused of high treason and said to have "drowned in a butt of malmsey".

BELOW: the elegant Royal Pump Rooms at Royal Leamington Spa.

A medieval doorway at Ford's Hospital.

But some historic buildings remain – **St Mary's Guildhall** with its spectacular Arras tapestry is a reminder of Coventry's wool-trading past; and **Ford's Hospital** is an outstanding medieval building which has functioned as an almshouse since 1509 – it was restored following bomb damage in the 1940s. For a change from the urban, head for the peaceful canal towpath, where 5½ miles (9km) of waterside art make up the **Coventry Canal Art Trail**.

Birmingham

Birmingham ㉛, at the forefront of the 19th-century Industrial Revolution and still one of the major manufacturing centres, has a history studded with the names of industrial greats – like James Watt, inventor of the steam engine and Matthew Boulton, who pioneered gas lighting. In the 1960s, the innovative city also became one of the country's most famous examples of revolutionary urban planning. However, thirty years on, Birmingham had lost momentum and was looking decidedly down-at-heel. It embarked on a journey of transformation and is emerging as a great centre for services, shopping and cultural activities, as exemplified by the dramatic redevelopment of the glass-covered environment of the **Bullring** shopping centre.

Whether you approach via the everbusy road network or by rail, you will be struck by the vivacity, if not by the beauty, of the city affectionately known as Brum. From New Street, Cannon Street climbs to **St Philip's Cathedral**, an outstanding example of English baroque, with the glorious stained-glass windows designed by Edward Burne-Jones (1833–98). Other members of the Pre-Raphaelite Brotherhood are also represented in the city: in Chamberlain Square the **Museum and Art Gallery** (Mon–Sat 10am–5pm, Thur from 10.30am, Sun 12.30–5pm; free) has a matchless collection of their work. A pedestrianised area makes a link on one side with **Victoria Square**, where the grandiose 19th-century Town Hall, modelled on the Temple of Castor and Pollux in Rome, and the Council House contrast with some monumental contemporary sculptures.

Coventry Cathedral

The ruins of the old cathedral, which form a poignant introduction to the city, are now a place of contemplation, and the venue for Mystery Plays, held every two years, as a symbol of peace and reconciliation.

The new cathedral, designed by Sir Basil Spence and built from 1955 to 1962, stands strikingly juxtaposed with the beautiful ruined shell of the old. The broad steps leading to the entrance on the university side are guarded by a striking bronze figure by Sir Joseph Epstein of St Michael triumphing over the devil, while the vast glazed screen is engraved with saints and angels.

Inside, the eye is led past slender supporting columns to Graham Sutherland's celebrated tapestry showing Christ in Glory surrounded by symbols of the Evangelists. The baptistry is dominated by a window of equal scale and renown, the abstract stained glass the work of John Piper and Patrick Reyntiens, and by a font consisting of a rugged boulder brought from Bethlehem. The small Chapel of Gethsemane is protected by a screen in the form of the crown of thorns, designed by Spence himself.

For further information about the building, call at the Visitors' Centre, where there is a spectacular audio-visual show, treasures from the old cathedral and gifts from well-wishers round the world.

On the other side of Victoria Square, a bridge crosses a section of Queensway to the Hall of Memory and **Centenary Square**, one of the city's newer public spaces and setting for the huge **International Convention Centre**. Its Symphony Hall has been acclaimed as one of the world's finest auditoriums. The pedestrianised area leads on to **Gas Street Basin**, once the hub of a transport network on Birmingham's canals – whose mileage is greater than that of Venice – now converted into a vibrant development of bars and restaurants baptised **Brindleyplace**. The site is home to the **National Sea Life Centre** (Mon–Fri 10am–4pm, Sat–Sun until 5pm; charge), which has a completely transparent underwater tunnel. On a more intimate scale, the **Ikon Gallery** (Tue–Sun 11am–6pm; free), housed in a Victorian building, is a laid-back venue for contemporary art with a good café-cum-tapas bar.

Stroll south along the water's edge to come to the **Mailbox**, an exclusive complex of designer shops and eateries, not to mention the shiny new home of BBC Birmingham.

Further south

On the fringes of Chinatown, the National Trust's **Back to Backs** (times vary; by guided tour only, booking recommended, tel: 0121-666 7671) is Birmingham's last surviving courtyard of working people's houses which were built literally back to back, a common feature in the industrial towns of 19th-century Britain.

Visitors are taken through four of the dwellings, restored and decorated to reflect the lives of chosen inhabitants from the 1840s, 1870s, 1930s and 1970s. The retro, fully operational sweet shop hugging the end of the row is a great touch. Three more houses can be rented as holiday accommodation.

A short bus or train journey from the city centre is the University of Birmingham at Edgbaston, home of the **Barber Institute of Fine Arts** (Mon–Sat 10am–5pm, Sun noon–5pm; free), an Art Deco building housing an unmissable collection of paintings, from the Renaissance artists to the Impressionists. The museum also houses one of the finest collections of Byzantine coins anywhere in Europe. ❑

South of Birmingham is the garden village of Bournville, laid out in the 19th century by the Quaker Cadbury family and the site of their cocoa factory. ***Cadbury World*** *(tel: 0845-450 3599) tells the story and offers chocolate tastings. Nearby is delightful Selly Manor (tel: 0121-472 0199), with its Tudor interior and small herb garden.*

BELOW:
Selfridges department store in Birmingham's Bullring shopping centre.

CAMBRIDGE

Like Oxford, Cambridge isn't car-friendly. But, with most of its architectural glories concentrated along a short stretch of the River Cam, it is an easy place to find your way around on foot

In 1209, when riots in Oxford resulted in the hanging of three students, a group of scholars settled in the market town of **Cambridge**, already a thriving community, and the seeds of England's second university were sown, although the first college was not founded until 1284. Feuds between townspeople and students ("town and gown") soon erupted and continued for six centuries, although the university's dominant role was established in the 1440s by the demolition of a large tract of the medieval centre to make way for the construction of King's College. Today there are 31 colleges in Cambridge; most of them are open to the public although restrictions apply during the examinations period (late Apr–mid-June). Some of the more famous ones – King's, Queens', St John's, Trinity and Clare (which has limited opening hours) – charge an admission fee.

Start your walk at **King's College** ⒶA, which was founded in 1441 by Henry VI, although the pinnacled gatehouse was added nearly 400 years later by Gothic revivalist William Wilkins and the classical Fellows' Building on the west side is an 18th-century structure. To the right soars the beautiful Perpendicular **King's College Chapel** (Mon–Fri 9.30am–3.30pm, Sat 9.30am–3.15pm, Sun out of term 10am–5pm, with some variations) with the largest fan-vaulted stone ceiling in the world, its only apparent support the slender columns of the nave. There are also some exquisite stained-glass windows, the work of 16th-century Flemish and English craftsmen. The intricately carved rood screen, donated by Henry VIII, is a magnificent example of Early Renaissance woodwork. The chapel also contains a stunning painting: Rubens' *Adoration of the Magi*. The renowned **King's College Choir**, whose carol performance is broadcast live across the world on Christmas Eve, sings here daily during term time and visitors are welcome to attend services.

Main attractions
KING'S COLLEGE CHAPEL
TRINITY COLLEGE
FITZWILLIAM MUSEUM
MUSEUM OF ZOOLOGY
CHRIST'S COLLEGE GARDEN
PEPYS LIBRARY, MAGDALENE
KETTLE'S YARD

PRECEDING PAGES: punting on the River Cam. **LEFT:** a custodian of King's College. **BELOW:** graduating students.

An angel on King's College Chapel.

Leave the chapel by the north gate to visit **Clare College**, founded in 1326 and resembling an elegant palace. From Clare Bridge, the oldest of the college bridges, there are good views of the river where punts drift sleepily past. Exit into Trinity Lane and turn left to Trinity Hall, one of the smaller, more intimate colleges, with a delightful Tudor brick library which has survived almost intact – it can only be admired from outside. From the main entrance, go down Senate House Passage, where you'll pass the domed Gate of Honour of Gonville and Caius College, one of the earliest Renaissance stone structures in the city, before reaching the **Church of Great St Mary** ⓑ, where the great 16th-century Protestant martyrs – Hugh Latimer and Archbishop Thomas Cranmer – preached. From the tower (123 steps) there is a wonderful view of the town (charge). This church is regarded as the very centre of Cambridge, the point from which all distances are measured.

Go north on Trinity Street to the **Cambridge University Press Bookshop** ⓒ, the oldest bookshop site in Britain: books have been sold here since 1581. On your left you will see the Great Gate of **Trinity College** ⓓ, the largest and richest college, founded by Henry VIII just before his death in 1546. Trinity has produced 32 Nobel Prize winners, six prime ministers and numerous poets, philosophers and scientists – Francis Bacon, Lord Byron, Isaac Newton, Ernest Rutherford, Lord Tennyson and Vladimir Nabokov among them. You can visit the Elizabethan **Dining Hall** (daily 3–5pm) with an intricately carved minstrels' gallery; and the **Wren Library** (term time, Mon–Fri noon–2pm, Sat 10.30am–12.30pm), one of the finest classical buildings in the country, designed by Sir Christopher Wren as a gift to the college. The 16th-century Great Court is the site of the Great Court Run, in which students must try to run round the perimeter (400 yards/metres) within the time it takes the clock to strike 12 (43 seconds); a scene memorably captured in the 1981 film *Chariots of Fire*. The Olympic runner, Lord Burghley, was the first successful contestant (in 1927).

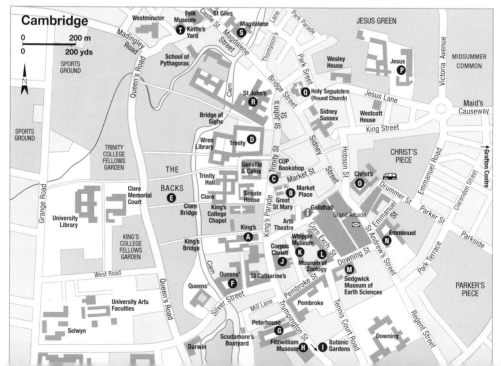

Leaving the college, cross **Trinity Bridge** to visit **The Backs** **E**, the lawns, meadows and gardens that back on to the Cam and are particularly beautiful in spring. The view of the colleges from the rear illustrates the wide variety of architectural styles employed. Beyond the back entrance to King's, turn left into Queens' Green and on to Silver Street to reach **Queens' College** **F** (summer daily 10am–4.30pm, varies at other times of the year). The Old Court is a fine example of a medieval quadrangle, and Cloister Court, flanked by the President's Lodge, a half-timbered building, makes a delightful setting for summer-evening performances of Shakespearean plays. The Cam divides the college in two and is spanned by the **Mathematical Bridge**, an early 20th-century copy of the one designed in 1749 by William Etheridge – and not Isaac Newton, as the myth runs.

From Queens', head south down Trumpington Street to **Pembroke College**, best known for its chapel, the first work to be completed (1663–65) by Sir Christopher Wren. Almost opposite stands **Peterhouse College** **G**, the oldest and most traditional of the colleges, founded in 1284 by the Bishop of Ely. The Gothic chapel on the east side is its most outstanding building. Sir Frank Whittle, inventor of the jet engine, was a student here, as was Charles Babbage whose work led to the modern computer.

To the right of Peterhouse is the **Fitzwilliam Museum** **H** (Tue–Sat 10am–5pm, Sun noon–5pm; free), revitalised by a £12 million Courtyard Development. The museum contains a priceless collection of paintings, books and manuscripts belonging to the museum's founder, Viscount Fitzwilliam; antiquities, sculpture, sarcophagi, ceramics and jewellery from Egypt, Asia, Greece and Rome; and masterpieces by Italian Renaissance artists, Flemish masters, and French Impressionists. The fan gallery has new displays of European and Oriental fans.

After this you might like to walk down Trumpington Road to the **Botanic Gardens** **I** (daily Apr–Sept 10am–6pm, Nov–Jan 10am–4pm, Feb–Mar and Oct 10am–5pm; charge), one

William Pitt the Younger (1759–1806), an early starter, came up to Pembroke at the age of 14, and became Britain's youngest prime minister only 10 years later.

LEFT: the Mathematical Bridge.

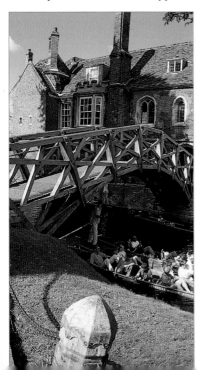

Fact File

By car 60 miles (100km) from London on the M11 (approximately 1½ hours).

By coach National Express services from London Victoria, via Stansted airport, www.nationalexpress.com.

By rail 50 minutes by train from London King's Cross; 1 hour 15 minutes from London Liverpool Street, tel: 08457-484 950, www.nationalrail.co.uk.

Nearest airport Stansted, 39 miles/48km (direct hourly train service to Cambridge).

Nearest port Harwich, 68 miles/110km.

Parking The city centre is closed to traffic Mon–Sat 10am–4pm; park in car parks: Adam and Eve Street, Castle Hill, Park Street, Queen Anne, Grafton Centre; or look for Park and Ride signs as you enter the city. From these, bus services run to the centre every 10–20 minutes.

Major colleges King's, Queens', Trinity, St John's (www.cam.ac.uk).

Best museums Fitzwilliam; Museum of Zoology; Kettle's Yard.

Activities Punting on the Cam, tel: 01223-359 750, www.scudamores.com for boat hire or go to the Quayside, Bridge Street, or to Mill Pond.

Annual events May Week; Folk Festival (July).

Tourist information Wheeler Street, tel: 0871-226 8006.

The atmospheric Eagle Pub, one of Cambridge's most popular drinking establishments.

BELOW: Trinity College fountain.

of the finest in the country. A huge variety of plants provide all-year colour; there are also a Water Garden, a Winter Garden, glasshouses full of tropical plants and a Genetics Garden, which illustrates how genetic variation plays on the appearance of plants. It's a reminder that the garden was established by Professor Henslow, the tutor who inspired Charles Darwin.

Retracing your steps past Pembroke College you come to **Corpus Christi** ❶, the only college founded by trade guilds. Its Old Court has resisted 18th-century refurbishment and looks much as it would have done in the 14th century. At the back of Corpus, on the other side of School Lane, lies the **Whipple Museum of the History of Science** ❸ (Mon–Fri 12.30–4.30pm; free) housing a selection of scientific and navigational instruments dating from the 14th century. Close by is the **Museum of Zoology** ❹ (in vacations Mon–Fri 10am–4.45pm; free); among its exhibits are specimens discovered by Charles Darwin on his 1831 voyage on the *Beagle*: most famous of these are some of the Galapagos finches.

Cross Downing Street to the **Sedgwick Museum of Earth Sciences** ❹ (Mon–Fri 9am–1pm, 2–5pm, Sat 10am–1pm; free), which houses Britain's oldest intact geological collection. Exhibits include the skeleton of one of the smallest known dinosaurs, the Compsognathus. The adjacent **Museum of Archaeology and Anthropology** (Tue–Sat 2–4.30pm; free) is devoted to prehistory. Downing Street leads east into St Andrew's Street where you will find the imposing **Emmanuel College** ❹, the first Protestant college, founded in 1584. The chapel was designed by Christopher Wren and the garden known as The Paddock has a large pool where Dominican monks used to fish, before Henry VIII dissolved their friary.

Going north up St Andrew's Street brings you to **Christ's College** ❹. The Fellows' Building is attributed to Inigo Jones; some have their doubts, but it is a splendid piece of 17th-century Classicism. **Fellows' Garden** (Mon–Fri 9.30am–noon, 2–4pm) is a magical oasis in the city centre. Milton's Mulberry Tree (said to have shaded the poet John Milton as he worked) was one of several planted by James I in 1608 to stimulate the silk industry. The most famous alumnus is Charles Darwin and a garden has recently been created to mark his achievements.

Head north up Sidney Street and turn right on Jesus Lane to **Jesus College** ❹, founded by the Bishop of Ely on the site of a Norman nunnery, to which the lovely **Cloister Court** belonged. The exquisite Early English arches, part of the Chapter House, were found under plasterwork in 1893. The chapel dates from 1200 but was restored by the Victorian Gothicist Augustus Pugin, and the new ceilings designed by William Morris's firm. Behind the college lies **Jesus Green**, a pleasant spot with an open-air swimming pool, tennis courts and bowling green; on the other side of Victoria Avenue is **Midsummer Common**.

Now retrace your steps to Bridge Street and turn right towards the 12th-century **Church of the Holy Sepulchre ◐** (daily 10am–5pm), one of only four surviving Norman round churches in England. Take St John's Street opposite to visit **St John's College ◑**, entered through an ornate 16th-century gate tower. The neo-Gothic chapel, inspired by Sainte-Chapelle in Paris and designed by George Gilbert Scott, can be visited (Mon–Fri 10am–5pm, Sat–Sun 10am–5pm; charge). The college was founded in 1511 by Lady Margaret Beaufort, mother of Henry VII, and her statue rests above the carved doorway of the Dining Hall.

The delicate **Bridge of Sighs**, modelled on its Venetian namesake, was built in the 19th century to link the older buildings of the college with New Court. From St John's, continue up Bridge Street where, on your right, you will see **The Quayside**, a popular spot in summer, when café tables are set out beside the river and punts can be hired for trips on the Cam.

Crossing the river, you come to **Magdalene College ◓** on your right.

The college showpiece is the **Pepys Library** (Mon–Sat summer 11.30am–12.30pm, 2.30–3.30pm, winter 2.30–3.30pm; free). Samuel Pepys bequeathed his 3,000-volume collection to the college in 1703. The library's greatest treasure is the original manuscript of the great man's diary, recording daily life in the 1660s.

Continue up Magdalene Street and you come to the **Folk Museum** (Tue–Sat 10.30am–5pm, Sun 2–5pm; charge), filled with the evidence of local life since 1700. Almost next door is **Kettle's Yard ◑** (house: Tue–Sun summer 1.30–4.30pm, winter 2–4pm, gallery: Tue–Sat 11.30am–5pm, Sun 2–5.30pm; free), an unusual museum in four cottages which Tate Gallery curator Jim Ede restored and made into his home in the 1950s.

With Kettle's Yard, Ede founded a haven of peace and welcome, filled with works by Ben Nicholson, Henry Moore, Barbara Hepworth and many other artists and sculptors; and one where music, light and natural objects, such as pebbles, would also greet the senses. ❑

St John's Dining Hall is hung with portraits of illustrious college members, including the poet William Wordsworth, and Lord Palmerston, the 19th-century prime minister.

LEFT: the Bridge of Sighs links old and new.

The Hidden Head

Sidney Sussex College in Sidney Street is one of the smallest colleges, founded in 1596 on the site of a dissolved Franciscan friary. It is not the most interesting college visually (although it does have attractive shady cloisters), but it is the last resting place of the head of Oliver Cromwell, leader of the Roundheads in the English Civil War. He had briefly been a student here, until his father's death obliged him to return home and take on family responsibilities. In 1643 he returned as military leader, looted the colleges – which supported King Charles I – and requisitioned their courts as barracks.

Cromwell was buried in Westminster Abbey in 1658, but after the restoration of the monarchy two years later his relics were exhumed and his body hung up at Tyburn Gallows, while his head was impaled on a spike at Westminster Hall for 20 years. When the skull eventually blew down it was spirited away and passed through various hands over the centuries before being offered to the college in 1960. It is buried somewhere under the ante-chapel floor, in the vicinity of the plaque. Sidney Sussex College has a reputation for mathematical expertise: many of the people who worked on decoding Enigma at Bletchley Park in World War II came from the college. More recent mathematical alumni include TV presenter Carol Vorderman.

EAST ANGLIA

The main attractions include boating on the Norfolk Broads, exploring the Fenlands, discovering medieval churches and following in the footsteps of John Constable

London

East Anglia, in medieval times, was one of the most densely populated and commercialised regions of England. Hard to believe now, when driving through the empty landscapes and sleepy villages of Suffolk and Norfolk. The broad acres of chalk and grassland provided ideal grazing for sheep, and huge quantities of wool were exported, boosted by the arrival of expert Flemish weavers in the mid-14th century. The main evidence of this era of wealth and prosperity is the region's medieval churches – more than 1,000 of them – from Saxon and Norman to Gothic Perpendicular. The great timber-framed houses you will see were also built on the proceeds of wool.

Our tour begins in **Cambridge ❶** (*see pages 161–65*) and first goes some 15 miles (24km) south on the A1301 to **Saffron Walden ❷**, which gets its name from the orange crocus dye that made the town wealthy. Today it's a delightfully unspoilt market town with a number of timber-framed buildings, several of them decorated with ornamental plasterwork called pargeting. The huge church that dominates the town is a fine example of Perpendicular style.

About 1 mile (1.5km) west is **Audley End House** (Apr–Sept Wed–Sun 11–5pm, grounds: 10am–6pm, Nov Wed–Sun 11am–4pm, grounds: 10am–5pm). The biggest house in England at the time, it takes its name from Sir Thomas Audley, Henry VIII's Lord

Chancellor, who adapted the buildings of Walden Abbey. This mansion was enlarged in grandiose Jacobean style in 1614 for his grandson Thomas Howard, the Lord Treasurer to James I who described it as "too large for a king, but it might do for a Lord Treasurer". Substantial changes were made in the 18th century when Robert Adam (1728–92) remodelled the Great Drawing Room and many other parts, although the Great Hall retains its hammer-beam ceiling and Jacobean oak screen. Lancelot "Capability" Brown landscaped the

Main attractions
ELY CATHEDRAL
SANDRINGHAM HOUSE
NORFOLK BROADS
FLATFORD MILL
LAVENHAM

LEFT: detail of Little Hall in Lavenham.
BELOW: fresh crabs at Cromer.

When Ely was an inaccessible island the surrounding marsh-land seethed with fish and eels, and it's the latter that gave the city its name: elge was the Saxon word for "eel district".

grounds at the same time. Just across the road is a miniature railway (tel: 01799-541 354). The Service Wing gives a fascinating insight into life "below stairs" in Victorian times.

The Fens

Now head in the opposite direction, to the flat Fenland of north Cambridgeshire, which was marshland until it was drained in the 17th century. About 16 miles (25km) north of Cambridge on the A10 stands **Ely ❸**. Rising shiplike above the city and surrounding fenlands is the great **Cathedral of Ely** (summer daily 7am–7pm, winter Mon–Sat 7.30am–6pm, Sun 7.30am–5pm; charge). The cathedral dominates the fens from its perch on what used to be called the Isle of Eels – after the staple diet of the villagers – earning it the title of "Ship of the Fens". The Isle, a knoll of dry land, was selected as a monastery site by St Etheldreda in AD 673, while the present cathedral dates back to the 11th century. Some 400 years later it made an ideal refuge for Hereward the Wake when pursued by William

the Conqueror. Hereward seemed unreachable on Ely (then an island), but eventually the monks tired of the siege and showed the conqueror's men the secret pathway through the marshes, giving Hereward away.

The splendour of Ely Cathedral lies in its unusual situation and in its unique lantern. In the evening, the lantern – an octagonal tower of wood and glass built high on the back of the nave in an extraordinary feat of engineering – reflects the rays of the dying sun. By night its glass gleams with the light within. The **Lady Chapel** is the largest of its kind in the country. A museum in the south triforium traces the history of stained glass.

Follow the A10, and the River Ouse, to the north, and branch off on the A1101 towards **Wisbech ❹**, a market town that styles itself the capital of the fens. The two imposing Georgian streets – South Brink and North Brink – illustrate the prosperity that marsh drainage brought. The eccentric **Wisbech and Fenland Museum** (Tue–Sat 10am–3.45pm; free) has the complete furnishings of a Victorian post office.

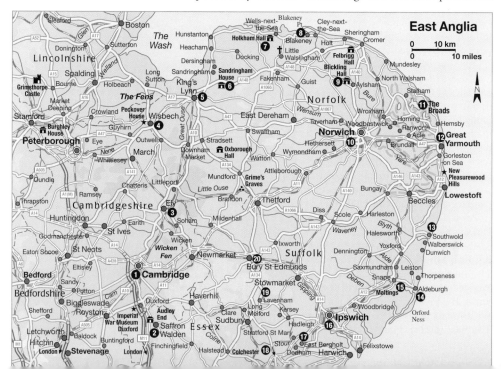

Peckover House (mid-Mar–end Oct Mon–Wed and Sat–Sun 1.30–4.30pm, garden: Mon–Wed and Sat–Sun noon–5pm; charge), built in 1722, is an interesting townhouse on North Brink renowned for its rococo decoration and with an outstanding Victorian garden, with a summerhouse, orangery and croquet lawn. Opposite stands the **Octavia Hill Birthplace Museum** (mid-Mar–end Oct Mon–Wed and Sat–Sun 1–4.30pm; charge). Hill (1838–1912) was a Victorian reformer and a co-founder of the National Trust.

Take the A47 for about 12 miles (20km) to the next stop, **King's Lynn** ❺, a port and market town on the Great Ouse, south of the Wash. Its port is still active and the heart of the town has retained its character with some fine Georgian houses and medieval monuments. Worth seeing are the elegant Custom House; St Margaret's Church on the Market Place; and the 15th-century Trinity Guildhall, where, in the Old Gaol House, you can take an audio-visual tour through some of the more gruesome aspects of the town's history. A relatively new attraction is

Green Quay, a discovery centre focusing on the unique wildlife of The Wash (daily 9am–5pm; free).

Take the A149 now, and turn right for **Sandringham** ❻ (tel: 01553-612 908; www. sandringhamestate.co.uk; Mar–Oct daily 11am–4.45pm, Oct until 3pm, closed last week in July; charge), built in 1870 by the Prince of Wales, who later reigned as Edward VII. Largely 18th-century in style, it has many Edwardian embellishments, and it is now the Queen's country retreat and the place where she has traditionally spent Christmas. There are extensive grounds, with lakes and nature trails, and a museum of royal motor cars.

A coastal route

Continue on the A149, now a coast road, past **Hunstanton**, a popular resort with broad sandy beaches and 60ft (18-metre) cliffs with distinctive

Royal limousines at Sandringham.

LEFT: Sandringham, the royal retreat.

Fact File

Location The counties of Essex, Suffolk, Cambridgeshire and Norfolk between the Thames Estuary and The Wash.

By car From London, Colchester is about 60 miles (100km) on the A12 and Norwich is 115 miles (185km) on the A12/A140; journey time from Norwich to Cambridge about 80 minutes; Norwich to King's Lynn 1 hour.

By bus National Express from London Victoria to Norwich, about 4 hours 30 minutes; www.nationalexpress.com.

By rail 50 minutes by train from London Liverpool Street to Colchester; 1 hour 50 minutes to Norwich; London King's Cross to King's Lynn 1 hour 40 minutes; tel: 08457-484 950, www.nationalrail.co.uk.

Nearest airport Stansted; four train services per hour to London Liverpool Street; hourly train service to Cambridge.

Nearest port Harwich (to Hook of Holland and Hamburg).

Major towns Colchester, Ipswich, King's Lynn, Norwich.

Attractions The Broads; medieval churches; wool towns.

For **children** New Pleasurewood Hills, Lowestoft, tel: 01502-586 000, one of the largest theme parks in England.

Tourist information Bury St Edmunds, tel: 01284-764 667; Colchester, tel: 01206-282 920; Ipswich, tel: 01473-258 070; King's Lynn, tel: 01553-763 044; Norwich, tel: 01603-213 999.

A town crier in Elm Hill, Norwich's most picturesque cobbled street.

BELOW: the approach to Blickling Hall.
RIGHT: Blakeney Point seals.

strips of carrstone and red and white chalk. It's the only East Anglian resort facing west, and you get some glorious sunsets over The Wash. The A149 follows the coast east through a series of small villages, seven of which have "Burnham" in their names. At Holkham is one of Norfolk's finest stately homes, **Holkham Hall** ❼ (www.holkham.co.uk; June–Sept Sun–Tue, Thur noon–4pm, May, Oct Sun, Mon, Thur noon–4pm; charge, grounds free). Set in magnificent parkland, the sombre Palladian facade hides a grandiose hall and state rooms with paintings by Van Dyck, Rubens and Gainsborough. The stunning sandy beach at Holkham famously featured in the closing scenes of the film *Shakespeare in Love*. Access is via Lady Anne's Drive on the A149.

East of Holkham lies **Wells-next-the-Sea**, a genuine working port with coasters along the quay and fishing boats bringing in crabs and shrimps.

It's also a popular holiday spot, with masses of amusements and fast-food outlets by the quay. A light railway from Wells will take you inland to **Little Walsingham**, still a place of pilgrimage for Catholics, with a well-preserved medieval high street.

A little further on from Wells, **Blakeney** ❽ is a pretty coastal village of flint-cobbled cottages, known for its sand-and-shingle spit. **Blakeney Point** at its tip is the summer home for a dozen species of seabirds, including terns, oystercatchers, plovers and redshanks. Common and grey seals bask on the sands when the tide is low, and in summer they can be spotted on a ferry trip from Morston Quay.

The last coastal stop for the moment is at **Cromer**, a pleasantly old-fashioned resort with a long sand-and-shingle beach and a town centre dominated by the soaring church tower. There's a Victorian pier, too, on which stands the Pavilion Theatre, still putting on shows. Fishing boats bring in the famous Cromer crabs, which you can buy throughout Norfolk in the summer months.

Inland to Norwich

Head inland now on the A140 to Aylsham and **Blickling Hall** ❾ (Mar–end Oct Wed–Sun 11am–5pm, mid-July–early Sept also Mon, park: all year; charge), one of England's greatest Jacobean houses. Covered with turrets and gables, bordered by lawns and huge yew hedges, it is also known for its spectacular Long Gallery, fine furniture and tapestries. The gardens are colourful all year round and the park offers splendid walks.

Continue south on the A140 to **Norwich** ❿. Before the Industrial Revolution this was one of the most prosperous cities in England. Set amid rich agricultural land it rose to prominence in the Middle Ages as a market and trading centre. This prosperity is evident in the 32 medieval churches and a host of historic houses. There's also a large and colourful **market**, a pub for every day of the year, and a pleasantly relaxed atmosphere. The 12th-century **Castle** (Mon–Fri 10am–4.30pm, Sat 10am–5pm, Sun 1–5pm; charge) has a museum in its keep, with collections of archaeology and natural history, as well as galleries displaying works by the Norwich School of landscape painters and visiting exhibitions from the Tate. It also has the world's largest collection of ceramic teapots.

Down in the town, close to the lively market, is an elegant Art Nouveau thoroughfare, the **Royal Arcade**, where you'll find the **Mustard Shop**. For nearly 200 years regional farmers have been growing mustard for the firm of Colman's, and this specialist shop-cum-museum stocks products and souvenirs. The magnificent **Cathedral** (daily) was founded in 1096 by Bishop Losinga. There are over 1,000 carved and painted bosses throughout the building, and the cloisters are the largest in England. Within the outer flint walls is a modern version of a Norman refectory, designed by Sir Michael Hopkins. You can admire the cathedral spire from **Pull's Ferry**, a medieval flint-and-stone watergate on the River Wensum.

Sir Hopkins also designed the **Forum**, a horseshoe-shaped building encompassing the regional library and

Blickling Hall was the childhood home of Anne Boleyn, Henry VIII's second wife, but little of that house remains. Most of what you see today is 17th century.

BELOW:
market day in Norwich.

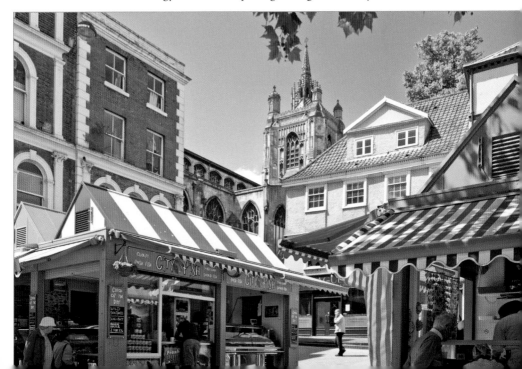

tourist office. At the University of East Anglia don't overlook the newly refurbished **Sainsbury Centre for Visual Arts**, (Tue–Sun 10am–5pm, Wed 10am–8pm; free), which houses a splendid European collection featuring Picasso, Henry Moore and Giacometti. Highlights include Moore's *Mother and Child*, and an Inca llama effigy, which would probably have been buried by a human sacrifice.

From the Broads to the Maltings

You can take the A1151 northeast, or the A47 or B1140 east from Norwich to reach **The Broads ⑪**, a network of navigable rivers and lakes in Norfolk and Suffolk, formed by the flooding of medieval peat diggings. Catering for every type of craft, and uninterrupted by locks, these 200 miles (320km) of quiet waterways are a haven for boating enthusiasts. Many people spend their holidays on the water in a narrow boat, but you can also hire a sailing boat or motor cruiser, by the hour or by the day. There are also trips to see the wildlife of the area. The floating

Broadland Conservation Centre (Apr–Oct daily 10am–5pm) at Ranworth offers a wealth of information and a boardwalk trail.

If you're doing your navigating through the Broads by road the A47 will take you to **Great Yarmouth ⑫**, where Charles Dickens (1812–70) set part of *David Copperfield*. The town once flourished on its herring catch, but over-fishing killed the industry and now, as the most popular resort on the Norfolk coast, it relies mainly on tourism. Golden sands are hidden from view behind helter-skelters and roller-coasters. The nicest area of town is the historical part around **South Quay**, where the **Old Merchant's House** (Apr–Sept daily; charge) with its Jacobean plaster ceilings, is worth a visit.

Some 10 miles (16km) south is **Lowestoft**, England's most easterly town, which still retains a small fishing fleet. About 15 miles (24km) down the coast lies **Southwold ⑬**, a remarkably unspoilt and rather old-fashioned little place. Set on a cliff top it is distinguished by its open greens, created after a fire destroyed much of the town

BELOW: testing the temperature at Southwold, Suffolk.

in the 17th century. Victorian seafront terraces, Georgian houses and fishermen's cottages blend smoothly together, and colourful beach huts face the sea across a sand-and-shingle beach. The **Southwold Museum** (Easter–Oct daily 2–4.30pm; free) is largely devoted to the Battle of Sole Bay, fought against the Dutch in 1672. The church of **St Edmund** is said to be the finest medieval seaside church in England.

You have to go around the estuary of the **River Blyth** to pick up the B1125 to **Aldeburgh** ⓮, the birthplace of the international music festival which now takes place at Snape. But Aldeburgh – an unspoilt and pleasant town which has been a port since Roman times – is still very much a festival centre and its hotels and restaurants cater well for visitors to nearby Snape Maltings. The High Street, lined with galleries and bookshops as well as food shops, runs parallel to a steeply shelving shingle beach where fresh fish is sold straight from the boats. The brick and timber-framed **Moot Hall**, which houses a small museum, stands near the promenade, but used to be some way inland,

until erosion ate away the land.

Take the A1094 inland, then turn left to reach the well-signposted **Snape Maltings** ⓯ on the River Alde, the 19th-century red-brick granaries and malthouses converted by Benjamin Britten (1913–76) into a concert hall in 1967. Born in Lowestoft, Britten moved to Snape in 1937 and his opera *Peter Grimes* was performed here eight years later. The main **Aldeburgh Festival** takes place in June (www.aldeburgh.co.uk; box office tel: 01728-687 110) but other events are held throughout the summer, and riverside galleries and craft, furniture and antiques shops are open all year.

Constable and Camulodunum

Get on the A12 now for **Ipswich** ⓰, the county town of Suffolk. The centre is mostly modern, but there's an atmospheric Victorian dockland on the River Orwell, and a local museum and gallery in the **Christchurch Mansion** (daily 10am–5pm; free), which has a splendid collection of Constable's paintings *(see box, page 174)* as well as

TIP

Left-hand turns off the B1125 between Southwold and Aldeburgh take you to Dunwich *(see box below)*; to the Sizewell Nuclear Power Station; and to Thorpeness, with its "House in the Clouds" and pleasant boating lake.

LEFT: Aldeburgh's Moot Hall.

Disappearing Dunwich

Dunwich is best known as the town that isn't. It was once the capital of medieval East Anglia, a prosperous town with eight churches, two monasteries, two hospitals, major shipyards and a population half the size of London. But coastal erosion changed all that. It was kept at bay for two centuries but a terrible storm in 1328 deposited vast amounts of sand and shingle in the harbour and ended its role as a port. Constant erosion over the centuries has reduced the village to a handful of cottages, a pub, one church, and a beach with a café and a few fishing boats. All that remains of medieval Dunwich are the ruins of Greyfriars monastery and those of the Leper Chapel by the church. A solitary tombstone is sole testimony to All Saints', the last of the medieval churches, which collapsed into the sea in 1921. Locals say that when a storm is threatening, the sound of the bells tolling can be heard from beneath the waves.

Dunwich Museum (daily Apr–Sept 11.30am–4.30pm, Oct noon–4pm, tel: 01728-648 796 for winter hours; free) charts the potted history of the town from Roman times to the present day, showing all the buildings lost to the sea. At the present rate of erosion, with recent storms scooping up more of the steeply shelving beach, the museum has about 70 years to go.

A circular route through Constable Country starts at the car park near Flatford Mill and takes in East Bergholt and Dedham. Guided walks visit the scenes of paintings (National Trust Information Centre at Bridge Cottage, tel: 01206-298 260).

works by Gainsborough. There's also 15th-century St Margaret's Church, with a wonderful hammer-beam roof and a Tudor gateway.

The pretty village of **East Bergholt** ⑰, birthplace of John Constable, lies to the left of the A12 between Ipswich and Colchester. A plaque on railings just before the church marks the painter's birthplace, and the graves of his parents lie in **St Mary's Churchyard**, where a large wooden cage houses the heaviest ring of five bells in England. From the church, follow the signs for **Flatford**, which take you to a car park from where a path leads down to the River Stour, to **Flatford Mill**, and **Willy Lott's Cottage**, both recognisable as subjects of *The Hay Wain*. Approaching **Dedham** on the B1029, you could stop to pet the farm animals at the **Dedham Rare Breeds Centre** (Mar–Sept daily 10am–5pm). In the village itself you'll see the soaring tower of the **Church of St Mary** (early 16th century), which features in several of Constable's paintings.

Now we're back on the road for **Colchester** ⑱. Set on the River Colne, this was Camulodunum, the first capital of Roman Britain, and a long section of Roman wall and a large gateway still stand. In 1076 William the Conqueror began his castle on the ruins of a Roman temple to Claudius. The great **Norman Keep** is all that remains: it houses the **Castle Museum** (Mon–Sat 10am–5pm, Sun 11am–5pm; charge), which features many hands-on and interactive displays on Roman, Norman and medieval history, the siege of Colchester during the Civil War, and a medieval prison.

From Colchester our route goes northwest on the A134 towards **Sudbury**, just north of which the village of **Long Melford** makes an interesting diversion, to see the mellow Tudor mansion **Melford Hall** (May–Sept Wed–Sun 2–5.30pm, Sat–Sun in Apr and Oct), where Elizabeth I once stayed; and the village church, which is one of the best examples of Perpendicular architecture in Suffolk.

Lavenham

Lavenham ⑲ (reached via the B1071) is one of the finest of the wealthy wool towns, with a huge number of medie-

Young Constable

John Constable was born on 11 June 1776 in East Bergholt House, at the heart of the 12 sq mile (30 sq km) valley of the Stour, which he was to paint for the rest of his life. His father, Golding, was a wealthy corn merchant and owned Flatford and Dedham mills, two corn-carrying vessels and some rich farmland. Two of his sisters, Ann and Mary, devoted their lives to horses and dogs; a third sister, Martha, was the only one to marry. His older brother, Golding, was mentally handicapped and so the youngest, Abram, eventually took over the family's affairs. At the age of seven, John was sent to boarding school 15 miles (24km) away, but eventually he returned to attend Dedham Grammar School, to which he walked each day. His talent was recognised at school, and in his free time he went on drawing expeditions with a friend, a plumber named John Dunthorne.

Local girls had their eye on the young painter. One, Anne Taylor, wrote: "So finished a model of what is reckoned to be manly beauty I never met with, while the report in the neighbourhood of his excellence in taste and character rendered him interesting in no small degree."

He finally married a local girl, Maria Bicknell (against the wishes of her family), grandchild of the local rector. He painted her when she was 12, and he was 24.

val buildings, many half-timbered and tilting at alarming angles. Best known is the lovely ochre-coloured **Little Hall** (Apr–Oct Wed–Thur, Sat–Sun 2–5.30pm; charge) in the market place. It dates back to the 14th century. The Perpendicular-style church has a magnificent tower, bearing the coats of arms of local cloth merchants; and the early 16th-century **Guildhall** (Apr–end Oct daily 11am–5pm, Mar Wed–Sun, Nov Sat–Sun only; charge), meeting place of the Guild of Corpus Christi, now houses a museum on the wool trade and a walled garden which contains dye plants used since the middle ages. Telegraph poles have been removed and the wires buried underground to preserve the village's Tudor appearance.

Bury St Edmunds

North of Lavenham is the last stop on our route, the ancient market town of **Bury St Edmunds** ⑳, aptly named to honour Edmund, the last Saxon king of East Anglia, who was canonised and buried here.

In *The Pickwick Papers*, Charles Dick-ens, who stayed here at the Angel Hotel, called Bury "a handsome little town of thriving and cleanly appearance". Nearby is **The Nutshell**, reputedly Britain's smallest pub. The town is now a mixture of architectural styles, but retains much of its original layout.

There are 980 listed buildings, including the 12th-century **Moyse Hall** (Mon–Fri 10.30am–4.30pm, Sat–Sun 11am–4pm), the oldest merchant's house in East Anglia, which is now a local museum. Inside are Bronze Age and Saxon artefacts found in the area.

The **Cathedral of St James** stands guard over the ruins of **St Edmunds Abbey**, one of the richest Benedictine foundations in England. It was here in 1214 that a group of barons swore to take up arms against King John if he did not sign the Magna Carta. The **Gate Tower**, the best-preserved feature, gives an idea of the abbey's former splendour. Origianlly founded in the 7th century, it was an important place of pilgrimage after the body of Edmund, last king of the East Angles who was killed by the Danes, was placed here in about 900. ❑

En route from Bury back to Cambridge you'll pass Newmarket, heart of English horse racing and home to the National Stud (tel: 01638-663 464 for tours Mar–Nov) and the National Horse Racing Museum (tel: 01638-667 333).

LEFT: Lavenham Guildhall.
BELOW: the ruins of St Edmunds Abbey.

CANTERBURY AND THE SOUTHEAST

The county of Kent is known for its fruit and fair women. It is also the cradle of Christianity in Britain, a land of castles, moated manors and delightful gardens

Main attractions
CANTERBURY CATHEDRAL
LEEDS CASTLE
SISSINGHURST GARDEN
CHARTWELL
IGHTHAM MOTE
BATTLE ABBEY

PRECEDING PAGES: fishing boat at Hastings. **LEFT:** Canterbury Cathedral. **BELOW:** Hastings old town seen from the castle.

Hops, apples, cherries and fair women are the traditional crop from the country's most southeastern county of Kent, known as "the Garden of England". Market forces and agricultural policies have driven all but the fair women to the wall, but the agriculture of the past has shaped the countryside, giving it distinctive hop kilns, while an abundance of wood has led to white weatherboard buildings. The High Weald is a lovely, rolling landscape, and at Dover the chalk Downs spill dramatically into the sea, giving England its ancient name, Albion, from the Latin *alba* (meaning white).

This is the nearest England gets to the Continent, and it was here that the invaders came: Julius Caesar in 55BC, Angles, Saxons and Jutes in the Dark Ages, William of Normandy in 1066. Christianity also arrived here with St Augustine in 597, establishing the Church at Canterbury. And it was in the skies over Kent that the ferocious dogfights of the Battle of Britain took place in 1940. Today England is linked to the Continent through the Channel Tunnel.

Charles Dickens country

The south, Kent side of the Thames estuary is Charles Dickens country. He drew inspiration from the bleak marshes, and the people who lived by the tidal river. Some marshlands remain, still bleak, but ideal for waders

and sea birds. Dickens lived at Gad's Hill in **Rochester ❶**. This ancient town on the River Medway has always been of strategic importance: Watling Street, the Roman road from Canterbury to London, passes through it and the Normans built a fine **castle** (daily Apr–Sept 10am–6pm, Oct–Mar 10am–4pm) with the tallest keep in England (113ft/32 metres). The Normans also built an exemplary **cathedral** (daily) here, on the site of an earlier Saxon cathedral which had been founded in AD 604, which is sturdy, simple and

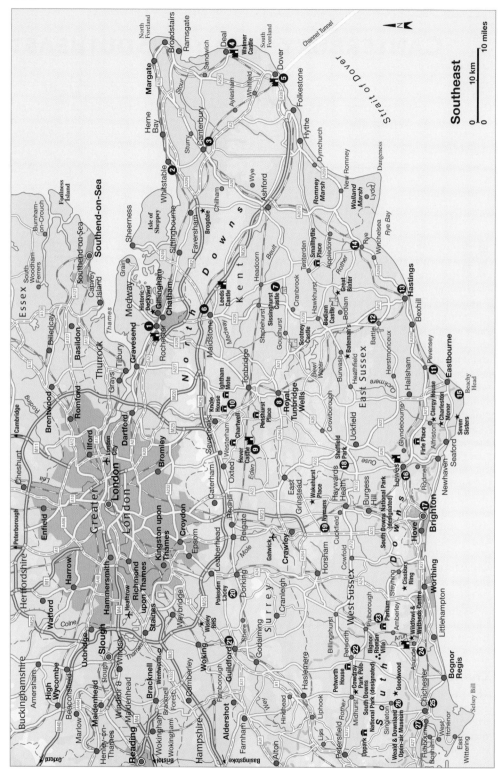

Southeast

reminiscent of their churches in France. The cathedral is an important place of pilgrimage and has been so since the 13th century. You can still see sites that inspired Dickens, notably Restoration House, Crow Lane, which was Satis House in *Great Expectations*. For free walking tours of the town (Apr–Sept) tel: 01634-721 886.

Chatham is a neighbour in this seamless clutter of Medway towns. Its famous Royal Navy dockyards, established by Henry VIII, were closed by the Admiralty in 1984 with a loss of 8,000 jobs but they found a new lease of life as a museum. The **Historic Dockyard** (end Mar–Oct daily 10am–6pm, mid-Feb–end Mar and Oct daily 10am–4pm, Nov Sat–Sun 10am–4pm; charge) covers 80 acres (32 hectares) and has the largest concentration of listed buildings in Britain. Visitors can see the shipbuilding sheds, the sail lofts and the impressive 1,140ft (350-metre) Ropery, built in 1792. Ships on display include the submarine HMS *Ocelot* and the last Victorian sloop, HMS *Gannet*. Nearby, at Chatham Maritime, is **Dickens World** (www.dickensworld.

co.uk; daily 10am–7pm; charge), a hi-tech recreation of Victorian England, complete with actors dressed as Dickensian characters. Aimed at families, it features a Great Expectations "dark" boat ride, a Victorian schoolroom and a "haunted house". There's also an animatronic show, telling the story of Dickens.

More of a backwater is **Faversham**, a pretty town also on Watling Street and on the River Swale. Among its ancient quays is a pervading smell from the local brewery, Shepherd Neame. Apples are prolific at nearby **Brogdale Orchard** (daily Nov–Easter 10am–4.30pm, Easter–end Oct 10am–5pm), which holds the national fruit collection. There are almost 2,000 varieties of apple alone, including the earliest known in England and the variety that is said to have fallen on Newton's head when he mused on gravity. Back on the coast, another attractive town is **Whitstable ❷**, known since Roman times

Charles Dickens, tireless writer and social campaigner.

LEFT:
Wheelers Oyster Bar at Whitstable.

Fact File

Main town Canterbury.
By car M2 and A2 from London, 50 miles (80km).
By train From London Charing Cross.
By sea Dover is the principal ferry port to France; the Channel Tunnel is outside nearby Folkestone (from Dover on the M20, London is 75 miles/120km, Canterbury 20 miles/32km on the A2).
By air Gatwick Airport (www.gatwickairport.com) is in Surrey, 28 miles (45km) south of London. Fast trains link the airport with Victoria station approximately every 15 minutes. Journey time 30 minutes.
Big attraction Canterbury Cathedral.
Best garden Sissinghurst Castle.
Best train ride Romney, Hythe and Dymchurch Railway.
What to eat and drink English wines from Lamberhurst and Tenterden; hundreds of types of fruit at Brogdale Orchard; lamb from Romney Marsh.
Annual events Summer concerts at Leeds Castle; opera and theatre companies tour historic buildings in summer, particularly National Trust properties.
Tourist information Canterbury, 12 Sun Street, tel: 01227-378 100; 01304-205 108; Royal Tunbridge Wells, The Pantiles, tel: 01892-515 675.

Canterbury Cathedral

The Church of England's spiritual home is a delightful hotchpotch of styles. For a detailed ground plan, see page 398.

Canterbury, the birthplace of Christianity in England, is the mother church of the Anglican Communion, its archbishop the Primate of England. In AD 597 Pope Gregory the Great sent St Augustine to England to convert the English, whose religion had lapsed after the Romans had departed. He converted King Ethelbert of Kent, who gave him land on which he founded a monastery (outside the city walls) and the cathedral (within).

In 1170 four knights, thinking they were doing King Henry II a favour, murdered the "turbulent priest", Archbishop Thomas Becket, in the northwest transept. Becket was promptly canonised and in 1174 Henry performed a penance at his tomb. From then until the Reformation, the cathedral was a place of pilgrimage, not just in England, but throughout Europe. The 14th-century poet Geoffrey Chaucer gives a vivid account of the characters who joined the pilgrimages in the prologue to *The Canterbury Tales*. In 1220 Becket's bones

were transferred to a shrine in the Trinity Chapel and in 1935 T.S. Eliot's play about Becket, *Murder in the Cathedral*, was first performed in the Chapter House leading off the Great Cloister.

The cathedral (summer Mon–Sat 9am–5.30pm, winter until 5pm, Sun 12.30–2.30pm, last entry 30 mins before closing; charge). The oldest part is the well-lit crypt, from the 11th century, and there are traces of earlier work; some of its fine carved capitals are unfinished. Four years after Becket's death a fire resulted in the building of the Trinity Chapel to contain his tomb and remodelling by William of Sens of the choir, which was used by the monks of the adjoining monastery for singing daily psalms.

The glorious, soaring, Perpendicular nave, rebuilt in the late 14th century, is the longest medieval nave in Europe; above the central crossing rises the main Bell Harry Tower (249ft/90 metres), added a century later. Among the many noble tombs perhaps the finest is that of the Black Prince in the Trinity Chapel, a copper effigy encumbered in full armour.

The cathedral's stunning stained glass dates from the 12th and 13th centuries and rivals the best in France. The windows in the Trinity Chapel portray the life of Jesus; a noted window of Adam, formerly part of a series showing the ancestors of Jesus in the choir and Trinity Chapel, is now in the west end of the cathedral.

During World War II a 24-hour watch for enemy planes was kept on the cathedral roof. The town was badly bombed, but the cathedral remained miraculously unscathed. ❏

LEFT: Henry II and Becket.
ABOVE: Chaucer's Canterbury pilgrims.

for its oysters. Buy them in the old harbour or try them at the seafront Whitstable Oyster Fishery Restaurant, or at Pearsons Crab and Oyster House, the pub and restaurant opposite. In 1830 George Stephenson built one of the first passenger railway lines which ran the half dozen miles from here to Canterbury.

Canterbury

Canterbury ❸ is the cradle of English Christianity. Its main attraction is, of course, the **cathedral** *(see left)*, which is steeped in history and redolent of its glorious and infamous past. As a place of pilgrimage for Christians from all over Europe, it provided the setting for one of the first great works of English literature, Geoffrey Chaucer's *Canterbury Tales* (1387). In St Margaret's Street the **Canterbury Tales** (daily 10am–5pm, Nov–Feb until 4.30pm; charge) promises a "medieval adventure" with the sights, sounds and even the smells of the journey made by five of Chaucer's characters.

Despite German aerial bomb attacks in 1942, much of Canterbury's medieval character remains. The town's delights include parts of the original Roman wall which once enclosed it. Also worth visiting are the excavated ruins of **St Augustine's Abbey** (Easter–end June Wed–Sun 10am–5pm, July–end Aug daily 10am–6pm, Sept–end Mar Sat–Sun 11am–5pm or dusk; charge). Further east along Longport is **St Martin's Church** (Sat, Tue, Thur 11am–4pm, winter until 3pm; free) where continuous Christian worship has taken place since AD 597. It was St Augustine's first base in Canterbury. The cathedral, the abbey and the church are all part of a Unesco World Heritage Site. In the 4th century this area was selected by rich Romans for their villas, and remains can still be seen. The **Museum of Canterbury** (all year Mon–Sat 10.30am–5pm, June–Sept also Sun 1.30–5pm; charge) is located in Stour Street.

Further east is **North Foreland**, the tip of the duck's tail of Kent and Britain's most easterly spot. Immediately below is **Broadstairs**, a pretty old-fashioned seaside town, with a sandy bay

In "The Canterbury Tales", which runs to 17,000 lines of prose and verse, 29 characters meet up in London to make the pilgrimage to Canterbury, and on the journey most of them tell the stories of their often rather bawdy lives.

BELOW: Canterbury Cathedral.

and landscaped cliffs, which Dickens described as being "left high and dry by the tide of years". When he knew it, the clifftop **Bleak House** was called Fort House. He spent many long summer holidays there in the 1850s and 1860s. It was here that he wrote much of his novel, *David Copperfield*.

Sandwich lies along the River Stour, 2 miles (3km) from the sea. In the 9th century it was an important port, but by the 17th century progressive silting of the estuary left it high and dry, and it is now surrounded by a 500-acre (200-hectare) coastal bird sanctuary. In the 11th century, Sandwich became one of the original Cinque Ports (pronounced "sink"), a string of harbours from here to Hastings with special trading privileges granted in return for maintaining vessels to defend the English Channel from the French. **Walmer Castle** (Apr–Sept daily 10am–6pm, Mar and Oct 10am–4pm) in **Deal** ❹ is still the official residence of the Lord Warden of the Cinque Ports, a post held by the Queen Mother for 24 years. Here, too, is the simple camp bed where the

great Duke of Wellington, who vanquished Napoleon at Waterloo, chose to die like a simple soldier. On the beach of this small resort Julius Caesar landed in 55BC.

Sandwich, Deal and **Dover** ❺ are now billed as "White Cliffs Country", and at Dover, Britain's busiest passenger port, the chalk massif of the South Downs dramatically drops into the sea. On these cliffs the Romans built a lighthouse, the Normans a **castle** (Apr–Sept daily 10am–6pm, Oct 10am–5pm, Nov–end Mar 10am–4pm, Nov–Jan Tue–Wed; charge), where you can experience a medieval siege and visit tunnels used by the military in World War II. The recently excavated Roman Painted House (Tue–Sat 10am–5pm, Sun 1–4.30pm) in York Street is also worth a visit. Built around AD 200, it was probably an official hotel for those crossing the channel. The neighbouring channel port of **Folkestone** is also built beside steep cliffs. The town has a large market by the sea on Sunday where you can buy, among many things, dried dogfish called "Folkestone beef". The nearby

Channel Tunnel provides fast train and car-shuttle services between England and France. **Ashford**, which along with new station Ebbsfleet, on the high speed rail link from France to London, is a handy jumping-off point for the rest of Kent.

Maidstone ❻ is the county town of Kent, built alongside the River Medway. Places to visit are just out of town: the **Museum of Kent Life** (Apr–Oct daily 10am–5pm, Sat–Sun until 6pm) in Sandling on the north side of the town, has Britain's last working oast house and hop-pickers' huts, and tells the story of how Kent was once filled with seasonal workers from the East End of London. Southwest at Yalding, near Paddock Wood, is the **Hop Farm Country Park** (daily 10am–5pm; charge), based around a large collection of oast houses; shire horses, which once pulled the brewers' drays, are on display. There are various attractions for children, including a Victorian-style carousel. Six miles (10km) to the south of Maidstone, **Leeds Castle** (www.leeds-castle.com; Apr–end Sept daily 10am–6pm, last entry 4.30pm, Oct–end Mar

daily 10am–5pm, last entry 3pm; charge) dates back to the 12th century and later passed into royal hands, becoming the residence of the widowed queens of medieval England. Henry VIII, with his wife Catherine of Aragon visited frequently. This fairy-tale place, built on islands in a lake, is one of England's finest castles in a lovely setting among 500 acres (200 hectares) of parkland. As well as visiting the grand interior of the castle itself, visitors can see the quirky museum of dog collars – some of which date back 500 years and wander through the elaborate yew maze. The extensive grounds include a vineyard, cottage garden and "duckery". Black swans swim on the large lake. Grand open-air concerts and *son-et-lumière* shows are put on in the grounds in summer.

Sissinghurst Castle ❼ (mid-Mar–end Oct Fri–Tue 11am–6.30pm or dusk, Sat–Sun from 10am; charge) is

The Roman pharos, or lighthouse, at Dover Castle.

LEFT: Walmer Castle. **BELOW:** Sandwich.

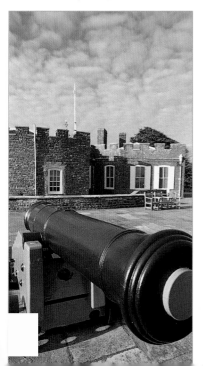

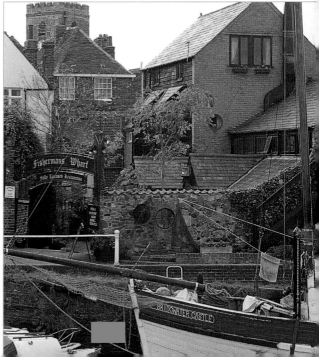

There are a number of good vineyards between Tenterden and Penshurst. Look out for signs offering winery and cellar tours.

RIGHT: oast houses.

not a castle at all, but the ruins of a 16th-century manor house and a perfect backdrop for one of the most popular gardens in England. During the Seven Years' War it served as a prison for captured French soldiers. It was bought by Vita Sackville-West (1892–1962), poet, novelist and gardener, and her politician husband Harold Nicolson in 1930. The beautiful gardens arranged as "outdoor rooms" are delightful, though belated revelations about Vita's love life – which included a passionate affair with the writer Virginia Woolf – no doubt have helped to bring the curious. The White Garden has a stunning array of white foliage and blooms and is particularly appealing. There is a vegetable garden that supplies the licensed restaurant with fresh fruit and vegetables. Visitors can also see the room where Vita sat and wrote.

Weavers and the Weald

The surrounding white weatherboarded High Weald towns of **Tenterden**, **Cranbrook** and **Goudhurst** are peaceful country places. In 1747 the villagers of Goudhurst locked themselves in the church while a gang of smugglers from nearby **Hawkhurst** fought the local militia in the churchyard. From this half-timbered village there are wonderful views south over hop and fruit country. These Wealden towns grew rich on wool and weaving. Large, half-timbered hall houses remain. Among the most interesting are **Smallhythe Place**, near Tenterden (Easter–Oct Sat–Wed 11am–5pm, Mar Sat–Sun 11am–5pm; charge), a charming 16th-century house where the actress Ellen Terry lived, and **Great Dixter** (Apr–Oct Tue–Sun, house: 2–5pm, gardens: 11am–5pm; charge) in Northiam, a rival of Sissinghurst which was home to the horticulturalist Christopher Lloyd, who set major trends in gardening in recent years. Nearby is **Bodiam Castle** (Feb–Oct daily 10.30am–6pm, Nov–late Dec Wed–Sun 10.30am–

The Hop Gardens of Kent

A distinctive feature of the landscape of Kent is the white painted angled, wooden cowls of the round (and later square) hop-drying kilns known as oast houses. These once turned with the wind to act as chimneys above the slatted wooden floors over which hop flowers were scattered above some form of heating. After the hops were dried they were cooled and stored and packed into bags before being dispatched to the breweries. There are only a handful of hop farms left in Kent and most kilns have been converted for residential use, though hop bines, which have a pleasant smell, often decorate pubs. There was a time, however, when hops, a principal ingredient of English ale, were a mainstay of the local agriculture. They were also an integral part of the lives of the working-class families from the East End of London, who every September would come down to Kent in their thousands, living in special hopper huts and harvesting the bines, the long plants that spiral clockwise around taut twine attached to wires supported by hop poles.

Much of it is aching, overhead work, and after the shout of "pull no more bines" the evening's rewards were singsongs and gatherings on the farms or in the local pubs. For many, this week or two would be the only holiday they had, and there are Eastenders still alive who look back on those working holidays as among the best times in their lives.

4pm, Jan–early Feb Sat–Sun 10.30am–4pm; charge), a classic medieval fort, dating from 1385 and set in a generous moat; while **Scotney Castle** (Mar–end Oct Wed–Sun garden: 11am–5.30pm, castle: until 5pm), 5 miles (8km) southwest, is a thoroughly romantic spot with a ruined 14th-century moated castle, and gardens landscaped in the 18th-century pictorial tradition.

Taking the waters in Tunbridge Wells

To the west, halfway down the A21 between London and Hastings, lies **Royal Tunbridge Wells ❽**, a place supposedly full of blimpish retired colonels who write letters to the *Daily Telegraph* and sign themselves "Disgusted of Tunbridge Wells". Dudley, Lord North, a hypochondriac, brought fame and fortune to the town in 1606 when he discovered the health-giving properties of a spring on the common. Court and fashion followed, and the waters, rich in iron salts, were, and still are, taken at the Pantiles. This terraced walk, with

shops behind a colonnade, is named after the tilework laid in 1638, some of which is still there.

Penshurst Place (www.penshurst place.com; Apr–Oct daily, house: noon–4pm, grounds: 10.30am–6pm, Mar also Sat–Sun; charge), just to the northwest of Tunbridge Wells, is one of Kent's finest mansions, dating from 1340. Home of the Viscount de L'Isle, it was for two centuries the seat of the Sidney family, notably Sir Philip Sidney, the Elizabethan soldier and poet. A few miles to the west lies **Hever Castle ❾** (www.hevercastle.co.uk; Apr–Nov daily, castle: noon–6pm, gardens: 10.30am–6pm, Mar Wed–Sun until 5pm; charge). Henry VIII, who first met Anne Boleyn in this, her father's house, seized Hever after her execution and murdered her brother. William Waldorf, first Viscount Astor, (1848–1919) applied his American millions to make massive and sympathetic improvements to the moated castle, 35-acre (15-hectare) lake and gardens where flowerbeds are laid out exactly as they were in Tudor times 400 years ago.

TIP

The Kent and East Sussex Railway (tel: 01580-765 155) starts its journey to Bodiam from Tenterden. Full-sized steam trains run daily in July and August and weekends the rest of the year. Try Sunday lunch in the restaurant car.

BELOW: Bodiam Castle.

Chartwell

Some 10 miles (16km) to the north on the B2026 is **Westerham**, where General James Wolfe, who decisively drove the French from Canada in 1759, was born. His birthplace, **Quebec House** (Mar–end Oct Wed–Sun 1–5pm; charge, National Trust), has memorabilia. Squerryes Court, also in Westerham, is a fine 17th-century manor house that belonged to a friend of Wolfe (Apr–Oct Wed, Sun 12.30–4.30pm; charge).

South of the village is **Chartwell**, (Apr–Oct Wed–Sun, bank holiday Mon 11am–5pm, July–Aug also Tue; charge), where Sir Winston Churchill lived from 1924 until his death in 1965. There is often quite a queue to see his home and studio where many of his paintings are on display. The grounds contain the famous brick wall that he built, and a fine kitchen garden – as well as the views of the Kentish Weald that inspired him.

Sevenoaks is 5 miles (8km) to the east on the far side of the A21 and on its outskirts is **Knole** ❿ (Apr–Oct Wed–Sun 12.30–4pm, Tue mid-July–

end Aug; charge), one of the largest private houses in the country and the birthplace of Vita Sackville-West. It was the Archbishop of Canterbury's residence until confiscated by Henry VIII. It has 365 rooms, 52 stairways and seven courtyards. There are exceptionally fine portraits of the Sackville family by Gainsborough and Van Dyck (though protective low lighting makes some hard to see), as well as some rare furniture. In the 1,000-acre (400-hectare) deer park there is a fascinating Gothic folly birdhouse.

Southeast of Knole is **Ightham Mote** (mid-Mar–end Oct Thur–Mon 11am–5pm; charge), a stunning 14th-century timber and stone, secluded, moated manor house. Ightham Mote has many special features including a Great Hall, a Tudor Chapel with hand-painted ceiling, and a Grade I listed dog kennel in the courtyard, built for a St Bernard.

William the Conqueror's country

In the Levels to the east, **Pevensey** ⓫ has the most considerable Roman

monument in Sussex, but the Roman fort was incomplete and could not withstand the landing in 1066 of William, Duke of Normandy, the last man successfully to invade Britain. The Norman conqueror did not meet up with Harold of England until some 10 miles (16km) inland; Senlac Field, the spot where Harold fell, his eye pierced by an arrow, was marked by William, who built upon it the high altar of the abbey church at **Battle** ⓬ as a thanksgiving. An imposing 14th-century gatehouse leads to the grounds and ruins of the **abbey** (daily Apr–Oct 10am–6pm, Nov–Mar 10am–4pm; charge). You can experience the dramatic events with the aid of an audio visual tour of the battlefield.

The place where William prepared for battle is just 6 miles (9km) southeast of Battle. The hill-top Norman castle at **Hastings** ⓭ stands above a warren of caves where Smugglers' Adventures (daily 10am–5pm, winter until 4pm) are re-enacted. It is now a ruin, but a siege tent inside tells the battle story on which the town has thrived. On the Stade, the stretch of

Sheds for drying fishing nets, on the shore at Hastings.

shingle beach, tall, black weatherboarded sheds used by fishermen for hundreds of years for storing nets are architectural fantasies.

To the east is the ancient town of **Rye** ⓮, which has suffered from floods and the French and now lies high and dry. Edward III (1327–77) gave Rye its walls and gates. The **Landgate** and **Ypres Tower** (Apr–Oct Mon, Thur–Sun 10.30am–5pm; charge) survive, as well as much half-timbering.

Rye has long been a home to writers: Lamb House (mid-Mar–mid-Oct Thur–Sat 2–6pm; charge) in Mermaid Street was the home of Henry James from 1898 to 1916, and later, E.F. Benson, whose Mapp and Lucia books were inspired by life in the town.

From Rye the land lies flat across the great expanse of **Romney Marsh**, a strange, haunted area of a special breed of sheep, of water weeds and wading birds such as the Kentish plover.   ❑

BELOW:
the 15th-century
half-timbered
Mermaid Inn at Rye.

BRIGHTON AND THE DOWNS

Londoners do like to be beside the seaside and its resorts have a raffish air. Around about are the bracing hills of the Downs with hill forts, horse racing and welcoming pubs

The Downs, a parallel chalk range that stripes the south of England, gives the region a distinctive outdoor flavour. Here are the famous horse-racing tracks of Epsom, Goodwood, Fontwell and Kemp Town; the fine golf course at Wentworth; the parklands of Petworth, Glyndebourne and Sheffield Park; tennis at Eastbourne; polo at Cowdray; as well as many fine flowering gardens. Close to the capital, the whole area is well explored and much of the northern "home county" of Surrey is suburban. A few people commute to the city from as far away as the Sussex coast, which has long been a favourite place for a day's outing (5 million visit each year), particularly Brighton, one of the world's first bathing resorts.

The **South Downs** were a highway into Britain for early settlers who started clearing land for farming here 6,000 years ago, leaving it crew-cut by sheep and striated by plough shares. Today in the high spots where Iron-Age forts and flint mines flourished, the wind whispers through copses, windmill sails and woodland clumps which rise over voluptuous gullies and coombs, remnants of the last Ice Age which scooped out devils' dykes and punchbowls. Along the crest runs the white streamer of the South Downs Way, Britain's first designated long-distance bridleway, and a popular path for walkers of all abilities. The beauty of the area led to it being given National Park status in 2009, though the boundaries will not formally be designated immediately. The area will stretch from the East Sussex coast to inland West Sussex and Hampshire.

The South Downs make their final majestic bow at **Beachy Head** ⑮, where chalk cliffs reach 530ft (160 metres) and yearly crumble into the sea. The lighthouse has recently had to be moved further inland, and the steps down the cliff at Birling Gap are only temporary. From the clifftop there is a view down on **Eastbourne**, a pristine

Main attractions
BEACHY HEAD
LEWES
THE ROYAL PAVILION, BRIGHTON
SHEFFIELD PARK
WISLEY GARDENS
PARHAM HOUSE
CHICHESTER

PRECEDING PAGES: Brighton's Royal Pavilion. **LEFT:** Seaford Head Cliffs, Sussex. **BELOW:** the Gay Pride Parade in Brighton.

Literary Friends in the South

The Bloomsbury Set, which started in London, ended up in the country, where its cultural traces can still be seen

In his 1903 *Principia Ethica* the philosopher G.E. Moore stated that "By far the most valuable things are the pleasures of human intercourse and the enjoyment of beautiful objects. It is they that form the rational ultimate end of social progress." This served as a springboard from old, stern Victorian values, into a new spirit of freedom. It was a spirit that infused a group of friends who began to meet two years later at 46 Gordon Square in Bloomsbury near the British Museum. Among them were the writers Virginia Woolf and Vanessa Bell (then the Stephen sisters), Lytton Strachey and E.M. Forster, the economist John Maynard Keynes, and the artists Duncan Grant and Roger Fry.

Little evidence of their creative spirit remains in London, but a visit to a number of sites in the south gives a clue of this intimate and influential group. Virginia and Leonard Woolf bought Monk's House

in Rodmell in 1919, seven years after they married. Virginia's sister, Vanessa Bell, took over Charleston near Firle, a delightful small house and garden, now fully restored with their hand-painted cupboards and doors.

Woolf also found a good friend in Vita Sackville-West, who was born at Knole in Kent and, with her husband Harold Nicolson, bought Sissinghurst Castle *(see page 185–6)*. Woolf's 1928 novel *Orlando* is based on their friendship; a copy of the manuscript is displayed at Knole *(see page 188)*.

Part of the interest in these literary figures was their private lives, and the sexual ambiguity and freedom that they relished. Duncan Grant, though homosexual, was Vanessa Bell's lover and father of her daughter Angelica; Angelica later married David "Bunny" Garnett, who had been Duncan's lover; Vita Sackville-West, whose husband was homosexual, had many lesbian affairs: as well as the famous fling with Virginia Woolf, she also had a long relationship with Violet Treyfusis, daughter of the mistress of Edward VII.

World War II ended the good times. The south of England was a dangerous place. Virginia Woolf, who had suffered from mental illness for most of her life, found her sensitivity tried by the incessant drone of fighters and bombers overhead. Finally one day she walked across the meadows from her house to the River Ouse, filled her pockets with stones, walked into the water and drowned. The 12th-century church of St Michael and All Angels at nearby Berwick suffered bomb damage and after the war Angelica and Quentin Bell painted it in the bright country colours they had grown up with at Charleston.

In recent years a retrospective of the group's works at London's Tate Gallery confirmed their popular appeal – and many critics' belief that they were merely dilettantes. Today Vita Sackville-West is best remembered for the stunning garden she and Harold created at Sissinghurst. ❏

ABOVE: Vita Sackville-West.
LEFT: the garden at Charleston.

resort which in sunshine can gleam like a slice of the French Riviera. The town was well planned from the start, around the middle of the 19th century, by the 7th Duke of Devonshire: shops are banned from the seafront and there are 200 acres (80 hectares) of public parks. Each year 1.8 million visitors come to see the pier, fortress, and other attractions, including lawn tennis courts in Devonshire Park where women's championships are held prior to Wimbledon each year. West of Eastbourne, Beachy Head is the highest of seven undulating waves of chalk hills known as the **Seven Sisters**. Behind them the **Seven Sisters Country Park** leads into the the **Cuckmere Valley**, a good place for walks, especially starting around the pleasant village of **Alfriston** where the **Clergy House** (mid-Mar–end Oct Sat–Mon, Wed and Thur 10.30am–5pm, end Oct–mid-Dec Sat–Mon, Wed and Thur 11am–4pm; charge), a 14th-century thatched hall, by the village green, was the first property to be acquired by the National Trust, in 1896.

Bloomsbury on Sea

Between the two world wars, this corner of England was a favourite spot of London's literary Bloomsbury set *(see left)*. At **Charleston** (Apr–Oct Wed and Sat 1–5pm, July–Aug from noon, Fri, Sun 1–5pm; guided tours; charge), an 18th-century farmhouse, Vanessa Bell and Duncan Grant drew the literary crowd, and their enthusiastic painting and decoration gives the house great charm. The family's handiwork can also be seen at the nearby church at **Berwick**. In 1919 Vanessa Bell's sister, the writer Virginia Woolf and her husband Leonard bought **Monk's House** (Apr–end Oct Wed, Sat 2–5.30pm; charge), a weatherboarded building among thatched houses in **Rodmell**. The village lies in the meadowlands around the River Ouse, where Virginia Woolf drowned in 1941.

Nearby **Firle Place** (June–Sept Wed–Thur, Sun 2–4.15pm; charge) in West Firle was refashioned in the 18th-century Georgian style from the Tudor original. Firle has been in the Gage family for more than 500 years; Sir Thomas Gage was Commander-in-Chief of the British forces in America during the skirmish of Lexington that began the American War of Independence in 1775. In the Great Hall are paintings by Reynolds, Gainsborough and Van Dyck and a 17th-century map of New York shows Wall Street running behind the city wall.

On the other side of the A27 is **Glynde Place** (May–Aug Sun, Wed and bank holidays house: 2–5pm, charge, garden: noon–5pm, free), an Elizabethan manor belonging to Viscount Hampden with portraits of a family that has owned this land for 800 years. A mile to the north is **Glyndebourne** (www.glyndebourne.com), where John Christie and his wife, the opera singer Audrey Mildmay, built an opera house in their Elizabethan home. Opera-goers have picnic dinners on the extensive lawns.

Bateman's, the 17th-century Jacobean house of Rudyard Kipling at Burwash.

Fact File

County towns Lewes (East Sussex), Chichester (West Sussex), Guildford (Surrey).

By car Brighton is 50 miles (80km) from London, and the journey takes about 75 minutes, depending on traffic.

By train Trains go from London Victoria to Chichester, Worthing, Brighton and Eastbourne.

By air Gatwick, London's second airport, is half way between Brighton and London: trains from Gatwick to Brighton and Worthing take about 30 minutes.

By sea Ferries and Seacats from Newhaven to Dieppe.

Best family day out Weald and Downland Open-Air Museum.

Local words Twitten (passages between streets), catcreeps (steps between streets on different levels).

The cultural year Brighton Festival (major multifarious events, three weeks in May); Glyndebourne opera (July).

The sporting year Eastbourne Women's Lawn Tennis Championship (June); Glorious Goodwood horse racing (August); National Bowls Championship, Worthing (August).

Tourist information Brighton, tel: 09067-112 255; Chichester tel: 01243-775 888; www.visitbrighton.com.

TIP

South of Lewes is the port of Newhaven where ferries run to Dieppe in France. Look out for traders from Dieppe who regularly come and set up their stalls in Brighton, selling French cheeses and other produce.

The county town of Lewes

Lewes ⓰, the county town of East Sussex, has been the scene of battles since Saxon times and today it is best known for its explosive Guy Fawkes celebrations on 5 November. Lewes is also an antiques and antiquarian book centre. Thomas Paine, author of *The Rights of Man*, which helped to fuel American Independence, lived at Bull House in the High Street from 1768–74. The Barbican in the High Street is the entrance to the **Norman castle** and **Museum of Sussex Archaeology** (Tue–Sat 10am–5.30pm, Sun–Mon 11am–5.30pm), the high point of the town, built by William de Warrene in the wake of the Norman Conquest. From here there are views over Harry Hill where in 1264 Simon de Montfort and England's barons defeated Henry III, forcing him to sign the Mise of Lewes, which brought about parliamentary government to England.

From 1890 the anglophile New England art collector Edward Perry Warren lived with a "male brotherhood" in Lewes House, now occupied by the local council. He commissioned from the French sculptor Auguste Rodin a version of *The Kiss*, with instructions that the man's genitals should be "seen in their entirety". The result horrified the town council and it was only briefly displayed; today it is in the Tate Britain gallery in London. The High Street drops steeply to the River Ouse and over the bridge is Harvey's, brewers of one of the best Sussex beers, and **Anne of Cleve's House** (Mar–Oct Sun–Thur 10am–5pm, Nov–Feb Sat 10am–5pm, Sun 11am–5pm; charge), a 16th-century timber-framed hall house given to Anne of Cleves in her divorce settlement with Henry VIII. Beyond it are the outline foundations of **Lewes Priory**, once one of the greatest Cluniac priories in Europe.

Raffish Brighton

London's favourite resort is an hour's train journey from the capital. The story of **Brighton** ⓱ begins with a local doctor, Richard Russell, who in a tract in 1750 extolled the efficacy of sea water, both to drink and to bathe in. The practice became so sociably desirable that when Russell opened an

BELOW: Bonfire Night celebrations at Lewes.

establishment with attendants called "bathers" (for men) and "dippers" (for women), he could count on the patronage of the Prince Regent (later George IV). It became the favourite haunt of "Prinny" and in 1784 he drove a coach from London on a new, direct road in 4 hours, 30 minutes. Today the journey is accomplished in less than a quarter of that time. At weekends in summer day trippers arrive at **Brighton Station** where a vast market fills its car park on Sundays. From there it's a short walk down Queen's Road and West Street to the promenade, the stony beach and sparkling sea.

The town has a raffish air, attracting artists, street performers and alternative lifestylers, who are catered for in a variety of good, inexpensive restaurants and bars. Much of the enjoyment in the town is simply in walking the streets. From the station, heading into the old town, the first encounter is with an area called **North Laine** Ⓐ. Here there remains a spirit of the 1960s, with candle and craft shops, vegan specialists, and tattoo parlours. A recent influx of independent boutiques now caters for the town's increasingly wealthy population. The town also has a reputation for antiques. The more respectable shops are in **The Lanes** Ⓑ, a warren of alleys between North Laine and the sea. The Lanes have various etymologies, but they follow an agricultural pattern, possibly from former fields where hemp was grown to make fishermen's nets. They are one of the best places to head to when it's time for something to eat.

North Laine and the Lanes are divided by Church Street where the Pavilion Gardens provides the entrance to the excellent **Brighton Museum and Art Gallery** Ⓒ (Tue 10am–7pm, Wed–Sat 10am–5pm, Sun 2–5pm; free) fills an ornate Victorian building. Its eclectic contents and recently redeveloped galleries exhibit everything from some fine Victorian paintings and an extensive collection of Art Deco furniture, to contemporary

clothing and a scientific facial reconstruction of a Saxon man, made from a skull discovered locally. The museum is part of an interesting assortment of buildings, which includes the **Dome Theatre** in the old Royal Stables, the **Corn Exchange** in the old riding house, and **The Pavilion Theatre**.

These all lie on the north side of the town's great attraction, the **Royal Pavilion** Ⓓ (Apr–Sept 9.30am–5.45pm, Oct–Mar 10am–5.15pm; charge). In 1785 the Prince Regent rented a small farm on the Old Steine, and on this site Henry Holland and John Nash, inspired by the architecture of Mughal India, built his lavish Pavilion. The brilliant Oriental interiors, designed by Frederick Grace and Robert Jones, are decorated with golden dragons, chinoiserie, burnished palms and coloured glass. The opulent Banqueting Room is laid ready for a feast from the ballroom-sized Great Kitchen which has 500 copper pieces in its *batterie de cuisine*.

North Laine in Brighton.

BELOW:
the main gate to Lewes Castle.

Looking out onto Brighton's beach and pier.

Concerts are sometimes held in the lovely Music Room. On the first floor Queen Victoria's bed has several mattresses.

Across the Old Steine down by the seafront is the **Sea Life Centre ⓔ** (daily 10am–5pm, Sat–Sun until 6pm; charge), which has a modern walk-through aquarium, and the **Palace Pier ⓕ**. With pubs, fish-and-chip shops and amusements arcades, this 1,700ft (500-metre) protuberance is an English institution. The **West Pier** is a listed building, but years of neglect, some ferocious storms and a disastrous fire have left it in a sorry and perilous state. On the east side of the Palace Pier is Madeira Drive, where the London to Brighton Veteran Car Run ends up every November. The Volks Railway goes more than a mile (2km) from here along the sea front, passing the nudist beach. Built in 1883, this is said to be the oldest electric railway in the world.

The road above, Marine Parade, leads to **Brighton Marina**, a man-made harbour said to be the largest in Europe, lined with bars, restaurants, shopping arcades, supermarkets and cinemas.

Most of the seafront action takes place on the other side of the pier, along the lower promenade, where bands play in the summer and impromptu dancing can break out at any time. By the small **Brighton Fishing Museum ⓖ** (daily 9am–5pm; free), barely bigger than the clinker-built fishing "punt" inside it, stalls sell cockles and whelks and other delights of the deep. Behind it is the historic Old Ship Hotel, from where Charles II escaped to France: every year the dash is re-enacted in a small boat race.

The best-known hotel is the **Grand Hotel ⓗ**, the ritzy joint on the seafront that became synonymous with naughty weekends. Following the dramatic IRA bomb attack on the building during the 1984 Conservative Party Conference, which left two dead and more than 30 injured, the hotel was defiantly restored to its former glory.

Four miles (6.5km) east of Brighton is **Rottingdean**, a pleasant village by

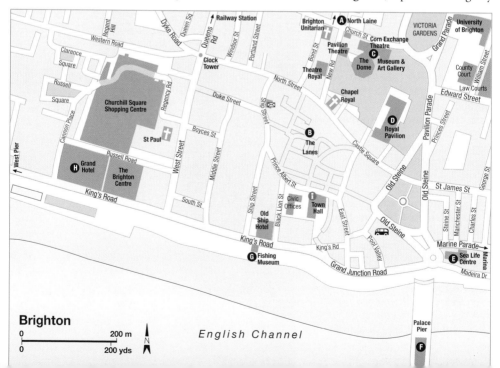

Brighton

English Channel

the sea, though rather cut off from it by the the A259 coastal road. From 1897 to 1902 Rudyard Kipling, the great literary figure of Britain's Empire days, lived at The Elms where he wrote *Kim*, *The Just So Stories* and *Stalky & Co*. His 18th-century house cannot be visited but its walled garden on The Green is open to be enjoyed. He was related to the Pre-Raphaelite painter Edward Burne-Jones (1833–98) who lived in North End House on the west side of The Green.

To the west of Brighton urban ribbon development connects the Sussex resorts of **Worthing**, **Littlehampton** (there is a good sandy beach at **Climping**, on the west side of Littlehampton) and **Bognor Regis**. Worthing is perhaps the most amiable of these resorts. Shaking off its image as a place for retired gentlefolk, it has recently become a popular centre for hi-tech industries. Oscar Wilde took its name for his main character, John Worthing, in his 1895 play *The Importance of Being Earnest*, which he wrote while staying here, and every year he is remembered in the town's August festival.

Just inland from Worthing is the fine church at **Sompting**, visible from the main A27. Dating from AD 960, it is the only Saxon church in the country with a Rhenish helm spire. Faithful parishioners have embroidered views of the Downs on the hassocks.

Iron-Age forts

Behind Worthing are **Chanctonbury** and **Cissbury Ring**s, sites of Iron-Age hill forts. There is little actually to see, but they are atmospheric places and make excellent walks. Cissbury was named after the Saxon leader Cissa, but the hill fort was built long before him, in 240 BC. It covers 650 acres (260 hectares), making it the second largest in the country after Maiden Castle in Dorset. For the ramparts a wooden wall was constructed to contain 60,000 tons of chalk excavated from the ditch. The site had already been occupied for around 4,000 years when some 300 flint mine shafts were dug, to a depth of up to 75ft (23 metres), using deers' antlers as digging tools. The thick grass is springy underfoot; it has never been ploughed, and the rich and ancient

Nobody can be altogether good in Brighton and that is the great charm of it.

Richard Jeffries (1848–87)

BELOW:
Brighton Pier.

We Do Like To Be Beside the Seaside

England's coastal resorts have long attracted a holiday crowd in search of bracing air and a little fun.

The Brighton Parish register of 12 November 1641 records the burial of a woman who "came for cure". This is thought to be the earliest record in England of anyone using the sea for its curative properties. Within a century, before Dr Russell made the sea cure fashionable, bathing in the sea had become a pastime for visitors to this fishing village and elsewhere. A 1735 print from Scarborough, on the Yorkshire coast, shows bathing machines on the beach. These wooden huts on wheels, used as changing rooms, were drawn by horses into the sea where men were attended by "bathers", women by "dippers". At Margate "Modesty hoods" were fitted over the steps of these machines, designed by a local Quaker. Male bathers did not always wear costumes at first and, though there are instances of female bathers also swimming naked in Brighton and Scarborough, they generally wore long flannel gowns. An 18th-century writer records how telescopes were used to inspect female bathers "as they kick and sprawl and flounder like so many mad Naiads in flannel smocks". But some actually learned to swim, Dr Samuel Johnson, who came to Brighton in the 1760s, among them.

The fashionable arrived, and the populace followed just as soon as there were railways to take them there. Wakes Week in Lancashire took cotton workers to Blackpool in their thousands and it became the first resort to reach borough status in 1876. Brighton burgeoned and was looked on as London-on-Sea (a popular title it still bears today), though Southend and Margate on the Thames Estuary became just as accessible. On bank holidays, introduced in 1871, special trains ran; entertainments were laid on and songs about the seaside were whistled in cities and played by promenade bands.

A hero of the hour was Captain Webb. In 1875 this dashing former captain of the Cunard line, covered in porpoise oil and wearing a scarlet costume, swam the English Channel in 21 hours 41 minutes. It was the world's first marathon aquatic event.

England's seaside resorts manage to retain a Victorian air: seafront promenades with deckchairs and bandstands; rusting piers in need of repair, and racks of the celebrated Donald McGill style saucy postcards. An aroma of vinegar may mingle with the ozone: fish and chips was England's first fast food. Even nudist enclaves (Brighton's was the first, in 1981) have an innocence that makes them seem a million miles from the fleshpots of the world.

Some resorts – Bournemouth, Eastbourne – are smart addresses. But even their airs and graces cannot hide the breezy cheeriness that earlier generations of holidaymakers brought to the English seaside. However, the English seaside is not just about "kiss me quick" hats. In recent years the seaside resort has enjoyed something of a renaissance: celebrities have settled in Brighton, Whitstable has attracted some trendy "second homers" who want a beach retreat, and some fashionable bars and restaurants have opened all along the coast. ❏

LEFT: Victorian bathers. **TOP LEFT:** the first Channel swimmer, Captain Webb.

flora includes eight kinds of orchids and fleawort, used in bedding to fend off fleas.

Chanctonbury, just to the north, is privately owned by the Goring family. In 1760 Charles Goring planted a beech copse around the hill fort, and it maintains mythical properties: run round it seven times on a moonless night to evoke the Devil. Chanctonbury can be reached from **Steyning** (pronounced Stenning), a pleasing small town of 61 listed buildings. Its church of St Andrews has the most impressive Norman nave in Sussex and it gives an idea of the importance that this town, formerly on a navigable river and with its own mint, once had.

Gardens

There are a number of outstanding gardens in Sussex and Surrey, all in the hands of the National Trust. **Bateman's** (gardens: mid-Mar–end Oct Sat–Wed 11am–5pm, Nov–Dec Wed–Sun until 4pm; charge) in Burwash was home of the writer and Nobel laureate Rudyard Kipling from 1902 to 1936. This lovely Jacobean building is full of mementoes of the Empire Kipling so powerfully evoked, and there is a romantic garden where plays and music are put on in summer. North of the Downs, between East Grinstead and Lewes, is **Sheffield Park** ⑱ (tel: 01825-790 231 for details; all year; charge), laid out in the 18th century by "Capability" Brown with lakes, waterfalls and cascades. There is a generous show of bluebells in spring and the Bluebell Railway steam train runs from here. **Nymans Garden** ⑲ near Hayward's Heath (house: mid-Mar–Oct Wed–Sun 11am–4pm, gardens: all year) is a fine Wealden garden with an historic collection of flora. Northeast of Nymans is **Wakehurst Place** (daily 10am–6pm; charge) is an outstanding botanical garden and home of the Millennium Seed Bank, the world's largest seed conservation project. The best of the North Downs flora can be seen at **Polesden Lacey** ⑳ (mid-Mar–Oct Wed–Sun 11am–5pm,

gardens: mid-Feb–mid-Oct daily 10am–5pm, mid-Oct–Feb 10am–4pm; charge) near Great Bookham, Dorking. This large Regency villa is where George VI and Queen Elizabeth spent their honeymoon in 1923.

The Royal Horticultural Society has its showpiece at **Wisley Gardens** (Mar–Oct Mon–Fri 10am–6pm, Sat–Sun 9am–6pm, Nov–Feb Mon–Fri 10.30am–4.30pm, Sat–Sun 9am–4.30pm; charge), just north of **Guildford** ㉑ on the A3 and England's many serious gardeners make regular visits. Surrey's county town, Guildford, has a castle with Norman walls and a modern cathedral. There are a number of attractive small towns nearby, including **Farnham**, **Godalming**, **Haselmere** and **Shere**.

A trio of stately homes lies to the south of Guildford. **Uppark** near Petersfield (Apr–Oct Sun–Thur 12.30–4.30pm, gardens: 11.30am–5pm; charge), magnificently restored by the National Trust, dates from the 17th century. Looking like a fabulous dolls' house, it has an art and decorative arts collection and a grand view from its

Emma Hart, 17, danced on the dining table at Uppark to entertain its reprobate owner, Harry Fetherston-haugh. She later married his nephew, Lord Hamilton, and became Horatio Nelson's mistress.

BELOW:
Rudyard Kipling's home, Bateman's.

high point 350ft (106 metres) on the top of the South Downs. **Petworth** ㉒ is a town of myriad antique shops overshadowed by the great wall of **Petworth House** (tel: 01798-343 929 for details; Mar–Oct; charge). This has been home to the Percy family since 1150 and it contains the National Trust's largest painting collection, with works by Van Dyck, Gainsborough, Reynolds, Blake and Turner, who had a studio here and executed many paintings of the house and extensive deer park, landscaped by "Capability" Brown. **Parham House** ㉓ (Easter–Sept Wed–Thur, Sun and bank holidays Mon 2–5pm, gardens: Tue–Fri, Sun noon–5pm; charge), between Petworth and Arundel, is one of the finest Elizabethan buildings in England, and its gardens include a 4-acre (1.6-hectare) walled garden, orchard, maze and heronry.

Due west of Parham, on a high point of the Downs by Bury Hill, is **Bignor Roman Villa** (June–July daily 10am–6pm, Mar–Apr Tue–Sun 10am–5pm, May daily 10am–5pm, Sept–Oct daily 10am–4.30pm;

charge). The site dates from the first century and covers more than 4 acres (1.8 hectares) where, beneath thatched buildings, there are mosaics depicting gladiators, Venus and Medusa. Nearby is the delightful village of Amberley, with mellow, robust thatched, flint-stone houses. The castle ruins are all that remains of the palace of the bishops of Chichester.

To the south of Amberley the River Arun cuts through the South Downs to reach **Arundel** ㉔, home of the Dukes of Norfolk. Its fairytale **castle** (www.arundelcastle.org; Easter–Oct Tue–Sun noon–5pm, grounds: 10am–5pm; charge), which had a Victorian makeover and provided the backdrop for films such as *The Young Victoria* and *The Madness of King George*, dates from 1070. The Norfolks are the premier Catholic family in England: the parish church is intriguingly divided between Anglican church and Catholic Chapel, the two separated by a glass wall.

The castle is surrounded by 2 sq miles (5 sq km) of landscaped parklands which contain a lake and a **Wildfowl and Wetlands Centre** (daily late

Mar–late Oct 9.30am–5.30pm, late Oct–late Mar 9.30am–4.30pm; charge).

Cathedral of modern masters

Chichester ㉕ is a small market town centred on a traditional Market Cross with many Georgian buildings. The modern Festival Theatre, a theatre-in-the-round, has a reputation for excellence. It lies in Priory Park by the old Norman motte and bailey and the remains of the city wall. The **Cathedral** (daily subject to services; free) is light and graceful and full of interest. Construction was begun in 1091 and its mixture of Gothic and Norman is enhanced by works of modern art from Marc Chagall, Graham Sutherland, Patrick Procktor and, most notably, John Piper, who created the altar tapestry in 1966. Pallant House in West Pallant has further works collected by Walter Hussey, Dean of the Cathedral from 1955–77. Together with Bishop Bell, he was instrumental in giving modern art a place in the cathedral.

North of Chichester, on the top of the Downs, is **Goodwood**, where the racecourse has a wonderful Downland setting. "Glorious Goodwood" is an annual meeting at the beginning of August. Just beyond it is **The Weald and Downland Open-air Museum** ㉖ (daily Mar–Oct 10.30am–6pm, Nov–Feb 10.30am–4pm, Jan–early Feb Wed, Sat–Sun only; charge). Nearly 50 historic buildings, ranging in age from 13th-century to 19th-century have been brought to this 50-acre (20-hectare) site. They include houses and shops, mills and barns as well as a farmhouse uprooted in the building of the Channel Tunnel.

Chichester grew up as a port, and the sea is not far away. In 1960 the largest Roman domestic building north of the Alps was found at **Fishbourne** ㉗ (tel: 01243-785 859; all year; charge). Begun in AD 75, it had a quayside and 100 rooms, with impressive mosaic floors, but it was burnt down some 200 years later.

Among **Chichester Harbour**'s tidal estuaries, **Bosham** stands out as the most timeless, attractive backwater. Its Saxon church, claims to be the oldest site of Christian worship in Sussex. ❑

TIP

Chichester Harbour is a safe place to learn to sail and has many sailing clubs to choose from. If you just want a 90-minute trip round the harbour, boats leave from Itchenor.

BELOW: Arundel Castle.

THE ENGLISH GARDEN

England's temperate climate encourages a great diversity of gardens which blend the grand and the homely in a cosmopolitan range of styles

The formal gardens of great houses have both followed fashion and set the style for the nation's favourite hobby. In medieval times, fruit trees, roses and herbs were grown in walled enclosures. In the 16th century, aromatic plants were incorporated in "knots" (carpet-like patterns). Tudor Gardens (like those at Hatfield House in Hertfordshire) were enclosed squares of flowers in geometric patterns bordered by low hedges and gravel paths.

A taste for small flower beds persisted through the 17th and 18th centuries when fountains and canals began to be introduced.

The Art of the Landscape

In the 1740s a rich banker, Henry Hoare, inspired by Continental art during his Grand Tour, employed William Kent (1685–1748) to turn his gardens at Stourhead in Wiltshire into a series of lakes dotted with buildings in the classical style. This was the birth of the landscape garden, known as *le jardin anglais*.

"Capability" Brown (*see panel, right*) rejected formal plantings in favour of natural parkland and restricted flowers to small kitchen gardens. But Humphry Repton (1752–1815) reintroduced the formal pleasure garden. The Victorians put the emphasis on plants and Gertrude Jekyll (1843–1932) promoted the idea of planting cycles to ensure that colour lasted through the year.

LEFT: Classical statues graced many gardens in the 17th century. This one is at **Belvoir Castle**, Leicestershire. Until the late 18th century many statues were made of lead.

ABOVE: This Wiltshire garden at Stourhead, birthplace of England's landscape movement, is dotted with lakes and temples and has many rare trees and shrubs. The artful vistas were created in the 1740s, and their magnificence contrasts with the severe restraint of the Palladian house (1721–24).

ABOVE: The 4th Duke of Marlborough employed "Capability" Brown *(see right)* in 1764 to impose his back-to-nature philosophy on **Blenheim Palace**. Brown's most dramatic change was to create a large lake by damming the River Glyme.

ABOVE: Hidcote Manor A 17th-century Cotswold house at Mickleton in Gloucestershire, has one of the most beautiful English gardens, mixing different types of plot within various species of hedges. Although covering 10 acres (4 hectares), it's like a series of cottage gardens on a grand scale, prompting Vita Sackville-West to describe it as "haphazard luxuriance".

LEFT: This example at Henry VIII's Hampton Court Palace outside London shows the Tudor liking for knots – small beds of dwarf plants or sand and gravel laid out in patterns resembling embroidery. Topiary, statues and mazes provided a counterpoint to the mathematical order.

THE GREAT GARDENERS

Lancelot Brown (1715–83) was nicknamed "Capability Brown" when he rode from one aristocratic client to the next pointing out "capabilities to improvement". His forte was presenting gardens in the "natural" state, and his lasting influence lay in his talent for combining quite simple elements to create harmonious effects.

Brown liked to create elegant lakes for his parks, as at Blenheim Palace in Oxfordshire. He was also involved with the gardens at Stowe in Buckinghamshire, which the National Trust today describes as "Britain's largest work of art", and with the gardens at Kew, Britain's main botanical establishment, just outside London.

One of the 20th century's most influential gardeners was Vita Sackville-West (1892–1962), below, who developed her gardens at Sissinghurst Castle in Kent. She revived the 16th-century idea of dividing a garden into separate sections, combining a formal overall style with an informal choice of flowers.

BELOW: Thanks to the influence of the Gulf Stream, sub-tropical flora can flourish at England's south-western tip. **Tresco Abbey Gardens**, on the Isles of Scilly, were laid out on the site of a Benedictine priory and contain many rare plants.

HAMPSHIRE, WILTSHIRE AND DORSET

The area's highlights include the splendid cathedral town of Salisbury, the ancient stone circle of Stonehenge, Stourhead's stunning gardens, and some of the best beaches in England

London

This tour offers plenty of variety, as it includes the ports of Portsmouth and Southampton, the offshore Isle of Wight, the cathedral city of Winchester and the monument of Stonehenge, as well as the New Forest itself.

Portsmouth ❶ is a good place to start: it's a large and confusing city, due to post-war reconstruction, but the main sites are clearly signed. "Historic Ships" signs lead you to the *Mary Rose*, HMS *Victory* and HMS *Warrior*. An inclusive ticket allows you to visit all three and to explore a number of museums and sites dotted around the **Historic Dockyard** (daily Apr–Oct 10am–5.30pm, Nov–Mar 10am–5pm; charge). The **Mary Rose Exhibition** details the history of Henry VIII's flagship, sunk in 1545, and the **Mary Rose Ship Hall** displays the recovered ship itself. The tour of **HMS Victory**, on which Lord Nelson died at the Battle of Trafalgar in 1805, gives a good idea of life for an 18th-century sailor. On **HMS Warrior**, the first iron-clad warship, you can take a tour or explore independently. The city's most striking attraction is the contemporary **Spinnaker Tower** (daily 10am–6pm; charge), which soars high above the harbour: it's taller than the London Eye. The tower has 3 viewing platforms: the first has a glass floor; the second has multimedia displays on the harbour's history, and the third is open to the elements.

Southampton and "the island"

The M27 motorway will take you the short distance to **Southampton ❷**, the port from which the *Mayflower* sailed to America in 1620, and the *Titanic* set out on its ill-fated voyage in 1912. It is still a busy port which, like Portsmouth, suffered badly in World War II. Post-war planning left much to be desired, but it makes the most of its heritage. The **Maritime Museum** (Sun 1–4pm, Tue–Sat 10am–4pm; charge) on the Town Quay is a mag-

Main attractions
PORTSMOUTH HISTORIC DOCKYARD
THE NEW FOREST
SALISBURY CATHEDRAL
STONEHENGE
THE JURASSIC COAST
HARDY'S COTTAGE

PRECEDING PAGES: re-enactment at Corfe Castle.
LEFT: the Spinnaker Tower, Portsmouth.
BELOW: HMS *Victory* in Portsmouth Dockyard.

The Medieval Merchant's House in Southampton.

nificent building with interesting exhibits; the nearby **Museum of Archaeology** (same hours) packs a huge amount of information into a small space; and the 13th-century **Medieval Merchant's House** (Apr–Oct Sun noon–5pm; charge) has been furnished to reflect how it would have appeared in the 14th century.

From Southampton you can take a ferry or hydrofoil to the **Isle of Wight** ❸. It's a pretty little place with an old-fashioned feel. **Osborne House** (daily Apr–Sept 10am–6pm, Oct 10am–4pm; charge) at **East Cowes**, designed by Prince Albert in 1845, was Queen Victoria's private residence. She died here in 1901 and the richly furnished Italianate house remains much as it was then.

Just outside **Newport**, in the centre of the island, is **Carisbrooke Castle** (Apr–Sept 10am–5pm, Oct–Mar 10am–4pm; charge). A 12th-century keep survives but most of the rest is 16th-century.

Charles I was imprisoned here in 1647 before being taken to London for trial and execution. The star attraction is the 18th-century treadmill, still operated by donkey-power.

Winchester

Back in Southampton, it's a brief journey on the M3 to **Winchester** ❹, which once shared with London the honour of joint capital of England. Start your tour at the **Cathedral** (visits Mon–Sat 9am–5pm, Sun 12.30–3pm; charge; tours on the hour Mon–Sat 10am–4pm; for pre-booked tour tickets (groups) tel: 01962-857 225). All architectural styles are represented, from the 11th-century Romanesque north transept to the glorious Perpendicular-style nave. Look out for the oldest choir stalls in England (c.1305); the grave of Jane Austen (1775–1817) in the north aisle; the Edward Burne-Jones windows in the Epiphany Chapel; and contemporary sculptor Anthony Gormley's bronze in the crypt. The precious 12th-century Winchester Bible is displayed in the library.

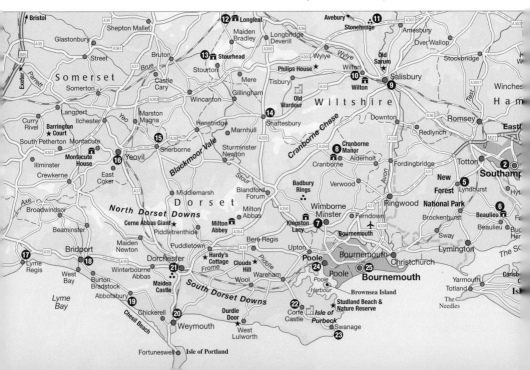

There's much else to be seen in the town: the **Great Hall** (daily 10am–5pm) which houses the **Round Table**, improbably linked with King Arthur and his knights, is all that remains of William the Conqueror's castle. **Winchester College** (1382; tel: 01962-621 227; guided tours only; charge) has a chapel rich enough to rival the cathedral; and the ruined **Wolvesey Castle** (Apr–Sept daily 10am–5pm) was the former home of the Bishops of Winchester.

The New Forest

Head southwest now on the M3/M27 motorways to **Lyndhurst ❺**, capital of the **New Forest**. You can learn about the area at the excellent **New Forest Centre** (daily 10am–5pm; charge for museum), which contains a museum, visitor centre and tourist information. There's information in the museum on Alice Liddell, the girl for whom Lewis Carroll (1832–98) wrote *Alice in Wonderland*. She became Mrs Reginald Hargreaves and it is under that name that you'll find her tomb in **Lyndhurst Church**, an exuberant building full of stained glass by William Morris and Edward Burne-Jones, with life-sized angels supporting the timber roof.

Many people come to the New Forest especially to visit **Beaulieu ❻** (www.beaulieu.co.uk; mid-May–Sept 10am–6pm, Oct–mid-May 10am–5pm; charge), one of the first stately homes to open its doors to the public. The magnificent **Cistercian Abbey** (now a ruin) was built in the 13th century. The cloister, the best-preserved part, is now planted with herbs, and the monks' refectory has been converted into a parish church. The abbey was confiscated and sold by Henry VIII during the 1530s Dissolution and in the 19th century the abbey gatehouse was turned into the baronial-style **Palace House**; beautifully vaulted ceilings survive and the walls are hung with portraits.

From here you can walk through attractive gardens to the ugly building that houses the **National Motor Museum**; hop on an open-topped bus for a tour of the grounds; or queue for a ride on the monorail that encircles them, and gives a fine aerial view. The museum holds a huge collection cover-

Ponies wander freely in the New Forest.

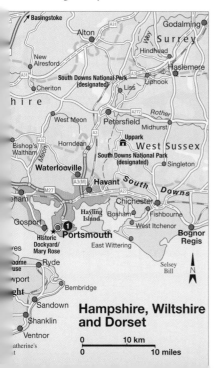

Hampshire, Wiltshire and Dorset

0   10 km
0   10 miles

Fact File

By car The region is easily accessible from most parts of England, although the A3, A4/A36, M3 and M27 are very busy with commuter traffic during rush hours.

By coach National Express services to Dorchester, Portsmouth, Salisbury, Bournemouth and other main towns: www.nationalexpress.com.

By rail Salisbury, Sherborne, Portsmouth and Winchester are on main Intercity lines; from Southampton there are local trains to the heart of the New Forest; tel: 08457-484 950, www.nationalrail.co.uk.

By ferry Daily car and passenger ferries operate from Poole, Portsmouth and Southampton to Bilbao, Caen, Cherbourg, Le Havre and St Malo; contact Brittany Ferries, tel: 0871-244 0744, www.brittany-ferries.co.uk or P&O Ferries, tel: 08716-645 645, www.poferries.com; Red Funnel Ferries, tel: 0844-844 9988, www.redfunnel.co.uk, operate services to the Isle of Wight.

New Forest Animals Tel: 023-8028 2052 or 023-8028 3141 (to report animals injured or in distress).

Tourist information Portsmouth, tel: 023-9282 6722; Dorchester, tel: 01305-267 992; Lyme Regis, tel: 01297-442 138; Southampton, tel: 023-8022 1106; Salisbury, tel: 01722-334 956; Lyndhurst New Forest Museum and Visitor Centre, tel: 023-8028 2269.

Beaulieu Palace House has been the ancestral home of the Montagu family since 1538.

RIGHT: Burne-Jones' stained glass window in Winchester Cathedral.

ing more than a century of motoring, concentrating more on the social history of the car than the mechanical aspects. There are also displays of cars that have broken the land-speed record; and trams, buses and fire engines for children to clamber on. Beaulieu also houses an exhibition on Britain's Secret Army, the World War II special operations executive (SOE), who completed their training there.

West to Wimborne

Leave the forest on the A31 for **Wimborne Minster ❼**, where the imposing twin towers of the church rise above Georgian houses. The original minster was built in 705, then destroyed by the Danes; the present one is Norman. Opposite stands the **Priest's House Museum** (Apr–Oct Mon–Sat 10am–4.30pm; charge), an interesting little place whose attractions include a Victorian kitchen and stationer's shop, an archaeology gallery, a fine garden and a tea shop.

West of town is **Kingston Lacy** (Apr–Oct Wed–Sun 11am–5pm; charge), a 17th-century mansion containing works by Rubens, Titian and Van Dyck, and set in grounds farmed by traditional organic methods. North now on the B3078 to **Cranborne Manor ❽** (Mar–Sept Wed 9am–5pm; charge) where, set around the Jacobean house (not open to the public), is one of England's most appealing gardens, originally planted with roses, clematis and topiary hedges by John Tradescant in the 17th century. The village is pretty, too.

Salisbury to Stonehenge

The best place to begin a visit to **Salisbury ❾** is on a windswept hill just outside it, **Old Sarum**, where extensive ruins of the earlier town are set within the ramparts of an Iron-Age hill fort. Salisbury itself is dominated by the

A Forest Trail

An exploration of the forest could begin at Lyndhurst, going south to Brockenhurst where one of England's oldest trees, a magnificent 1,000-year-old yew, stands in the churchyard. Stock up with picnic provisions in the village, then follow Rhinefield signs to three beauty spots. The first, Ober Water, is a forest stream alive with minnows where boggy margins support such flowers as the bog asphodel and insect-eating sundew plant. Information boards at the car park indicate a choice of walks.

About 1 mile (2km) on, you come to Rhinefield Drive, an arboretum planted with rhododendrons, azaleas and giant conifers. Again, there is a choice of marked walks. A right turn off the A35 will take you to Bolderwood Drive, another 19th-century arboretum where you can follow marked walks, keeping an eye out for red, fallow and roe deer.

Heading towards Ashurst you'll find the New Forest Otter, Owl and Wildlife Park (www.ottersandowls.co.uk; tel: 02380-292 408; daily except Mon–Fri in Jan, 10am–5.30pm) where an array of small mammals, including three species of otter and several species of owl, live in old farm buildings and forest enclosures that approximate their natural habitat. Most people go there to please the children, then find themselves fascinated by the place.

creamy-white limestone **Cathedral** (daily; charge) with its wonderful spire (the tallest in Britain), timber roof and Decorated-style cloister. It was built in the 13th century and is a stunning example of the Gothic style. In the Chapter House is displayed one of the four original copies of the Magna Carta (1215). The cathedral is not the only attraction; stroll around the town enjoying the gracious Queen Anne buildings, or stop for tea or a light lunch at one of them, the National Trust-run **Mompesson House** (Sat–Wed 11am–5pm; charge).

Only 3 miles (5km) west of Salisbury is **Wilton** ❿, dominated by **Wilton House** (May–end Aug Sun–Thur 10.30am–5.30pm; charge), the estate of the Earl of Pembroke. The 17th-century house was designed by Inigo Jones and the grounds – which can be visited separately – have a marvellous adventure playground.

Between Wilton and Salisbury, the A360 leads about 11 miles (16km) north to **Stonehenge** ⓫ (daily June–end Aug 9am–7pm, mid-Mar–end May and Sept–mid-Oct 9.30am–6pm, mid-Oct–mid-Mar 9.30am–4pm; charge), which stands on **Salisbury Plain**. England's most famous ancient monument, it has been declared a Unesco World Heritage Site. It spans the period 3,000–1,600 BC (the central ring of stones dates from circa 2,000 BC) and was built in phases. Part of it is constructed of large bluestones, hauled here from the Preseli Mountains in Pembrokeshire, 200 miles (320km) away – the final part of their journey was probably by water. There are also enormous sarsen stones which outcrop locally.

Its purpose has baffled archaeologists and other experts for centuries and engendered many myths. Inigo Jones, one of the first to formally investigate the monument, at the behest of James I in the 17th century, concluded it was a Roman temple to Uranus. Though the alignment of the major axis with the midsummer sun-rise suggests a religious significance, no firm evidence has been found, and theories about it range from the practical – that it was some kind of calendar – to the extraterrestrial. Whatever its purpose, its builders must have had some knowledge of mathematics and astrology. It is popularly associated with the Druids, but in fact predated them by about 1,000 years. Regardless of this, present-day Druids and many other people regard it as a place of ritual and worship on Midsummer Eve, and the police regard it as a priority to stop them trespassing.

Stonehenge was part of the ancient Kingdom of Wessex, a region that was later immortalised in the novels of Thomas Hardy. The name referred to "West Saxons", and part of what was Wessex has more ancient sites than the Norman land of the New Forest.

From Stonehenge, visitors can make a detour north on the A360/361 to the village of **Avebury**, the site of one of the most important megalithic monuments in Europe, as well as Bronze Age burial mounds. Northwest of Stonehenge, on the A303/A36, you

TIP

Near Stonehenge look for signs to the Hawk Conservancy (Feb–Oct daily 10.30am–5.30pm; tel: 01264-773 850), which has one of the largest collections of raptors in the world.

BELOW: the graceful arches of Salisbury Cathedral.

TIP

At Sparkford, Yeovil, the Haynes Motor Museum (daily Apr–end Sept 9.30am–5.30pm, Oct–end Mar 10am–4.30pm; charge) has a spectacular collection of historic cars and motorcycles.

reach **Warminster** and **Longleat**  (tel: 01985-845 420 for times of tours; www.longleat.co.uk; house: daily, safari park: Feb–end Mar Sat–Sun, Apr–Nov until 4pm, 5pm Sat–Sun and school holidays; charge). The property of the Marquess of Bath, this was the first stately home to be opened to the public (in 1948). The house, Elizabethan in origin and with an eclectic mixture of styles spanning the past four centuries, is splendid, but it is the safari park, where animals roam freely in grounds originally landscaped by "Capability" Brown, which is now the greatest draw.

After your safari, return to the A303 then take a right turn at **Mere** to visit **Stourhead**  (house: Mar–end Oct Fri–Tue 11am–5pm, garden: all year 9am–6pm; charge). The Palladian-style house, built for banker Henry Hoare in the 18th century is surrounded by one of the loveliest landscaped gardens in England. Classical temples dedicated to Flora and Apollo stand beside the dark waters of the lake. In spring the walks are vivid with azaleas and rhododendrons.

Returning to the A303, retrace your route a short way and take the A350 to **Shaftesbury** , one of southern England's few hill towns. Climbing cobbled **Gold Hill**, lined with 18th-century cottages and the remaining wall of a demolished abbey, is like stepping back into a picturesque version of the past. Thomas Hardy (1840–1928) used Shaftesbury, renamed Shaston, as the setting for his 1896 novel *Jude the Obscure*.

Heading west on the A30, our next destination is **Sherborne** , the burial place of two Saxon kings. There is a wealth of medieval buildings, including the Abbey Church and Almshouse. **Sherborne Castle** (Apr–Nov Tue–Thur, Sat–Sun 11am–4.30pm, last admission; charge) is an interestingly eccentric pile, built for Sir Walter Raleigh (1552–1618).

At **Yeovil** , 5 miles (8km) west, is the Elizabethan **Montacute House** (Mar–Oct Wed–Mon 11am–5pm; charge), built in golden stone with ornamental gazebos for the lawyer who prosecuted Guy Fawkes, one of the conspirators who tried to blow up

BELOW: the great circle of Stonehenge.

the Houses of Parliament in 1605. In the church at **East Coker**, 3 miles (5km) south, are the ashes of T.S. Eliot (1888–1965), whose ancestors emigrated to the USA. "In my beginning is my end" he wrote in the poem named after the village.

The Dorset coast

Continue west on the A30 and drop down to the coast at **Lyme Regis** ⓱ just east of the Devon border. This old fishing town was once as fashionable as Bath. Regency bow windows and trellised verandas on Victorian villas line The Parade on the way to the tiny harbour and the projecting arm called **The Cobb**. It was here that the Duke of Monmouth landed in 1685, aspiring to the crown, and here on the steps called Granny's Teeth that Jane Austen's Louisa Musgrave tumbled in *Persuasion*. **Bay Cottage** at the harbour's end, now a café, is thought by some to be where Austen (1775–1817) lived while writing much of the novel: the Jane Austen garden marks the location of a cottage where she certainly stayed. More

recently, the sea-lashed walls formed a backdrop for Meryl Streep in the 1981 film of John Fowles's novel *The French Lieutenant's Woman*.

The road east takes you to **Bridport** ⓲. It is 2 miles (3km) from the sea, yet there is no denying its marine character. **West Bay** is Bridport's improbable harbour, a narrow channel dug in the shingle bank and flanked by two high piers only feet apart. In the old days, coasters had to be hauled in with ropes.

The next town is **Burton Bradstock**, a pretty spot with thatched cottages, smoky stone and bright window boxes, and a stream that used to drive the flax mills until the last one closed in 1931. Here the **Chesil Bank** begins, curving away eastwards until it becomes the slender link that means the Isle of Portland is not really an island at all, but a peninsula. Chesil Bank has no mercy: to bring a boat in here spells almost certain disaster. Stretching eastwards to Exmouth and westwards to Studland Bay, this 95 miles (153km) of coastline has been named the "Jurassic Coast" and designated a World Heritage Site for its geological importance.

Thomas Hardy, who used Dorset locations for most of his novels, renamed Bridport, Port Bredy.

BELOW: a view of The Cobb, Lyme Regis.

English Heritage looks after Maiden Castle.

Charmouth is the prime location for finding fossils, such as ammonites, on the beach. Before you start searching, take a Fossil Hunting Walk. There's a small charge, but they last 2 hours and are extremely informative. To book, contact Charmouth Heritage Coast Centre, tel: 01297-560 772.

Portland is a place apart: Hardy called it "the Gibraltar of Wessex" and claimed the people had customs of their own. Everything is made of Portland stone, the material used for many of London's best-known buildings. The lighthouse on the southern tip overlooks the water of the treacherous Portland Race. Portland's harbour will be the location for the sailing events in the 2012 Olympics.

St Catherine's Chapel on a green hill above the bank at **Abbotsbury ⑲** is a vital mark for sailors and fishermen, as well as a place of prayer. On the land side it overlooks a surprising sub-tropical garden, the ruins of a substantial 15th-century monastic barn, built as a wheat store and a swan sanctuary.

George III put **Weymouth ⑳** on

the map when he went there to convalesce in 1789, and much of the character of an 18th-century watering place remains. The king's statue stands at the end of the Esplanade, which is lined on one side with stuccoed terraces, on the other by an expanse of golden sands. From Brewers' Quay you could take a trip through history at the **Timewalk Journey** (daily 10am–5.30pm, until late in Aug; charge), which includes entrance to the **Weymouth Museum**. A regular ferry service from the jetty runs to the Channel Islands.

Turn inland now and take the A354 some 8 miles (13km) towards Dorchester. Just outside the town you will come to **Maiden Castle**, a massive Iron-Age hill fort: excavations show that the hilltop was occupied some 6,000 years ago. The name derives from "mai dun" meaning great hill; the fort is believed to be the world's largest earthworks.

Dorchester

Dorchester ㉑ is the county town of Dorset and a place well aware of its

RIGHT: Hardy's Monument.

Thomas Hardy

Thomas Hardy (1840–1928) was born at Higher Bockhampton, near Dorchester, the son of a stonemason, and although he spent considerable periods of time in London and travelled in Europe, all his major novels are set in the region. He trained as an architect, but after the success of *Far From the Madding Crowd* in 1874 he was able to concentrate on writing.

A recurrent theme in Hardy's work is the indifference of fate and the arbitrary nature of the suffering it inflicts on mankind. In his own time he was widely criticised for his pessimism, and it must be said that many of his novels, particularly the later ones such as *Jude the Obscure*, are extremely gloomy. In his later years Hardy turned to poetry, which he considered a superior art form, but it is for his novels that he is remembered.

Hardy sites that can be visited, as well as the Dorset County Museum and the Hardy Cottage, mentioned above, are Max Gate, in Alington Avenue, Dorchester (Apr–Sept Mon, Wed, Sun 2–5pm; National Trust), which he designed himself and inhabited from 1885 until his death; and the churchyard at Stinsford, just east of town, where his heart was buried alongside his family, although his body was interred at Westminster Abbey.

past. It was the setting for Thomas Hardy's *Mayor of Casterbridge*, and there is a collection devoted to him, including the original manuscript of the 1886 novel, in the **Dorset County Museum** (Oct–June Mon–Sat 10am–5pm, July–Sept daily 10am–5pm; charge). **Hardy's Cottage** (mid-Mar–end Oct Sun–Thur 11am–5pm; charge), the writer's birthplace, is 3 miles (5km) northeast of the town *(see box, previous page, for more Hardy memorials)*.

But Dorchester isn't all Hardy: it's a pleasant town in its own right, where the pace of life is a little slower than elsewhere. It has another claim to fame (or infamy) in the **Shire Hall**, the courtroom where six farmworkers, who became known as the **Tolpuddle Martyrs**, were sentenced to transportation in 1834 for the crime of forming a branch of the Labourers' Union. Such was the public outcry that the men were returned to England after serving two years in Australia, rather than the seven their sentence demanded. The village of Tolpuddle lies just off the A35 to the east of Dorchester, and there is a monument to the men, who became heroes of the later union movement.

To the north of town, on the A352, is the village of **Cerne Abbas**, which has a magnificent tithe barn but is best known for the **Cerne Abbas Giant**, the 180ft (55-metre) tall priapic club-wealding fertility figure carved into the chalk downs nearby. Some believe he dates from the time of the Roman occupation, but there are no written records of him until the 17th century.

Also worth a stop as you head east from Dorchester on the A35 is **Athelhampton House** (Mar–end Oct Sun–Thur 11am–4.30pm; charge), a fine medieval hall surrounded by impressive Victorian gardens adorned with fountains, statuary and topiaried pyramids.

Corfe Castle and the Isle of Purbeck

Turn off the A35 on to the A351 for **Corfe Castle ㉒** (daily Apr–Sept 10am–6pm, Oct, Mar 10am–5pm, winter until 4pm; charge) at Wareham. Sitting on a rocky pinnacle, this

TIP

An alternative route from Dorchester to Corfe Castle is on the A352, but this cuts out several of the Hardy sites, as well as Athelhampton House.

LEFT: the Cerne Abbas Giant.
BELOW: the impressive ruins of Corfe Castle.

Bournemouth's sedate Town Hall

is one of England's most impressive ruins and has been an important stronghold since the time of the Norman Conquest. Its finest hour was during the Civil War when the owner, Lady Bankes, defended it against a six-week siege by Parliamentary troops, who later demolished it to prevent any repetition. Corfe Common nearby is rich in wildlife and there are splendid views from the folly of Crech Grange Arch.

Head for the coast now (staying on the A351) to **Swanage ㉓**, between Durlston and Swanage bays, "lying snugly between two headlands as between a finger and a thumb", as Hardy put it when he fictionalised the village as Knollsea. Look out for a stone globe 10ft (3 metres) in diameter, flanked by panels giving sobering information on the nature of the uni-

verse; and for the ornate 17th-century Town Hall facade, made from the famous local marble.

This region is the **Isle of Purbeck** (although it is not an island at all) and is famous both for its marble and for its wonderful white sandy beaches. A whole swath of the coast is National Trust land, designated the **Studland Beach and Nature Reserve**. As well as one of the best beaches in England, the area supports a variety of rare birds and plants, butterfly habitats and other wildlife. There are a number of public paths and nature trails, plus car parks and the usual National Trust facilities. There is also a cliff-top walk westwards to lovely **Lulworth Cove** and the strangely eroded rock formation of **Durdle Door**.

At **Studland Heath**, the eastern tip of the area, a car ferry goes from Shell Bay to Sandbanks, giving access to Poole. Alternatively, take the A351/A350 via Wareham. **Poole ㉔** is a thriving port sitting on a huge harbour and has a delightful quayside. Curving steps meet under the portico of the **Customs House** with its coat of arms

representing an authority the Dorset smugglers never acknowledged. The **Waterfront Museum** (mid-Mar–Oct Mon–Sat 10am–5pm, Sun noon–5pm, Nov–Mar Tue–Sat 10am–4pm, Sun noon–4pm) has a section devoted to the Boy Scout movement, founded by Sir Robert Baden-Powell in 1908 after running the first Scout camp on nearby Brownsea Island.

From the quay, ferries run regularly to **Brownsea Island** (daily Mar, Sept–end Oct 10am–4pm, Apr–mid-July Sept 10am–5pm, mid-July–end Aug 10am–6pm; charge), which is now National Trust-owned although part of it is leased to the Dorset Wildlife Trust as a nature reserve. A lovely area of heath and woodland, the island is a haven for the now-rare red squirrel, and has a waterfowl sanctuary. The island is also accessible by ferry from Poole, Sandbanks and Bournemouth.

Bournemouth

Sedate and elegant **Bournemouth** **㉕** was established as a resort at the end of the 19th century and has remained popular ever since, largely due to a great sweep of sandy beach and the attractive parks and gardens that cover its surrounding cliffs. It has all the accoutrements of a modern seaside resort: amusement arcades, and clubs and bars. If you are there during the summer months, it's worth getting tickets for a performance by the Bournemouth Symphony Orchestra.

Bournemouth's best museum is the **Russell-Cotes Art Gallery** (Tue–Sun 10am–5pm), which has good Oriental exhibits. East of town, next to a ruined Norman castle, stands **Christchurch Priory**, which has an impressive Norman nave, although most of the remainder dates from the 13th–16th century. If you've seen enough churches and castles for a while, you might just like to climb nearby **Hengistbury Head** for splendid views over the Channel, or go a little further to **Mudeford**, where bright beach huts line the shore. ❏

The chain ferry connects Poole and Studland.

LEFT: Studland Beach. **BELOW:** on the way to Studland Bay.

BATH

Visitors no longer come to Bath to take the curative waters, but most go away feeling a lot better after even a short stay in this lively and beautiful city

Map on page 222

Cradled in the folds of the Mendip Hills and dissected by the River Avon, **Bath** has a long history. The Romans built the baths which give it its name – they are among the most impressive Roman remains in the country – and after years as a popular spa it was transformed, early in the 18th century, into one of the most beautiful cities in Europe. In 1988 Bath was designated a Unesco World Heritage Site. The transformation of the city was largely thanks to three men: Richard "Beau" Nash, a dandy and gambler and the town's master of ceremonies; Ralph Allen, a far-sighted businessman; and John Wood, an innovative architect. Their influence will be seen everywhere on this tour.

Our tour of Bath begins at the **Pump Room** Ⓐ which was built in the 1790s. Here the therapeutic waters could be sampled in comfort but it was also a social arena complete with musical entertainment, a place to see and be seen. Admire the room from one of the elegant tables, entertained by the Pump Room Trio or the regular pianist, with a Bath bun and coffee to hand. At the far end of the room, a statue of Beau Nash presides over the scene, and in an alcove on the south side, overlooking the King's Bath, spa water is dispensed from a lovely late 19th-century drinking fountain graced by four stone trout.

The greatest attraction are the **Roman Baths** Ⓑ (www.romanbaths.co.

uk; Mar–June, Sept–Oct 9am–5pm, July–Aug 9am–9pm, Nov–Feb 9.30am–4.30pm; charge). The Great Bath, seen below on entering, was discovered in the 1880s during investigations into a leak in the King's Bath that was causing hot-water floods in local cellars. The Victorians were excited by archaeology and the past and the discovery was greeted with great interest throughout Britain.

From here the route leads down to the heart of the baths, the **Temple Precinct**, excavated in the early 1980s.

Main attractions
THE ROMAN BATHS
THE PUMP ROOM
BATH SPA
BATH ABBEY
ROYAL CRESCENT
PULTENEY BRIDGE

LEFT: the Roman Baths.
BELOW: the restaurant in the Pump Room.

Bath's mythical founder, Bladud, is commemorated everywhere. Even the acorns topping the pediment of the Circus allude to his swineherd past.

The temple was built around AD 60, on the site of the native Sanctuary of Sulis, a Celtic goddess associated with healing whom the Romans identified with their own goddess of healing, Minerva. Finds from the period include coins, votive offerings and petitions to the goddess. There are also curses inscribed on pewter or lead sheets, some written backwards. Other highlights include the gilded bronze head of Minerva, discovered in 1727 by workmen, the first intimation of the marvellous Roman ruins below the medieval buildings; the Gorgon's head which would have adorned the main temple's pediment; the corner blocks of a sacrificial altar; and the sea beast mosaic.

The museum emerges next to the **Great Bath**, from where free guided tours leave every 15–20 minutes, taking in the East and West baths, and the medieval King's Bath. The Great Bath is the best place to see the water at close quarters, bubbling up at a temperature of 115°F (45°C) and laden with 43 minerals, including iron which stains the stone red. Its

green colour is caused by light reacting with algae: when the baths were roofed over in Roman times, the water would have been clear. The **King's Bath**, overlooked by the Pump Room, is named after King Bladud, mythical founder of Bath, who, as a prince, suffered from leprosy and roamed the countryside as a swineherd. According to legend he was miraculously cured when he stumbled upon some hot springs. Duly rehabilitated, he went on to found the city on the site of the curative waters.

The ancient abbey

From the Baths it is a short hop across Abbey Churchyard to **Bath Abbey** ⓒ (Apr–Oct Mon–Sat 9am–6pm, Sun 1–2.30pm, 4.30–5.30pm, Nov–end Mar Mon–Sat 9am–4.30pm, Sun 1–2.30pm and 4.30–5.30pm; donations welcomed; tower tours Mon–Fri hourly from 10am–4pm, Sat 10am–5pm; charge), the heart of medieval Bath. In 675 a Convent of Holy Virgins was founded here, and although there is no further record of the convent, there is evidence that a Saxon

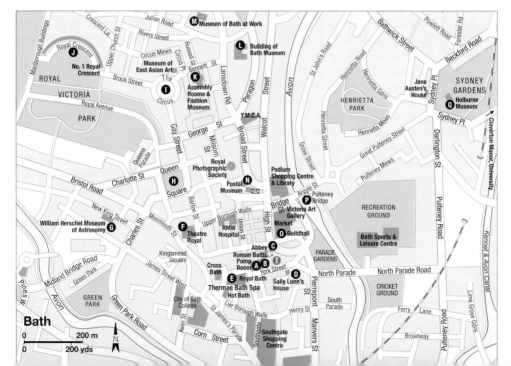

Bath

abbey existed by 757. Edgar, the first king of all England, was crowned in the abbey church in 973. He introduced the Benedictine monks who were to control the abbey and the town for the next 500 years.

In 1107, in the wake of the Norman conquest, the Bishop of Somerset moved the seat of the bishopric from Wells to Bath and built a Norman church on the site of the Saxon one. This lasted until 1499, when Bishop Oliver King rebuilt the church in the Perpendicular style characterised by flying buttresses, wide windows and fan vaulting. The Dissolution of the Monasteries by Henry VIII in 1539 brought the work to a halt, leaving the nave without a roof for many years.

The entrance to the abbey is through the **West Front**, with its Jacob's Ladder ("the angels of God ascending and descending on it": *Genesis 28: 12–17*). Inside, the vast windows fill the abbey with light. The east window depicts 56 scenes from the life of Christ in brilliant stained glass. Overhead stretches the lovely fan vaulting. One of the delights of the abbey are the memorials to famous residents and guests who died in Bath for want of the desired cure. Don't miss the one dedicated to Beau Nash ("Ricardi Nash, Elegantiae Arbiter"), who died at the age of 86, impoverished and enfeebled.

A door on the south side leads to the **Heritage Vaults** (Mon–Sat 10am–4pm), tracing the history of the abbey from Saxon times to the present day.

Not far from the abbey, along North Parade Passage, you may want to visit **Sally Lunn's House D**, a restaurant-cum-café occupying the oldest house in Bath (15th-century, with a prettified 17th-century facade). It is famous for a highly versatile bun, made on the premises since the 1680s, and served with sweet or savoury toppings.

West of the Pump Room, along colonnaded Bath Street, the state-of-the-art luxury **Thermae Bath Spa E**

Sally Lunn's famous traditional bun.

LEFT:
Bath Abbey

Fact File

Location Set in the Mendip Hills, on the River Avon, some 110 miles (175km) from London.

By car Easily accessible from London and the Midlands on the M4 and M5 motorways.

By coach National Express service from London Victoria Coach Station every 2 hours; journey time approx. 3 hours 45 minutes; tel: 08705-808 080, www.nationalexpress.com.

By train First Great Western rail service from London Paddington to Bath Spa, journey time 1 hour 20 minutes; tel: 08457-484 950.

By air Bristol Airport, near the M4/M5 junction; tel: 0871-334 4344, www.bristolairport.co.uk.

Guided walks From outside the Pump Room, Sun–Fri 10.30am and 2pm, Sat 10.30am, also Tue and Fri at 7pm May–Sept; free.

River and canal trips Tel: 01225-312 900 or 07974-560 197.

Excursions The American Museum at Claverton Manor; tel: 01255-460 503; www.americanmuseum.org.

Tourist Information Abbey Chambers, Abbey Churchyard, tel: 09067-112 000, cost 50p per minute; for accommodation bookings, tel: 0844-847 5256, www.visitbath.co.uk; free publications such as *This Month in Bath* and *Bath Guide* provide detailed listings of what's on where.

Rooftop pool at Thermae Bath Spa.

heir after bathing here. The modern complex includes a roof-top pool with views over the historic centre.

Georgian elegance

Head now to Sawclose and the **Theatre Royal** N, one of the oldest and loveliest theatres in England, which attracted some of the best-known actors of the late 18th century – such as David Garrick and Sarah Siddons. The Royal presents a year-round programme of plays, opera, dance and concerts (tel: 01225-448 844) and there are backstage tours on the first Wednesday and the following Saturday of the month at 11am.

(daily 9am–10pm; tel: 0844-888 0844; www.thermaebathspa.com) complex has been created from a cluster of historic baths harnessing the waters of two of Bath's three hot springs. They include the **Cross Bath**, built by Thomas Baldwin in 1791, the neighbouring **Hot Bath**, and the **New Royal Bath**. During the 17th century the Cross Bath had a reputation for curing sterility, and Mary of Modena, the wife of James II, conceived a much-needed

From the theatre, go up Monmouth Street and turn left for the **Herschel Museum of Astronomy** N (Feb–mid-Dec Sat–Sun 11am–5pm, Mon–Tue, Thur–Fri 1–5pm; charge), the home and observatory of Herschel, who came to Bath from Hanover in 1761 as an organist, and became musical director of the Assembly Rooms. From this garden, with the aid of a home-made telescope, he discovered Uranus in 1781. A replica of the tele-

scope is in the museum. He was subsequently appointed Director of the Royal Astronomical Society.

Queen Square  is our next stop. It was built in the 1730s by John Wood the Elder, the architect credited with introducing the Palladian style to Bath. The north side, with Roman portico, is particularly striking. Up Gay Street now to **The Circus** ❶, again designed by John Wood, although completed after his death by his son. This was England's first circular street and there is a wealth of architectural detail, not least the three types of column on the facades: Doric at the bottom, Ionic in the middle, and Corinthian at the top.

John Wood the Younger designed another architectural first: the **Royal Crescent** ❶, built from 1767–74, a short walk west of The Circus. This is Bath's star turn, set in a dramatic position above Royal Victoria Park, and comprising 30 separate properties. **No. 1 Royal Crescent** has become a museum (Feb–Oct Tue–Sun 10.30am–5pm; charge), restored and furnished by the Bath Preservation Trust as it would have been in the 18th century. The crescent had its share of famous residents: Isaac Pitman, inventor of shorthand, lived at No. 17; and Elizabeth Linley, who was painted by Gainsborough and who eloped with playwright Richard Sheridan, lived at No. 11.

Retrace your steps now past The Circus to the **Assembly Rooms and the Fashion Museum** ❸ (daily 10am–5pm, Mar–Oct until 6pm; tel:

The Assembly Rooms, once the centre of Bath's social scene.

LEFT: the Theatre Royal.

The Season

The elegant environment created by Nash, Allen and Wood drew the cream of fashionable society during the 18th century who came to see and be seen.

The main "season" was September to May, with most visitors staying from six weeks to three months. From the moment the abbey bells pealed out to welcome the new arrivals, days were a round of bathing, visiting, play-going and dancing, so finely captured by Jane Austen (1775–1817) in her novels.

Mornings began with a dip in the baths followed by a turn around the Pump Room and breakfast in the Assembly Rooms; afternoons were divided between shops, coffee houses and gaming tables. Twice a week a ball was held at one of the assembly rooms; other nights might be spent at the theatre, where Sarah Siddons held audiences spellbound during the 1770s, or at a concert by the castrato Venanzio Rauzzini, for whom Mozart wrote *Exultate Jubilate* in 1773.

At the end of the century Bath began to lose its lustre, as the upper classes deserted it for Tunbridge Wells, Cheltenham and, later, Brighton, where George IV had built the flamboyant Pavilion.

Bath turned into a residential city favoured by the professional classes in search of a comfortable but relatively inexpensive living.

Building, business and banquets

Go north from here, up Paragon, to the **Building of Bath Museum** ❶ (Sat–Mon 10.30am–5pm; charge), which offers an illuminating account of the talents and techniques that created the facades of the city. The particular crafts involved in Georgian interior design are explained in sections including furniture making, painting, wallpaper, soft furnishings and upholstery.

The next stop, in nearby Julian Road, is the **Museum of Bath at Work** ❿ (daily Apr–Oct 10.30am–4pm, Nov–Mar Sat–Sun only; charge). The museum relates the story of a 19th-century family firm which operated for 100 years without, it seems, ever throwing anything away. You can wander through the workshop, storeroom, office and factory and imagine yourself back in a less-fashionable part of Bath.

Retrace your steps down Paragon to Broad Street and the **Bath Postal Museum** ❻ (Mon–Sat 11am–5pm, Sun 2–5pm), from where the world's first postage stamp, the Penny Black,

Artefacts on display at the Museum of Bath at Work.

BELOW: the shop-lined Pulteney Bridge.

01225-477 173 to check it is not booked for functions; free to rooms, charge to museum). The magnificent ballroom is lit by cut-glass chandeliers, and there are separate rooms for gambling and taking tea. The Fashion Museum is dedicated to the fickleness of fashion over the past four centuries, with the exhibits on the Georgian period being the most fascinating. The collection was started by Doris Langley Moore, who gave her collection to Bath in 1963.

was sent in May 1840. Exhibits track the history of the postal service and touch on some delightful peripheral topics, such as a collection of cupid-covered Victorian Valentine cards.

It's not far now to the **Guildhall ◯**, designed in the Adam style in the 1770s by the young Thomas Baldwin, who went on to become the city architect. The **Banqueting Hall** (Mon–9am–5pm; free) is splendid, lined with portraits of city notables and lit by the finest chandeliers in the city.

Next door is a covered market, a lively cut-through to **Grand Parade**, and then the **Victoria Art Gallery** (entrance on Bridge Street; Tue–Sun 2–5pm; charge). Several Sickerts and a Whistler are on display along with Gainsborough portraits and J.M.W. Turner's *West Front of Bath Abbey*.

Bridge Street leads to **Pulteney Bridge ◯**, designed by Robert Adam from 1770 to 1774 and lined, like the Ponte Vecchio in Florence, with tiny shops on either side. On the right side of the bridge steps lead down to the Avon, from where river cruises depart every hour or so, and there are river-side walks to North Parade Bridge. There's a little café below the bridge with views over the weir.

At the east end of imposing **Great Pulteney Street** (another Thomas Baldwin design) is the **Holburne Museum ◯**, housed in an elegant 18th-century mansion which was originally the Sydney Hotel. It is closed for major refurbishment until at least 2011, but when it re-opens visitors will once again be able to see paintings by Turner, Stubbs, Reynolds and Gainsborough. The latter made his name in Bath, portraying the rich and famous.

The museum stands on the edge of **Sydney Gardens**, which are frequently mentioned in the letters of Jane Austen, who lived nearby at No. 4 Sydney Place from 1801 to 1804, as the scene of public galas and fireworks displays. In the 19th century they were the site of daring balloon ascents. The gardens are dissected by Brunel's Great Western Railway (1840–41) and the Kennet and Avon Canal (1810), elegantly incorporated by means of landscaped cuttings and pretty stone and cast-iron bridges. ❏

TIP

Bath International Music Festival, late May to early June, presents 16 days of music featuring well-known orchestras, ensembles and soloists; tel: 01225-463 362 for details.

LEFT: on parade at the American Museum.

The American Museum

Visiting an American Museum in a city with a Roman and Georgian heritage may seem odd, but this one is rather special. It is housed in Claverton Manor, set in grounds based on George Washington's garden at Mount Vernon, overlooking a beautiful wooded valley, yet barely 3 miles (5km) from the city.

A series of rooms have been furnished in different styles: there's the 18th-century Deer Park Parlor from Maryland; the Greek Revival Room, based on a mid-19th century New York dining room; and the New Orleans Bedroom which, with blood-red wallpaper and ornate Louis XV-style bed, evokes the ante-bellum world of Scarlett O'Hara.

There are also galleries devoted to the history of Native Americans, to westward expansion, to whaling, and to American crafts such as quilting and Shaker furniture. The Library holds over 11,000 books and periodicals, and is free to use by appointment. There is also a superb collection of maps, most dating back to the 16th century. A programme of special events features re-enactments of Civil War camp life and Independence Day displays. Opening hours: mid-Mar–end Oct Tue–Sun noon–5pm; tel: 01225-460 503. You can reach the museum by bus to the university then 10 minutes' walk; or by car via the A36 towards Bradford-on-Avon.

THE WEST COUNTRY

A tour around England's southwestern corner offers a wide variety of scenery, architecture and activities, and the best climate in the country in which to enjoy them

The West Country is many things to many people. For some it's the bleak moorlands of Bodmin, Dartmoor and Exmoor; for others it is quaint fishing villages and artists' colonies, or the gardens for which Cornwall is famous. This chapter will attempt to offer a little of everything.

The tour starts at **Bath ❶** (*see page 221*) then goes 8 miles (13km) east to the former mill town of **Bradford-on-Avon ❷**, which focuses on the picturesque main bridge, and has one of the best Saxon churches in the country – St Laurence's, founded in 700.

Bristol to Exmouth

After this we go northwest of Bath on the A4 to **Bristol ❸**, a major port since the time of the Phoenicians and in the 18th and 19th centuries an important gateway to the British Empire. Attractions and museums have flowered around the redeveloped docks, including **At-Bristol** (daily Mon–Fri 10am–5pm term time, Sat–Sun and daily in school holidays 10am–6pm; charge), an interactive science museum geared to children. Nearby, the **Watershed** is a pleasant complex of shops, bars and restaurants on the Floating Harbour. Further round the dock you can visit the *SS Great Britain* (Apr–Oct daily 10am–6pm, winter until 4.30pm). Designed by Brunel (1806–59), the ship represents Bristol's heyday as a shipbuilding centre, a theme explored further in the nearby **Maritime Heritage Museum** (same hours as ship). Bristol's newest planned attraction is the Museum of Bristol, due to be completed by 2011. Housed in harbourside buildings that were once home to the Industrial Museum, the museum aims to present the history of the city and its people and is part of a major redevelopment of the waterfront.

In the city centre, uphill from the waterfront, is the **Cathedral**, founded in 1140 (tours Sat 11.30am and 1.30pm; donations welcome). From

Main attractions
WELLS CATHEDRAL
WILD MOORS – DARTMOOR, EXMOOR, BODMIN
EDEN PROJECT
LOST GARDENS OF HELIGAN
ST IVES
CORNISH MINING HERITAGE
TINTAGEL CASTLE

PRECEDING PAGES: tightly-packed houses in Polperro. **LEFT:** riding the waves. **BELOW:** Glastonbury Tor.

TO THE TOR FOOTPATH

West Country

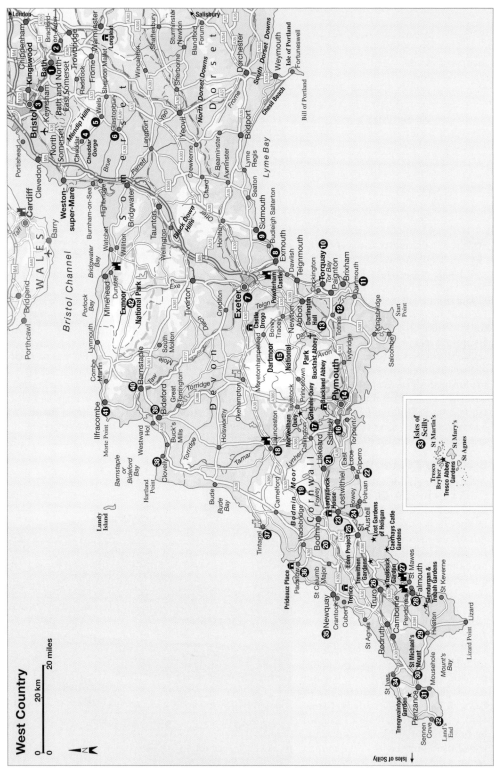

Isles of Scilly ↓

0 —— 20 miles

0 —— 20 km

here, Park Street rises to Bristol University, the City Museum and Art Gallery, and Clifton Village, where Isambard Kingdom Brunel's **Suspension Bridge** spans the Avon gorge (to get there, board bus No 8 or 8A from Bristol Temple Meads station).

From Bristol take the A38 towards **Cheddar Gorge ❹**, at 3 miles (5km) long the biggest gorge in England, carved out of karst limestone by the River Yeo. **Gough's Caves** (July–Aug daily 10am–5.30pm, Sept–June 10.30am–5pm; charge) were discovered by Richard Gough in 1890, and 13 years later the skeleton of the 9,000-year-old Cheddar Man was found here. A walkway leads through a series of stalactite-encrusted chambers. The **Cheddar Gorge Cheese Company** (daily 10am–4.30pm; charge) in the lower Gorge, has a viewing gallery where you can watch England's most popular cheese being made.

The A371 leads southeast from Cheddar to **Wells ❺**, a market town centred on the stunning **Cathedral Church of St Andrew** (daily Oct–Mar 7am–6pm, rest of year 7am–7pm; donations welcomed; *floorplan, see page 398*). Among the highlights of this early-English Gothic building are the intricately carved West Front, the Choir, with England's oldest Jesse Window, and the 14th-century scissor arches. Look out for the stunning clock, which dates back to 1390. The face shows the universe as imagined before Copernicus – with the earth at the centre. On the quarter hour, jousting knights appear and race around the clock.

Also well worth a visit is the **Bishop's Palace** (Easter–end Oct Sun–Fri 10.30am–6pm, Sat 10.30am–2pm), approached over a drawbridge spanning the moat. The ruins of the 13th-century Great Hall stand in tranquil grounds, where you can see the springs which gave the town its name.

Now it's time to get on the M5 motorway and go straight to the university town of **Exeter ❼**. The Roman city wall was completed in AD 200: much of it still stands and most main sites are within its circumference. The focal point is the **Cathedral ❹** (Mon–Sat 9.30am–5pm; charge), largely 14th-

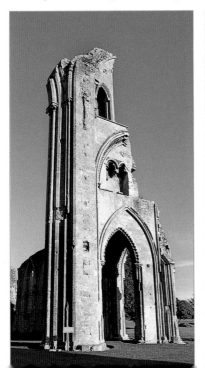

LEFT: Glastonbury's ancient abbey.

Glastonbury

Glastonbury **❻** is best known these days as the site of a hugely popular rock festival held over the summer solstice, its profits donated to charity. But Glastonbury is also the site of the oldest Christian foundation in Britain. The ruined abbey is built on the site of an earlier church, founded in the 1st century when Joseph of Arimethea, the man who gave his tomb to Christ, is believed to have brought here either the Holy Grail or the Blood of the Cross. The winter-flowering hawthorns in the abbey grounds are said to have sprung up when Joseph dug his staff into the ground and it rooted. An omen that he should settle here. Three early kings – Edmund I (died 946), Edgar (died 975) and Edmund Ironside (died 1016) – are buried here.

The existing buildings date from 1184–1303, when Glastonbury was the richest abbey in England, after Westminster. They fell into ruin after the Dissolution of the Monasteries in the 1530s. The remains of a warrior and his female companion interred deep beneath the Lady Chapel are identified by local legend as those of King Arthur and Queen Guinevere.

Glastonbury Tor, high above the little town, offers views as far as the Bristol Channel. On this spot the last abbot and his treasurer were executed in 1539 for opposing Henry VIII.

There are over 230 panes of glass in the windows of Mol's Coffee House.

century but with two Norman towers. The most significant feature is the fan vaulting of the world's longest Gothic vault. The building contains hundreds of carved images of "green men", pagan symbols of fertility. In the elegant Cathedral Close the most eye-catching building is 16th-century **Mol's Coffee House B**, sadly a coffee house no longer, where Sir Francis Drake (1540–96) is popularly rumoured to have met his sea captains.

Beneath the pavements of the nearby pedestrianised High Street are the **Underground Passages C** (June–Sept and school holidays Mon–Sat 9.30am–5.30pm, Sun 10.30–4pm, Oct–June Tue–Fri 11.30am–5.30pm, Sat 9.30am–5pm; charge), 14th-century subterranean aqueducts through which you can take an entertaining guided tour. At the top end of Gandy Street (enlivened with murals) is the **Exeter Phoenix Arts Centre D**, which has a popular café and a heavy schedule of events. Straight ahead stands the **Royal Albert Memorial Museum E** (currently closed for redevelopment). Descending to the River Exe and the cobbled **Quayside F** you'll find shops and cafés, plus bikes and canoes for hire. Visit the **Quay House Visitor Centre** (Apr–Oct daily 10am–5pm, Nov–Mar Sat–Sun 11am–4pm; free) for an audio-visual local history presentation.

Sand, sea and sanctuary

South of the city, where the estuary meets the sea, is **Exmouth 8** (take the A376). Its 2 miles (3km) of golden sand are the finest in East Devon, and made it the county's first beach resort, in the 18th century.

To the east (A3052) is **Sidmouth 9**, the most attractive and best preserved of East Devon's resorts. Narrow lanes back on to a grand seafront dominated by Regency houses and the shingle beach is framed by cliffs. Just east of the town is the **Donkey Sanctuary** (tel: 01395-578 222; daily 9am–dusk; free), a home for abused and abandoned donkeys, which has cared for over 9,000 donkeys over the years.

Head west after this short diversion,

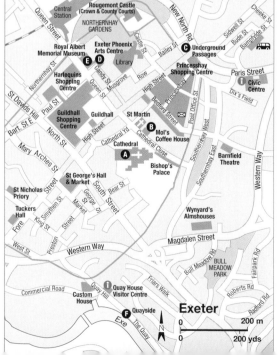

Exeter

via the A379, down the west side of the estuary, to **Powderham Castle** (Apr–end Oct daily 11am–4.30pm; guided tours; charge). This dramatic medieval fortress is set in a deer park, and has a lakeside picnic area and a Children's Secret Garden.

The English Riviera

The road continues via **Teignmouth**, to the great sweep of Tor Bay, and **Torquay** ⑩, a town which likes to emphasise its Mediterranean influences. At night, with the illuminations on, palm trees rustling and people promenading, it could almost be part of the French Riviera. The **Pavilion** (now a shopping arcade) on the seafront is a wonderful example of Edwardian wedding-cake architecture.

On the north side of town, reached by the **Oddicombe Cliff Railway** (Apr–Sept), an attraction in itself, is the **Babbacombe Model Village** (Apr–early Dec daily; tel: 01803-315 315 for varied closing times), a microcosm of contemporary England that is particularly inviting when the lights go on at dusk. A couple of miles east is

Kent's Cavern (summer daily 10am–4pm, tel: 01803-215 136 for winter hours; charge), a network of caves with a massive bear fossilised in a chamber roof. The guided tour is good, but many of the best remains are in the **Torquay Museum** (summer Mon–Sat 10am–5pm, mid-July–Sept also Sun 1.30–5pm) at the foot of Babbacombe Road. The museum also has a gallery devoted to the crime writer Agatha Christie who spent much of her life in the town and a reconstruction of a 19th-century farmhouse.

Torquay blends seamlessly into Paignton, which has little of the former's elegance, but does have two of the region's best stretches of sand, one off the promenade, the other at **Goodrington**, reached by the **Paignton and Dartmouth Steam Railway** (Apr–Oct), which chugs through attractive scenery. Behind Goodrington is **Paignton Zoo** (tel: 01803-697 500; summer daily 10am–6pm, winter until dusk; charge), where there are six recreated habitats providing a home for a variety of animals.

Brixham is the third town in Torbay,

Safe at the Donkey Sanctuary.

LEFT: beach huts near Torquay.

Fact File

The gateways to the West Country are Bath, Bristol, Exeter, Plymouth and Newquay.

By rail Trains leave from London Paddington for all the above destinations. Journey times: about 1 hour 30 minutes to Bath and Bristol; 2 hours 30 minutes to Exeter; 3 hours to Plymouth. For all rail information, tel: 08457-484 950.

By coach National Express coaches from London Victoria are slower, but cheaper. For information, tel: 0870-580 8080, www.nationalexpress.co.uk.

By car Bath and Bristol are easily accessible from London via the M4, Exeter via the M5, fed from London by the M4, from the north by the M6, Plymouth via the M5/A38.

By air Air Southwest operate flights to Plymouth and to Newquay from London Gatwick and Manchester among other places; tel: 0870-241 8202, www.airsouthwest.com.

Best museum Tate Gallery, St Ives, tel: 01736-796 226.

Walking trails Information on guided walks around Dartmoor, tel: 01822-890 414.

Tourist Information Exeter, tel: 01392-665 700; Plymouth, tel: 01752-306 330; Penzance, tel: 01736-362 207; Torquay, tel: 01803-211 211.

a pretty resort where tourism and fishing harmoniously co-exist. The harbour area, with its active fish market, has real character, and there's a full-size reconstruction here of the *Golden Hind*, the ship that took Sir Francis Drake around the world.

Maritime towns

Take the A379 south now to Kingswear, clinging to the steep banks of the Dart Estuary, from where it is a short ferry ride to **Dartmouth ⓫**, where the waters are thick with boats in one of England's best anchorages. Dartmouth has a long maritime history and a strong naval presence, with the Britannia Royal Naval College on the hill. The town focuses on the **Boat Fleet** (an inner harbour) and the streets running off it, crowded with historic buildings with fine frontages.

Just outside town, clamped to a shoulder of rock, is the formidable, well-preserved **Dartmouth Castle** (Apr–Oct daily 10am–5pm, July–Aug until 6pm, Nov–Mar Sat–Sun 10am–4pm; charge). It comprises the original 14th-century castle, a Victorian fort

BELOW: a steep
climb in Dartmouth.

and 17th-century St Petrock's Church.

From Dartmouth head inland to **Totnes ⓬**, an elegant town often described as Elizabethan although its history goes back much further than that. Its face has not changed for centuries, the castle concealed from view by a tumble of houses and the arch of the East Gate spanning the main street.

The **Guildhall** is a lovely building with a pillared portico, and 15th-century St Mary's Church has a delicate Saxon rood screen. In the granite-pillared Butterwalk an Elizabethan market is held on summer Tuesdays, with traders in period dress. Turn right, and **Totnes Castle** (Apr–Oct daily 10am–5pm, July–Aug until 6pm, Oct until 4pm; charge) soon comes into view, a perfectly preserved Norman motte and bailey structure.

Just off the A384, 2 miles (3km) north of Totnes, is the gracious 14th-century **Dartington Hall ⓭**, the nerve centre of the Dartington Estate, run by philanthropists Leonard and Dorothy Elmhirst. The hall has a cobbled quad and magnificent hammer-beamed Great Hall; outside, sculptures and a grassy-banked amphitheatre are set in mature woodland. Most visited is the **Dartington Cider Press Centre** (Mon–Sat 9.30am–5.30pm, Christmas–Easter also Sun 11am–5pm Easter–Christmas), a group of shops and workshops, whose high-quality products reflect the Dartington emphasis on local crafts.

Follow the road to the A38, where you will find **Buckfast Abbey** (Mon–Thur 9am–6pm, Fri 10am–6pm, Sun noon–6pm), an 11th-century foundation bought in 1882 by a group of French Benedictines who dedicated their lives to its restoration. Today, the monks keep bees and make and sell tonic wine.

Now take the A38 straight to **Plymouth ⓮**, the largest conurbation in Devon. Being a naval base, it was badly bombed during World War II. Subsequent building leaves much to be

desired. The **Hoe** survived, a broad grassy shoulder between town and sea, where Francis Drake was playing bowls when the Spanish Armada was sighted (1588). **Smeaton's Tower** (the current lighthouse) stands on the Hoe, not far from the formidable walls of the **Royal Citadel** (guided tours May–Sept 2.30pm). Further along the seafront is the Barbican, where the huge **National Marine Aquarium** (Apr–end Sept daily 10am–6pm, Oct–Mar until 5pm) has impressive displays that recreate the different levels of aquatic habitat, from high moorland to deepest ocean. Among the species on show are sharks, turtles and several species of seahorse, which have been successfully bred at the centre.

Dartmoor National Park

Dartmoor National Park ⓯ covers some 368 sq miles (954 sq km). Reaching 2,000ft (600 metres), the moor is the highest land in southern England: around half is open moorland, the rest steep wooded valleys with secluded villages. We enter from **Tavistock** on the B3357, which leads to the **High**

Moorland Visitor Centre – with well-presented displays, and information on guided walks – and **Princetown**, the highest, bleakest settlement, with Dartmoor Prison looming nearby. The road continues to **Widecombe-in-the-Moor**, a captivating little place with two claims to fame: the well-known song which advertises its annual fair in September *(see left)*, and its church, known as the cathedral of the moor, because of the height of its tower. Narrow lanes south lead to two pretty villages, **Buckland-in-the-Moor**, with some of the most photographed thatched cottages in Devon; and **Holne**, birthplace in 1819 of writer Charles Kingsley – author of *The Water Babies* – where you'll find the 14th-century Church House Inn.

Back on the B3357 you will soon reach **Hay Tor** (1,490ft/450 metres), with far-reaching views; and **Becky Falls** (mid-Feb–end Oct daily 10am–

Sir Francis Drake looks out to sea at Plymouth Hoe.

LEFT: Buckfast Abbey after its restoration.

West Devon Highlights

Saltram House (tel: 01752-333 500; mid-Mar–Oct Sat–Thur noon–4.30pm) set in 470 acres (190 hectares) of grounds in Plymouth's eastern suburbs. Virtually all the furnishings are original, which is rare. This National Trust property contains fourteen portraits by Sir Joshua Reynolds (who was born in Plympton) and a magnificent salon, reworked by Robert Adam in the 1770s.

Buckland Abbey (tel: 01822-853 607; mid-Mar–Oct Fri–Wed 10.30am–5.30pm, daily July–Aug, Nov–early Dec and late Feb–early Mar Fri–Sun 11am–4pm) was a 13th-century Cistercian monastery, and the vast barn and abbey church are original. Sir Francis Drake (1540–96), the first Englishman to navigate the globe, and the man who brought potatoes and tobacco from Virginia to England, bought it in 1580, and the rooms house an exhibition devoted to his life. Look out for Drake's Drum – it is said that it beats when England is in danger and needs his help: the last time it was heard was at Dunkirk.

Morwellham Quay (tel: 01822-832 766; Apr–Oct daily 10am–5pm), set in a Designated Area of Natural Beauty at the highest navigable point on the Tamar, is a superbly presented reconstruction of industry and transport in Victorian times. A small railway takes visitors into the disused copper mine.

Most of Dartmoor is still in private hands. Prince Charles, as the head of the Duchy of Cornwall, is the largest single landowner.

5pm, last entry 4pm; charge), where there are nature trails and woodland walks through pleasant woodland, plus a restaurant, gift shop and picnic area surrounding the waterfalls. Nearby the little granite-built town of **Bovey Tracey** is worth a stop for the **Devon Guild of Craftsmen** (tel: 01626-832 223; daily 10am–5.30pm), housed in an historic riverside mill. You will find a high-quality selection of ceramics, glass and textiles on display and for sale.

Take the A382 towards Okehampton, where a right turn leads to Drewsteignton and **Castle Drogo** (tel: 01647-433 306; mid-Mar–end Oct daily 11am–5pm, early Mar and early Dec 11am–4pm; charge), the last castle to be built in England, begun in 1910, and designed by Sir Edwin Lutyens. The formal terraced gardens are open all year (Sat–Sun only in winter) with access to various walks through the beautiful River Teigh Gorge.

Now join the A30 to visit the market town of **Okehampton**, where the **Museum of Dartmoor Life** (end Mar–Oct Mon–Sat 10.15am–4.30pm,

tel: 01837-52295 for details of Sun times; charge) offers detailed visitor-friendly insights into life on the moor. Okehampton's **Castle** (daily Apr–end Sept 10am–5pm; charge) has been a ruin since seized by Henry VIII in 1538 but its hilltop setting, with a riverside picnic area below, is delightful. Our tour follows the road south past lovely **Lydford Gorge** back to Plymouth and into Cornwall.

Across the Tamar

It is said that nothing has done more to keep Cornwall Cornish than the River Tamar. To get a sense of how different from Devon it is, cross via Brunel's **Royal Albert Bridge** (toll payable) at **Saltash** ⑯. Eighteenth-century houses cluster on the quayside and the home of Drake's first wife, **Mary Newman's Cottage**, can be visited in summer (Wed 2–4pm, Sat–Sun noon–4pm; charge). Outside town (off the A38) stands the imposing Norman church of **St Germans**, and there are several stately homes in the vicinity: **Trematon Castle** (also Norman) can only be glimpsed from the road, but

BELOW: Launceston steam railway.
RIGHT: rock formations on Bodmin Moor.

Antony House (Apr–Oct Tue–Thur 1–5pm, June–Aug also Sun; charge) and **Mount Edgcumbe House** (Apr–Sept Sun–Thur 11am–4.30pm, charge for house; country park: daily 8am–dusk, free) can be visited. Our route takes you north, leaving the main road to visit **Cotehele Quay** ⓱ (mid-Mar–end Sept 11am–4.30pm; charge), perched above the wooded river banks, where there's a medieval house, remarkably unchanged, and a collection of wharf buildings, including a watermill, forge and cider press.

Rejoin the main road now (A388) to **Launceston** ⓲, Cornwall's only walled town, founded in the 11th century. **Launceston Castle** (Apr–Oct daily 10am–5pm, July–Aug until 6pm, Oct until 4pm; charge) sits in immaculate grounds, with views across Bodmin and Dartmoor. The castle was once a prison, where George Fox, the founder of the Quakers was held in 1656. The 16th-century parish church, **St Mary Magdalene**, covered with decorative motifs, is the town's other most interesting building. The **Launceston Steam Railway** (tel: 01566-775 665, www.launceston sr.co.uk; daily July–Sept, check for times rest of year), with a museum, workshop and buffet, will take you on a trip down memory lane.

Broody Bodmin

Pick up the A30 here and follow it through the brooding, magnificent **Bodmin Moor** ⓳. The road enters the moorland at Altarnun, where you can visit the **Wesley Cottage** (summer Tue, Fri, Sat 10.30am–3.30pm) where John Wesley (1703–91), founder of Methodism, stayed when preaching in Cornwall. At Bolventor you cannot miss the **Jamaica Inn**. The attached Smugglers' Museum (Apr–Oct daily 10am–5pm) gives a theatrical presentation of Daphne du Maurier's story and has a collection of smuggling relics.

A minor road follows the River Fowey passing **Dozmary Pool**, in the wildest part of the moor. Fed by underground springs it is the stuff of legend:

Brunel's bridge at Saltash.

BELOW: sunset over Lostwithiel's Castle.

St Mary Magdalene Church at Launceston.

BELOW: the waterfront at East Looe.

according to Alfred Lord Tennyson, it was here that King Arthur's sword was consigned to the waters after his death. A little further south is **St Cleer's Holy Well**, whose waters were reputed to cure madness.

You are close to Liskeard (pronounced "Liskard") here, and roads to the coast, but an exploration of the moor is best rounded off by a visit to **Bodmin ⑳**, the western gateway, an old trade route from Ireland which attracted early saints. St Petroc, Cornwall's senior saint, founded a priory here in the 6th century (only fragments remain) and the 15th-century **Church of St Petroc** (Apr–Sept daily 11am–3pm) houses a cask containing his remains. This is the county's largest church.

Bodmin Museum (Easter–end Sept Mon–Fri 10.30am–4.30pm, Sat 10.30am–2.30pm, Oct Mon–Sat 10.30am–2.30pm; free) has good exhibitions on local life through the ages.

There's a nostalgic taste of sulphur on the **Bodmin and Wenford Steam Railway** (tel: 01208-73666, www.bodmin andwenfordrailway.co.uk; end May–end Sept daily, also other times Mar–Dec). Bodmin's bypass skirts the grounds of **Lanhydrock House** (end Mar–Oct Tue–Sun 11am–5pm, Apr–Sept until 5.30pm; charge), an enormous country house with 50 rooms to explore and a pleasing lived-in atmosphere. Highlights are the long gallery with a splendid plasterwork ceiling, the servants' quarters and extensive grounds planted with rare shrubs. Double back now to **Liskeard ㉑** on the A38. Its tin mining heyday is long gone, but there's still a wealth of Georgian buildings, a Regency Market Hall and the **Stuart House**, where Charles I spent several nights during the Civil War (1642–46).

Jewels of the coast

Down to the coast now to **Looe Bay**, where East and West Looe are linked by a bridge. The former is the larger and more prosperous, dependent on tourism and the revived fishing indus-

try. The **Old Guildhall Museum** (Easter and May–end Sept Sun–Fri 11am–4pm) is devoted to fishing and smuggling.

Go west a few miles to **Polperro** ㉒, which lives up to its reputation as one of Cornwall's most picturesque fishing villages. Clinging to the steep hillside, colour-washed cottages bedecked with flowers crowd the narrow alleys. The paths winding up the hill offer splendid views over the harbour.

Inland now to **Lostwithiel** ㉓, once Cornwall's capital, a serene, rather French-looking place beside the Fowey. There are many attractive Georgian buildings in the town, and the 14th-century **Duchy Palace** stands in Quay Street. **Lostwithiel Museum** (Easter–Sept Mon–Sat 10.30am–4.30pm) has an excellent collection of local photographs, and domestic and agricultural implements.

Fowey ㉔ (pronounced Foy), at the mouth of the river of the same name, is a lovely place, its houses huddled daintily above a deep-water harbour, one of the south coast's best sailing areas. Henry VII built a fort above

Readymoney Cove: **St Catherine's Castle** contains the mausoleum of the locally powerful Rashleigh family: their town house is now the Ship Inn. For many years Fowey was the home of Daphne du Maurier, and there is a festival in her honour each May.

The **Fowey Town Museum** (May–Sept Mon–Fri 10am–5pm; charge), housed in part of the Town Hall, commemorates the town's maritime past.

From Truro to Land's End

Leaving Fowey, take the A3082 which joins the A390 to **St Austell** and the **Eden Project** ㉕ (www.edenproject.com; daily Apr–Oct 9.30am–6pm, Nov–Mar 10am–4.30pm; charge) where a vast global garden, incorporating huge domed conservatories, has become one of Cornwall's major attractions. Eden was created on the site of a huge, disused china clay pit. The biomes, as the conservatories are called, recreate rainforest and Mediterranean habitats. The lush Rainforest biome is filled with all sorts of exotic plants, including chocolate, bananas, cola and sugar. The Mediterranean biome contains plants such

Jamaica Inn, on the borders of Bodmin Moor.

BELOW:
the geodesic domes of the Eden Project.

On the way to Falmouth you'll see the sign for Come-to-Good, a thatched Quaker meeting house built in 1710 after the Tolerance Act ended their persecution. (For good, read God.)

as olive trees, vines, citruses and cork trees. The aim is not just to entertain but to educate, and there's plenty of non-preachy information on the impact that people have on plants and habitats all over the world. There are also extensive gardens outside. On from here to **Truro** ㉖ – every inch a city, although the ring road has separated its heart from its maritime heritage. The triple towers of the neo-Gothic **Cathedral** soar above the rooftops of 18th-century houses. **Lemon Street** is one of the most homogenous Georgian streets in England. The past is well documented in the **Royal Cornwall Museum** (Mon–Sat 10am–4.45pm; free), which has an Egyptian room (boasting an unwrapped mummy) and a superb collection of archaeological finds, local and natural history, ceramics and costume.

Turn off the A39 onto the B3289 to reach **St Mawes** ㉗, on the Roseland Peninsula. Ferries bustle in and out of the harbour, and yacht owners fill the Victory Inn. Thatched cottages line the seafront road to the three huge circular bastions of **St Mawes Castle** (Apr–end Sept Mon–Fri and Sun 10am–5pm, July–Aug until 6pm, Oct 10am–4pm, Nov–Mar Fri–Mon 10am–4pm; charge), built by Henry VIII in 1543 as defence against a French attack from the sea. The garden of **Lamorran House** (Apr–Sept Wed and Fri 10am–5pm) in Upper Castle Road has a Mediterranean feel, with sub-tropical plants flourishing on the hillside (*see below right for more Cornish gardens*). Level with the top of the tower below, the lych-gate of the church of **St Just-in-Roseland** frames what may be the most perfect view in Cornwall. The 13th-century church itself, reflected in St Just Pool, is almost as pleasing.

On the other side of the estuary called the Carrick Roads lies **Falmouth** ㉘ (there are ferries in summer; otherwise return to Truro and continue on the A39). The town developed after Sir Walter Raleigh (1552–1618) decided it would make a good harbour. Henry VIII built **Pendennis Castle** (daily Apr–end June and Sept 10am–5pm, July–Aug 10am–6pm, Oct–Mar until 4pm, until 4pm Sat

BELOW: Pendennis Castle

year round; charge) at the same time as the one at St Mawes, but the expected French attack never came. The town received a charter in 1661 and the church of King Charles the Martyr was built the following year.

On the newly developed Discovery Quay, the new **National Maritime Museum** (daily 10am–5pm) occupies a splendid building. Lots of interactive exhibits make it popular with children as well as marine enthusiasts. The **Falmouth Art Gallery** (Mon–Sat 10am–5pm; free) in the central square, The Moor, has frequently changing exhibitions of paintings, sculpture, photographs and textiles.

Helston ㉙ is the next important port of call. It really comes alive on 8 May, the celebration of Flora Day, a pagan ritual to welcome spring. The **Helston Folk Museum** (Mon–Sat 10am–1pm, until 4pm during school holidays) has interesting displays on life in the region in days gone by. Just outside Helston is The **Flambards Experience** (all year, check www.flambards.co.uk or tel: 01326-573 406 for hours), a theme park with various rides, as well as exhibitions including an authentic re-creation of a Victorian village.

The A394 takes you west to the rocky island of **St Michael's Mount** ㉚ (tel: 01736-710 507; Apr–end Oct Sun–Fri 10.30am–5pm, Nov–Mar guided tours Tue and Fri as tide and weather permit). A Benedictine monastery was founded here in the 12th century (the Priory Church crowns the summit), then fortified by Henry VIII after the Dissolution as part of his string of coastal defences.

Across **Mount's Bay** lies **Penzance** ㉛, the star of the Cornish resorts and the warmest place in the British Isles, with sub-tropical plants flourishing in **Morrab Gardens**, off Morrab Road. At the other end of the road, in Penlee Park, the **Penlee House Gallery and Museum** (Easter–end Sept Mon–Sat 10am–5pm, Oct–Easter 10.30am–4.30pm; charge) displays a collection

Fisherman in Falmouth bay.

LEFT: Cornwall's mild climate produces lush, exotic plants and palms.

Cornish Gardens

Cornwall's mild climate has produced some beautiful gardens. Among the best are:

Glendurgan, which is set in a wooded valley near Falmouth. Rare and exotic sub-tropical plants and an unusual 19th-century laurel maze; tel: 01326-250 906.

Trebah, Falmouth. Hydrangeas, rhododendrons and azaleas plus a water garden and cascades; colour all year round; tel: 01326-252 200.

Lost Gardens of Heligan, Pentewan, St Austell. These "lost" Victorian gardens have been superbly restored. The Italian garden, kitchen garden, walled garden and "jungle" area have been returned to their former glory; tel: 01726-845 100. A must on your itinerary.

Trelissick, near Truro. This is a plantsman's garden, famous for its tender exotic plants and shrubs, as well as its delightful setting. Woodland and riverside walks, with wonderful views down to Falmouth; tel: 01872-862 090.

Trewithen, Truro. Internationally known for its camellias, rhododendrons, magnolias, plus many rare trees and shrubs; tel: 01726-883 647.

Caerhays Castle, Gorran, St Austell. An informal woodland garden overlooking the sea. Camellias, magnolias and rhododendrons; tel: 01872-501 310.

The Old Post Office at Tintagel

BELOW: Tintagel castle and coastline.
RIGHT: sculpture in the garden at the Barbara Hepworth Museum.

of paintings from the Newlyn School.

Take the A30 now to **Land's End** ❷, the most westerly point in England. No longer the romantic, isolated spot it once was, it has now been developed. The **Land's End Centre** (tel: 0871-720 0044; daily 10am–dusk, from 10.30am Nov–end Mar; charge) has a discovery trail and underground exhibitions; there's also a beached trawler, a theatre and lots of shops and restaurants.

The ship-eating **Isles of Scilly** ❸ (pronounced "silly") 28 miles (45 km) west of Land's End can be reached by ferry or helicopter from Penzance. Phoenician traders landed here before the birth of Christ in search of tin, copper and other metals. Five of the islands are inhabited and all but one, Tresco, are part of the Duchy of Cornwall. Highlights are the **Tresco Abbey**

Gardens (daily 10am–4pm; charge), which contain the Valhalla collection of figureheads; and the **Isles of Scilly Museum**, St Mary's. In summer there are races of six-oar gigs off St Mary's.

Mines, legends and artists

On the road to St Ives (the B3306 which hugs the coast) you'll pass **St Just**, where Cornish miracle plays are performed in a grassy amphitheatre called the Playing Place; and **Botallack**, which has the most picturesque of the ruined mine buildings. The **Levant Steam Engine** (tel: 01736-786 156) is the oldest working beam engine in Cornwall. Along the cliff is the **Geevor Tin Mine Museum** (Easter–end Oct Sun–Fri 9am–5pm, Nov–Mar until 4pm, last tours one hour before closing; charge). A little further up the coast is **Zennor**, a place of magic and legends. The **Wayside Folk Museum** (daily May–Sept 10.30am–5.30pm, Apr and Oct 11am–5pm) is an unusual, privately owned collection of local history and lore.

But our goal is **St Ives** ❹, the liveliest and most interesting of the resorts.

Its most distinguishing point is the "island", which divides the Atlantic surfing beach of Porthmeor from the harbour and beach of Porthminster, with the little granite chapel of St Nicholas on its topmost point. St Ives grew prosperous on pilchards and tin mining, and the houses of the pilchard fishermen still crowd the tangled streets of Downalong, while the tin miners lived in Upalong. Both industries collapsed, but the town was saved by its scenic beauty and the quality of its light, which attracted artists here.

The **Tate St Ives** (Mar–Oct daily 10am–5.20pm, Nov–Feb Tue–Sun 10am–4.20pm; charge) has a small permanent exhibition of works by artists connected with the region complemented by temporary exhibitions of modern art.

Nearby on Barnoon Hill is the **Barbara Hepworth Museum** (hours as above) where her work is displayed in her studio and garden. For more paintings, go to the Wills Lane Gallery, the excellent **St Ives Society of Artists Gallery**, in Norway Square, and the Penwith Gallery.

Continue up the north coast, beautiful despite the plethora of seaside bungalows and caravan sites, to **Newquay ㉟**, the largest, brashest resort on the coast, with beautiful sandy beaches popular with surfers. Inland, at Kestle Mill, is **Trerice** (Mar–Oct Sat–Thur 11am–5pm; charge), an exquisitely decorated and furnished Elizabethan manor house.

Padstow and Tintagel

Our route continues inland (A392/A39) to reach **Padstow ㊱** on the River Camel estuary, a picturesque little place with a small harbour and cobbled streets. If you're here on 1 May you'll see the famous **Padstow 'Obby 'Oss** (Hobby Horse) and his colourful entourage in a procession celebrating the coming of summer. **Prideaux Place** (Easter and May–end Sept Sun–

Exhibits in the Tate St Ives.

BELOW: St Michael's Mount.

TIP

The Tarka Trail *(see page 247)* stretches from Ilfracombe to Meeth, via Barnstable. For more information on hiring bikes for this traffic-free cycle route, tel: 01271-24202.

Thur 1.30–4pm, grounds 12.30–5pm), which overlooks the town and deer park, is one of the stops on the procession's route, and one of the nicest of Cornwall's stately homes.

Pick up the A39 at Wadebridge and turn left at Camelford for **Tintagel** ㊲, where the **Old Post Office** (Apr–end Sept daily 11am–5.30pm, Oct 11am–4pm; charge), a 14th-century yeoman's farmhouse, has been restored. It's amazing that so much remains of **Tintagel Castle** (Apr–Sept daily 10am–6pm, Oct until 5pm, Nov–Mar until 4pm; charge), on a headland of black craggy cliffs, accessible only by footbridge. Once a Celtic stronghold, then home to the earls of Cornwall, it's best known as the legendary birthplace of King Arthur, and home to Merlin the magician. Carry on north to **Bude**, where surfers flock to the golden sands and strong waves.

Westward Ho!

Here we cross back into Devon to visit **Clovelly** ㊳ a perfectly preserved fishing village, where steep cobbled streets lined with brightly-painted houses

RIGHT: going home from the beach at Bude.

lead up from the harbour. It was made famous by Charles Kingsley (1819–75) in *Westward Ho!* The resort of this name, a 19th-century development, lies nearby.

Follow the road round Barnstaple Bay to the pleasant town of **Bideford** ㊴, also closely associated with Kingsley. There's an impressive medieval bridge, and the quay is the mainline station for **Lundy Island**, a peaceful sliver of land 11 miles (18km) offshore, home to puffins and a wealth of other bird and marine life.

Nearby **Barnstaple** ㊵, on the Taw estuary, is best known for its glass-roofed 19th-century Pannier Market, the finest in Devon, where fresh produce is on sale.

The major resort on Devon's north coast is **Ilfracombe** ㊶, although its beach is not remarkable. (For the finest beach in Devon, turn off on the B3343 and wind down to the sands and dunes of **Woolacombe**.) But Ilfracombe has a port full of character, and a highly eccentric **Museum** (tel: 01271-863 541; Apr–Oct 10am–5pm, Nov–Mar Tue–Fri 10am–1pm).   ❑

Exmoor National Park

Exmoor ㊷ contains a great variety of landscape and wildlife; parts are open heather-covered moor, but it also includes some of Britain's most dramatic and beautiful coastline. It is not as high as Dartmoor and is more extensively farmed, with habitation more widely spread; many of its hills are topped with Iron Age forts. Among many highlights (starting from Combe Martin on the moor's western edge) are:

The Great Hangman, with breathtaking cliff scenery.
The Cliff Railway (daily 8am–7pm) linking Lynton and the pleasant seaside town of Lynmouth.
Valley of the Rocks, a dramatic land formation.
Doone Valley, made famous by R. D. Blackmore's novel.
Culbone Church, said to be England's smallest parish church.
Selworthy, a picture-book pretty village.
Dunster, with a castle and circular Yarn Market.
Dunkery Beacon, the highest spot (1,704ft/519 metres).
Landacre Bridge a medieval structure on the River Barle.
Tarr Steps, a clapper bridge near Withypool.
For information, or details of guided walks or routes for independent walkers, contact the Visitors' Centre, 7/9 Fore Street, Dulverton, TA22 9EX, tel: 01398-323 841.

West Country Writers

Whether crafting poetry or thrillers, family sagas or anthropomorphic tales, writers find the West Country inspirational

The West Country is a region that has both produced and inspired numerous writers, some of whose works have been immortalised in place names. R.D. Blackmore's *Lorna Doone* (1869), set in the 17th century, gave its name to the Upper East Lyn, which became the Doone Valley. Much of mid-Devon has been christened Tarka Country, after *Tarka the Otter* (1927), written by Henry Williamson (1895–1977).

Charles Kingsley (1819–75), whose father was vicar of Clovelly, wrote *Westward Ho!* (1855) while living in nearby Bideford, and the name was borrowed for the resort.

Other writers associated with Devon are Sir Arthur Conan Doyle (1859–1930), who used Dartmoor as the location for *The Hound of the Baskervilles* in 1902; and John Galsworthy (1867–1933), who wrote *The Forsyte Saga* series while living in Manaton on the east side of the moor. Two centuries earlier, John Gay (1685–1732), author of *The Beggars' Opera* (1728), was born and educated in Barnstaple.

Perhaps the most famous of Devon's writers is Agatha Christie (1890–1976), Britain's most prolific author, whose thrillers still sell about 4 million copies a year. She was born in Torquay and wrote two of her books while staying at the Art Deco hotel on Burgh Island.

Greenway, Christie's family home, overlooking the River Dart, is now managed by the National Trust, and is open to the public. Pre-booking essential if arriving by car, tel: 01803-842 382.

Cornwall, too, has its share of literary figures. D.H. Lawrence (1885–1930) wrote *Women in Love* at Zennor where he set up a small and short-lived group of like-minded people during World War I, intent on isolating themselves both from London and from the conflict. Virginia Woolf (1882–1941) used early memories of Godrevy Lighthouse in her 1927 novel *To The Lighthouse*. Sir John Betjeman (1906–84) also spent childhood holidays in Cornwall, in Trebetherick at the mouth of the Camel estuary. His early poems, such as *Summoned by Bells*, reflect bicycle trips to churches, and he described travelling by rail to Padstow as "the best train journey I know".

More recently, Winston Graham, in his immensely popular Poldark novels, has drawn on the 19th-century mining industry around Perranporth.

Most inextricably associated with Cornwall, however, is Daphne du Maurier (1907–89). She wrote several of her early works at Bodinnick, near Fowey, and later ones at Menabilly. She used Jamaica Inn on Bodmin Moor as the setting for the eponymous novel, and gave evocative Cornish settings to *Frenchman's Creek* and *Rebecca*, the latter published in 1938 and later memorably filmed by Alfred Hitchcock. ❑

ABOVE: Daphne du Maurier as a young woman.
RIGHT: Agatha Christie.

HEREFORD AND THE WELSH BORDERS

The border counties play host to literary and arts festivals, produce world-famous pottery, and lay claim to some splendid castles and cathedrals and the world's first iron bridge

The great border castles of Herefordshire are a legacy of the time when this green and pleasant region was a fiercely disputed frontier between England and Wales, where the Norman lords established the Marches. This chapter explores the castles and valleys, the pretty towns of the Wye valley and takes in the world's first iron bridge at Telford, and the pottery town of Stoke-on-Trent.

We start with a visit to **Ross-on-Wye ❶**, which stands on a red sandstone cliff above a bend in the River Wye. The slender spire of **St Mary's Church** which tops the cliff can be seen for miles around. The church is known for its hedgehogs: stone ones, wooden ones, painted and embroidered ones. The area of parkland that surrounds the church is called The Prospect, and it does indeed offer a wonderful prospect across the river. Ross is a busy market town centred on a 17th-century arcaded **Market Hall** which is set in a square where markets are still held.

The **Ross International Festival** in the last two weeks of August is a feast of high-quality theatre, music and film which is well worth visiting, but the town gets very busy so accommodation should be organised in advance.

Amazing diversions

From Ross, make a diversion some 8 miles (13km) southwest to **Symonds Yat ❷**, a rocky outcrop with stunning

views over the Wye. The ferry that links Symonds Yat East and West across the river runs on an overhead chain and is operated by hand. The **Amazing Hedge Puzzle** (daily 11am–5pm, Oct and Mar until 4pm, Nov–Feb until 3pm; charge), along with the Jubilee Maze and the adjoining Museum of Mazes, explain some of the mysteries of maze-making.

Symonds Yat is a springboard for walks in the **Forest of Dean**, a former royal hunting ground, over the border in Gloucestershire. The forest's ancient

Main attractions
HEREFORD CATHEDRAL AND THE MAPPA MUNDI
IRONBRIDGE GORGE MUSEUM
LUDLOW CASTLE
WEDGWOOD MUSEUM
HAY-ON-WYE

PRECEDING PAGES: the iron bridge over the River Severn. **LEFT:** Ross-on-Wye. **BELOW:** Staffordshire figurines in Stoke.

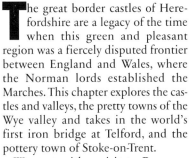

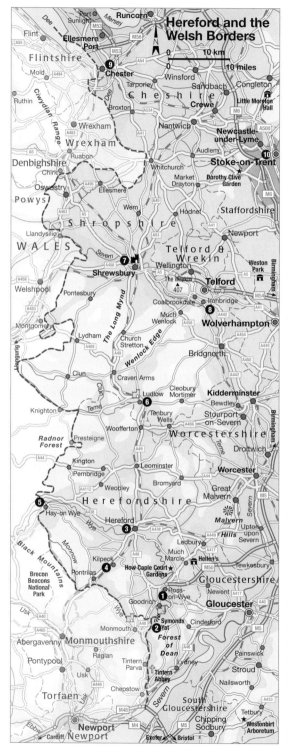

mining industry can be explored at **Clearwell Caves** (mid-Feb–end Oct 10am–5pm; charge) near Coleford.

On your way back to Ross, take a look at **Goodrich Castle** (daily Apr–end June, Sept–Oct 10am–5pm, July–Aug 10am–6pm, Nov–Feb Wed–Sun 10am–4pm; charge, English Heritage), the best-preserved and most intact of the border fortresses.

From Ross, take the A449/B4224 towards Hereford. There are opportunities for riverside and woodland walks. To the left of the road is **How Caple Court** (mid-Mar–mid-Oct 10am–5pm; charge), which has 11 acres (4.5 hectares) of beautiful gardens (including a Florentine sunken garden) with great views, interesting walks, a plant shop and a café.

To the right of the road, at **Much Marcle**, is **Hellens** (Easter–Sept Wed, Thur, Sun; guided tours at 2pm, 3pm and 4pm), a Tudor house set in extensive grounds with fish ponds and coppices. There's also a ridge-top picnic spot near Much Marcle.

Hereford

Ignoring all other tempting diversions, make your way now to **Hereford ❸**, the pleasant cathedral city that is capital of the Wye Valley. Its greatest treasure is the 12th-century **Cathedral** (daily 7.30am–6.30pm; tours at 11am and 2pm in summer; donations welcomed), with a lovely early-English Lady Chapel and the restored Shrine of St Thomas of Hereford. The **Mappa Mundi Centre** (Apr–Oct Mon–Sat 10am–4.15pm, Sun 11am–4pm, Oct–Mar Mon–Sat only, until 3pm; charge) displays the largest and finest medieval map of the world, as well as the famous **Chained Library**. Here is an amazing collection of books and manuscrips dating from the 8th–18th century. Every three years the cathedral plays host to the world's oldest music festival, the **Three Choirs Festival** (www.3choirs.org; August 2012, 2015 and so on). On other years the festival is held in Worcester or Gloucester.

The **Hereford Museum and Art Gallery** (Tue–Sat 10am–5pm, Apr–Sept also Sun 10am–4pm; free) opposite the cathedral offers a good introduction to the city and area, plus changing art exhibitions. In Edgar Street on the ring road the **Courtyard Centre for the Arts** is a light and modern venue for theatre, music and dance; it also has an art gallery and restaurant. You may just want to wander along pedestrianised Church Street, linking the cathedral to **High Town**, where you can visit the **Old House** (Tue–Sat 10am–5pm, Apr–Sept also Sun 10am–4pm; free), a handsome half-timbered Jacobean house. In the other direction, south of the cathedral, is the Old Bridge, from where you can walk along the Wye.

The village of **Kilpeck** ❹, about 8 miles (13km) south on the Abergavenny road, has the most wonderfully ornate, red sandstone Norman church in England. **St Mary and St David** was built around 1134–45 and is well preserved, with unusual carvings on the south door, chancel arch and the semicircular apse.

Secondhand book centre

Books for sale at Hay-on-Wye.

Backtracking a little on the A465, take a left turn on to the B4348 for the trip to the border town of **Hay-on-Wye** ❺ (most of the town is in Wales). Hay became a major book centre in the 1970s when an eccentric businessman, Richard Booth, seeing how many shops and cinemas were losing business to the bigger towns, began converting the empty premises into bookshops. Financial difficulties foiled his plan to rule the town unchallenged, and other booksellers moved in. Today, Hay is a

LEFT:
the Hay-on-Wye
Festival.

Hereford Cider

Herefordshire is the place to go for cider. If you are there in spring you will see orchards of trees loaded with pale pink apple blossom, in late summer with rosy cider apples. Perry (made from pears) is also produced. Numerous cider breweries open their doors to visitors, providing demonstrations of cider making, tastings and opportunities to buy. Among the most interesting are Lyne Down Cider (tel: 01531-660 691), Newton Court Cidery (tel: 01568-611 721), which offers orchard tours on request and Dunkerton Cider Mill (tel: 01544-388 653), which has a well-stocked cider shop. Then there's award winning newcomer Once Upon a Tree (tel: 01531-670 263), which produces fine ciders and apple juices. Call in advance for tours. If you want to explore the history of the industry in more detail, visit the Cider Museum and King Offa Distillery (tel: 01432-354 207; www.cidermuseum.co.uk; Tue–Sat Apr–Oct 10am–5pm, Nov–Mar 11am–3pm; charge) in Ryelands St Hereford (the museum is signposted on the ring road), which has a well-stocked shop and café. All these distilleries suggest that you check availability in advance if you would like a tour.

If you fancy exploring Hereford's cider producers by bike or staying on a cider-producing farm, check out the website www.ciderroute.co.uk. It also details any upcoming festivals or special events to do with cider.

book enthusiast's paradise, and in late May/early June the **Hay Festival** (www. hayfestival.com) attracts thousands of readers and high-profile writers to the little town.

Into Shropshire

The A438/A4112 leads via Leominster to **Ludlow** ❻, a lovely town where lie the ashes of A.E. Housman (1859–1936), the poet who immortalised the dreamy slopes of this part of rural England in *A Shropshire Lad*. It's an architecturally pleasing town, with 13th-century taverns and Tudor market buildings. **Ludlow Castle** was the seat of the presidents of the council of the Marcher lords, and it was here that John Milton's play, *Comus*, was first performed in 1634.

More recently Ludlow has spearheaded an English gastronomic revival that has produced more Michelin stars than any town in the UK. West of Ludlow (and just over the Welsh border) is Knighton, a good centre for exploring **Offa's Dyke**. This 8th-century earthwork built by the Saxon King Offa to protect England from the marauding

Welsh runs the length of the England–Wales border and was the first official boundary between England and Wales. Its exact purpose – military or administrative – is uncertain. Compared to Hadrian's Wall, built to keep the Scots at bay, it can hardly be regarded as a serious line of defence. This 1,200-year-old barrier has vanished along some of its route, but walkers can trace its course on the long distance Offa's Dyke Path (www.offas-dyke.co.uk). Hay-on-Wye, Monmouth and Knighton, 17 miles (28km) west of Ludlow are good access points.

North on the A49 lies **Shrewsbury** ❼, beautifully situated on a meander in the River Severn, crossed by the English bridge and the Welsh bridge. It has 15th-century houses, some quaint half-timbered shop fronts, and some fine parks and gardens. The pink sandstone castle near the station was converted into a museum by Thomas Telford (*see next page*) and now incorporates the **Shropshire Regimental Museum** (Easter–mid-Sept daily 10.30am–5pm, Sun until 4pm, Sept–mid-Dec Tue–Sat 10.30am–4pm). The solid and unas-

Fact File

Location The area follows the Welsh border from south to north, taking in parts of Herefordshire, Shropshire and Cheshire.

By car Via the M4/M5/M50 from London to Ross-on-Wye; M5 from Birmingham; M56 from Manchester to Chester.

By coach Tel: 08705-808 080, www.nationalexpress.co.uk.

By rail London Paddington to Hereford, journey time approx. 2 hours 45 minutes; tel: 08457-484 950.

Main events Hay Festival, literature and the arts, (www.hayfestival). com; Ross-on-Wye International Arts Festival, Hereford Three Choirs Festival (www.3choirs.org).

For children Alton Towers Theme Park, tel: 08705-204 060; Gladstone Working Pottery Museum. Come along and make a souvenir to take home (tel: 01782-237777; charge).

Most famous sons Industrial pioneer Abraham Darby (1678–1717); naturalist Charles Darwin (1809–82); poet Wilfred Owen (1893–1918).

Tourist information Hay-on-Wye, tel: 01497-820 144, www.hay-on-wye.co.uk/tourism; Hereford, tel: 01432-268 430, www.visithereford-shire.co.uk; Ludlow, tel: 01584-875 053, www.ludlow.org.uk; Ross-on-Wye, tel: 01989-562 768; Stoke-on-Trent, tel: 01782-236 000, www.visitstoke.co.uk.

suming **Cathedral** is built of the same reddish stone as the castle.

Shrewsbury is the birthplace of scientist Charles Darwin (1809–82), whose *Origin of the Species* revolutionised Victorian ways of thinking. The World War I poet Wilfred Owen (1893–1918) was also born here.

Ironbridge to Chester

East of Shrewsbury on the A5/M54 is **Telford**, a new town named after the 18th-century engineer Thomas Telford. Initiated in the 1960s, the ambitious project takes in **Coalbrookdale** and **Ironbridge** ❽ on the River Severn, where the world's first iron bridge was built by Telford in 1773. It was in Coalbrookdale, a region rich in natural resources which had been a mining centre since the time of Henry VIII, that Bristol brassmaker Abraham Darby pioneered the use of coke to smelt iron, thus making the process much cheaper while retaining high quality, and turning the area into the busiest industrial centre in the world.

Nine different museums, which include original furnaces, foundries, brick works, the Coalport china works and a recreated Victorian town, are incorporated in the splendid **Ironbridge Gorge Museum** (daily 10am–5pm; a passport ticket allows repeated entry to all museums for one year).

Our next port of call (north on the A442/A41) is **Chester** ❾, the most northerly and the most exciting of the timbered Tudor towns of the Welsh Marches. Its particular architectural character can be seen in the so-called **Rows** of double-tiered and covered walkways as you walk down Eastgate, Westgate or Bridge Street. The oldest of the Rows dates from 1486, and most of them from the 16th century.

In Roman times Chester was an important stronghold called Deva; part of an amphitheatre can be seen just outside the city walls, by St John's Street.

The Market Hall in Ludlow.

BELOW: the Wye from Symond's Yat.

Screams galore at Alton Towers.

The **Grosvenor Museum** (Mon–Sat 10.30am–5pm, Sun 1–4pm; free) records the Roman legacy with models of the ancient fortress city. Under the Normans, Chester became a near-independent state governed by a succession of earls. The tidal estuary of the River Dee allowed the city to flourish as a port until the 15th century, when the estuary began to silt up. After that, shipping was transferred to the natural port of Liverpool.

The 2-mile (3km) walk around the city walls will help you to get orientated. This is one of the few British cities with its medieval walls still intact, with those on the north and east sides following the original Roman plan. The **Cathedral** was a Benedictine abbey until the Dissolution of the Monasteries under Henry VIII. An unusually square building, it has a massive south transept featuring a grand Victorian stained-glass window.

Due east of the city via the A54/34 is **Little Moreton Hall** (mid-Mar–end Oct Wed–Sun 11am–5pm; charge), an ornately decorated, half-timbered and moated manor house, built in the late 15th century, which is worth an expedition if you have time.

The Potteries

Stoke-on-Trent ⑩ was made famous by Arnold Bennett (1867–1931) in his novels of the "Five Towns", in which he described provincial life with a discernment and attention to detail that has rarely been matched.

Thousands of people come here simply to pick up a bargain at the factory shops, selling everything from dinner services to ceramic jewellery, and with "seconds" on sale at reduced prices. But Stoke is also a progressive town with a lively centre and the newly opened **Cultural Quarter** where the Victoria Hall stages classical and rock music, comedy and children's shows and the Regent Theatre hosts touring productions of opera, ballet and musicals.

All the big names in pottery were once represented here, but many have sadly closed down in recent years. **Wedgwood** however, has a visitor cen-

tre (Mon–Fri 9am–5pm, Sat–Sun 10am–5pm; charge) which – in an imaginative and entertaining way – allows you to explore the history and craft of ceramics, to have a go at throwing or painting a pot and, of course, to visit their working factory. Beside the visitor centre is a excellent new Wedgwood Museum (combined tickets available with visitor centre), which tells the story of Wedgwood with interactive displays and fascinating exhibits covering 250 years of ceramic history. The collection includes a vase thrown by Josiah Wedgwood himself.

When you've had enough of pottery, there are a number of places to visit in the vicinity. About 7 miles (12km) north of Stoke-on-Trent is **Biddulph Grange Garden** (mid-Mar–Oct Wed–Fri 11am–5pm, July–Aug also Mon–Tue, Nov–early Mar Sat–Sun only 11am–3pm; charge), an unusual Victorian garden in which visitors are taken on a miniature tour, from an Egyptian Court to a mini-Great Wall of China, as well as a pinetum and a fernery. Or there's the **Dorothy Clive Garden** (mid-Mar–end Sept daily 10am–5.30pm; charge) near Market Drayton, which is glorious in early summer when the rhododendrons are in full bloom and has pleasant woodlands at any time of the year; and the **Shugborough Estate** (Apr–Oct daily 11am–5pm; charge), the magnificent ancestral seat of the Earls of Lichfield which is being restored as a 19th-century working estate. The stable block houses the original 18th-century kitchens, there is a walled garden and, of course, the mansion itself. The grounds contain eight nationally important monuments, including the Shepherd's Monument, which many believe has links to the Holy Grail.

When the children have tired of all this, cart them off on the short trip to **Alton Towers** (Mar–Nov daily), the country's leading theme park, which is constantly updating its thrills and spills. The rides range from adrenalin-filled Nemesis, to gentle ones that are suitable for small children. There's a new pirate themed aquarium, a water park – even a hotel and a spa. ❑

Chester Cathedral's south transept.

BELOW: pottery gilding in Stoke-on-Trent.

DERBY TO THE EAST COAST

The Pilgrim Fathers, Robin Hood and D.H. Lawrence all have links with this region, which spans the Midlands, incorporating bulb fields and family-friendly beaches

Settled snugly in the centre of England, **Derby** ❶ is a useful jumping-off point for the Peak District *(see page 271)* but it's also a lively city in its own right, with plenty to see and do, and with good public transport making a car unnecessary. In Irongate, the oldest (and most upmarket) part of town, there's the **Cathedral** (daily 8.30am–6pm; donations welcomed) with a fine wrought-iron screen, as well as boutiques and restaurants. Nearby, on the Strand, is the **Derby Museum and Art Gallery** (Mon 11am–5pm, Tue–Sat 10am–5pm, Sun 2–5pm; free), home to the world's largest public collection of works by 18th-century local artist Joseph Wright. On Friar Gate is Pickford's House Museum (hours as Derby Museum), a fine Georgian house where interiors recreate the appearance of the house in its heyday. On the top floor is a servant's bedroom with a straw mattress. The house also contains a large costume collection. The city's lively in the evening, with plenty of bars and cinemas.

Kedleston Hall (mid-Mar–end Oct Sat–Wed, house: noon–5pm, park: 10am–6pm; charge), 5 miles (8km) from the city centre, is a splendid 18th-century Palladian mansion complete with Robert Adams interiors, a huge collection of paintings, and an **Eastern Museum**, housing objects collected by Lord Curzon, the owner, when Viceroy of India (1899–1905). The property, which has extensive grounds, was used as a location in the film *The Duchess* starring Keira Knightley.

A town without a sheriff

Return to Derby (or skirt it to the south) and take the A52 to **Nottingham** ❷, the cultural and nightlife hub of the East Midlands, with two popular universities. It's an attractive city centred around a broad market square, with two large shopping centres, the original Paul Smith shop (the designer is a local lad), a major arts complex

Main attractions
JOSEPH WRIGHT PAINTINGS AT DERBY MUSEUM
CLUMBER PARK
LINCOLN CATHEDRAL
BURGHLEY HOUSE

PRECEDING PAGES: National Fishing Heritage Centre, Grimsby. **LEFT:** Ferris Wheel, Nottingham. **BELOW:** Derby Cathedral.

Lincoln Cathedral.

tours of the castle caves (Mon–Sat, 11am–2pm, 3pm; charge) but be warned, they are quite strenuous.

Nottingham is also famous as the birthplace of the writer D.H. Lawrence *(see opposite)*, and for its lace making. To discover more about the history of life in the city, visit the Museum of Nottingham Life (daily 10am–4.30pm; charge) in Brewhouse Yard at the base of the castle rock. Set in five 17th-century cottages, it covers 300 years of social history and contains a reconstructed Victorian schoolroom.

Go west of the city and you'll come to **Wollaton Hall** (daily Apr–Oct 11am–5pm, Nov–Mar 11am–4pm; free), a fine Elizabethan mansion that is also home to the city's Natural History Museum and Industrial Museum. The house was recently restored and visitors can now see the Tudor kitchens, as well as the Regency Dining Room and Salon.

Go to Ravenshead in the northern outskirts to visit **Newstead Abbey** (house: Apr–Sept Fri–Mon noon–5pm, gardens: year-round 9am–dusk; charge). The ancestral home of Lord

and myriad bars and restaurants. In popular imagination, the city is still associated with Sherwood Forest, Robin Hood and the evil sheriff. The Norman gatehouse of **Nottingham Castle** remains intact, set in impressive grounds, and houses the **Castle Museum and Art Gallery** (daily Mar–Sept 10am–5pm, Oct–Feb 10am–4pm; charge) with collections of silver, glass, armour and paintings. There are also

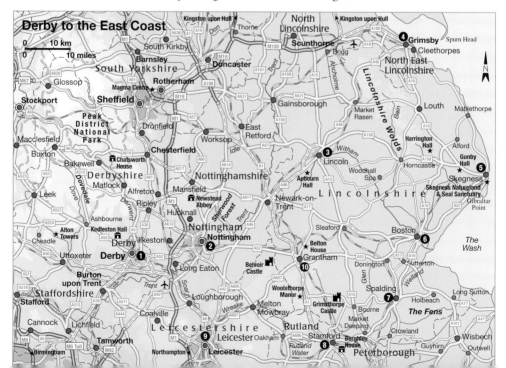

Byron, the house is surrounded by lakes, terraces and Japanese and Spanish gardens. A little further north is **Clumber Park** (park: daily during daylight hours, walled garden: Apr–Oct Mon–Fri 10am–5pm, end Oct–end Jan daily), one of Nottingham's famous "Dukeries" or large hunting estates, consisting of park-, farm- and woodland, a serpentine lake, and a walled garden enclosing a Victorian apiary, fig house and vineries.

Lincoln

Take the A57 now towards **Lincoln ❸**, which towers impressively over its flat Fenland setting. It's a city with Roman, Norman, medieval and Georgian influences, with a well-preserved historic area at the top of the hill, and the modern town below. You can get a good look at the city by taking a canal trip on the *Brayford Belle* (daily, summer only; tel: 01522-881 200).

The three towers of its magnificent **Cathedral** (Mon–Sat 7.15am–6pm, Sun until 5pm, end June–end Aug Mon–Fri until 8pm, Sat–Sun until 6pm; charge) dominate the skyline

from afar. The building, which featured as a location in the film the *Da Vinci Code*, is an attractive blend of Norman and Gothic, and has some fascinating misericords in the choir stalls. Concerts, recitals and exhibitions are staged here (tel: 01522-561 600 for details).

Lincoln Castle (Apr and Sept 10am–5pm, May–Aug 10am–6pm; Oct–Mar until 4pm) is also Norman in origin, although there have been many

The entrance gate at Lincoln Castle.

LEFT: England's oldest pub, Ye Olde Trip to Jerusalem, on Brewhouse Yard, Castle Road, Nottingham.

D.H. Lawrence

The first thing that most people associate with D.H. Lawrence is *Lady Chatterley's Lover*, first published in 1928, but later banned because of its sexual content. It was not published unexpurgated until 1963 after an unsuccessful prosecution for obscenity. This was his last but one novel, finished when he was already slowly dying of tuberculosis, and was the culmination of a prolific writing career that included collections of short stories and poems as well as novels.

Born in Nottingham in 1885, Lawrence was the son of a miner, and a product of the Victorian concern to make education available to the poor. But while far more working-class children were reading books, few were writing them. His mother, an ex-teacher, was determined he should not follow his father down the pit, and encouraged him to study – he eventually won a scholarship to Nottingham University College. The bond between mother and son was recreated in the autobiographical *Sons and Lovers* (1913). In 1912 he met his future wife, Frieda (already married to one of his professors); their life together was turbulent and peripatetic, as they travelled in Australia, the USA and Mexico. His last years, when in failing health, were spent in Italy and the south of France. He died in France in 1930. Visit his Birthplace Museum (daily 10am–5pm, winter until 4pm) in the village of Eastwood.

later additions. For 900 years it served as the town prison. It contains a copy of the Magna Carta, one of only four left in the country, signed and sealed by King John at Runnymede in 1215.

Among the city's many fine Norman and medieval buildings is the **Jew's House** in The Strait, dating from the 1170s, a reminder when a large Jewish community flourished here, and believed to be the oldest surviving example of domestic architecture in the country.

If you have time for only one museum or gallery, make it the **Usher Gallery** (daily 10am–4pm; free) in Lindum Road where there are works by Peter de Wint, J.M.W. Turner, L.S. Lowry and Walter Sickert, as well as memorabilia relating to the Lincolnshire-born Poet Laureate Lord Alfred Tennyson (1809–92), whose statue stands in the cathedral grounds. The gallery has joined forces with the new, adjacent archaeological museum to form **The Collection**, which includes a wealth of artefacts from the Iron Age and the Roman, Saxon, Viking and medieval eras.

RIGHT: statue of Robin Hood in front of Nottingham Castle.

The Lincolnshire coast

Grimsby ❹ (about 50 minutes' drive northeast of Lincoln on the A46) is situated on the east coast at the mouth of the River Humber, with access to miles of safe and sandy beaches. Sadly, the fishing industry which brought prosperity to the town in the 19th century has dwindled to almost nothing in recent years, but the ethos and atmosphere remain.

At the **National Fishing Heritage Centre** (summer Mon–Fri 10am–4pm, Sat–Sun 10.30am–5.30pm, winter Mon–Fri until 4pm, Sat–Sun until 3pm) some superior interactive displays take you on a credible trip through old Grimsby and its port, and allow you to roam around a restored 1950s trawler. Afterwards, you can buy good smoked fish from **Alfred Enderby Traditional Fish Smokers** in Fish Dock Road (tel: 01472-342 984).

Popular family resorts on this coast include Cleethorpes (closest to Grimsby), Mablethorpe and, best known of all, **Skegness** ❺, with 6 miles (10km) of safe and sandy beaches. Here, accommodated in one

Fact File

Location Lying just to the south of the Peak District (for which Derby and Nottingham are good jumping-off points) and covering a swath of middle England between The Wash and the mouth of the River Humber.

By car The M1 to Derby or Nottingham (Exit 25) takes about 2 hours from north London (allow at least 3 hours from central London).

By coach National Express coach service from London Victoria, about 3 hours, tel: 08705-808 080, www.nationalexpress.co.uk.

By train About 1 hour 40 minutes to both Derby and Nottingham from London St Pancras, tel: 08457-484 950.

For children Butterfly and Wildlife Park, Spalding; the beaches of Skegness, Cleethorpes and Mablethorpe; Skegness Natureland Seal Sanctuary, www.skegnessnatureland.co.uk

Best theatres Nottingham Playhouse.

Famous sons (and daughter) Alfred, Lord Tennyson; D.H. Lawrence; Sir Isaac Newton; Lady Thatcher.

Tourist information Derby, tel: 01332-255 802, www.visitderby.com; Leicester, tel: 0844-888 5181, www.goleicester.com; Lincoln, tel: 01522-873 213, www.visitlincolnshire.com; Nottingham, tel: 0115-915 5330, www.visitnottingham.com.

of the many small hotels or bed-and-breakfast establishments, children can build sandcastles and enjoy donkey rides, and parents can take advantage of gardens and bowling greens as they did in the days before the Costa Brava beckoned. It was here in 1936 that Billy Butlin opened the first Butlin's Holiday Camp.

The **Magic World of Fantasy Island** (tel: 01754-615 860; Easter week and May–Nov daily 10.30am, closing times vary) offers entertainment when the beach palls or the weather is bad; and the **Skegness Natureland Seal Sanctuary** (tel: 01754-764 345; daily 10am–5pm, winter until 4pm) in North Parade aims to combine education and conservation with entertainment. Many unusual animals have been guests at the sanctuary, including dolphins, whales, oiled seabirds and injured birds of prey.

American connections

From Skegness the A52 parallels the coast, then turns inland a short way to **Boston ⑥** on the banks of the River Witham. It's an attractive little town,

and has one of the finest produce markets in Lincolnshire, held each Wednesday and Saturday. On Wednesday, produce is auctioned in Bargate Green, an entertaining event even if you don't intend to buy. Boston also has the tallest working windmill in England, the Maud Foster Windmill, and a church tower, known as the Boston Stump, which soars to 272ft (83 metres).

Modern artists are much in evidence here: murals are created all over town to disguise empty or neglected properties; the Memorial Gardens Archway is a modern piece in forged steel; and gracefully poised welded steel sculptures of human figures by artist Rick Kirby are displayed in Friary Court.

Most of all, Boston is known for its American connections. It was here that the Pilgrim Fathers were tried and imprisoned for trying to leave the country. The **Guildhall** (Wed–Sat 10.30am–3.30pm; charge) contains the cells where the Pilgrim Fathers were confined in 1607, and the **Pilgrim Fathers' Memorial** stands on the river bank near the sea, on the spot where they were arrested.

TIP

Lincolnshire is well known for its markets, which are held throughout the county. If you enjoy the bustle of a market and the chance to buy fresh produce, contact the local tourist offices for times and venues.

LEFT: St Botolph's Church, whose tower is known as the Boston Stump.
BELOW: Boston town centre.

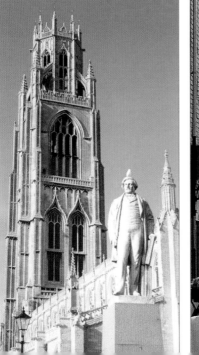

Stamford High Street in the rain.

Spalding to Stamford

From Boston we head southwest on the A16 to **Spalding** ❼, the heart of the Lincolnshire bulb industry. If you come here in spring you will see acres of tulips, hyacinths and daffodils, and all summer long you can visit the **Bulb Museum** (Apr–Oct daily 10am–4pm; free), which depicts the industry from 1880 to the present. **Spalding Tropical Forest** (daily 10am–5.30pm; charge) offers more exotic delights, with rainforests, Oriental gardens, waterfalls, orchids and sweet-scented climbing flowers; while the **Butterfly and Wildlife Park** (Mar–end June daily 10am–5pm, end June–early Sept until 5.30pm, rest of Sept–end Oct until 4.30pm; charge) keeps its butterflies in a free-flying environment and stages birds of prey flying displays twice daily (usually at noon and 3pm).

Keep to the A16 to reach **Stamford** ❽, a mellow stone-built town with five medieval churches, and some streets and squares in which all the buildings pre-date the Victorian era. The **Stamford Museum** (Mon–Sat 10am–4pm; free) gives a good historical background to the town, but its best-loved exhibits, with adults and children alike, are the wax models of Daniel Lambert, once England's fattest man (who collapsed and died at Stamford Races in 1809) and Tom Thumb, the smallest. The museum also produces useful Town Trails, to make sure you don't miss anything, from the peaceful water meadows to the 12th-century priory.

Just to the south of Stamford is **Burghley House** (www.burghley.co.uk; end Mar–end Oct daily 11am–5pm; charge), one of the most glorious Elizabethan mansions in the country. Built in the late 16th century for William Cecil, the first Lord Burghley and treasurer to Elizabeth I, this has been a family home ever since, which gives it a special atmosphere lacking in many stately homes.

The state rooms hold a wonderful collection of paintings, furniture, porcelain and tapestries; and the deer park, landscaped by "Capability"

Brown, is delightful. A newly planted sculpture garden is open on the same days as the house.

Leicester and Grantham

Due west on the A47 lies **Leicester ❾**, a busy modern city with ancient origins. **Castle Park** is the historic heart: the castle gardens and riverside are tranquil spots for walking, and the city's Saxon, Roman and medieval forebears are all represented. Visit the **New Walk Museum** (Mon–Sat 10am–5pm, Sun 11am–5pm) for a wonderfully eclectic display, ranging from Ancient Egyptian artefacts to dinosaurs. The museum's art collection contains works by Bacon, Durer and Lowry as well as examples of German Expressionism.

Leicester's markets are also worth seeing: the great food hall in the **Market Centre** (Tue–Sat 7am–6pm) and the outdoor **Retail Market** (Mon–Sat 7.30am–6pm) both offer a vast selection of fresh food and other goods.

From here you can return to Nottingham or head south to London on the M1, but if you have time, pay a visit to **Grantham ❿**, a pleasant old town of red-brick and half-timbered houses with a steepled parish church. It used to be famous for its connections with Sir Isaac Newton (1642–1727), who propounded the theory of gravitation, and who was born at nearby Woolsthorpe Manor, but these days it is better known as the birthplace of Margaret Thatcher, the Conservative prime minister who dominated British politics in the 1980s; she was brought up here above her father's grocer shop. Friendly little **Grantham Museum** (Mon–Sat 10am–4pm; free) in St Peter's Hill explores the town's links with both of them, and much more.

Just north of the town on the A607 is the elegant 17th-century **Belton House** (mid-Mar–end Oct Wed–Sun 11am–5pm; charge) with a formal topiaried walk and an Orangery. For those too young to be interested in such things as houses and gardens, there's an adventure playground and an activity room. ❑

Leicester's historic heart.

LEFT: Leicester's Concert Hall.
BELOW: a tranquil spot in Castle Park.

THE PEAK DISTRICT

Bleak and challenging in parts, but threaded
with pure rivers and dotted with idyllic villages
and some splendid stately homes, the Peaks
are a walker's paradise

The Peak District is a region of outstanding beauty lying at the southern end of the Pennines. It's the last knobbly vertebrae on "the backbone of England" and the first real hill country encountered by travellers heading north from London. Over the years, as a centre of lead mining, then of silk and cotton production, it has been much changed by man, but retains some wild and wonderful walking country. Today, it is highly acccessible, and much visited: surrounded by the conurbations of the North and the Midlands, it has over 100 roads running through the area. It is the nearest National Park to London (and also the first, founded in 1950) and easily reached by the M1 motorway.

Our tour will begin in Matlock, in the southern Peaks, the largest town and the administrative centre of the district. Modern **Matlock ❶** was created by John Smedley, a 19th-century industrialist who watched over its development from **Riber Castle**, which overlooks the town from its commanding hilltop to the south. From here, take the A6, crossing the bridge over the River Derwent and passing into the Derwent Gorge, where high limestone crags crowd in on the left. Soon the biggest of the lot, the 300ft (90-metre) **High Tor** appears, almost overhanging the road, with rock climbers clinging to the rock face like flies on a wall. Just beyond High Tor the swinging gondolas of the **Heights of Abraham Cable**

Cars (tel: 01629-582 365; daily mid-Mar–end Sept 10am–5pm, Oct 10am–4.30pm; charge) can be seen. The Heights of Abraham, named after General Wolfe's 1759 victory in Quebec, are reached by turning left as you enter Matlock Bath. They include the **Rutland and Great Masson Caverns** (times as above), former lead mines that now provide exciting underground tours, picnic sites and nature trails up to the **Victoria Prospect Tower**, built in 1844 and commanding stupendous views across the gorge.

Main attractions
ARKWRIGHT'S MILL
DOVEDALE
CHATSWORTH HOUSE
CRESSWELL CRAGS
BAKEWELL
BUXTON

PRECEDING PAGES:
mill stones at
Stanage Edge.
LEFT: a climber on
High Tor.
BELOW: Matlock
Bath.

Mines, mills and Stilton cheese

Matlock Bath **②** became popular as a holiday spot in Victorian times when the railways arrived. Today, it is well known as a weekend destination for motor bikes and for its illuminations over the Lovers' Walks along the Derwent from late August to early October. Among its modern attractions is the **Peak District Mining Museum** (daily summer 10am–5pm, winter 11am–4pm; charge) in the Pavilion, a fascinating introduction to the world of the lead miner, with tunnels through which children can crawl. **Gulliver's Theme Park** (June–Aug daily 10.30am–4.30pm; times vary at other periods of the year, so tel: 01925-444 888 for details) is set high on a hillside above Matlock Bath and has river rides and a mine train.

Follow the A6 through Matlock Bath to **Cromford ③**. Richard Arkwright, one of the architects of the Industrial Revolution, came here in 1771 to build the world's first water-powered cotton mill and create an industrial village that was a wonder of the age. It was poor communications that stopped the Derwent Valley becoming one of the principal centres of that world-shattering revolution. **Arkwright's Cromford Mill** (daily 9am–5pm; charge for tour), a world heritage site, is clearly signposted. Tours around the village are arranged from the Arkwright Mill.

Cable cars to the Heights of Abraham.

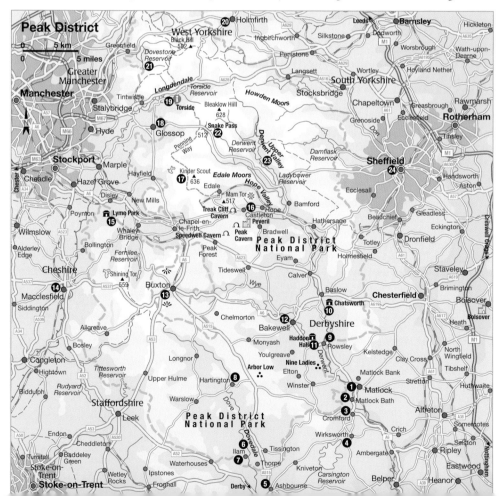

Workers' cottages in North Street off the Wirksworth road, completed in 1776, show how Arkwright wanted his workers to live.

A little further on is Cromford Wharf and the **High Peak Junction Workshops** (Apr–Sept daily 10.30am–5.30pm, Oct–Mar Sat–Sun 10am–4pm) of the **Cromford Canal**, which runs for 5 miles (8km) to Ambergate. Turn right at Scarthin Nick crossroads and left up a steep hill, passing the outstanding viewpoint of the **Black Rocks of Cromford**. Here there's a picnic site and access to the **High Peak Trail**, a route that follows the line of the former Cromford and High Peak Railway, completed in 1831 as an extension of the Cromford Canal. As the road enters quarry-scarred **Wirksworth ❹**, signs indicate the **National Stone Centre** (Apr–Sept daily 10am–5pm, Oct–Mar until 4pm), an exciting attraction with treasure trails, audiovisual shows and exhibitions, set in a former limestone quarry by the High Peak Trail.

Roam the narrow streets to appreciate the atmosphere of Wirksworth, which has been a lead-mining centre for centuries. Its story is graphically told in the **Wirksworth Heritage Centre** (Apr–end Sept Wed–Sat 10.30am–4.30pm, Sun 1.30–4.30pm; charge). Created in a former silk and velvet mill, this award-winning centre has three floors of interpretive displays and exhibits, including a replica quarryman's house from the early 20th century. There is also a licensed restaurant.

Wirksworth's sloping **Market Place** has many fine 18th- and 19th-century buildings, including the Moot Hall (not open to the public). The **Parish Church of St Mary** is mainly 13th-century, and contains a wonderful 7th-century carved coffin lid.

Continue along the B5035 to **Ashbourne ❺**, "the gateway to Dovedale". The **Parish Church of St Oswald** is one of the finest in the Peak District, and its soaring 14th-century spire is an elegant landmark. Nearby, in Church Street, is the beautiful gabled and mullion-windowed Elizabethan Old Grammar School (private). On the way to the cobbled Market Place, you will

Richard Arkwright invented a horse-driven spinning frame before the water-powered one at Cromford. He was knighted in 1786 and became high sheriff of Derbyshire the following year.

LEFT:
St Oswald's church spire dominates the skyline in Ashbourne.

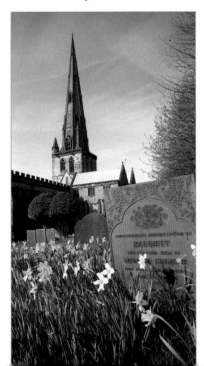

Fact File

By car About 2½ hours on the M1 motorway from north London; leave at Exit 28 (Matlock) for the southern dales, Exit 29 (Chesterfield) for the central and northern areas.

By coach National Express daily coach services from London and Manchester. A good coach service also links the main Peak District towns, tel: 08705-808 080.

By train About 2 hours from London St Pancras to Derby, Nottingham, Chesterfield and Sheffield. Local services link with the main Peak District towns, tel: 08457-484 950.

Main towns Matlock, Buxton, Bakewell.

Special events Buxton International Festival of Music and the Arts (late July); well-dressing ceremonies throughout the summer.

For children Chatsworth Farm and Children's Adventure Playground; Gulliver's Kingdom Theme Park, Matlock Bath; the Ranger Service runs children's fun days and activities throughout the summer, www.peakdistrict.gov.uk.

Local specialities Bakewell puddings; Stilton cheese.

Tourist information Bakewell, tel: 01629-816 558; Buxton, tel: 01298-25106; Chesterfield tel: 01246-345 777; Matlock tel: 01629-583 388.

*Honey for sale in
Hartington.*

BELOW: Ilam Hall.

come to the restored timber-framed **Gingerbread Shop**, which still makes the local delicacy on the premises. The **Tourist Information Centre** (tel: 01335-343 666) is in the Market Place.

Take the A515 Buxton road up a steep hill to the north, then turn left on a minor road signposted to Thorpe and Dovedale. Thorpe is an unpretentious limestone village standing at the foot of **Thorpe Cloud** (942ft/287 metres), one of the sentinels of **Dovedale 6**, probably the most famous and certainly the most popular and overused of the White Peak dales (National Trust; car park). Over a million people visit it every year, and the National Park and footpath authorities run a continuous programme of repairs to the 7-mile (11km) path that runs north through the dale to Hartington. Go beyond the famous **Stepping Stones** beneath Thorpe Cloud and Bunster Hill (many people don't) to the famous series of rock pinnacles and caves such as Tissington Spires, Ilam Rock, Pickering Tor and Reynard's Cave, with its natural archway.

Just beyond the Dovedale turn is the quaint estate village of **Ilam 7**, largely rebuilt by 19th-century shipping magnate Jesse Watts Russell in neo-Gothic style. Russell lived at mock-Gothic **Ilam Hall** (grounds and park: daily during daylight hours; hall private). In the grounds stands the beautiful **Church of the Holy Cross**, a mixture of Saxon, Norman and Early English.

Make your way back to the A515 and head north to **Hartington 8**. You'll cross the line of the Tissington Trail at the **Hartington Station National Park Visitor Centre**, housed in a railway-signal box – children love it because they can operate the signals. Hartington has a wonderful youth hostel in a Jacobean hall, and is the home of the **Stilton Cheese Factory**, one of only a few in the country. Return to the main road and take the A5012 back towards Matlock.

Some 10 miles (16km) up the A6 from Matlock is **Rowsley 9**, with the splendid 17th-century Peacock Hotel.

Opposite it, a road leads to **Caudwell's Mill and Craft Centre** (daily Apr–Oct 10am–6pm, Nov–Feb 10am–4.30pm; charge). This 19th-century mill on the Wye, one of few working water-powered roller mills, was lovingly restored by a group of enthusiasts and still produces and sells flour. Local craftspeople work in the former stableyard.

Stately homes

From here, the B6012 takes you to **Chatsworth House** ❿ (house: mid-Mar–end Oct daily 11am–5.30pm, charge; park: year round, free). Home of the Dukes of Devonshire for some 400 years, and known as "the Palace of the Peaks", this is one of the finest houses in England, and contains one of the most important private art collections in the country.

Highlights of the tour include the magnificent **Painted Hall** by Louis Laguerre, which shows scenes from the life of Julius Caesar, and is the setting for the annual Chatsworth Children's Christmas Party. The **State Rooms** are stunning in their opulence.

Note the superb 17th-century English tapestries in the Drawing Room, the wonderful painted ceiling, again by Laguerre, in the State Bedroom, and Jan Vandervaart's famous *trompe l'oeil* violin "hanging" behind a door. The **Great Dining Room** is where the young Princess Victoria had her first dinner with the grown-ups in 1832; it is notable for its gold-encrusted barrel ceiling and fine collection of paintings. On a different scale, but also impressive, is the series of small rooms known as the **Queen of Scots Rooms**, where the unfortunate monarch lodged during several stays between 1570 and 1581.

The house as we see it today is largely the creation of the 4th Earl and the Dutch architect William Talman, and it was built in the Palladian style between 1678 and 1707. The only part of the original 16th-century Tudor house that remains is the **Hunting Tower** (private), up through the trees of Stand Wood behind the house. Also in Stand Wood is the **Chatsworth Farm and Children's Adventure Playground**.

The Peak District is misleadingly named. Visitors seek in vain for sharply-pointed mountain tops. In fact, the name comes from the Old English peac, *which simply meant a hill. In the 10th-century Anglo Saxon Chronicle, the area was known as* Peaclond – *the hilly land.*

BELOW: Chatsworth House, the "Palace of the Peaks".

The Plague Village of Eyam

The village of Eyam (pronounced "eem") is perhaps the most evocative place in the Peak District. In September 1665 a piece of cloth for the tailor arrived from London. It was infested with rat fleas, the carriers of the bubonic plague. By May 1666, 73 villagers had died. So the villagers held a public meeting and agreed to place themselves under quarantine – cutting themselves off from the world to prevent the disease spreading further afield. Food and medicine was donated from nearby Chatsworth House and left at designated points. The villagers, now unable to flee, suffered terribly and, by the time the plague had run its course, 260 people were dead. Plaques mark plague houses and there are plague graves all over the village, including the churchyard.

Enjoying Chatsworth Playground.

Were you to go east now along the A619, you would soon reach **Chesterfield**, famed for the crooked 14th-century spire of the Parish Church. It has a spiral design and a distinct tilt. The design was deliberate, but the crookedness came from a lack of skilled workmen, due to the Black Death, and the use of green timber in construction.

Further east and into Nottinghamshire is a fine archaeological site in Welbeck, Worksop: **Creswell Crags** (Feb–Oct daily 10.30am–4.30pm; charge). This is a limestone gorge and caves which contain the only known examples of Ice Age rock art in Britain. There is a museum and new visitor centre, and guided tours to see the cave paintings are available (book first, tel: 01909-720 378).

Back in the Peak District and about a mile up the A6 from Rowsley is another famous stately home, **Haddon Hall ⑪** (Apr and Oct Sat–Mon noon–5pm, May–Sept daily noon–5pm; charge), home of the Duke of Rutland and known as "the most romantic medieval manor house in England", a description that is hard to dispute. Haddon is remarkably unrestored: most of what you see from the sloping **Lower Courtyard** dates from the 14th and 15th centuries. The time-worn steps and oak-panelled rooms breathe history. Among the highlights are: the wonderful **Banqueting Hall**, the very essence of a medieval manor house, complete with minstrels' gallery and massive 13th-century oak refectory table; the **Long Gallery**, with elaborate oak panelling featuring the boar's head and the peacock of the founding families; and the **Kitchen**, stone-flagged and stone-walled, with massive oak tables, chopping blocks and mixing bowls almost worn through with centuries of use.

The **Chapel of St Nicholas**, one of the oldest parts of the house, originally served the now-disappeared village of Nether Haddon. It contains some of the finest 14th- and 15th-century wall paintings in Britain. The tour ends with the famous terraced gardens: a riot of roses, clematis and other blossoms in summer.

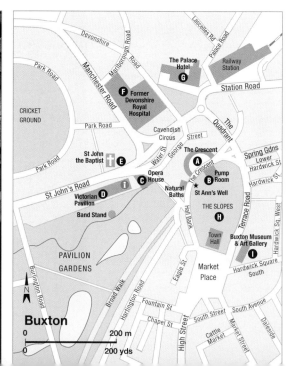

Buxton

0   200 m
0   200 yds

Bakewell

Beyond Haddon Hall you come to **Bakewell** ⑫ whose history goes back to the Saxons, as a visit to the parish church of **All Saints** will reveal: although heavily restored in Victorian times, the cruciform church still has fragments of Saxon and Norman work, and two of the finest Saxon preaching crosses in the Peak District are situated in the churchyard.

Just behind the church is the **Old House Museum** (Apr–Oct daily 11am–4pm), one of the finest local museums in the country. It is housed in a 1534 Tudor building, which was used in the 19th century by Richard Arkwright as accommodation for workers employed at his mill on the Wye. There are collections of memorabilia, costumes, lace, samplers and toys, and the Victorian kitchen is retained, along with recreated craftsmen's workshops.

Back in the centre of town, visit the **Old Market Hall National Park and Tourist Information Centre** (tel: 01629-816 558) in Bridge Street. The arcaded building dates from the 17th century, and was for many years used as a market hall. Displays tell the story of the town and the Peak District. There is a well-stocked shop where maps and guides are on sale.

Outside the Tourist Information Centre is the **Old Original Bakewell Pudding Shop**, one of three in the town that claim to hold the original recipe to this much-loved almond and puff-pastry confection. The story is that it was created when a flustered cook at the 17th-century Rutland Arms Hotel in nearby Rutland Square poured her pastry mix over the jam instead of the other way around. Whether this is true or not, the pudding (or tart, as it is known outside the region) has become synonymous with Bakewell.

The northern spa

Leaving Bakewell, follow the A6 through the pretty Wye Valley to **Buxton** ⑬. Start by admiring the elegant Corinthian-styled buildings of the

Crescent Ⓐ, now beautifully restored after many years of neglect. Designed by York architect John Carr in the 1780s, it was part of the master plan of the 5th Duke of Devonshire to make Buxton a fashionable spa town. The **Assembly Rooms**, once used for church services, have been restored as part of the public library. The **Thermal Baths** have become the Cavendish Shopping Arcade, but they retain a plunge pool complete with bosun's chair-type seat showing how some patients were encouraged to "take the waters".

Opposite the Crescent is the low classical structure built in 1894 and known as **The Pump Room** Ⓑ. The building is now closed to the public, but you can still use the drinking fountain outside, known locally as **St Ann's Well** – the scene during July of one of the town's well-dressing ceremonies. There are often queues of people waiting to fill containers with the warm, blue, slightly effervescent water.

Walk past the Natural Baths and up

Try the original Bakewell puddings.

BELOW: the Long Gallery, Haddon Hall.

BELOW: the Buxton
Opera House.
RIGHT: tropical
plants in the
Victorian Pavilion
Conservatory.

to the corner of The Square, where massive gritstone "cloisters" face the attractive Pavilion Gardens. Turn right at the corner and you'll see the ornate, twin-domed frontage of the **Opera House** Ⓒ, designed and built in the grand Edwardian style by the eminent theatrical architect Frank Matcham in 1905 and sensitively restored in 1979, after serving for many years as a cinema. It seats 1,000 people in a magnificently decorated auditorium lit by a massive gas-fired crystal chandelier. The theatre stages a varied programme of comedy, drama, ballet and concerts, as well as opera, and is the home of the widely acclaimed **Buxton International Festival of Music and the Arts**, held annually at the end of July.

Beside the theatre is the splendid **Victorian Pavilion** Ⓓ (1871), well supplied with restaurants and bars and now home to Buxton Tourist Information. Its recently renovated **Conservatory** houses a variety of tropical and native plants. In the centre of the Pavilion is the superb **Octagon**, or Concert Hall, which soars above the

Pavilion Gardens. Just beyond the Octagon is a large modern swimming pool, filled with warm spa water.

The **Pavilion Gardens**, which have been restored to their former glory (notably with the addition of a new bandstand) thanks to a Lottery grant, provide 23 acres (9 hectares) of pleasantly landscaped space by the banks of the River Wye. Although the gardens continue beyond Burlington Road, turn right into St John's Road to the parish church of **St John the Baptist** Ⓔ, a beautiful example of Italianate Georgian architecture standing in an oasis of green. Designed by Sir Jeffrey Wyatville, who worked closely with the 6th Duke of Devonshire at Chatsworth, it is built in a Tuscan style and contains some fine mosaics and stained glass behind a massive portico under an elegant tower rising to a copper dome.

Beyond the parish church is the great dome of the former **Devonshire Royal Hospital** Ⓕ (now a campus building for the University of Derby). It was originally the Great Stables, built in 1790 to house the horses of spa visi-

tors. The great dome that so dominates Buxton was begun in 1880, when, with the widest unsupported iron-framed dome in the world, spanning 152ft (46 metres), it was an architectural wonder. Across Devonshire Road stands the imposing facade of the **Palace Hotel** 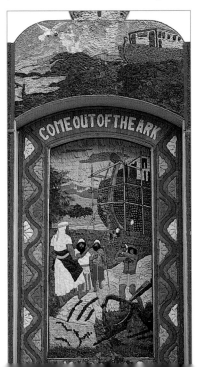, Buxton's largest and most prestigious, built at the height of the resort's popularity in 1868. It stands close to the **London and North Western Railway Station**, of which, unfortunately, only the facade remains, with its great semi-circular fan window.

From the station, walk down The Quadrant back to The Crescent and the steep paths that wind up **The Slopes** , designed to provide graded paths for exercise. At the top of The Slopes, which offer fine views across the town, is the **Town Hall**, designed by William Pollard and opened in 1889. Hall Bank leads steeply up from The Slopes to the Market Place and the area known as Higher Buxton, where the weekly street market is held. Turn left down Terrace Road to **Buxton Museum and Art Gallery** halfway down on the right (Oct–Mar Tue–Fri 9.30am–5.30pm, Sat until 5pm, Apr–Sept also Sun and bank holidays 10.30am–5pm).

This is an excellent little museum with an award-winning display entitled "The Wonders of the Peak", which takes you back in a time tunnel complete with sounds and smells.

Macclesfield and Lyme Park

Macclesfield was granted a charter by Edward I to establish a free borough in 1261, but the town's modern prosperity rests on the silk industry that began in 1742. Three excellent museums tell the story of the town's rise to fame as a silk producer, and the best place to start is the **Heritage Centre Galleries** (Mon–Sat 11am–5pm; charge) in Roe Street, which also has a café. The **Park Lane Galleries** (hours as before) in Park Lane, is the only museum in the country dedicated to the silk industry. The last handloom weaver in Macclesfield retired in 1981, but you can see 25 working Jacquard handlooms at the **Paradise Mill Working Silk Museum** (guided tours only Mon–Sat 12.15, 1.30 and 2.45pm; charge), which is a few minutes' walk

LEFT: a well-dressing tableau at Buxton.

Well Dressing

Nothing to do with fashion, well dressing is a Peak District custom that takes place in many villages – about 20 in all – throughout the summer months. Pagan in origin – it was probably an act of thanksgiving for the spring well-water on the high, dry limestone plateau – the ceremony was gradually taken over by the Christian religion, which absorbed what it could not suppress, and is now usually linked to the day that honours the patron saint of the local church, at the beginning of what is sometimes known as Wakes Week.

Designs, usually on biblical themes, are etched into malleable clay on a wooden background, then brought to life, like a natural mosaic, with leaves, berries, bark, grass and flower petals. It is a skillfull art involving the whole village and can take up to ten days to complete. The tableau is carried in a procession and placed over the local well, where it is blessed by the village priest in a ceremony that generally coincides with the local summer fête.

Well dressing can be seen in Wirksworth and Ashford in May; Rowsley, Bakewell and the Hope Valley at the end of June; in Bamford and Buxton in July; in Eyam in August; and in numerous other villages. Consult the local tourist office or the informative *Parklife* (available free from tourist offices) for details of dates and places.

Working on a Jacquard handloom at Paradise Mill.

RIGHT: walking the Peaks is a popular weekend activity.

away. All-inclusive tickets are available for these museums. An interesting way of exploring the past is to follow the Silk Trail (details from the Tourist Information Centre). The town has one other museum, the West Park Museum (Tue–Sun 2–5pm), which houses some ancient Egyptian artefacts and works by wildlife artist Charles Tunnicliffe.

From Macclesfield take the B5470 to **Lyme Park ⑮** (house: mid-Mar–Oct Fri–Tue 11am–5pm, park: Apr–Oct daily 8am–8.30pm, Nov–Mar daily 8am–6pm; charge). Lyme is one of the Peak District's most impressive stately homes. Originally Tudor, the present Palladian mansion was designed by Leone Leoni in 1720, and its three-storey Ionic portico on the south front is reflected in a peaceful lake. The interior is famous for its intricate carvings by Grinling Gibbons, its clock collection and its beautiful orangery, but Lyme Park's more recent claim to fame has been as a location for the BBC's 1995 television adaptation of Jane Austen's *Pride and Prejudice*. The extensive 1,320-acre (534-hectare) park is famous for its red deer, the largest herd in the Peak District, and it backs on to the moorland of Park Moor, where the hunting tower known as the Cage is a prominent landmark.

Castleton

From Lyme Park, get on the A6 as far as **Whaley Bridge**, a pleasant little town where colourful canal boats are moored in the canal basin. From here you can follow a minor and at times extremely steep road to the **Goyt Valley**, where there is good rock climbing for the intrepid and, for the rest, lovely views over the Fernilee and Errwood reservoirs, and a forest trail to what is left of Errwood Hall, demolished when the valley was flooded to provide water for Stockport.

After this detour, take the A6 again for about 5 miles (8km) then turn right towards **Castleton ⑯**, the "capital" of the **Hope Valley**. Prominent in the village is the parish church of **St Edmund** with some lovely 17th-century box pews. It plays an important part in Castleton's **Garland Ceremony** on Oak Apple Day (29

Walking the Peaks

If you are a seasoned and adventurous walker you will have a fair idea of where you want to go and what kind of terrain to expect in the Peak District, but for those who would like to ramble but are a bit hesitant there is an extensive scheme of Park Ranger-led walks. Some 250 walks cater for differing interests (some specialise in archaeology or botany, for example) and different levels of experience. There are gentle walks that are suitable for children and that are wheelchair-accessible, and tougher hikes for experienced hill walkers.

You can do a rugged 12-mile (20km) moorland walk to Kinder's Waterfall, learn about wildlife in the Goyt Valley, walk the hills above Dove Valley, or gently discover the Upper Derwent. The starting point of most walks can be reached by public transport – use it whenever you can, to help cut down on traffic.

All guided walks are free, but for some you need to book in advance. For more information, ring the National Park Authority's Field Services Hotline, tel: 01629-816 290, check out www.peakdistrict.gov.uk or ask a local tourist office for the (free) *Parklife*, which gives full details. A selection of maps and trail guides are available from visitor centres and tourist offices. Don't forget you need sturdy shoes, waterproofs and a packed lunch for the longer walks.

May), when the Garland King and Queen, on white horses, lead a procession, the King encased from head to waist in the "garland", a wooden cage covered in flowers. The procession stops at all the village pubs, where a special tune is played and children dance, then ends up at the church, where the garland is strung from the top of the tower and left to wither. The custom is thought to have its origins in a pagan ceremony to welcome the return of spring.

Castleton owes its fortune to its strategic importance and its geography. Ever since the Celtic Brigantes tribe built their massive hill fort on the windswept 1,698ft (517-metre) summit of **Mam Tor** (National Trust) this has been a military and administrative centre, although the modern village only came into existence when William Peveril, William the Conqueror's illegitimate son, built **Peveril Castle** (Apr–end June and Sept–Oct daily 10am–5pm, July–Aug 10am–6pm, Nov–Mar Thur–Mon 10am–4pm; charge). Situated on a limestone spur between the precipitous slopes of Cave Dale and the huge chasm of Peak Cavern, the castle is as impregnable as a castle could be. Not much remains of Peveril's early structure, but the views from the ramparts are fabulous.

Caverns and caves

But most people come to Castleton to visit the famous show caves which display the unique semi-precious mineral known as Blue John. The oldest of the caves is **Peak Cavern** (Apr–Oct daily 10am–5pm, Nov–Mar until 5pm). Its entrance is said to be the largest in Europe, at 40ft (12 metres) high and 100ft (30 metres) wide, beneath a cliff of limestone over which towers Peveril Castle. Inside, the spacious entrance area was once home to a community of rope-makers, whose equipment still survives. The roof is still blackened with the soot from their sunless homes.

In the **Speedwell Cavern** (Apr–Oct daily 10am–5pm) at the foot of the

Winnats Pass (National Trust), you are transported to the Bottomless Pit by a boat that is legged along a flooded lead mine drainage level like a barge in a canal tunnel. The Winnats Pass is a spectacular limestone gorge formed after the last Ice Age. The scene of the tragic murder of a pair of lovers in the 18th century, it is now the only road out of the Hope Valley to the west, since constant landslips from the crumbling slopes of Mam Tor led to the closure of the former A625 turnpike road in the early 1970s.

Treak Cliff Cavern (daily Mar–Oct 9.30am–4.20pm, Nov–Feb 10am–3.20pm, guided tours only; charge) probably has the most spectacular formations, and it is one of the few sources of the semi-precious banded fluorspar known as Blue John. Ornaments made from this brilliant brittle mineral are sold here and in the village.

The fourth of Castleton's caves, the **Blue John Cavern** (daily 9.30am–5.30pm, or dusk if earlier, guided tours; charge), is the deepest of all and reached by turning right and right

The Garland King at the Castleton Garland Ceremony.

BELOW: National Park Study Centre at Castleton.

again at the top of the Winnats Pass. This cavern was discovered 300 years ago when miners in search of Blue John broke into the previously unknown range of caves.

The Pennine Way

From Winnats Pass you can take the steep, narrow road between Mam Tor and Rushup Edge which drops steeply down into the Vale of Edale, with magnificent views of **Kinder Scout** , the district's reigning summit (2,088ft/636 metres). At **Edale** is a **National Park Visitor Centre** (Easter–Oct Mon–Sat 9.30am–5.30pm, Sat–Sun until 5.30pm, Nov–Easter Mon–Sat 10am–3.30pm, Sat–Sun 9.30am–4.30pm, closes for lunch year round), for this is the southern point of the great long-distance path, the 268-mile (429km) **Pennine Way**, which marches along Britain's backbone between the Peaks and the Scottish border. This is serious walking country, and weather forecasts are available at the centre, which doubles as a mountain rescue point.

Serious walkers might also want to head up to the northern moors: high,

BELOW: Snake Pass winding through the valley.

wild country of desolate moorland and long valleys, where the trans-Pennine roads are often closed by snow in winter. To do so, get back on the A6, then the A624 to **Glossop** ⓘ, a small industrial town with a surprisingly elegant main square. Glossop's wealth was founded on textiles: there were nearly 60 cotton mills here in the 19th century. **Old Glossop** still has a pleasing pre-industrial air and a range of 17th-century gritstone houses. The history of the region is well told in the **Glossop Heritage Centre** (Mon–Sat 10am–4pm) just off Norfolk Square (the 11th Duke of Norfolk was a patron of Glossop).

From Glossop head for the A628. Passing through the hamlet of Tintwistle (pronounced "Tinsel"), you enter the dramatic cross-Pennine valley of **Longdendale**, an important packhorse route for centuries. The Woodhead Railway ran through the valley in 1847; it included the Woodhead Tunnel, then the longest in the world, and was built at the cost of many lives. The line is closed now and redesignated the **Longdendale Trail**, a cycle trail, part of the **Trans-Pennine Trail** which links the Irish and the North seas. It is served by a **Peak National Park Information Centre** at **Torside** ⓘ (summer weekends and bank holidays) near the sailing club on Torside Reservoir.

At nearby **Crowden**, you again cross the line of the Pennine Way, which drops from the peaty heights of **Bleaklow** (2,077ft/633 metres) to the south to climb the boggy wastes of **Black Hill** (1,908ft/582 metres) to the north, on one of the toughest sections of the Pennine path. **Crowden Youth Hostel** (tel: 0845-371 9113) to the left of the road, converted from a row of cottages by the National Park authority in 1965, creates a vital first overnight stopping place for northbound walkers.

Risqué cards and risky roads

From Crowden, take the A6024 to **Holmfirth** ⓴, a pretty town where some of the earliest silent films were produced. The long-running BBC Television comedy series *Last of the Summer Wine* was set here and there is a small exhibition devoted to the series (Mon–Fri 10.30am–3.30pm, Sat–Sun 10am–4pm; charge). *Last of the Summer Wine* mini bus tours leave from outside the church most days (tel: 01484-687 231).

Head back now across **Wessenden Head Moor**, recrossing the line of the Pennine Way again, then take a sharp turn just before Greenfield to beautiful **Dovestone Reservoir ㉑**, with good surrounding walks and a thriving sailing club. Head back to Glossop through Stalybridge (in the eastern suburbs of Greater Manchester), then get on the A57 which will take you across the Snake Pass to Sheffield. Best not to try it in winter: the **Snake Pass ㉒** is one of the highest and most exposed roads in Britain – it reaches 1,680ft (512 metres) at the summit – and is always one of the first to be closed in winter, and the last to reopen.

The road runs above Holden Clough, passing the peat banks of **Featherbed Moss**. It levels out at the summit where the unmistakable line of the Pennine

Way is crossed. From the summit, the road swings down in a series of sharp bends to **Lady Clough** then to the isolated **Snake Pass Inn**, a welcome landmark, and sometimes a life-saving one, for walkers or stranded motorists.

As the A57 continues towards Sheffield you pass, on the right, the western arm of the **Ladybower Reservoir** (the largest in the Upper Derwent) and on the left, the **Upper Derwent Valley ㉓**, a man-made landscape, from its reservoirs and dams to the surrounding conifer woods, which has proved so popular that minibus and cycle-hire services are provided at weekends to keep traffic from choking the entrance road.

The main road continues over the Ashopton Viaduct to the western suburbs of **Sheffield ㉔**. Once the steel capital of Britain, the city is recovering from the industry's decline, and while many see it simply as a convenient base for visiting the Peaks, it does have its own attractions. ❑

Sid's cafe in Holmfirth, featured in the long-running sitcom Last of the Summer Wine.

LEFT: Sheffield Winter Gardens, home to more than 2,000 plants.

Things to Do in Sheffield

An enlightened attitude to public transport makes Sheffield easy to get around. The Supertram, a glossy modern tramcar, is a pleasure to ride. A popular university also ensures a lively atmosphere and plenty of bars, clubs and cheap-ish restaurants. Try visiting:

Abbeydale Industrial Hamlet (Apr–early Oct Mon–Thur 10am–4pm, Sun 11am–4.45pm) a museum of the industrial past. Craftsmen demonstrate their skills in this restored steelworks by the River Sheaf.

Bishops' House (Mon–Fri pre-booked educational tours only, Sat 10am–4.30pm, Sun 11am–4.30pm; free), dating from 1500, is the best-preserved timber-framed house in Sheffield.

The Millennium Galleries (Mon–Sat 10am–5pm, Sun 11am–5pm) at Arundel Gate comprise four galleries in one, displaying arts, crafts and contemporary design. They also include the Ruskin Gallery, the collection of the Guild of St George, the movement started by the Pre-Raphaelite John Ruskin (1819–1900). Adjacent is the city's **Winter Garden**, a spectacular new glasshouse.

The Weston Park Museum (Mon–Sat 10am–5pm, Sun 11am–5pm) the new showcase for the city's collections of archaeology, natural history, art and social history, formerly housed within the Sheffield City Museum and Mappin Art Gallery.

THE NORTHWEST

Liverpool, home of the Beatles, also has a great
waterfront and excellent galleries, while
Manchester has emerged as a thriving metropolis,
and Blackpool remains a seaside institution

The Northwest is not a prime holiday destination, but with two
vibrant and exciting cities – Liverpool and Manchester – and the
smaller historical city of Lancaster, as
well as Blackpool, one of the country's
best-known seaside resorts, and the
lovely Ribble Valley, the region has
lots to offer.

City on the Mersey

It is possible to visit **Liverpool ①** and
avoid references to the Beatles, but it's
not easy – the group are still the main
reason many people come here. **The
Beatles Story** (daily 9am–7pm, last
entry 5pm; charge) in Albert Dock will
take you through their whole career
"eight days a week" and features the
Yellow Submarine and a stroll down
Penny Lane. The attraction is expanding all the time. The **Cavern Club**, a
new building on the old site, is open
every day; the childhood homes of
Paul McCartney and John Lennon can
now be visited on a National Trust tour
(tel: 0151-427 7231; advance booking
essential); and **Magical Mystery Tours**
run daily at 2.30pm (tel: 0151-236 9091
for reservations) to all sites of interest
to Beatles fans and 1960s enthusiasts.

But there is much more to see and
do. Liverpool was the European Capital of Culture for 2008 which led to a
flurry of regeneration and large parts
of the city, including the renovated
Albert Dock, a busy development with
a variety of shops, bars, restaurants,

museums and galleries, were put on
the Unesco World Heritage List in July
2004. The **Merseyside Maritime
Museum** (daily 10am–5pm; free) documents the 800 year old history of the
port, and incorporates the new **International Slavery Museum** which
offers a poignant and thought-
provoking view of the slave trade and
its legacies. Nearby is the new **Museum
of Liverpool**, which is replacing the
Museum of Liverpool Life and will
explore the city's fascinating social history. It's due to open at the end of 2010.

Main attractions
THE BEATLES STORY
MANCHESTER UNITED FOOTBALL
  GROUND
BLACKPOOL PLEASURE BEACH
MORECAMBE BAY
CARNFORTH STATION

PRECEDING PAGES:
Liverpool
Metropolitan
Cathedral.
LEFT: the Mersey
ferry.
BELOW: beer and
the Beatles.

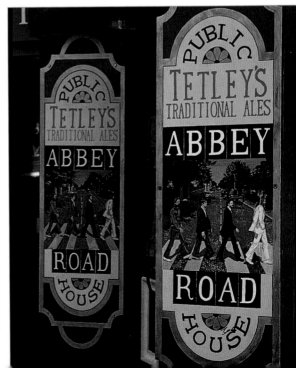

B of the Bang public sculpture by Thomas Heatherwick.

BELOW: Beetham Tower is the tallest building in Manchester.

Among the fine galleries are the **Tate Liverpool** (daily 10am–5.50pm, winter Tue–Sun 10am–5.50pm; charge for special exhibitions, permanent collection free), which has the largest collection of modern and contemporary art outside London and hosts some great temporary exhibitions; and, away from the waterfront, the neoclassical **Walker Art Gallery** (daily, 10am–5pm), sometimes known as "the National Gallery of the North" which has an outstanding collection that ranges from the 14th century to the present, and includes works by Rembrandt.

Liverpool's architecture is on a grand scale. Down by the docks it includes the three buildings known as "The Three Graces": the imposing **Royal Liver Building**, with the mythical liver birds sitting atop the two clock towers; the Cunard Building and the Port of Liverpool Building. All three were built in the early 20th century, when the city and the port were at the height of their prosperity.

Liverpool also has two modern churches, of which the **Roman Catholic Metropolitan Cathedral**, designed by Sir Frederick W. Gibberd and consecrated in 1967, is the most striking: a circular structure topped with a spire that represents the Crown of Thorns. The crypt, begun in 1930, was the work of Sir Edwin Lutyens, and was the only part of his original design to be carried out before lack of cash halted work.

The **Anglican Cathedral**, Britain's largest, by Giles Gilbert Scott, was begun in 1904 and completed in 1978 after two world wars delayed its construction, but its neo-Gothic style gives it the appearance of a much older building.

There is a good Pre-Raphaelite art collection, along with some Turners and Constables, at **the Lady Lever Art Gallery** (daily 10am–5pm), built by William Hesketh Lever, later Lord Leverhulme (1851–1928), to house the collection he had assembled to "enrich the lives of his workforce". The gallery sits in formal gardens in the delightful model village of Port Sunlight, across the Mersey in Wirral. Leverhulme, a paternalistic philanthropist and enlightened employer, funded the village for employees of his soap empire.

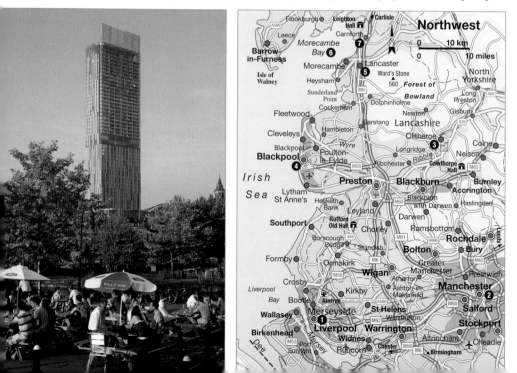

The village is a fascinating place, tranquil and seemingly detached from 21st-century life. It is a Conservation Area, and each of the 900 Grade II listed buildings is different from its neighbour. To reach **Port Sunlight**, take Queens Way across the Mersey if you are driving, and follow the signs, or use the Merseyrail Wirral Link to Port Sunlight or Bebington stations.

The changing face of Manchester

Manchester ❷ is changing so fast it's hard to keep up with it. The city came to prominence during the 19th century when it was at the forefront of the Industrial Revolution. Its "dark satanic mills" sprang up when cotton production was revolutionised by Richard Arkwright's steam-powered spinning machines in the late 18th century. When a railway line linked the city with Liverpool in 1830, and the Manchester Ship Canal was completed in 1894, Manchester's prosperity was sealed, and the huge Victorian civic buildings we can see today are evidence of a city that believed in its own destiny.

The tenements in which the mill workers lived were razed by slum-clearance projects in the 1950s.

But Manchester's docks went the way of many others, and for years the city centre was drab, under-used and under-populated, before a huge revitalisation process began. Now the centre throbs with life. There's a shiny new shopping centre; a colourful Chinatown; a Gay Village, spanning out from a canal-side promenade; and three universities. Some things to include on a visit are the extensive **Museum of Science and Industry** (daily 10am–5pm; free), an award-winning museum with full working machinery; the **City Art Gallery** (Tue–Sun 10am–5pm; free), which has a permanent collection that includes works by Ford Maddox Brown and Millais; the **Whitworth Art Gallery** (Mon–Sat 10am–5pm, Sun noon–4pm; free) and the **Manchester Jewish Museum** (Mon–Thur 10.30am–4pm, Sun 1–5pm; charge), where a record of the city's Jewish history is housed in a restored synagogue. Try to book for a performance by the resident Hallé Orchestra at the splendid **Bridgewater**

> **TIP**
>
> Manchester's most famous attraction is Old Trafford, the home of Manchester United Football Club. The club museum is open daily 9.30am–5pm, and stadium tours are available daily 9.40am–4.30pm: www.manutd.co.uk.

LEFT: the Ribble Valley.

Fact File

By car Connections to Merseyside via the M6, M56, M58 and M62, about 4 hours from London; to Manchester via the M6, M62, M56, about 3 hours 30 minutes.

By train InterCity services from London Euston to Liverpool, about 2 hours 50 minutes; about 3 hours to Manchester from London Euston; tel: 08457-484 950.

By coach National Express services from London, Birmingham and many other cities to Liverpool, Manchester, Lancaster and Blackpool; tel: 08705-808 080.

By air Manchester Airport, 10 miles (16km) south of the city centre, tel: 08712-710 711; Liverpool John Lennon Airport, 9 miles (15km) southeast of the city, tel: 0871-521 8484.

Bridgewater Packet Boat Service Tel: 0161-748 2680 for trips around Manchester's canals.

Manchester United Museum and Tour Tel: 0161-868 8000.

Manchester City Stadium Tel: 0870-062 1894.

Liverpool Football Club Museum and Tour Tel: 0151-260 6677.

Tourist Information Centres Liverpool, tel: 0906-680 6886; 0151-907 1057; Manchester, tel: 0871-222 8223; Blackpool, tel: 01253-478 222; Lancaster, tel: 01524-582 394; Morecambe, tel: 01524-582 808.

The main political parties take it in turns to hold their annual autumn conferences in Blackpool.

Hall (tel: 0161-907 9000); or make tracks for the City of Manchester Stadium where the spiky, 184ft (56-metre) **B of the Bang**, a starburst in steel, is the tallest sculpture in the UK and a triumph of engineering.

To the west of the city, on Salford Quays, the multi-media **Lowry Centre** (gallery: Sun–Fri 11am–5pm, Sat 10am–5pm; free) has the world's largest collection of local artist L.S. Lowry's work; opposite the centre, a stunning new building houses the **Imperial War Museum North** (daily Mar–end Oct 10am–6pm, Nov–end Feb 10am–5pm; free).

Down in the valley

To reach the **Ribble Valley**, take the A666 north, past Blackburn, and head for **Clitheroe ❸**, a pleasant little town for an overnight stop if you want to explore the area. From the remains of its ancient castle, perched on a limestone crag, there are splendid views of the valley. Nearby stands the remains of the 13th-century Cistercian **Whalley Abbey**, and a parish church with Saxon crosses outside. To the west,

RIGHT: all lit up in Blackpool.

Ribchester, a pretty village with a 17th-century bridge over the river, has the remains of a huge Roman fort, part of which has been excavated to reveal the foundations of two granaries.

Beside the seaside

Leaving the peaceful valley, the B5269 joins the M55 motorway for the short trip (about 12 miles/20km) to **Blackpool ❹**, which became a popular seaside resort when the arrival of the railways in the mid-19th century enabled Lancashire cotton workers to enjoy a day beside the sea. Fast-food stalls, and restaurants, bingo halls and amusement arcades line the **Golden Mile**, which parallels long, wide stretches of sand, where sand-surfers and kite flyers have the time of their lives. Trams trundle along the prom, three piers offer traditional summer entertainment, and the **Pleasure Beach** has every ride imaginable. The famous 518ft (158-metre) **Blackpool Tower** looms above it all: in September and October it is outlined in coloured lights as the centrepiece of the spectacular **Blackpool Illuminations**.

Lancashire's Finest

Two of Lancashire's finest stately homes are not far off our route and easily accessible either by car or by public transport:

Gawthorpe Hall (Apr–Oct Tue–Thur and Sat–Sun 1–5pm, garden: all year daily 10am–6pm) is an Elizabethan masterpiece in Padiham, near Burnley, which was restored in the 19th century by Sir Charles Barry, who created many of the magnificent interiors. The collection of paintings includes some on loan from the National Portrait Gallery in London, and there is a rare collection of needlework, displaying exhibits of samplers and lace work. There is a rose garden and a tea room and special children's interactive sessions during term time (tel: 01282-771 004 for details).

Rufford Old Hall (house: mid-Mar–Oct Sat–Wed 11am–5pm, garden: Sat–Wed 11am–5pm and Nov–late Dec Fri–Sun noon–4pm) is one of Lancashire's finest 16th-century buildings, especially well known for the Great Hall with a hammer-beam roof and carved wooden screen. It is said that Shakespeare performed here for the owner, Sir Thomas Hesketh, whose family owned the house for 400 years. The Carolean Wing has collections of 17th-century furniture and tapestries. The Old Kitchen Restaurant serves light lunches and teas. There are Victorian-style gardens and a wildflower meadow.

City of the red rose

Head north now on the A588 to **Lancaster ❺**, the county town of Lancashire, founded by the Romans. In 1322 Robert Bruce razed the castle and much of the town to the ground but it was rebuilt by John of Gaunt, and his **Gateway Tower** is a fine specimen. During the 15th-century so-called Wars of the Roses, the House of Lancaster was symbolised by the red rose, the House of York by the white. The **castle** (daily 10am–5pm; charge) and the Shire Hall can be visited, although some parts of the castle are not accessible when the Crown Court is in session. There's also a priory church, **St Mary's**, with a fine Saxon doorway and beautiful choir stalls.

Shrimps and sands

Morecambe Bay ❻ is known for its shrimps and its sands. The shrimps are small, brown and tasty and are gathered in nets taken across the sand by horse and cart. The sands, a vast spread of tidal flats that are home to thousands of sea birds, can be very dangerous: the tide sweeps across the bay and performs a pincer movement around the sandbars, then spreads over the flats, and in no time at all a peaceful expanse of sand becomes a choppy sea. There are guides who will lead you, when the tide is right, all the way round the bay. The best way to see the sands and their bird population is by train on a track that trundles over viaducts from Ulverston (*see page 298*) to Arnside. **Morecambe** is a pleasant holiday resort on the bay, which claims to have originated the idea of autumn illuminations in order to lengthen the summer season.

Carnforth ❼ is the last stop on our route, a small town just north of Morecambe, whose main claims to fame are the rejuvenated **Carnforth Station and Visitor Centre** (Tue–Sun 10am–4pm, Easter–Sept also Mon; free), including the refreshment room made famous in the film *Brief Encounter*; and **Leighton Hall** (May–Sept Tue–Fri, Sun 2–5pm), home of the Gillow furniture family. In the extensive grounds there are plenty of paths to explore, as well as a walled garden and ornamental vegetable plot.　❏

TIP

You should not attempt to cross the sands of Morecambe Bay without a guide. To book a Cross Bay Walk (approx 9 miles/14km) tel: 01524-824 693.

LEFT:
Morecambe Bay shrimps.
BELOW:
overlooking the Lakes from Morecambe.

THE LAKE DISTRICT

The landscape that inspired the Lakeland poets continues to exert its spell on visitors, who come to walk the fells, to sail the waters, or simply to enjoy the breathtaking scenery

London

Main attractions
FURNESS ABBEY
BEATRIX POTTER'S HILL TOP
DOVE COTTAGE
CASTLERIGG STONE CIRCLE
DERWENT WATER
TARN HOWS
AIRA FORCE

The **Lake District**, in northwest England, is a small area, but extremely beautiful, with the varied delights of soft hills and woodland, the panoramas of the great lakes, the unexpected discoveries of the smaller waters or tarns, the bare contours of the fells and high ground and the awe-inspiring power of the more remote mountains and mountain passes. The poet William Wordsworth, who was born here at Cockermouth in 1770 and spent most of his life here, rightly remarked: "I do not know any tract of country in which, within so narrow a compass, may be found an equal variety in the influences of light and shadow upon the sublime or beautiful features of landscape."

The Lake District is more frequently visited, both by day tourists and holidaymakers, than any other region of outstanding natural beauty in the British Isles. On the whole it copes remarkably well with the vast numbers of visitors, but traffic congestion can be a big problem in summer.

The two routes that were popularised by the first tourists in the 1760s and 1770s still carry the greatest share of summer traffic. One is from Penrith to Ambleside by the west shore of Ullswater (scene of Wordsworth's poem *The Daffodils*) and over the Kirkstone Pass, now the A592; the other is from Keswick to Windermere by the side of Thirlmere, Grasmere, Rydal Water and Windermere, now the A591.

Away from these routes you can find quiet areas of great beauty – particularly if you avoid the high summer – and experience the sense of solitude and oneness with nature that was valued so highly by the 19th-century Romantic poets *(see page 303)*. The central area of mountains was never much affected by industry or quarrying, and the 19th-century shipbuilding, iron manufacturing and coal mining that once flourished by the coast have now almost entirely disappeared. Sheep farming was the tradi-

PRECEDING PAGES: Coniston Water. **LEFT:** High Dam, Windermere. **BELOW:** wooden sculpture in Grizedale Forest.

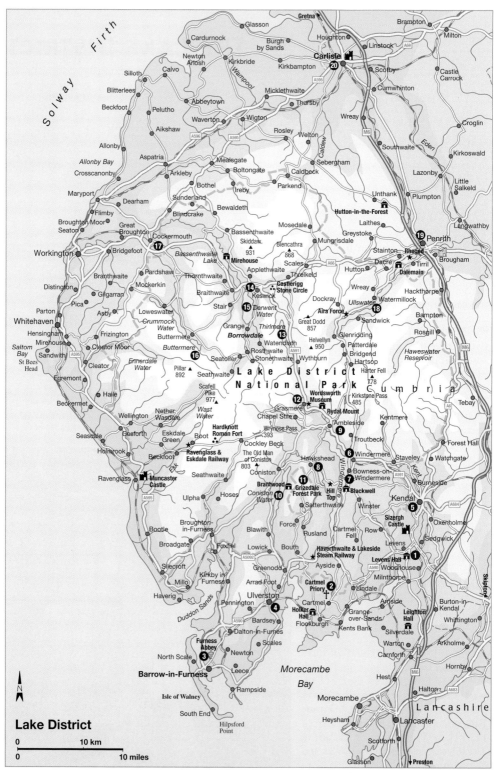

Lake District

0   10 km

0   10 miles

tional way of life of the hill folk, and it continues today throughout the area covered by the Lake District National Park, often on farms owned and leased by the National Trust.

Gardens, halls and abbeys

Approaching from the south along the M6, turn off at Junction 36 to Levens. **Levens Hall ❶** (Apr–Sept Sun–Thur, house: noon–4.30pm, garden: 10am–5pm; charge) is an Elizabethan house furnished in Jacobean style, and built around a 13th-century pele tower (impregnable tower at the core of a building). The famous topiary garden is little changed since its trees were first shaped in the 17th century.

The A590 south from Levens leads to **Cartmel Priory ❷** (daily except during services, summer 9am–5.30pm, winter 9am–3.30pm), near the resort of Grange-over-Sands. It was founded around 1189 by the Baron of Cartmel and was saved from destruction at the time of Henry VIII's Dissolution of the Monasteries by the quick-wittedness of local people who claimed that it was their parish church. Only the gatehouse

and the church remain. Inside the latter there is good medieval carving and old glass; the lovely east window dates from the 15th century, as does the tower. A mother and son who drowned while crossing Morecambe Bay sands are buried next to the font; in the days before the railway linked Cartmel and Lancaster, the treacherous old low-tide route was risked by many. Nearby, the splendid home of the powerful Cavendish family, **Holker Hall** (late Mar–Nov Sun–Fri 11am–4pm, gardens 10.30am–5.30pm; charge), is set in attractive gardens. Look out for the Great Holker Lime, planted in the early 17th century it is one of the largest lime trees in the country. The Lakeland Motor Museum (daily Feb–end Oct 10.30am–4.45pm; charge), with its extensive collection of vehicles and related memorabilia, is located here. Holker Hall also hosts a noteworthy annual garden festival in June.

Furness Peninsula, the southern tip of Lakeland, was in medieval times the heart of a great Cistercian estate farmed by the monks of **Furness Abbey ❸** (Apr–end June, Sept Thur–

A Cumbrian sheep farmer.

LEFT: Levens Hall topiary garden.

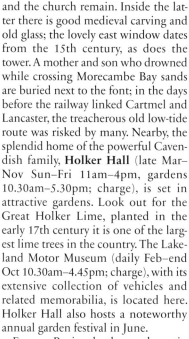

Fact File

Location 250 miles (400km) from London, 75 miles (120km) north of Manchester, the Lake District covers 30 miles (48km) north–south, and 20 miles (32km) east–west.

By train London Euston to Penrith or to Oxenholme (with a connecting service to Windermere); journey time about 4 hours 30 minutes. From Edinburgh to Carlisle, about 1 hour 30 minutes; tel: 08457-484 950.

By coach National Express from London Victoria to Kendal; journey time about 6 hours 30 minutes; tel: 08705-808 080.

By car About 5 hours from London via the M40/M6.

By air Manchester Airport, near the M6, is approximately 80 miles (130km) south of Windermere.

Most famous Lakelanders Children's writer Beatrix Potter (1866–1943); the poet William Wordsworth (1770–1850).

For children The World of Beatrix Potter; Grizedale Forest Sculpture Playground; Cumberland Pencil Museum; Brockhole Visitor Centre.

Festivals Appleby Horse Fair (June); Ambleside Rushbearing Festival (July); Kendal Mountain Film Festival (Nov).

Tourist information Coniston, tel: 01539-441 533; Hawkshead, tel: 01539-46946; Kendal, tel: 01539-797 516; Keswick, tel: 01768-772 645; Windermere, tel: 01539-446 499 or 601.

The area in which Furness Abbey stands is known as the Vale of Deadly Nightshade because these sinister plants once grew here in such profusion.

Mon 10am–5pm, July–Aug daily 10am–5pm, Oct–end Mar 10am–4pm; charge). The abbey, which lies in a lovely setting, was the second-richest Cistercian establishment in England at the time of its suppression in 1537. Its red sandstone buildings, standing out against green lawns, date from the 12th and 15th centuries. The abbey lies to the north of **Barrow-in-Furness**, the peninsula's main town, and once a major shipbuilding centre. **The Dock Museum** (Tue–Sun, Mon in high summer; tel: 01229-876 400 for details) charts the town's social and industrial history.

Head north now on the A590 to the historic town of **Ulverston ➍** on an old ship canal, where you can visit the **Laurel and Hardy Museum** (Feb–Dec daily 10am–4.30pm; charge). It sounds incongruous, but Stan Laurel was born here in 1890. Back on the A591 near Levens, where we began, you will come to **Sizergh Castle** (Apr–Oct Sun–Thur house: noon–5pm, garden: 11am–5pm; charge), whose medieval defensive appearance is softened by attractive

RIGHT: the Abbot Hall Museum.

gardens. About 3 miles (5km) on you reach **Kendal ➎**, which is a good centre for exploring the Lakes. It is still a working town, not just a holiday centre, carrying on its daily life in the midst of fine 17th- and 18th-century buildings. The church is a Perpendicular structure, and the lively Brewery Arts Centre is worth a look. Beside the church stand **Abbot Hall Art Gallery** and the **Museum of Lakeland Life** (Jan–Dec Mon–Sat 10.30am–5pm, Nov–Mar until 4pm; charge), housed in an 18th-century mansion and its stable block. The former has paintings by John Ruskin and J.M.W. Turner and by local artist George Romney; the latter concentrates on local trades and crafts, and has two rooms devoted to *Swallows and Amazons* author Arthur Ransome (1884–1967), whose books have a Coniston Water setting.

The Southern Lakes

The A591 runs from Kendal to the town of **Windermere ➏** and the lake of the same name. It's a Victorian town, which really came into being

Taking to the Water

Looking at lakes, in scenery such as this, is wonderful, but at some point most people actually want to get on the water, whether to get from one point to another, to view the fells from a different perspective or simply to feel at one with the water.

Ullswater Steamers are the best way to enjoy the lake and the mountains around it. In the summer season there are services every day between Glenridding, Howtown and Pooley Bridge, in addition to one- and two-hour cruises. You can take a one-way trip and walk back if you prefer that option. Tel: 01539-721 626 or 01768-482 229 (Glenridding Pier).

Windermere Lake Cruises operate a fleet of launches and steamers all year round between Ambleside, Bowness and Lakeside, with connections for the Lakeside and Haverthwaite Steam Railway, the Brockhole Visitor Centre and the Aquarium of the Lakes. Steamers have licensed bars and coffee shops and are heated in the winter: www.windermere-lakecruises.co.uk.

Coniston Water has the National Trust steam-powered yacht, the *Gondola*, launched in 1859 and now renovated, which takes visitors on memorable cruises, tel: 01539-41288. The *Gondola*, sails from Coniston Pier (½ mile from Coniston village).

when the railway arrived. In a pretty lakeside setting is **Windermere Steamboats and Museum** (closed for redevelopment), which has a large collection of mementos from the age of steam (including the 1850 steam-launch *Dolly*, said to be the oldest mechanically powered boat in the world). Windermere is closely associated with the children's writer Beatrix Potter (1866–1943) and **The World of Beatrix Potter** (daily summer 10am– 5.30pm, winter 10am–4.30pm; charge) in the Old Laundry at Crag Brow recreates her characters in a lively exhibition. You can walk down Lakes Road to **Bowness-on-Windermere** ❼, the most popular resort, which has a very attractive centre but is almost always too crowded for comfort.

You can also take a car ferry to Near Sawrey and **Hill Top**, Potter's home (mid-Mar–end Oct Sat–Wed 10.30am– 4.30pm; charge), a fine example of a 17th-century Lakeland farmhouse, with a traditional cottage garden. To the south of Bowness just off the A507, is **Blackwell** (daily 10.30am–5pm, Nov–Mar until 4pm; charge), the dis-

tinctive Arts and Crafts house designed by M.H. Baillie Scott for a wealthy Manchester brewery owner. The design is asymetrical and the light-filled main living areas face south, away from the lake. Two of the upstairs bedrooms have been converted into galleries where craft exhibitions are held.

In Main Street in nearby **Hawkshead** ❽ on the west side of the lake is the **Beatrix Potter Gallery** (mid-Mar–end Oct Sat–Thur 10.30am– 4.30pm; charge), housed in the office of her solicitor husband. It has changing displays of many of her original drawings and watercolours from her famous children's books.

William Wordsworth (1770–1850; *see page 303*) attended the **Grammar School** at Hawkshead (Apr–Oct Mon– Sat 10am–1pm, 2–5pm, Sun 1–5pm, Oct until 3.30pm; charge). Downstairs,

Hill Top, Beatrix Potter's home.

BELOW: Kendal, famous for Kendal Mint Cake.

The Wordsworth Museum contains many rare first editions.

BELOW: Old Man of Coniston.

remains of a group of 15th-century manorial buildings constructed when the Cistercian monks from Cartmel ruled much of the area. Further west, just off the B5285, is **Tarn Hows**, considered by many to be the prettiest lake in the district. Only a half-mile (800 metres) long, it was originally three smaller lakes but joined after a dam was built. There are adequate National Trust car parks (including designated parking close to the lake for disabled people) and a good footpath right round the tarn, and takes about an hour to to walk all the way around.

You can continue on the west side of the lake towards Ambleside, but if you take the A591 from Windermere you will also be able to visit **Troutbeck**, a delightful village which has several roadside wells dedicated to various saints; a church with a Pre-Raphaelite east window (the combined work of Edward Burne-Jones, William Morris and Ford Maddox Brown); and an atmospheric 17th-century farmhouse, **Townend** (Apr–end Oct Wed–Sun and Bank Holidays 11am–5pm; charge), built by yeoman George

it suggests little of the excellence of its teaching in the 1780s when the Wordsworth brothers studied there. But upstairs is a superb library with books dating from the foundation of the ancient school by Archbishop Sandys in 1585. **St Michael's Church** preserves wall paintings of scriptural texts. From beneath its east window you can take in the view of this tiny, whitewashed town.

West of Hawkshead stands the medieval arched **Courthouse**, all that

Browne, which has a wonderful collection of carved woodwork and domestic implements.

The Browne family collected over 1,500 books between the 16th and 20th centuries, and the existence of this lovingly preserved library is historically significant.

Ambleside 9 is a Victorian town of splendid slate buildings. If you arrive by boat during peak tourist times you can hop on the trolley that runs between Waterhead pier and Ambleside town centre (1 mile/1.5km). Spanning the beck beside Rydal Road, the tiny **House on the Bridge** accommodates a National Trust information centre. There is also a glass-blowing workshop and an old corn mill with waterwheel. The entertaining **Homes of Football** gallery (daily, hours vary, tel: 01539-434 440) displays a selection of vibrant images by acclaimed sports photographer Stuart Clarke.

Old Man and eminent men

Instead of continuing north from here you could make a diversion on the A593 to **Coniston Water 10** where the **Old Man of Coniston** (2,635ft/803 metres) can be climbed via a well-marked route from the village. In St Andrew's Church, John Ruskin (1819–1900), the art historian and critic, is buried. The **Ruskin Museum** (Easter–mid-Nov daily 10am–5.30pm, mid-Nov–Easter Wed–Sun 10.30am–3.30pm) is a few minutes' walk from the church. Ruskin lived at **Brantwood** (Mar–Nov daily 11am–5.30pm, winter Wed–Sun 11am–4.30pm; charge), on the northeast shore of Coniston Water. Many of his paintings are preserved, and the house remains much as he left it. It's accessible by road (B5285) or by the renovated Victorian steam yacht *Gondola* from Coniston Pier, which is operating once more after lying wrecked in Nibthwaite Bay for many years. To the east of Coniston lies **Grizedale Forest Park 11**, a large tract of land the Forestry Commission has imaginatively given over to nature trails, modern sculptures and a small theatre.

Get back on the A593 now to Ambleside, then pick up the road towards Keswick. You'll soon come to

John Ruskin, the great Victorian art historian and writer on social and economic themes, was a resident of Coniston.

BELOW:
the *Gondola* steam yacht on Coniston Water.

Dove Cottage in Grasmere.

BELOW: Tarn Hows, surrounded by dense woodland.

Rydal Mount (Mar–Oct daily 9.30am–5pm, Nov–Feb Wed–Sun 11am–4pm; charge), which was the home of the Wordsworth family from 1813 until William's death in 1850. The house (still owned by a descendant) contains portraits and family mementos; the grounds were landscaped by Wordsworth and retain their original form. **Rydal Water** is a small reedy lake with a population of waterfowl, and red squirrels in the larches round the edge.

Two miles (3km) north lies **Grasmere** ⓬, a pleasant village on the lake of the same name: "the prettiest spot that man has ever found", according to Wordsworth. **St Oswald's Church** with its ancient timber roof is worth a visit in its own right, not just to see the Wordsworthian graves. The display of manuscripts and portraits of the poet's family and friends in the **Wordsworth Museum** (Feb–Dec daily 9.30am–5.30pm; charge) brings home the magnitude of the poetry that was written here and the importance that Wordsworth and his friend Samuel Coleridge (*see right*) held in the cultural life of their day. Entrance to the museum also gives access to whitewashed **Dove Cottage** from which William, his wife Mary, and sister Dorothy, had a view over Grasmere to the fells, although it's now hemmed in by later buildings.

Pencils for poets

The 17-mile (28km) journey to Keswick on the A591 passes **Thirlmere** ⓭, a reservoir created from two smaller lakes in 1890 to supply the water needs of Manchester. **Helvellyn**, the third-highest mountain in England (3,120ft/950 metres), rises steeply to the right. Close to Keswick you could turn off to **Castlerigg Stone Circle**, an ancient monument which Victorian tourists associated with the Druids. The views from here are tremendous.

Keswick ⓮ is a Victorian town with a much older centre, which has been popular with visitors since the 1760s. It has a **Moot Hall** (market hall), grand as a church, which now houses a helpful information centre. The town came to prominence through

the manufacture of pencils, using graphite mined in Borrowdale. The factory is now the **Cumberland Pencil Museum** (daily 9.30am–4pm) – pencil making can be traced to the discovery of graphite in the 16th century; local shepherds soon began to use it to mark their sheep. Keswick's **Museum and Art Gallery** (Easter–Oct Tue–Sat 10am–4pm; free) has mementos and manuscripts of Samuel Coleridge, Robert Southey and Hugh Walpole, who all lived nearby.

Lovely **Borrowdale Valley** has long been a favourite with both artists and walkers. The B5289 from Keswick skirts **Derwent Water 🟊**, which mirrors a range of splendid fells. To the left of the road are the **Lodore Falls** "receding and speeding, And shocking and rocking..." as Robert Southey wrote. Where the valley narrows to form the Jaws of Borrowdale (best seen from Friars Crag on the right as you leave Keswick) lies the pretty village of Grange, reached over a narrow bridge. A mile to the west is **Brackenburn** (private), the home of Hugh Walpole, who set *The Herries Chronicle* (1930–33)

in the region. From Grange you can walk beside the waters of the Derwent and through the oak woods.

Stay on the B5289 and you'll pass Rosthwaite and Seatoller. Between the two is **Johnny Wood**, with a nature trail. The road continues through **Honister Pass**, where fell walkers park their cars and make the relatively easy climb to the summit of **Great Gable** (2,949ft/899 metres). From here the road drops down to **Buttermere 🟊** at the foot of Fleetwith Pike (2,126ft/648 metres). You can walk round Buttermere (which is quieter than the other lakes), then stop at the **Fish Hotel** in the village, where the strength of the ale was recommended back in the 18th century. In **Buttermere Church** there's a plaque to Alfred Wainwright (1907–91), most famous of the fell walkers. Through the window (on a clear day) you can see **Haystacks Fell**, where his ashes were scattered.

Back on the road, turn left at the junction of the B5292 for **Cockermouth 🟊**, a pleasant market town of red sandstone, which is mostly visited by those keen to see **Wordsworth**

Lodore Falls.

The Lake Poets

There's no getting away from the Lake Poets – not that anyone really wants to. They were the first generation of English Romantics, united by their love of poetry, free thought, progressive causes and natural beauty.

William Wordsworth (1770–1850) was the focus. Born in Cockermouth, he lived most of his adult life in the district, accompanied by his wife Mary and sister Dorothy (1771–1855), whose journals provided inspiration for her brother's work. His line "I wandered lonely as a cloud..." must be one of the few that every English person knows. Samuel Taylor Coleridge (1772–1834) joined them in 1800, living in Greta Hall, Keswick, and continuing the intense friendship begun a few years earlier. It ended in an irrevocable quarrel 10 years later, by which time he was addicted to opium. Robert Southey (1774–1843) joined the group shortly afterwards; he took over Greta Hall and lived there for 40 years. He was appointed Poet Laureate in 1813. Thomas de Quincey (1785–1859) was more of a journalist than a poet, but closely associated with the group. He settled for a while in Grasmere, at Dove Cottage, previously occupied by the Wordsworths, and made his name in 1821 with *The Confessions of an English Opium Eater* – a subject on which he was well qualified to write.

RIGHT: Aira Force, Ullswater.

House (Apr–Oct Mon–Sat 11am–5pm). Recently renovated and enlivened by costumed characters and hands-on activities, this is where the poet was born.

The A595 leads straight to Carlisle from here, but our tour takes the A66 which skirts **Bassenthwaite Lake** for a while then passes Keswick, with Skiddaw Forest to the left. **Skiddaw** (3,0543ft/931 metres) and **Blencathra**, also known as Saddleback (2,847ft/868 metres), are the dominant fells. At the foot of Skiddaw lies **Mirehouse**, home of scholar James Spedding 1808–81 (Apr–end Oct, house: Sun, Wed 2–5pm, last entry 4.30pm, Aug also Fri, grounds: daily 10am–5.30pm). Children will delight in roaming the estate's four woodland adventure playgrounds.

From Ullswater to Carlisle

It's only a 15-mile (24km) drive from Keswick to the old town of Penrith, but there are a few interesting diversions to be made en route. You could incorporate a visit to **Dacre**, a few miles before the town on the right. It has a largely

Norman church, even earlier carvings and views of 14th-century **Dacre Castle**. Nearby is **Dalemain** (Easter–end Oct Sun–Thur 11am–4pm; charge), a former manor house that dates back to the 14th century and is essentially unaltered since 1750, with fine interiors (including a Chinese drawing room with 18th-century wallpaper), paintings and a pleasant garden.

Dalemain lies just off the A592, which leads past **Ullswater** ⓲ and over the Kirkstone Pass to Ambleside. Ullswater is the second-largest lake after Windermere, and it was here that the Wordsworths saw the dancing daffodils. There are steamers on the lake *(see page 298)* from which one can enjoy magnificent views of Helvellyn and other surrounding mountains. **Aira Force**, on the north shore beneath **Gowbarrow Fell**, is one of the most impressive waterfalls in the Lake District, tumbling 60ft (18 metres) in a gorge flanked by trees. The fell, a former deer park, is a good place to wander, enjoying magnificent views without too much strenuous effort.

Heading north now on the A592,

Walking the Fells

Walking is the most popular activity in the Lake District. The travel shelves of local bookshops are crammed with books, most of which describe circular and not-too-arduous routes. The Lake District National Park organises walks and details are given in their free newspaper, which is available at any information centre.

For more experienced walkers – those who believe there is no substitute for the fell-walking books written and illustrated by Alfred Wainwright – there are some great challenges: a circuit taking in the Langdale Pikes, beginning and ending at the Dungeon Ghyll car park at the head of Great Langdale, is one of the most popular. In the east of the region, the summit of Helvellyn can be approached from either Thirlmere or Ullswater – one route from the latter being up the magnificent Striding Edge. In Central Lakeland, Great Gable can be climbed from Honister Pass, while Wasdale Head is the most popular starting point for those wishing to conquer Scafell Pike. The southern fells are dominated by the Old Man of Coniston, while Skiddaw looms 3,053ft (977 metres) above Bassenthwaite Lake.

Information centres stock local maps showing walks suitable for people with disabilities. The Wainwright Society, based in Kendal, organises memorial lectures and walks in honour of the great Lakeland walker Alfred Wainwright: www.wainwright.org.uk.

Rheged – The Village in the Hill (daily 10am–5.30pm) lies at the junction with the A66. Housed in Europe's largest grass-covered building, this innovative tourist attraction takes the visitor through 2,000 years of Cumbria's history.

After this diversion, it's on to **Penrith** ⑲, a sturdy working town of red sandstone buildings, where the 14th-century castle is a picturesque stump in a park near the station, and a collection of ancient stones, known as the Giant's Grave, stand in the churchyard of 18th-century St Andrew's. **Brougham Castle**, just southeast of Penrith, is a Norman structure built on the foundations of a Roman fort. The ruins are impressive: the top gallery of the keep has fine views and is worth the effort of climbing. During the 9th and 10th centuries, Penrith was the capital of Cumbria, a semi-independent region which was once considered part of Scotland.

Just north of the town, at Little Salkeld, stands an impressive Bronze Age stone circle known as **Long Meg and her Daughters**. On the B5305 is a stately home worth a visit: **Hutton-in-the-Forest** (Apr–Oct Wed, Thur, Sun and Bank Holidays 12.30–4pm; charge). It's a gracious building, with a 14th-century tower and a splendid 17th-century Long Gallery, a walled garden and pleasant woodlands.

Carlisle ⑳, 21 miles (34km) north of Penrith on the M6, is our last stop. It's also the last city before the Scottish border on the northwestern side of the country. Now the capital of Cumbria, it has suffered numerous attacks over the centuries, and the Norman **Castle** obtained its unusual outline when its roof was strengthened to carry cannons. From the castle, take the footbridge or underground walkway to **Tullie House Museum and Art Gallery** (Apr–June, Sept–Oct Mon–Sat 10am–5pm, Sun noon–5pm, July–Aug from 11am on Sun, Nov–Mar until 4pm; charge) containing an eclectic collection of Roman artefacts, wildlife displays and Pre-Raphaelite paintings. Carlisle is a good starting point for Hadrian's Wall (*see page 342*). A special bus operates daily in summer from the town centre (tel: 01434-322 002). ❏

Dacre church with carved stone bear effigies.

LEFT: Rheged Visitor Centre.
BELOW: Ashness Bridge and Skiddaw.

HOWZAT!

England's special gift to the world is cricket. Most countries don't want it, and the ones that do have proved to be much better at it

A Frenchman reporting on the state of cricket in England in 1728 wrote: "Everyone plays it, the common people and also men of rank. They go into a large open field and knock a ball about with a piece of wood. I will not attempt to describe this game." Apart from a lack of sensitivity to the music of leather balls on willow bats, this foreigner was sensible in not attempting a description of a game which involves two teams of 11 players, two wickets, two umpires, tea and sandwiches and, in county and international Test matches, takes five days to play. It has been said that the English, not being spiritual people, invented the game to give themselves some conception of eternity.

Batting for a Better World

Many see cricket as a civilising influence. Writing on the French Revolution, the historian G.M. Trevelyan reflected, "If the French noblesse had been capable of playing cricket with their peasants, their châteaux would not have been burnt." In this idealised pursuit the village blacksmith had the opportunity to hurl balls down at the Lord of the Manor. It was a very English sporting spirit, in which one did one's best, never cheated, and played with a "straight bat" – one which traditionalists feels has been tarnished by the new Twenty20 game which is faster, less subtle and far more commercial.

RIGHT: Bowlers use the raised seams of the cricket ball to make the ball deviate in direction, both through the air and when hitting the surface of the cricket pitch.

ABOVE: Cricket is still played on village greens. Games last all afternoon, with a break for tea, and there's beer when stumps are pulled.

ABOVE: One delight of the game is seeing in what bizarre circumstances it might be played. The players pictured here in the Solent on the south coast meet for a 90-minute match once a year, the only time when the Brambles Sandbar is revealed by an abnormal tide.

W.G. GRACE, HERO AT THE WICKET

The colossus of cricket was William Gilbert "W.G." Grace, depicted here in *Vanity Fair* magazine in 1877. He was a giant on the field, knocking up runs with consummate ease. Born in Bristol, he played for a Gloucester team of Gentleman v Players at the age of 16. He twice captained England and toured the US and Canada. At home crowds flocked to see him wherever he appeared. He had a doctor's practice, and remained a gentlemen player, though this amateur status did not prevent him making money from the game where he could. His reputation for fairness and a straight bat overshadowed the odd occasion when he would replace bails claiming that the wind had blown them off. He went on playing until he was 66 and Sir Arthur Conan Doyle watched him in old age, recording, "At the end of a century he had not turned a hair."

ABOVE: Howzat! If a batsman is thought to be out, a cry goes up for the umpires to adjudicate. The headgear shows that it can be a dangerous game.

ABOVE: Lords cricket ground in London is home to the Marylebone Cricket Club (MCC), the game's governing body whose members are identified by red and gold ties, known as "egg and bacon" *(right)*. Lords hosts international matches known as Tests.

YORK

This venerable city of the north, easily explored on foot, has a vast Minster and strong links with the Romans, Vikings and the golden age of railways

E ngland's most ancient northern city lies on the River Ouse in the centre of the Vale of York between the Yorkshire Dales and the North York Moors. It was once the principal town of Yorkshire, and it remains the see of the Archbishop of York, Primate of England, second to the Archbishop of Canterbury in the hierarchy of the Church of England. Its streets, walls and buildings mark the pageant of its history, from Roman and Viking ancestry to medieval heart and Georgian elegance. A child-friendly city, its Viking, Castle and Railway museums have plenty to engage young people as well as adults.

The starting point of any visit is **York Minster Ⓐ** (www.yorkminster.org; daily 7am–6.30pm), England's largest medieval church *(see next page)*, which dominates the city. The **Minster's Visitor's Centre** is beside it in St William's College, founded in 1461 as the home of the chantry priests who sang Masses for the souls of the founder. In Dean's Park on the north side of the minster is the **Minster Library**. The Archbishop's Palace once covered this area, and the library, which is the largest cathedral library in the country, is in its former chapel. To the right of the chapel is the **Treasurer's House** (Mar–Oct, house and garden Sat–Thur 11am–4.30pm, Nov 11am–3pm; charge, ghost cellar open selected days only, tel: 01904-624 247). Built in 1419, it was fully restored at the end of the 19th century, but ghosts of Roman legion-

naires are said to continue to march through its cellar. The Roman city was walled but the walls that can be seen today date largely from the 14th century and are the longest remaining medieval walls in Britain. **Monk Bar Ⓑ**, which lies on the north side of the Minster, gives access up on to the Bar Walls. Walking round the wall to the left brings you to the city gate of **Bootham Bar Ⓒ**, which once led out to the Forest of Galtres; armed guards used to wait here to protect travellers, it is said, from wolves and robbers in the forest.

PRECEDING PAGES: York Minster. **LEFT:** the National Railway Museum. **BELOW:** street busker.

The Magnificent Minster

With fine medieval stained glass, this is the most elegant building in the north. For a detailed floor plan see page 396.

The Minster is the largest Gothic cathedral north of the Alps and is both a cathedral – because of its archbishop's throne – and a minster because it has been served since Saxon times by a team of clergy. It has the widest Gothic nave in England, stands 196ft (60 metres) high, is 525ft (160 metres) long and 250ft (76 metres) wide across the transept. The finest stained glass in the country give an immediate impression of airy lightness. The first church was founded in 627, followed by two Norman cathedrals and the present Gothic one, completed in 1472. Major restoration was needed after two 19th-century fires, and one in 1984, caused by lightning, destroyed the south transept roof.

The nave is Decorated Gothic in style and was completed in the 1350s. The pulpit on the left has a brass lectern, in use since 1686. The 14th-century West Window, painted in 1338, is known as the "heart of Yorkshire" because of the shape of the ornate tracery. Shields in the nave arches are the arms of nobles who fought against the Scots in the 14th century. The dragon's head peeping out from the upper gallery is a crane used to lift a font cover. To the right of the nave is the Jesse Window of 1310. The north transept is dominated by the Five Sisters' Window from 1260, the oldest complete window in the Minster.

The Chapter House (charge) off the transept was the architectural wonder of its age. It has a beautiful domed roof and some of the finest medieval carvings on the canopied stalls. Beside the entrance to the Chapter House, the astronomical clock commemorates World War II airmen, while 400-year-old figures of Gog and Magog chime the striking clock to the right.

The screen in the crossing is decorated with the statues of 15 kings of England from William I to Henry VI. Daily services are held behind it in the choir. The Great East Window at the east end of the church has the world's largest area of medieval stained glass, with scenes from the Bible. On the south side of the choir St Cuthbert's Window (1435) shows scenes from the life of the saint. The Norman crypt contains the coffin of the minster's founder, St William.

The south transept, restored after the 1984 fire, has mirrored tables to see the new carvings, six designed by children. The Rose Window, which commemorates the end of the Wars of the Roses in 1486, escaped destruction in the fire. Walls of the Norman churches and remains of the Roman forum lie beneath the central tower in the Foundations Museum and Treasury.

Visitors who are feeling energetic can climb the 275 steps to the top of the tower, which offers superb views of the city and the surrounding countryside. The charge to the Minster includes an informative guided tour, separate charges apply to the tower. ❑

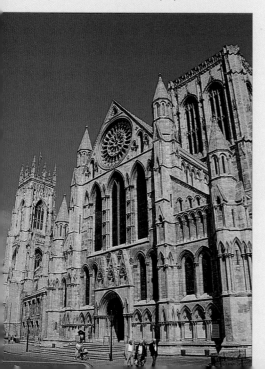

LEFT: the minster's exterior.
ABOVE LEFT: detail of the Archbishop's throne.
ABOVE RIGHT: the Rose Window.

From here descend to Exhibition Square where there is a fountain and statue of the local artist William Etty whose work can be seen in the nearby **City Art Gallery** (daily 10am–5pm), which displays 600 years of British and European paintings and pottery. Behind the gallery, set within the 10-acre (4-hectare) site of Museum Gardens, is the **Yorkshire Museum D**. One of the oldest museums in the country, it has important geology, natural history and archaeology collections, including a marble head of Constantine the Great who was proclaimed Roman Emperor in this city in 306. The museum is closed for refurbishment, and will re-open with five new galleries.

Into the old town

Cross the street in front of the museum and head straight into the old town to arrive at **Stonegate E**, the finest street in York, which follows the route of the Roman Via Praetoria. Elegant shops now use the 15th- and 16th-century houses: No. 52A is the 1180 **Norman House**, the oldest surviving house in the city. Another historic site is Coffee Yard where coffee houses were once meeting places described by the 19th-century author Laurence Sterne as "chit chat" clubs.

Stonegate leads down towards the River Ouse where the **Guildhall F** and **Mansion House** lie. The Mansion House is the residence of the city's Lord Mayor, the only one outside London to be accorded the title of The Right Honourable; the building was completed in 1730, 10 years before London's Mansion House. The arched passageway alongside this pretty building leads to the **Guildhall** (Mon–Fri 9am–5pm, May–Oct also Sat 10am–5pm, Sun 2–5pm). First mentioned in 1256, it was rebuilt in the 15th century, and since 1810 the city's business has been conducted from the council chamber rich with Victorian carved desks and chairs, and with a view over the river. Hooks on the ceiling were used for hanging meat. Committee Room No. 1 is where the Scots received payment in silver from the Parliamentarians in 1646 for handing over Charles I who had fled to Scotland.

Parliament Street pals.

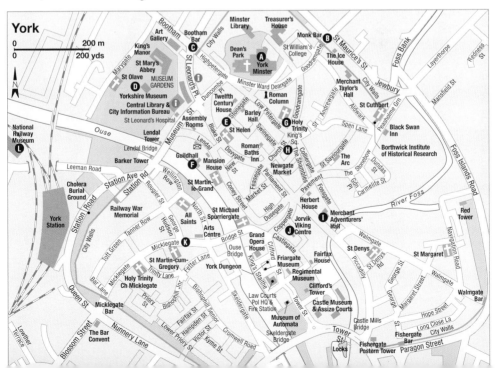

Clifford's Tower.

RIGHT: the former butchers' quarter, The Shambles.

The cash was counted out on the table. The impressive, oak-beamed Common Hall is a replica: the original was destroyed by German bombs.

Petergate, at the opposite end of Stonegate, leads to **Goodramgate** where boutiques and antiques shops occupy Tudor buildings. Eleven tenements from the 11th century are known as Lady's Row; opposite is a 1960s error, an eyesore of concrete arches which brought strict controls on subsequent developments.

Halfway down the street is **Holy Trinity G**, one of the most delightful of the city's churches, it has a two-tiered pulpit (1785) and a reredos with the Ten Commandments, Creed and Lord's Prayer.

Heart of the old town

Goodramgate leads down to **King's Square** and Colliergate where the shortest street in York has the longest name: Whipmawhopmagate. A plaque suggests this is 16th-century dialect for "What a gate!". King's Square is the place to be in summer: buskers, jugglers and street artists provide some of the best free entertainment in the north of England. Leading off the square is **The Shambles H**, York's most famous street and one of the best-preserved medieval streets in all Europe. Once called Fleshammels (the street of the butchers), its broad windowsills served as shelves to display meat. The half-timbered houses lean inwards and neighbours can shake hands across the street. Three narrow alleyways lead to **Newgate Market**, open daily with stalls selling everything from fish to fashions. The original main market area was on **Pavement**, on the other side of Newgate Market. This was the first paved street in the city, a place of punishment (whipping, pillorying) and execution.

Fossgate, which leads from Pavement down to the River Foss, is where the richest of the city's medieval merchants used to live. Just before the river on the right is a stone portal leading to the **Merchant Adventurers' Hall I** (Apr–Sept Mon–Thur 9am–5pm, Fri–Sat 9am–3.30pm, Sun noon–4pm, Oct–Dec Mon–Sat 9am–3.30pm; charge). Still the home of the most

Fact File

Location 164 miles (264km) from London, 167 miles (269km) from Edinburgh.

By car M1 motorway from London to Leeds, the last 36 miles (60km) on the A1(M) and A64. Allow 3 hours.

By train Direct from London's King's Cross (approx 2 hours, leaving every 30 minutes) and Edinburgh (2 hours 30 minutes).

Nearest airport Leeds Bradford Intl (www.leedsbradfordairport.co.uk).

Boat trips Cruises on the Ouse include one-hour trips downstream to the Archbishop's Palace at Bishopthorpe.

Most famous site The Minster.

Best for Yorkshire high teas Betty's Café Tea Room, St Helen's Square.

Festivals Jorvik Viking Festival (February), three-day Ebor Festival at Knavesmire horse-race track – "the Ascot of the North" (August).

Historic emblem The white rose: the Wars of the Roses, immortalised in Shakespeare's *Richard III*, were fought between the House of York (white rose) and the House of Lancaster (red rose).

Royal connection The second son of a monarch is traditionally given the title Duke of York.

Tourist information Tel: 01904-550 099; www.visityork.org.

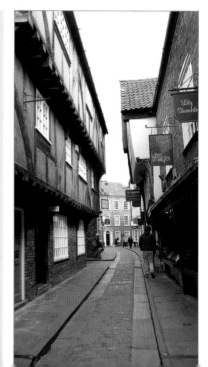

powerful of the York guilds, the hall has a massive, timber-framed roof and a 14th-century undercroft used for receptions.

The other end of Pavement leads to Coppergate and the **Jorvik Viking Centre** ❿ (www.jorvik-viking-centre.co.uk; Apr–Oct daily 10am–5pm, Nov–Mar 10am–4pm; charge). The museum is based on an archaeological dig at Coppergate in the 1970s which revealed wicker houses and shoulder-high walls, the best-preserved Viking settlement in Britain.

Visitors are whisked back to a reconstructed settlement in "time capsules". Background chatter of the ancient Norse language and evocative smells of middens and latrines give a convincing atmosphere.

The age of horse and steam

Castlegate behind the Viking Centre ends in a great earth mound topped by **Clifford's Tower**, thrown up by the Normans in their conquest of England. The **Castle Museum** (www.york castlemuseum.org.uk; daily 9.30am–5pm), housed in what were a female and a debtors' prisons, is a folk museum with a reconstruction of a complete Yorkshire street and a glimpse of lost ways of life. There is still evidence of the former prison: the cell of the highway robber Dick Turpin is preserved; in 1739 he was sentenced next door in the Assize Court and hanged on St George's Field.

On the south side of the River Ouse is **Micklegate** ❿, once York's most important street, as it was the road into the city from London. Many fine Georgian houses were built along it. But for a century and a half, visitors have been arriving by rail: York is famous for its railways, personified in George Hudson, the 19th-century "Railway King". **The National Railway Museum** ❿ (www.nrm.org.uk; daily 10am–6pm) is one of the greatest in the world. Exhibits include Queen Victoria's favourite travelling "home", a replica of Stephenson's *Rocket*, the legendary *Flying Scotsman* and the only "bullet train" outside Japan. Visitors can also see *Mallard*, the fastest steam train in the world.❑

George Hudson, three times Lord Mayor of York, was York's "Railway King", obsessed with "makin' all t'railways coom to York". But by 1847 his speculations had ruined him.

LEFT: Micklegate Bar, the four-storey high gatehouse.
BELOW: the Jorvik Viking Centre.

YORKSHIRE

The Dales and Moors of Yorkshire are
as rugged and resolute as their inhabitants.
Beyond York are the great former abbeys
of Whitby, Fountains and Rievaulx

Yorkshire is England's Big Country. Until 1974 this region north of the River Humber was divided into three Yorkshire "Ridings", from the Old Norse trithing, meaning three administrative parts. North Riding (now largely North Yorkshire) was larger than any other county in England. Characterised by miles of moorland, the three modern counties of Yorkshire extend from the Pennines to the North Sea, and include two national parks – the Yorkshire Dales to the west of York and the North York Moors to the north – separated by the Vale of York, where the A1 follows the old Roman Road heading for Hadrian's Wall.

Limestone, shale and sandstone of the Carboniferous Age shaped the Yorkshire Dales, which are cut through by fast-flowing rivers and douched with waterfalls. The Jurassic limestone of the North York Moors has been used for houses, castles and spectacular abbeys such as Fountains and Rievaulx. To the south, the Yorkshire Wolds are chalk hills rising to 800ft (240 metres), reaching the sea at Flamborough Head. Grouse are the prize of the moors; trout fill the short, fast rivers and streams of the Pennines and Dales.

Yorkshire is traditionally a sheep-rearing region, and incessant grazing means that, as in the rest of Britain, there is no true wilderness.

An overall pattern of dry-stone walls links the farms, villages and market towns. The buildings, constructed in local slate and stone, are unpretentious in style but perfectly suited to the needs of a pastoral community, from the farmhouse with its big, flagged, ground-floor rooms, to the field barns with just enough space to accommodate young cattle.

The farmers' way of life, evolving in isolation, bred a sturdy, independent type of person, the sort about whom James Herriot, the celebrated Dales vet (whose real name was Alf Wight), wrote in his best-selling books.

Main attractions
SALTAIRE
BRONTE PARSONAGE
YORKSHIRE DALES NATIONAL PARK
HAREWOOD HOUSE
FOUNTAINS ABBEY
NORTH YORK MOORS NATIONAL
  PARK
CASTLE HOWARD
RIEVAULX ABBEY

PRECEDING PAGES:
sunset over the
Yorkshire Moors.
LEFT: Danby Dale.
BELOW: Litton in the
Yorkshire Dales.

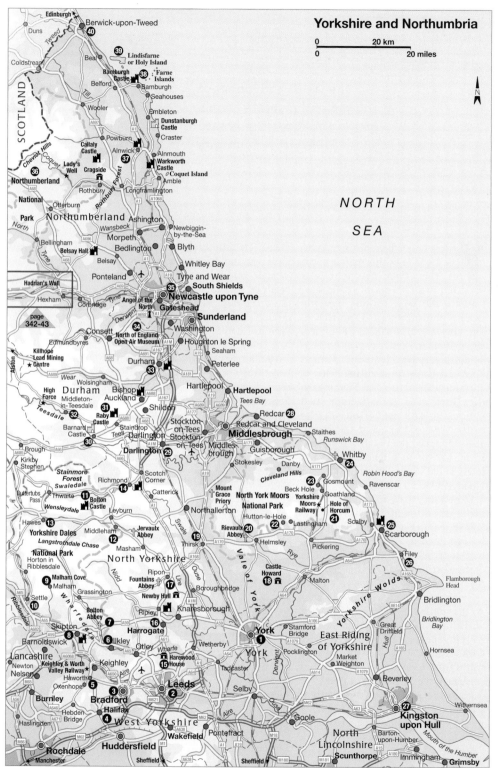

Yorkshire and Northumbria

0   20 km
0   20 miles

N

NORTH

SEA

SCOTLAND

Edinburgh
Duns
Coldstream
Berwick-upon-Tweed 40
Tweed
Lindisfarne 39
or Holy Island
Beal
Bamburgh 38
Castle
Belford
Bamburgh
Seahouses
Farne
Islands
Till
Wooler
Embleton
Dunstanburgh 37
Castle
Craster
Powburn
Callaly
Castle
Alnwick
Cheviot Hills
Coquet
Lady's
Well
Cragside
Alnmouth
Warkworth
Castle
36
Northumberland
Rothbury
Rothbury Forest
Longframlington
Coquet Island
Amble
National
Otterburn
Park
North
Ashington
Newbiggin-
by-the-Sea
Bellingham
Wansbeck
Morpeth
Belsay Hall
Bedlington
Blyth
Belsay
Whitley Bay
Tyne
Ponteland
Tyne and Wear
South Shields 35
Hadrian's Wall
Hexham
Corbridge
Angel of the
North
Newcastle upon Tyne
Gateshead
Sunderland
page
342-43
Consett
North of England 34
Open Air Museum
Washington
Houghton le Spring
Edmundbyres
Seaham
Killhope
Lead Mining
Centre
Durham
Peterlee
Alston
Wear
Wolsingham
Durham 33
High
Force
Middleton-
in-Teesdale
Bishop
Auckland
Hartlepool
Hartlepool
31
Raby
Castle
32
Shildon
Tees Bay
Teesdale
Staindrop
Tees
Redcar 28
Barnard
Castle
30
Darlington
Stockton-
on-Tees
Stockton-
on-Tees
Redcar and Cleveland
Staithes
Runswick Bay
Brough
Kirkby
Stephen
Darlington 29
Middles-
brough
Middlesbrough
Guisborough
Whitby 24
Stainmore
Forest
Swaledale
Richmond
Scotch
Corner
Stokesley
Danby
Cleveland Hills
Robin Hood's Bay
Ravenscar
Butterbuts
Pass
Thwaite
11
Bolton
Castle
Catterick
Mount
Grace
Priory
North York Moors
National Park
Beck Hole 23
Gosmount
Yorkshire
Moors
Railway
Goathland
Hawes
13
Wensleydale
Leyburn
Northallerton
Hutton-le-Hole
Hole
of
Horcum 21
Scalby
Scarborough 25
Yorkshire Dales
Langstrothdale Chase
Middleham 12
Jervaulx
Abbey
Swale
19
Rievaulx
Abbey 20
22
Lastingham
National Park
Horton in
Ribblesdale
Masham
Thirsk
Helmsley
Rye
Pickering
Filey
26
Malham Cove 9
North Yorkshire
Ripon
Fountains
Abbey
17
Ure
Boroughbridge
Castle
Howard 18
Malton
Flamborough
Head
Settle
Malham
Grassington
Newby Hall
Ouse
Yorkshire Wolds
A614
Bridlington
10
Ribblesdale
Nidd
Ripley
Knaresborough
Bridlington
Bay
Bolton
Abbey
7
Skipton
Bolton
Abbey
Wharfe
York 1
Stamford
Bridge
East Riding
of Yorkshire
Hornsea
8
16
Harrogate
Otley
Wetherby
York
Pocklington
Market
Weighton
Barnoldswick
Ilkley
Wharfe
Derwent
Hull
Lancashire
Newton
Nelson
Keighley & Worth
Valley Railway
Keighley
Harewood
House 15
Tadcaster
Beverley
Haworth
Oxenhope
5
Aire
Selby
Burnley
Bradford 3
Leeds 2
Kingston
upon Hull 27
Witherness
Haslingden
Hebden
Bridge
Halifax
4
West Yorkshire
Wakefield
Pontefract
Goole
North
Lincolnshire
Barton-
upon-Humber
Mouth of the Humber
Rochdale
Huddersfield
Manchester
Sheffield
Sheffield
Scunthorpe
Immingham
Grimsby

The wool towns

From Yorkshire sheep grew a wool trade which enriched the monasteries and the town of **York** ❶ *(see pages 311–15)*. After the Industrial Revolution, however, cloth manufacturing was centred on towns to the south of the Dales. England's third-largest and Yorkshire's main city, **Leeds** ❷, is one place to go to see the region's industrial heritage. **The Armley Mills Museum** (Tue–Sat 10am–5pm, Sun 1–5pm; charge), on the northwest side of this lively university city, was once the world's largest woollen mill and still demonstrates the machinery that once helped to make Britain the richest nation.

The Royal Armories Museum (www.royalarmouries.org; daily 10am–5pm; free) beside the River Aire at Clarence Dock contains an impressive collection of arms and armour organised around five themes: war, tournament, self-defence, hunting and the Orient. There is also a Craft Court, menagerie and a tiltyard, where you can watch demonstrations of jousting. **The City Art Gallery** (Mon–Tue 10am–8pm, Thur–Sat 10am–5pm, Wed noon–8pm, Sun 1–5pm; free) has works by Courbet and Sisley as well as Atkinson Grimshaw (1836–93), a local artist and one of the best painters of Victorian towns, and the great landscape painter John Sell Cotman (1782–1842). Contemporary crafts can be bought at the adjoining Craft Centre and Design Gallery. The sculptor Henry Moore, who was born not far away in Castleford in 1898, studied in Leeds and the Henry Moore Institute, with sculpture galleries, was added in 1995. His work is also to be seen at the **Yorkshire Sculpture Park** (www.ysp.co.uk; daily 10am–6pm; free), south of Leeds near Wakefield, where the sculptor Barbara Hepworth was born in 1903.

Bradford's ❸ famous artistic son is David Hockney, who was born in this mill town in 1935. Many of his paintings are on the walls of the **1853 Gallery** (Mon–Fri 10am–5.30pm, Sat–Sun 10am–6pm; free) in Salts Mill, **Saltaire**. This well-preserved "model" village, founded by 19th-century wool baron Titus Salt, was designated a Unesco World Heritage Site in 2001.

Among the chic shops in Leeds is Harvey Nichols. Marks & Spencer, the high-street clothing giant, started life in a market in this one-time "ready-to-wear capital of England".

LEFT: the cobbled streets of Haworth.

Fact File

Main cities Leeds, York *(see pages 311–15).*
Car The A1 goes through the Vale of York. Alternative transport is strongly encouraged within the National Parks.
Bus There is a network of services including extra Moorsbus (tel: 01845-597 000) and Dales (www.dalesbus.org, www.traveldales.org.uk) bus services in summer.
Train The Settle–Carlisle line and two steam railways: the North Yorkshire Moors Railway, from Pickering to Grosmont, and the Embsay and Bolton Abbey Steam Railway.
Local words Many of Old Norse origin: fell (hill), scar (cliff face), dale (valley), gate (street), happen (maybe).
National Parks North York Moors (www.northyorkmoors.org.uk); Yorkshire Dales (www.yorkshiredales.org.uk).
Best stately home Castle Howard.
Most famous family The Brontës.
Food and drink Wensleydale cheese, Yorkshire pudding, mushy peas, Yorkshire curd tart, Theakston's beer.
Tourist information Leeds, tel: 0113-242 5242; Harrogate, tel: 01423-537 300; www.yorkshire.com; Scarborough, tel: 01723-383 636; www.discoveryorkshirecoast.com.

The Brontës of Haworth

The reputation of Yorkshire's most talented literary family brings thousands of visitors to their moorland home every year.

With their Celtic background, it was inevitable that the writing of the Brontë girls – Charlotte, Emily and Anne – would be strong and imaginative. Their father, Patrick (1777–1861), was a poor Irish boy from Emdale in County Down who made good, changing his name from Brunty to Brontë after his hero Lord Nelson, who had been given the dukedom of Bronte by King Ferdinand of the Two Sicilies in 1799.

Patrick married Maria Branwell, from Penzance in Cornwall. She bore him six children in quick succession, but died of cancer in 1821 when they were all still young, leaving them in the care of their distraught father.

Patrick was to outlive all of his children, whose short, sad lives give the Brontë story a particular poignancy. The family moved to Haworth in 1820 after Patrick was appointed curate for life. His two oldest children, Maria and Elizabeth, died in 1825. The other four, often left to their own devices, created a fantasy world, writing tiny books with minuscule script. In 1846, using pseudonyms, the three girls wrote and published a book of poems, which sold just two copies.

Success came the following year with the publication of Charlotte's *Jane Eyre*, now regarded as a classic feminist novel. Ferndean Manor, described in the book, was probably the 16th-century home of the Cunliffes in Wycoller, reached by a 9-mile (15km) footpath from Haworth called the Brontë Way.

Charlotte's success was followed by Emily's *Wuthering Heights* and Anne's *Agnes Grey*. Charlotte had written: "Speak of the North – a lonely moor, silent and still and trackless lies." But it was Emily who most vividly described the atmosphere of Haworth's moors, which she saw as wild and savage. She used the landscape when portraying Heathcliffe in *Wuthering Heights*; he was described by Catherine, the object of his passion, as "an unreclaimed creature, without refinement, without cultivation; an arid wilderness of furze and whinstone".

Charlotte became a literary celebrity. In 1854 she married the Rev. Arthur Bell Nicholls. Both Emily and her brother Branwell died in 1848, aged 30 and 31. Branwell had become addicted to alcohol and opium – he used to buy the latter at an apothecary in Haworth, and his health had been compromised, leaving him easy prey to tuberculosis, the disease that also killed Emily. Anne died of the same disease a year later, aged 29, and Charlotte in 1855, aged 38 and pregnant. Patrick, last of the Brontës, died in 1861, aged 84. The parson's body was lowered into the vault within the altar rails and placed beside the coffin of Charlotte.

All the Brontës except Anne, who was buried in Scarborough, lie in the family vault near to where the Brontë's pew stood in the old church of St Michael and All Angels.

Still very visible is the congestion of old tombstones in the burial ground, recalling mid-19th century conditions here, when average life expectancy was 28 and the town was racked with typhus and cholera. ❑

ABOVE: Charlotte Brontë.
RIGHT: The Black Bull, Haworth, where Branwell Brontë drank.

Its design was influential in the "garden city" movement and illustrates the philanthropic paternalism of the time: Salt enshrined his ideals in a mill, hospital, school, library, church and almshouses, but religiously excluded pubs.

Two other famous sons are the composer Frederick Delius (1862–1934), who inspires regular festivals, and the writer J.B. Priestley (1894–1984), who wrote prolifically and with an acute eye for Yorkshire characters. Bradford also has the **National Media Museum**, which has one of the best photographic collections in the country, as well as hands-on film fun (Tue–Sun 10am–6pm; free). In the 1950s immigrants from the Indian subcontinent were encouraged to work in Bradford's mills, and today over 20 percent of the city's population is Muslim. There is no shortage of good quality curry restaurants in town.

Halifax ❹, west of Bradford, was another important wool town, noted for its carpets and yarns. Its 18th-century Piece Hall, set amid stunning scenery, is the only remaining cloth hall in York-shire. Cottage weavers sold their "pieces" in 315 small rooms in the collonaded galleries that provide an impressive shopping area today, and a market is still held here. To the southwest of Halifax lie the attractive Pennine woollen mill towns of **Hebden Bridge** and **Heptonstall**, both good bases for Pennine walks. A little further north is another Pennine mill village, **Haworth ❺**, the second most popular literary shrine in England after Shakespeare's Stratford. The Brontës moved to Haworth in 1820 *(see left)* and today more than a million visitors arrive each year to see the fine Georgian **Parsonage** (www.bronte.org.uk; Apr–Sept daily 10am–5.30pm, Oct–Mar 11am–5pm; charge), restored to look as it did when it was the writers' home. The main street of this hillside village was surfaced with stone setts, to provide horses with a good grip as they drew laden carts. The flanking gritstone houses were built right up to the edge of the street. Houses with a third storey and long, narrow windows were both the home and workplace of hand-loom weavers – in the time of the Brontës

LEFT: Malham Cove.
BELOW: preserving the valley railway.

more than 1,200 looms were chattering in the village. The parish church has a Brontë memorial chapel and an admirer from the USA paid for the stained-glass window on which Charlotte is commemorated. The walk to Top Withens, the inspiration for *Wuthering Heights*, is about 5 miles (8km). Haworth station is the headquarters of the working steam railway, **Keighley and Worth Valley Railway Preservation Society** (www.kwvr.co.uk; July–Aug daily, tel: 01535-645 214 for hours rest of year).

A dozen miles north of Haworth is **Ilkley** , a Victorian inland spa for the prosperous burghers of Leeds and Bradford. The 16–17th-century Manor House houses a small local history museum. Ilkley has immortalised its rugged climate in the Yorkshire anthem *On Ilkla Moor baht 'at*, which, translated, tells you that it is not prudent to venture forth on Ilkley Moor without a hat.

The Dales

To the north of Ilkley lies the 680-sq-mile (1,762-sq-km) **Yorkshire Dales National Park** (www.yorkshiredales.org.

uk), characterised by dry stone walls – each dale has its own distinctive pattern of dry-stoning – bustling market towns, lonely farmhouses and cathedral-like caverns. Dales are valleys, and they take their name from the rivers that created them – Ribblesdale, Wensleydale, Swaledale. Motorists, look out for cyclists and animals on the narrow winding roads or, better still, use the train and bus services within the park. The easiest excursion from Ilkley takes you into surrounding Wharfedale, an alluring mix of water, wood, crag and castle. **Bolton Abbey** (daily Nov–late Mar 9am–6pm, late Mar–end May, Sept–Oct 9am–7pm, June–end Aug 9am–9pm, last entry 2 hours before closing), 5 miles (8km) northwest of Ilkley, dates from the 12th century. Its picturesque ruins, surrounding footpaths and stunning location by the River Wharf, have long made it a major attraction and it can be reached by steam train from Embsay station.

West of Ilkley is the market town of **Skipton** , "the gateway to the Dales". Its position on the Leeds–Liverpool

canal brought it great prosperity during the Industrial Revolution. Many of the warehouses still stand, and so does the much older **Skipton Castle** (summer Mon–Sat 10am–6pm, Sun noon–6pm, winter Mon–Sat 10am–4pm, Sun noon–4pm; charge), home of the powerful Clifford family from the 14th to the 17th century. Skipton provides easy access to **Malham Cove** ❾, one of the great wonders of the Yorkshire Dales. Knee-cracking steps lead to the tip of this immense cliff where limestone pavement with clints (blocks of worn limestone with crevices known as "grykes") form a pattern like the whorls of a brain. The view from here is magnificent. It is possible to continue walking north along the Pennine Way. **Gordale Scar**, 1½ miles (2km) east of Malham, has 16ft (5-metre) overhanging cliffs described by the poet William Wordsworth as a lair "where young lions crouch".

To the west of Malham is the small market town of **Settle** ❿, separated from **Giggleswick** by the River Ribble. Beside Market Place, which comes alive on Tuesday, are The Shambles,

which, like York's, were once a butchers' domain. Ye Olde Naked Man Café got its name when it was an inn and fashion was deemed to be needlessly flamboyant. Settle is an excellent point from which to explore Ribblesdale or begin a circular tour of the flat-topped Ingleborough Hill, taking in the magnificent Ribblehead Viaduct, built from 1870 to 1875 to carry the Settle–Carlisle railway across Batty Moss. This trans-Pennine line has the highest mainline station in England, 1,150ft (350 metres) up, at **Dent**.

To the north, **Wensleydale** is broad and wooded and seems serene until the eye catches the forbidding **Bolton Castle** ⓫ (daily Apr–end Oct Tue–Sun 10am–5pm; charge), perched on a hillside. Tradition has it that the mortar was mixed with ox blood to strengthen the building. Wander through the stables area into the open courtyard which was once the Great Hall and you can easily imagine yourself transported back to 1568 when Mary, Queen of Scots was imprisoned here. The building was fortified in the 14th century by Richard le Scrope,

Wensleydale, the best-known cheese in Yorkshire.

BELOW: the Moors at Sutton Bank.

chancellor to Richard II. He was a friend of Chaucer and the poet used him as the model for his *Knight's Tale*. Nearby are the impressive **Aysgarth Falls**, where there is a National Park Centre and well-signposted spectacular walks. At the bottom of the dale is the town of **Middleham ⑫**, famous for its race-horse stables and **castle** (Apr–Sept daily 10am–6pm, Oct–Mar Mon–Wed, Sat–Sun 10am–4pm; charge), childhood home of Richard III. As Duke of Gloucester, he came to Middleham to be tutored by the Earl of Warwick, and he married the earl's daughter, Anne. His death in 1485 at Bosworth (near Leicester), the final battle in the Wars of the Roses, ended the 24-year reign of the House of York. The castle remains include a 12th-century keep, 13th-century chapel and 14th-century gatehouse.

Near the head of the dale and in the heart of the Yorkshire Dales National Park is the excellent **Dales Countryside Museum** (daily 10am–5pm; charge) at **Hawes ⑬** (from *haus*, a mountain pass). On view is a traditional dales kitchen and displays relating to dairy farming, industry, local crafts and community life. Nearby, approached through the Green Dragon Inn, is the impressive **Hardraw Force**, England's highest unbroken waterfall.

In neighbouring Gayle is the **Wensleydale Creamery Visitors' Centre** (Mon–Sat 9am–5pm, Sun 10am–4.30pm; free), where visitors can watch the production of Wensleydale cheese and taste the results.

Buttertubs Pass, at 1,726ft (526 metres) above sea level, links Wensleydale with **Swaledale** to the northeast ("buttertubs" are deep limestone shafts). Swaledale is steep and rocky, noted for its intricate patterns of dry-stone walls and field barns. It also has **Richmond ⑭**, a market town with a cobbled square, impressive Norman **castle** (Apr–Sept daily 10am–6pm, Oct–Mar Thur–Mon 10am–4pm; charge) and the splendidly restored Georgian Theatre Royal (tel: 01748-825 252).

Splendour and sulphur

There are other ways to leave Leeds than via Ilkley. Strike north on the A61 and, after 9 miles (14km), you reach

the ornate **Harewood House** ⓘ (www.harewood.org; Apr–end Oct daily grounds: 10am–6pm, state rooms: noon–4pm; charge). Its interiors are by Robert Adam, furniture by Thomas Chippendale and gardens by "Capability" Brown, and it has a remarkable bird park. Built in the 1760s by Edwin Lascelles, it is now the home of the Earl and Countess of Harewood.

Eight miles (13km) further along the A61 is **Harrogate** ⓘ, where the **Royal Pump Room** stands over the famous sulphur wells and still serves the strongest sulphur water in Europe. The museum (Mon–Sat 10am–5pm, Sun 2–5pm, Nov–Mar until 4pm; charge) has displays recalling Harrogate's heyday as the Queen of Inland Spas. Being on a hilltop and a late starter among Yorkshire towns, Harrogate was able to develop gracefully. Many 19th-century buildings have their original cast-iron canopies. The protected 200-acre (90-hectare) Stray gives the town a spacious appearance, added to by a number of gardens. **Harlow Carr Botanical Gardens** (daily 9.30am–6pm, winter until 4pm), sus-tained by the Northern Horticultural Society, is comprehensive, with a spectacular Streamside Garden and ornamental gardens. The woodland, arboretum and wildflower meadow are home to birds, squirrels, stoat and roe deer. Harrogate promotes a spring flower show and has the permanent ground for the three-day Great Yorkshire Show in July, the largest agricultural show in the north of England. The Northern Antiques Fair is held in the autumn.

Neighbouring **Knaresborough** is celebrated for **Mother Shipton's Cave** (daily Apr–end Oct and Feb half-term 10am–5.30pm), birthplace and home of England's most famous prophet. She foretold the Great Fire of London, the defeat of the Spanish Armada, the coming of the motor car, and her own death in 1561. In Castle Grounds are **Knaresborough Castle** and The Old Court House Museum (Easter–Sept daily 10.30am–5pm). Take the castle tour and then try a game of Medieval putting or bowling

Four miles (6.5km) to the north, **Ripley** is a village conceived in the

LEFT: boats on the River Nidd at Knaresborough.
BELOW: tempting eats at Betty's Café Tea Rooms, Harrogate.

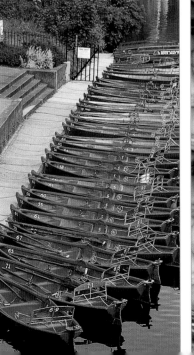

Wildlife on Moor and Dale

The wildness of the Yorkshire landscape attracts a variety of birds and encourages carpets of springtime flowers.

Among the region's varied wildlife, the red grouse, target of the sporting shooters, must hold pride of place. A bird that is endemic to Britain, it is also the only bird that remains on the open moor in winter. Its coarse yet cheerful call, uttered as it flies over the heather and often written as "go-back, go-back, go-back", is the archetypal sound of the North York Moors. In recent years its numbers have declined.

In spring the grouse is joined by snipe, plover and golden plover. The moors are also home to England's largest, though modest, populations of merlins. The Swainby moors are one of the strongholds of this small, darting hawk. Also seen on occasion is the hen harrier, a truly magnificent bird with an enormous wingspan that hunts by flying low over the heather and suddenly swooping sideways. Upland waders – curlews, redshanks, dunlins – fare best on the well-maintained grouse moors.

The Dales support a good population of dippers, with some kingfishers and, in spring and summer, grey wagtails and sandpipers. Mature woodland is home to green and greater spotted woodpeckers and flycatchers, while in the forest plantations of the moors are crossbills and nightjars.

Roe deer and, to a lesser extent, red and fallow deer can be found where there is woodland cover, and there are sika deer in Studley Royal, part of Fountains Abbey estate. Mink, introduced via Lancashire fur farms, have spread through the area, but in the rivers, otters are scarce. Crow Wood, home of the Moors Centre, has a bird hide and feeding station where visitors can observe woodland species such as goldfinches, nuthatches and green woodpeckers.

Several flower species reach their northern or southern limit on the moors. On Levisham Moor are two arctic-alpine species at the edge of their range – chickweed wintergreen and dwarf cornel, a kind of miniature dogwood. The early purple orchid shows up against the limestone of the Dales and the yellow mountain pansy is found in many areas. In the moist wooded ravines, such as Gunnerside Gill in Swaledale, are the star-shaped flowers of the spring sandwort.

In Kirkdale the rare May lily blossoms on its only native site in Britain. But while other common species, such as globeflower and bird's-eye primrose, are also found, it is perhaps the more familiar flowers that give most delight. The Farndale daffodils are famous, and there are carpets of bluebells at Glaisdale, Hasty Bank near Stokesley and other places. Nowhere are snowdrops prettier than on the banks of Mulgrave Old Castle, Sandsend. And on early-spring walks in the Forge Valley, or through the woods at Sunnington, popular flowers such as wood anemone, wood sorrel, violet and primrose, as well as shyer species like early purple orchid, brush the boots at almost every step. ❑

ABOVE: yellow mountain pansy.
LEFT: red grouse.

style of Alsace in France with a town hall labelled "Hôtel de Ville"; Sir William Amcotts Ingilby and his wife, who were largely responsible for rebuilding the town in the 1820s, were great Francophiles. **Ripley Castle** (Easter–Sept daily, Oct–Nov, Mar Tue, Thur, Sat–Sun, for times call 01423-770 152) has been the home of the Ingleby family for 700 years. There are regular tours of the castle, plus Castle Gardens, a deer park, and tearooms.

Ripon ⓱, further along the A61, developed around the sombre Saxon cathedral founded by St Wilfrid in the 7th century. The massive seven-light east window, 51ft (16 metres) high and half as wide, dates from the 14th century, but the most special feature is the crypt under the central tower, dating from 672, which is redolent of Saxon times. Nearby is **Newby Hall** (Apr–end Sept Tue–Sun, July–Aug also Mon, grounds: 11am–5pm, house: noon–4pm; charge), an Adam house set in 25 acres (10 hectares) of splendid garden.

Four miles (6km) to the west are the atmospheric remains of *Sancta Maria Fonctibus*, **Fountains Abbey** (Mar–Oct 10am–5pm, Nov–Feb 10am–4pm; charge), once Britain's richest Cistercian monastery. In 1132 monks first arrived in Skelldale, "thick-set with thorns, fit rather to be the lair of wild beasts than the home of human beings". Kitchens and dormitories survive, a tribute to old craftsmanship, giving today's visitor an unusually clear idea of medieval monastic life. In the 18th century the estate was landscaped with the 400-acre (160-hectare) deer park and the elegant **Studley Royal Water Garden** with ornamental lakes, temples and statues.

North York Moors

The North York Moors are a place apart. The most sharply defined of Britain's 15 national parks, they are bounded on two sides by steeply plunging escarpments and on a third by towering cliffs that defy the North Sea. Only where neighbouring farmland slopes up gradually from the Vale of Pickering do the moors lack an obvious frontier. Within their 553 sq miles (1,380 sq km) they embrace the largest unbroken expanse of heather moorland in England. In summer the heather flings a coat of regal purple across the full width of the moors, from the Vale of York to the sea. Other seasons have colours, too: the bright green of bilberries in spring, russet bracken in autumn, and in winter subdued greys and browns.

The moors can be approached directly from York or from the A1. On the eastern side of the Vale of York on the A64, is **Castle Howard** ⓲ (www.castlehoward.co.uk; Mar–end Oct daily 10am–5pm, last entry to house 4pm; charge). The first building to be designed by Sir John Vanburgh (1664–1726), it inspired 20th-century poet John Betjeman to write: "Hail Castle Howard! Hail Vanburgh's noble dome, Where Yorkshire in her splendour rivals Rome!" The centrepiece of the entire house is the marble-floored hall which rises up to the magnificent 70ft (21-metre) dome, across which charge great "Horses of the Sun". The principal

Friar Tuck, Robin Hood's fellow outlaw, is said to have been a monk at Fountains Abbey.

BELOW: Barden Moor, Skipton.

rooms contain paintings by Gainsborough, Reynolds and Rubens and furniture by Sheraton and Chippendale. The Pre-Raphaelite chapel has stained glass by Edward Burne-Jones. The west wing, a Palladian addition, has a magnificent Long Gallery. The stunning gardens and grounds include a walled rose garden, lakes, fountains, statues and woodland. There is also a plant centre and adjacent holiday park in Coneysthorpe village.

Just off the A1 is the thriving market town of **Thirsk** ⑲, now famous as the "Darrowby" of James Herriot's vet books, which translated into the successful 1980s television series, *All Creatures Great and Small*. Herriot's former surgery (daily; charge) is now a visitor centre devoted to the author.

Rievaulx Abbey

Approaching the Moors from this south-westerly direction, most visitors will arrive in **Helmsley**, whose quaint shops give it a distinctly "Cotswolds" feel. Nearby, tucked amid hanging woods and placid pastures deep in the Rye Valley, are the breathtaking ruins

of **Rievaulx Abbey** ⑳ (Apr–end Sept daily 10am–6pm, Oct Thur–Mon 10am–5pm, Nov–end Mar 10am–4pm; charge), an extensive Cistercian monastery founded in the 12th century. The now supremely beautiful setting was viewed as "a place of horror and waste" by the abbey's 12 founder monks who arrived directly from France in 1132. Larger than Fountain's Abbey *(see page 329)*, Rievaulx was both the first and biggest Cistercian abbey in the north of England. At its 13th-century peak it housed 150 monks and 500 lay brothers "so that the church swarmed with them, like a hive with bees". Because of the abbey's narrow site, between steep banks of the Rye, the church was aligned north–south. Its greatest glory is its chancel, from around 1230. Standing to its full height, with two tiers of lancet windows above cluster-column arches, it is a majestic example of the Early English style.

Northwest of Rievaulx, by the A19, is another romantic ruin, **Mount Grace Priory** (Apr–end Sept Thur–Mon 10am–6pm, Oct–end Jan Thur–Sun 10am–4pm; charge). This is the best

The End of the Monasteries

When Henry VIII issued the Suppression Act in April 1536 there were 800 monasteries, nunneries and friaries in England and Wales populated by 10,000 monks, canons, nuns and friars. The Act was ostensibly in response to a six-month survey by a team of royal visitors which found "manifest sin, vicious, carnal and abominable living daily used and committed amongst the little and small abbeys." But this was a smokescreen: Henry wanted the religious houses' wealth to replenish his own treasury. Most had agreed to acknowledge Henry as head of the new Church of England after his acrimonious break with the Catholic Church of Rome over his divorce arrangements. Only the smaller establishments were at first dissolved but the manner of their repression led to a rebellion, known as The Pilgrimage of Grace, as the dissolved houses were defiantly reinhabited, often with the support of the larger houses. The king retaliated, forcing the surrender of the larger monasteries. Four years after the Act was passed not a single monastery, nunnery or friary remained.

By the end of Henry's reign, two-thirds had been sold off, saving the king from bankruptcy. Their grandeur and wealth can be glimpsed at Fountains *(see previous page)* and Rievaulx *(see above)*, which are among the best preserved of Henry's ruins.

preserved of Britain's nine Carthusian monasteries. A monk's cell has been restored and an exhibition is housed in a handsome Jacobean mansion converted from the priory's gatehouse.

Ryedale is just one among a network of Dales penetrating the great dome of moorland. In some places they create dramatic natural features, such as the **Hole of Horcum** ㉑ above the Vale of Pickering; elsewhere they enfold villages and farmhouses built mainly of warm, honey-coloured sandstone. The prettiest villages include **Hutton-le-Hole** ㉒ in Farndale, with a broad green, and 17th- and 18th-century limestone cottages built by Quaker weavers. The **Ryedale Folk Museum** here (daily end Jan–mid-Dec 10am–5.30pm or dusk if earlier; charge) is the premier museum of moorland life. There are a number of vernacular buildings in the grounds, an iron age roundhouse and displays of traditional craft making, as well as an art gallery. Nearby Lastingham has a splendid Norman crypt.

On the northern flanks, above Eskdale, are **Goathland** and **Beck Hole** ㉓,

Ryedale Folk Museum.

the former the setting for the TV series *Heartbeat*, the latter a delightful hamlet with an arc of cottages facing a green. Quoits is played here, inquests afterwards being conducted in the Birch Hall Inn where beer is served through a hatch in a flagstone bar adorned with quoiting pictures. **The Moors Centre** (Apr–Oct daily 10am–5pm, Nov–Dec and Mar daily 10.30am–3.30pm, Jan–Feb Sat–Sun 10.30am–3.30pm; free), a showcase for the **National Park** and starting point for waymarked walks, is at **Danby** 12 miles (18km) west.

Heading north across the moors to the sea, from **Pickering** to **Grosmont**, is the steam-powered **North Yorkshire Moors Railway** (www.nymr.co.uk; Easter–Nov; talking timetable on 01751-473 535). A stop in Pickering should include a visit to the Beck Isle Museum of Rural Life (daily Mar–Oct 10am–5pm) where the photography of Sydney Smith (1884–1956) is a beautiful record of rural England in the first half of the 20th century. The most dramatic section of the railway journey is Newton Dale, with sheer cliffs 400ft (120 metres) high. For the more ener-

BELOW: around the Ryedale Folk Museum in Hutton-le-Hole.

Captain Cook, the Pacific explorer and Whitby's famous son.

getic, there is the 42-mile (68km) Lyke Wake Walk, which crosses the moors between Osmotherley and Robin Hood's Bay.

Coastal highlights

The moors end at the east coast, where breaks in the precipitous cliffs provide space for pretty villages and the occasional town. **Whitby** ㉔ is a picturesque fishing port with a jumble of pantiled cottages climbing from the harbour. On East Cliff are the 13th-century remains of **Whitby Abbey** (Apr–end Sept daily 10am–6pm, Oct–end Mar Thur–Mon 10am–4pm; charge), on which site a 7th-century monk wrote the *Song of Creation*, considered to mark the start of English literature. The ruins are said to have inspired Bram Stoker, author of *Dracula*. The Sutcliffe Gallery in Flowergate exhibits and sells the evocative Victorian photographs of Whitby and its hinterland by Frank Sutcliffe (1853–1941). The Antarctic and Pacific explorer Captain Cook (1728–79) lived in this former whaling port – a whale's jawbone still acts

as an arch to remind people of the town's former trade. **Captain Cook Memorial Museum** (daily Apr–Oct 9.45am–5pm, Mar 11am–3pm; charge) in Grape Street is the focal point of a heritage trail tracing his life throughout the region. To the north of Whitby, steep roads lead down to **Runswick Bay**, a self-consciously pretty assortment of fishermen's cottages, and Staithes, where the young Cook was briefly and unhappily apprenticed to a grocer. To the south, seekers after solitude can divert from the coastal road to find **Ravenscar** – "the resort that never was". It has fine walks, but never developed economically beyond one rather imposing cliff-top hotel.

Robin Hood's Bay, a popular resort close by, once offered sanctuary to the benign outlaw and was a haunt of smugglers. Off its main street run the snickets (narrow lanes) that, together with the diminutive dock, give Robin Hood's Bay its Toytown character. Time should be spent exploring the intimate network, full of odd corners and sunny squares.

BELOW: Whitby Abbey.
RIGHT: the cobbled streets of Robin Hood's Bay.

Further south lies **Scarborough** ㉕, whose origins as a posh watering hole are exemplified by the imposing frontage of the Grand Hotel, among the handsomest in Europe when it opened in 1867, now undergoing a £7 million refurbishment programme.

The 12th-century **castle** (Apr–Sept daily 10am–6pm, Oct–Mar Thur–Mon 10am–4pm; charge) is worth seeing. Anne Brontë – who, like so many invalids, came for the bracing air – is buried in the graveyard of St Mary's *(see page 322)*. The town also has an enviable theatrical reputation built around Alan Ayckbourn, the local-born playwright, who premiers most of his plays at the Stephen Joseph Theatre.

Filey ㉖ offers unpretentious delights, with amusement arcades, a splendid beach and Filey Brigg, the breakwater at the north end of the bay. Off the dramatic 400ft (130-metre) cliff at nearby Flamborough Head, John Paul Jones, commodore of a French squadron showing US colours, captured two British men-of-war in 1779.

The Yorkshire Wolds

Flamborough Head is where the chalk ridge of the Yorkshire Wolds meets the sea. Just to the south is **Beverley**, a picture-postcard mix of medieval and Georgian streets, but its main attractions are the Gothic minster and its former chapel, St Mary's, which between them contain one of the largest collections of carvings in the world. The minster dates from 1220 and among its wood and stone carvings are 68 misericords and the elegant Percy tomb of the 14th century.

At **Kingston upon Hull** ㉗, usually referred to simply as Hull, on the River Humber, **The Deep** (daily 10am–6pm; charge), a spectacular aquarium, has sharks and other sea creatures, including simulations of those species now extinct, seen from Europe's deepest viewing tunnel and the world's only underwater lift.

The house where William Wilberforce was born in 1758 is now a museum (Mon–Sat 10am–5pm, Sun 1.30–4.30pm; free), covering the history of slave trade which Wilberforce helped to outlaw. ❑

A rabbit carved on a portal in the chapel of St Mary's in Beverley Minster is said to have been the inspiration for Lewis Carroll's White Rabbit in Alice in Wonderland.

BELOW: Whitby pub. **LEFT:** the harbour at Staithes.

NORTHUMBRIA

The lands of the northeast are wild, wide-open spaces, littered with evidence of a turbulent past. Newcastle is its cultural capital, and Durham its most historic city

H istory is everywhere in these bleak northern hills – the last flourish of the Pennines before they cross the borders into Scotland. It was a grim posting for Roman soldiers stationed along Hadrian's Wall, but it appealed to the Christians, who chose lonely Lindisfarne on the wild, sandy Northumbrian shore as a bastion and exemplar of the early church. Incursions came from the Vikings, who left their language in such local dialect names as *stell* (sheepfold) and *beck* (stream): the local "Geordie" dialect is the strongest in England.

The Normans came next, ravaging Northumbria in their pitiless "harrying of the North"; but they were builders, too, and they raised the mighty cathedral at Durham. The Scottish border was always a volatile place and, for some 300 years until the early 17th century, rustic gangsters called reivers ruled the roost.

Coal mining put the area in the forefront of the Industrial Revolution and in the 20th century Britain's major shipbuilding yards grew up along the Tyne and Wear rivers, but those times are now passed.

The farming community, raising both sheep and cattle, is finding life as hard as anywhere in Britain. A tourism campaign has dubbed the north Pennines "England's last wilderness" and at Kielder (*see page 344*) the largest man-made forest has proved a great attraction.

Teesdale and the Pennines

The first beach resort in Northumbria is **Redcar ㉘**, a lively playground with a sandy beach which serves the former industrial centres of **Middlesbrough**, **Stockton-on-Tees** and **Darlington ㉙**. The region boomed in the 19th century as coal and iron were discovered and the railways pioneered an undreamed-of prosperity. George Stephenson's *Locomotion No. 1* built in 1825 is displayed at **Head of Steam**, Darlington's railway museum (Tue–Sun Apr–Sept 10am–4pm, Oct–

Main attractions
BOWES MUSEUM
DURHAM CATHEDRAL
BEAMISH OPEN AIR MUSEUM
HADRIAN'S WALL
ALNWICK CASTLE
LINDISFARNE

PRECEDING PAGES: Hadrian's Wall. **LEFT:** Lindisfarne Castle, Holy Island. **BELOW:** George Stephenson's *Locomotion No 1*.

BELOW: Bowes Museum, Barnard Castle.

Mar 11am–3.30pm; charge). It ran on the world's first railway line, from Darlington to Stockton.

Sixteen miles (25km) to the west on the River Tees is **Barnard Castle** ③, capital of Teesdale. Wednesday is market day on "the cobbles" of Butter Market, and the first Saturday of the month the town is crowded with farmers bringing their produce to be sold. The **Castle** (Apr–Sept daily 10am–6pm, Oct daily 10am–4pm, Nov–Mar Thur–Mon 10am–4pm; charge) stands on a bluff above the River Tees, with two towers and the remains of a 15th-century great chamber. Follow Newgate out of Barnard Castle to reach the extraordinary **Josephine and John Bowes Museum** (daily 10am–5pm; charge). Looking like a grand French château, its outstanding collection of French and Spanish paintings include El Grecos and Goyas. There are also tapestries, ceramics and lace exhibits.The highlight of the museum is the extraordinary, life-size, silver swan automaton, made in the late 18th-century and still in working order. Every day at

2pm and 3pm, visitors can watch as it dips its head and plucks a fish from the "water".

Just outside Barnard Castle is **Raby Castle** ③ (May–June, Sept Sun–Wed, July–Aug Sun–Fri and Bank Holidays, castle: 1–5pm, gardens: 11am–5.30pm), a fine medieval fortification set in a 200-acre (80-hectare) deer park. It has decorated period rooms, a 14th-century kitchen and stables full of period carriages. **Cotherstone**, just west of Barnard Castle, is many people's favourite Teesdale village, but **Middleton-in-Teesdale** ③ is the real centre for Upper Teesdale. A staging post on the Pennine Way, here the moors start to crowd in on the river, making it a superb centre for exploring such sites as **High Force**, a few miles to the west. This is the greatest waterfall in England, which crashes 70ft (21 metres). Continue on the B6277 to **Alston** in the valley of the River South Tyne where the **South Tynedale Railway** (tel: 01434-382 828) runs steam- and diesel-hauled passenger trips beside the river. Another local experience is the **Kill-**

Fact File

Main towns Newcastle, Durham.

By Rail 3 hours from London King's Cross; 2 hours from Edinburgh.

By Road A1 and M1 from London, about 4 hours.

By Ferry From North Shields to the Netherlands (14 hours).

Airports Newcastle International (www.newcastleairport.com).

Best wildlife The Farne Islands.

Most historic places Holy Island; Hadrian's Wall, Hexham Abbey.

Best for children Roman Army Museum; Discovery Museum; North of England Open Air Museum at Beamish.

Tourist information Northumbria, www.visitnortheastengland.com; Durham, tel: 0191-384 3720, www.durhamtourism.co.uk; Newcastle, tel: 0191-277 8000, www.visitnewcastlegateshead.com.

hope **Lead Mining Centre** (Apr–Oct daily 10.30am–5pm) to the east along the A689, where visitors can see the workings of the lead mines and go underground.

Between Barnard Castle and Durham at Bishop Auckland is **Auckland Castle** (Easter–Sept Sun–Mon 2–5pm, July–Aug Sun 2–5pm, Mon and Wed 11am–5pm; charge; Bishop's Deer Park: daily throughout the year 7am–sunset), residence of Durham's bishops since Norman times. Its throne room, state rooms, medieval kitchen and the largest private chapel in Europe are open to the public.

A tour of Durham City

The cathedral and castle of **Durham** ③, caught in a loop in the River Wear, are a Unesco World Heritage site. To tour this compact and friendly university town, start at the tourist information centre in Millennium Place next to the marketplace. On the north side are **St Nicholas' Church** ④, once part of the city walls, and **Guildhall** ⑤, with a Tudor doorway and balconies. South of the square, Saddler Street and

Owen Gate lead to **Palace Green** ⑥. From here there is a grand view of the the city's finest buildings, including the cathedral and legacies of a 17th-century benefactor, Bishop Cosin. On the left is the elegant 17th-century red-brick **Bishop Cosin's Hall** ⑦, and, bearing right, **Bishop Cosin's Library** ⑧, a favourite backdrop for photographs of students who have just graduated. A gateway to the right leads to University College in **Durham Castle** ⑨ (tel: 0191-334 3800; guided tours only: July–Sept daily 10am–noon, 2–4.30pm, otherwise Mon, Wed, Sat–Sun 2–4pm; charge). One of the finest Norman palaces in Britain, it was the domain of the powerful Prince Bishops of Durham, who had their own parliament, laws, coinage and army.

Across the Green is the **Cathedral** ⑩ (Sun 7.45am–5pm, Mon–Sat 7.30am–6.15pm, summer until 8pm; free), once voted Britain's favourite building. Inside, massive columns stride down the nave like a petrified forest; boldly incised with spirals, lozenges, zigzags and flutings, their impact is stunning. Largely completed

The Quakers who ran the London Lead Company built the model town of Nenthead in Cumbria where they introduced compulsory schooling for their employees and inaugurated the country's first free library.

BELOW: Durham Cathedral on the River Wear.

by 1133, it was the first major English church to be covered entirely by stone vaulting and is the finest example of early Norman architecture. Its outstanding features include the Galilee Chapel, with a tomb of England's first great historian, the Venerable Bede (died 735) and the Chapel of the Nine Altars, which contains the remains of St Cuthbert *(see page 347)*. **The Treasury Museum** (Mon–Sat 10am–4.30pm, Sun 2–4.30pm; charge) contains other relics of the saintly Bishop of Lindisfarne.

Turn right outside the cathedral down Dun Cow Lane to the **Durham Heritage Centre** (Apr–May and Oct Sat–Sun 2–4.30pm, June daily 2–4.30pm, July–Sept daily 11am–4.30pm), which has exhibitions and audio-visual displays of the city. From here descend to the Riverside Walk, a pleasant path beside the river which leads to **The Upper Room** , a sculpture of The Last Supper carved from 11 elm trees by Colin Wilbourn. Cross Prebends Bridge (1777) for a classic view of the cathedral or continue round to the Old Fulling Mill, home

of the **Museum of Archaeology** (Apr–Oct daily 11am–4pm, Nov–Mar Fri–Sun 11.30am–3.30pm), which displays local finds.

County Durham and the North Pennines

Durham's proud industrial legacy can be seen at the award-winning **North of England Open Air Museum** at **Beamish** between Chester-le-Street and Stanley on the A693 (Apr–Oct daily 10am–5pm, Jan–end Mar Tue–Thur, Sat–Sun 10am–4pm; charge). One of the leading attractions in Northeast England, it vividly re-creates the past with reconstructed buildings and shopkeepers and workers in period dress. There is a Victorian town, with cobbled streets, shops, a pub, stables, a park and railway station with a replica of George Stephenson's *Locomotion*, the first passenger-carrying steam train in the world. There is a farm with rare breeds and a colliery and engine house with the steam winder built in 1855 for the Beamish colliery. Nearby are the mine and pit cottages where the miners originally lived.

BELOW:
underground at North of England Open Air Museum, Beamish.

Newcastle upon Tyne

Nine miles (15km) from the mouth of the Tyne, **Newcastle upon Tyne** ❸ is the hub in a conurbation formed with Tynemouth, South Shields, Wallsend, Jarrow and Gateshead. A centre of coal mining and shipbuilding, industrial England never got grittier than this. But the grim working-class conditions which the popular novelist Catherine Cookson described can no longer be seen in this lively university town, which has a bright nightlife and well-supported football club. In recent years Quayside development has put the city into another league.

The old town, known as the Chares, is a small area of narrow streets and steep lanes on the north side of the river; around here are the **Custom House** (1766), **Guildhall** (1658) and **Castle Keep** (Mon–Sat 10am–5pm, Sun noon–5pm, last entry 4.15pm; charge). Constructed by the son of William The Conqueror on the site of a Roman fort, this was the "new castle" which gave the city its name. "New castle" by name, but it was the new technology of the steam train which defined the city's character and much of the castle was demolished in the 19th century to make way for the railway. The keep and the Black Gate remain and inside you can explore the royal accommodation, Great Hall and chapel. Just beyond is **St Nicholas' Cathedral** (Mon–Fri 7am–6pm, Sat 8.30am–4pm, Sun 7am–noon, 4–7pm, Bank Holidays 7am–noon), crowned by its distinctive Lantern Tower, a city landmark for over 500 years. It has a fine altar screen depicting Northumbria's many saints. Several museums are worth seeking out. The **Laing Art Gallery**, New Bridge Street (Mon–Sat 10am–5pm, Sun 2–5pm; free) has permanent 18th- and 19th-century collections and major contemporary exhibitions. **Discovery Museum**, Blandford Square (Mon–Sat 10am–5pm, Sun 2–5pm; free) celebrates history and scientific innovation on Tyneside. The city's newest museum is the **Great North Museum** (Mon–Sat 10am–5pm, Sun 2–5pm; free) at Barras Bridge, a few minutes' walk from Haymarket Metro station. Its collections include antiq-

TIP

To the southeast of Newcastle is the Old Hall in Washington village, ancestral home of George Washington, now run by the National Trust. A special event here celebrates Independence Day.

BELOW:
Newcastle at night.

"He crossed to Britain where he set many things to rights and built a wall 80 miles long to separate the Romans from the barbarians," wrote Spartianus, nearly 200 years after the event. Hadrian arrived at the Tyne in 122, five years after he had been made Roman Emperor. He enjoyed touring his vast empire, and on his journeys he would live as an ordinary legionnaire, in full uniform, but often bare headed, and marching 20 miles (32km) a day.

uities from ancient Greece and Egypt, as well as family-friendly displays of fossils and a large scale, interactive model of Hadrian's Wall.

An impressive collection of bridges span the River Tyne: the High Level Bridge built by George Stephenson who inaugurated the railway industry here; the Swing Bridge where the Roman bridge stood; and the **Tyne Bridge**, which when built in 1928 was the largest single span in the world. The latest addition is the **Gateshead Millennium Bridge**, the world's first tilting bridge. It has received a host of awards for architecture, design, innovation, and for the dramatic nighttime lighting which creates a stunning reflection in the river. Cross on foot to Gateshead and the **Baltic Centre for Contemporary Art** (daily 10am–6pm, Tue from 10.30am; free), one of the biggest art spaces in Europe for constantly changing exhibitions. Dominating Gateshead Quays is **The Sage**, a pioneering international centre for musical discovery designed by Sir Norman Foster. The concert schedule, which embraces music of all kinds, is complemented by programmes enabling everyone to become involved in music.

Approaching Gateshead by the A1 or A167, a 20-metre (66-ft) tall steel giant marks the entry into Tyneside. The *Angel of the North* stands on the site of a former coal mine and was created by Antony Gormley, partly in tribute to the coal miners who worked in darkness beneath its feet.

Hadrian's Wall: a tour of Rome's last outpost

Built by order of the Emperor Hadrian in AD 122 to consolidate the northern boundary of the Roman empire, Hadrian's Wall (www.hadrianswall.org) was 15ft (4.5 metres) high and ran 73 miles (117km), coast-to-coast, from the Solway to the Tyne: it was effectively an enormous customs post, controlling the flow of goods and people between the north and south. Thriving civilian settlements, known as *vici*, spread out to the south behind the protection of the wall, with houses, temples, shops and theatres, serving the needs of both the local Britons and the 10,000 auxiliary soldiers from all over the Roman Empire who were stationed here. In 1987 the Hadrian's Wall Military Zone was designated a World Heritage Site by Unesco. The Hadrian's

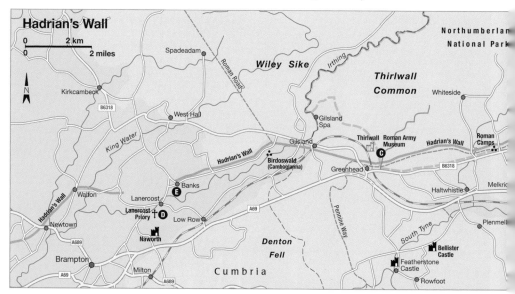

Wall National Trail is an 84 mile (135km) waymarked walking route, from Wallsend in the east to Bowness on Solway in the west. The walk can be broken into day-long stages. If you prefer to visit Roman military sites by car, this suggested route will take a full day. It starts at the historic market town of **Hexham** Ⓐ and ends at **Housesteads Fort and Museum**. Hexham Abbey (daily 9.30am–5pm, services permitting; donations welcome) was founded by Wilfrid *circa* 674. The Saxon crypt (from 11am and 3.30pm) and apse still remain but the present abbey is 12th-century.

Across the marketplace stands the Old Gaol (1333), the earliest documented purpose-built prison in England. Inside, the **Border History Museum** (for opening hours tel: 01434-652 351) tells the life and times of the Border Reivers. From Hexham take the A69 west through **Haydon Bridge** Ⓑ and Haltwhistle and turn off at Greenhead for the **Roman Army Museum** Ⓒ (daily Feb–Mar 10am–5pm, Apr–Sept 10am–6pm, Oct–Nov 10am–5pm; charge). The museum brings to life Roman frontier history with a variety of dramatic multi-media exhibits.

The A69 continues towards the busy little market town of Brampton, and 1 mile (2km) beforehand a minor road leads to the 12th-century Augustinian **Lanercost Priory** Ⓓ (Apr–Sept daily 10am–5pm, Oct Thur–Mon 10am–4pm; charge). Continue down this road to cross the vallum of the wall at **Banks** Ⓔ. Follow it eastwards through Gisland to the ruined 14th-century Thirlwall Castle built with masonry from the wall.

From here follow the B6318, the military road, about 6 miles (10km) to the **Once Brewed Northumberland National Park Centre** (Apr–Oct daily 9.30am–5pm, winter Sat–Sun only 10am–3pm). From here follow the Roman Stanegate (literally "stone road") 1 mile (1.5km) to **Vindolanda** Ⓕ Fort and Museum (daily Dec–Jan 10am–4pm, Feb–Mar, Oct–Nov 10am–5pm, Apr–Sept 10am–6pm; charge). This has a full-sized reconstruction of part of the wall and a turret, plus replica Roman temple, house and shop with various artefacts.

The most complete Roman fort in Britain is 2 miles (3km) away on the wall at **Housesteads** Ⓖ (daily mid-Mar–Sept 10am–6pm, Oct–Mar 10am–4pm; charge). There are extensive

Excavations along Hadrian's Wall.

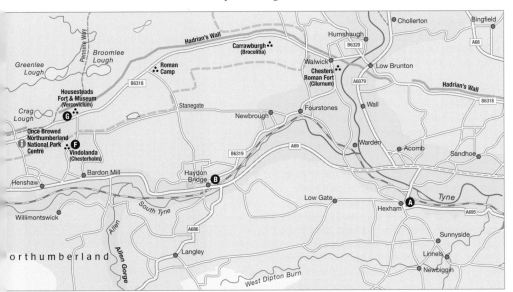

Alnwick Castle.

RIGHT: Kielder Water man-made lake.

remains of barracks, plus a bathhouse, hospital and granary.

National Park and the Cheviots

The **Cheviot Hills**, shared by England and Scotland, are quite distinct from the Durham Dales and the North Pennines. Rounded and covered in rough grass, they reach 2,000ft (610 metres) and their cloying blanket of peat is notorious to exhausted Pennine Wayfarers on the final leg of their 268-mile (429km) marathon from Edale in Derbyshire. **The Northumberland National Park ③** covers 405 sq miles (1,049 sq km) between Hadrian's Wall and the Cheviots. There is a visitor centre for the park on Bridge Street in the pretty market town of **Rothbury**, the capital of Coquetdale, and the town offers many opportunities for good walks. Just outside town is **Cragside House** (Tue–Sun Apr–Sept 1–5pm, from 11am school holidays, grounds: Mar–end Oct from 10.30am, Nov–Dec Wed–Sun 11am–4pm; charge), a fantastic mock-Tudor, mock-medieval building created by the inventor and arms manufacturer Lord Armstrong and the first house in the world to be lit by hydroelectricity.

The stunning setting is enhanced by splendid gardens of extraordinary scale and variety.

There is an important Iron-Age hillfort at **Lordenshaws**, built around 350 BC, and there are good walks along the **Simonside Ridge** from here. The views north towards the Cheviots are among the finest in Northumberland.

To the northwest is the delightful village of **Holystone** and the **Lady's** or **St Ninian's Well**. Set in a copse a short walk north of the village, it is a tranquil rectangular pool of clear water fed by a never-failing sparkling spring. A Celtic cross in the pool is a reminder that, on Easter Day in 627, 3,000 pagan Northumbrians were

Kielder, Man-made Wilderness

Kielder, in its own, totally artificial way, is a unique landscape. Situated between Hadrian's Wall and the Scottish border on the west of the Northumberland National Park, it has the largest man-made forest in Europe, covering 300 sq miles (777 sq km), complemented by Kielder Water, Europe's largest man-made lake, opened in 1982, with a 27-mile (43km) shoreline (www.visitkielder.com).

This artificial landscape, criss-crossed by hundreds of miles of track, has proved immensely popular with walkers, horse riders and cyclists, especially for visitors from nearby Tyneside. A new Lakeside Way allows visitors to walk all around the shore of the enormous lake. The Tower Knowe Visitor Centre (tel: 0845-155 0236) near Falstone is the gateway visitor centre for the area, with a café, shop and history displays. Visitors can take the Osprey ferry from here to explore the water.

There are self catering lodges and a bird of prey centre at Leaplish Waterside Park (tel: 01434-251 000) as well as cycle hire, sauna, solarium and restaurant. Kielder Village is a 1950s forestry community which is now the headquarters of the Forestry Commission's Border Forest operations, based in Kielder Castle, the late 18th-century castellated shooting lodge of the Duke of Northumberland which today has a Visitor Centre. It is the starting point for various mountain bike trails.

apparently baptised here by St Paulinus, a Roman missionary from Kent.

The coast, Lindisfarne and the Farne Islands

The Northumbrian coast has some of Britain's finest and least-spoilt beaches, and the 40 miles (65km) from **Amble** to the Scottish border has been designated an Area of Outstanding Natural Beauty. Just north of Amble is **Warkworth Castle** (Apr–Sept daily 10am–5pm, Oct daily 10am–4pm, Nov–Mar Sat–Mon 10am–4pm; charge), a masterpiece of late-medieval architecture. Not far from Morpeth, at Belsay on the A696, is **Belsay Hall** (Apr–Sept daily 10am–5pm, Oct daily 10am–4pm, Nov–end Mar Thur–Sun 10am–4pm; charge) with striking gardens, filled with exotic species.

Inland from Alnmouth further north is the ancient town of **Alnwick** ❸, and the stupendous **Alnwick Castle** (www.alnwickcastle.com; Apr–end Oct daily 10am–6pm, state rooms: 11am–5pm; charge). After Windsor, this is largest inhabited castle in England and has been home to the Percys, Earls and Dukes of Northumberland, since 1309. The **Garden** (daily summer 10am–6pm, winter 10am–4pm; charge) has recently been ambitiously redesigned with features including a "Grand Cascade", a maze, a poison garden and a huge, higgledy-piggledy **tree house** – actually a magical complex of furnished buildings linked by suspended walkways and one of the world's largest.

In the picturesque fishing village of **Craster**, the world-famous Craster kippers can be bought from Robson & Sons (herring smokers for four generations) or sampled in their restaurant during summer. A 30-minute coastal path leads to **Dunstanburgh Castle**, one of the most romantically sited ruins in Britain. Beyond is the busy little harbour town of **Seahouses**, where, from Easter to September, boats take visitors the 2–5 miles (3–8km) to the **Farne Islands** (www.farne-islands.com). Protected by the National Trust, the rich wildlife includes over 20 species of seabirds and a large colony of seals. Beyond Seahouses, atop a basalt outcrop over-

Northumbrian festivals involve a conflation of fire and music. The fires date back to Celtic, perhaps Viking times. Its musical small-pipes are like Scottish bagpipes inflated by an arm action. Some songs were collected by Sir Walter Scott in Minstrelsy of the Scottish Border (1803).

BELOW: one of the world's largest tree houses, in Alnwick Castle Garden.

*The ruins of
Dunstanburgh Castle.*

looking the Farne Islands, is **Bamburgh Castle ㊳** (mid-Mar–end Oct daily 10am–5pm, last entry 4pm; charge), said to be the finest castle in England. It has a Norman keep but was largely remodelled in the 19th and 20th centuries. As well as a fine armoury collection there are aviation and engineering artefacts and memorabilia.

To reach **Holy Island**, or **Lindisfarne ㊴**, it is necessary to turn inland and take the A1 for 6 miles (9km) to Beal. Before crossing the 3-mile (5-km) causeway, check the tide tables (to plan ahead call 01289-330 733) and never try to beat the treacherous tide. The island is cut off for about five hours a day. The 4-sq-mile (10-sq-km) island is a nature reserve and birdwatchers flock to the islands' breeding grounds. The romantic remains of **Lindisfarne Priory** (Apr–Sept daily 9.30am–5pm, Oct daily 9.30am–4pm, Nov–Jan Sat–Sun 10am–2pm, Feb–Mar daily 10am–4pm; charge) date from 1083. The adjacent museum displays Saxon carvings from the site and the adjoining church of St Mary's, which stands on the site of the original monastery founded by St Aidan in AD 635, contains copies of the famous Lindisfarne Gospels, beautiful illuminated manuscripts *(see right)*. **Lindisfarne Castle** (tel: 01289-389 244; mid-Mar–end Oct Tue–Sun, times vary with tides: 10am–3pm or noon–5pm, daily Feb school half term 10am–3pm; charge) is a 16th-century miniature castle transformed into an Edwardian country house with a charming walled garden by Gertrude Jekyll (daily all year 10am–dusk).

Berwick-upon-Tweed ㊵, the last town in England before Scotland, has changed allegiance between England and Scotland 11 times. Its most impressive feature is its perfectly intact Elizabethan walls and ramparts, built in 1558. ❑

St Cuthbert, the "Fire of the North"

From the Holy Island of Lindisfarne, this legendary local monk and animal lover inspired the spiritual life of the northeast.

Lindisfarne became a holy place in the 7th-century AD, when King Oswald of Northumbria, sent for St Aidan from the holy island of Iona in Scotland to spread the Christian message through his kingdom. Aidan and 12 companions founded the first monastery at Lindisfarne, a tiny rocky island, cut off by the tides from the mainland twice each day. This was to become the cradle of Christianity in northeast England and for the rest of Europe. After Aidan died in 651, he was succeeded by Cuthbert. Cuthbert, greatest of the northern saints, was born in the Scottish borders in 625. While tending sheep in the Lammermuir Hills he saw a vision of a great light and angels in the sky, and, taking this as a sign that he should spread the Christian message, he became a monk.

Cuthbert, "the Fire of the North", ignited the Christian flame in the region. News of his gift for healing spread far and wide and he was frequently called to other monasteries throughout the north both to preach and to heal. However, Cuthbert preferred solitude and he often withdrew to live the life of a hermit in a tiny cell on the rocky island of Inner Farne.

There are many legends associated with St Cuthbert, mostly related by the Venerable Bede, who wrote the invaluable first history of the English people *(Historia Ecclesiastica Gentis Anglorum)* up to the time of his death in 735 from his monk's cell in the monastery of Jarrow, near New-

castle. Bede said Cuthbert was: "unassumingly patient, devoted to unceasing prayer". One of the tales he told was of the sea otters drying Cuthbert's feet and warming him with their breath after he had spent a night praying in the cold North Sea. His love of animals was characteristic, and the eider ducks still found around the Farne Islands are known as St Cuthbert's ducks, or Cuddy's, because he had managed to tame them.

Cuthbert died in 687 and was buried on Lindisfarne. Shortly afterwards, an unknown monk began work on the famous Lindisfarne Gospels, a beautifully illuminated manuscript now in the British Museum. Cuthbert's body was not destined to stay on his beloved Lindisfarne. After a series of Viking raids on the coast, monks removed it, first to Chester-le-Street and later to Ripon, before it eventually arrived, in 995, on a peninsula on the River Wear known as Dunholme (which became today's city of Durham).

Today the remains of the famous Celtic saint reside in the Lady Chapel behind the altar of the great Norman cathedral *(see page 340)* while those of his great chronicler, Bede, are at the opposite end of the cathedral, in the Galilee Chapel. There is a waymarked walk, the St Cuthbert's Way, which runs from Melrose in the Scottish Borders to Lindisfarne. Stretching 65½ miles (100km), it can be broken into shorter sections. ❑

ABOVE: Lindisfarne Gospels.
RIGHT: a 12th-century wall painting of St Cuthbert in Durham Cathedral.

✗ INSIGHT GUIDES TRAVEL TIPS
ENGLAND

T RANSPORT

GETTING THERE
AND GETTING AROUND

GETTING THERE

By Air

Britain's two major international airports are Heathrow (mainly scheduled flights), which is 15 miles (24km) to the west of London, and Gatwick (scheduled and charter flights), which is 24 miles (40km) south of the capital. An increasing number of international flights now arrive at the regional airports of Birmingham, Manchester, Liverpool, Glasgow, Prestwick and Cardiff, and London's other airports, Stansted and Luton. The small London City Airport, a few miles from London's financial heart, is used by small aircraft to fly to European capitals.

London Airports

The Airport Travel Line, tel: 08705-747 777, gives information on coaches into Central London and between Heathrow, Gatwick and Stansted airports. Dot2Dot runs a door-to-door coach service from Heathrow and Gatwick airports to hotels in central areas of London. Booking is essential, tel: 0845-368 2368; www.dot2.com.

National Express also runs coach services connecting Heathrow, Gatwick, Stansted and Luton airports, and the first three airports with Victoria coach station in central London. For enquiries, tel: 08717-818 181; www.nationalexpress.com.

Heathrow Airport (www.heathrow airport.com) with five terminals, is sprawling – it can be a long walk to the central building.

There is a fast rail link, the Heathrow Express, between Heathrow and Paddington station. It runs every 15 minutes from 5am–midnight and takes about 20 minutes. Fares are £16.50 single and £32 return. Prices are lowest when buying online, increasing if you purchase from a machine or onboard. Paddington is on the District, Circle, Bakerloo and Hammersmith and City Line underground train lines (tel: 0845-600 1515; www.heathrowexpress.com).

The cheapest way into central London is by the *Underground* (known as the Tube), which takes about 60 minutes to the West End. The Piccadilly line goes from Heathrow directly to central areas such as Kensington, Piccadilly and Covent Garden. The single fare is £4. Keep your ticket. You'll need it to exit the Underground system. For all London Transport enquiries: tel: 020-7222 1234; www.tfl.gov.uk.

Heathrow is also well-served by taxis. A ride into town in a London black cab will cost £40–70, depending on your destination.

Gatwick Airport (www.gatwickairport. com) isn't on the Underground network, but has train and coach services into London and to other large cities. Gatwick Express trains leaves every 15 minutes from 5am until 12.35am, and take 30 minutes to London's Victoria station. For information, tel: 0845-850 1530; www.gatwickexpress.com. First Capital trains to Victoria and Southern Trains to London Bridge station are much cheaper and take only a little longer, but can be very crowded at peak hours with general commuter traffic.

A black cab taxi into central London costs around £77.

Luton Airport (www.london-luton. co.uk)has a regular express train service from Luton Airport Parkway (take the shuttle bus) to St Pancras Station, City Thameslink, Blackfriars and London Bridge, taking 25 minutes minimum. Alternatively, Green Line 757 coaches to London's Victoria Station take about an hour (tel: 0844-801 7261, or easyBus coaches (up to 1 hour 40 mins during peak times).

Stansted Airport (www.stansted airport.com) has the Stansted Express train service to London's Liverpool Street station. A frequent service operates 5.30am–12.30am and takes about 45 minutes (tel: 0845-850 0150; www.stanstedexpress.com). A non-stop coach service to London Victoria is run by Terrravision, and National Express has services to Stratford (east London) and Victoria.

For those heading elsewhere in Britain other than London, there are regular National Express bus links to nearby British Rail stations.

London City Airport's major strength is its proximity to the City

Flight Information

Birmingham Airport
Tel: 0844-576 6000
Gatwick Airport
Tel: 0844-335 1802
Heathrow Airport
Tel: 0844-335 1801
London City Airport
Tel: 020-7646 0088
Luton Airport
Tel: 01582-405 100
Manchester Airport
Tel: 0871-271 0711
Stansted Airport
Tel: 0844-335 1803

Centre (10 miles/16km; www.london cityairport.com). There is a London City Airport DLR station (about 50 metres from the airport terminal), whose service has direct connections with the Jubilee line (at Canning Town) and Northern, Central, Circle and Waterloo and City lines (at Bank). The Transport for London website (www.tfl. gov.uk) can be used to help plan your journey.

A taxi into Central London should cost £25–30.

English Regional Airports
Manchester Airport is 10 miles (16km) south of the city. Frequent rail services run to Piccadilly station (20 minutes) in central Manchester, from where there are regular InterCity trains to London and other major cities. Alternatives are local buses or a taxi (approximately £15–20). For information visit www.manchesterairport. co.uk.

Birmingham International Airport is 8 miles (13km) southeast of Birmingham. The free Air-Rail Link shuttle connects the airport with Birmingham International station, from where trains run every 10–15 minutes to New Street station in the city centre (about 15 minutes). InterCity trains from New Street to London Euston run every half hour (about 90 minutes).

Newcastle Airport is 6 miles (9km) northwest of Newcastle city centre on the A696 at Woolsington. The airport is a main station for the Metro underground system, which takes 23 minutes to Central Station where regular InterCity trains run to London (3 hours) and Edinburgh (1 hour 30 mins).

Liverpool John Lennon Airport is 9 miles (15km) southeast of the city centre. The Airport Airlink 500 bus runs to the city centre every 20 mins Mon–Fri and 30 minutes Sat–Sun and evenings. Taxis charge about £14 for the 20-minute journey.

Channel Tunnel
Eurostar's regular passenger trains link France and Brussels with Britain. Services run from Paris Gare du Nord (2 hours 15 minutes) and Belgium Midi (1 hour 50 minutes) to London's St Pancras International; some trains now stop in Ebbsfleet, Kent.

Booking is not essential, but there are offers on tickets bought in advance. For UK bookings, tel: 08705-186 186. From outside the UK, tel: +44 1233-617 575, or visit www. eurostar.com.

By Car
Eurotunnel trains travel through the tunnel from Nord-Pas de Calais in France to Folkestone in Kent. At least two departures every hour during the day with a reduced service overnight (journey time 35 minutes). Booking is not essential – just turn up and take the next service. Crossings are priced on a single-leg basis and prices vary according to the level of demand; the further ahead you book, the cheaper the ticket. For UK reservations and information, tel: 0870-535 3535; www.eurotunnel.com.

Sea Transport
Sea services operate between 12 British ports and more than 20 Continental ones. Major ferries have full eating, sleeping and entertainment facilities. The shortest crossing is from Calais in France to Dover in Britain, which takes about 90 minutes by ferry.

Brittany Ferries sails from St Malo, Caen and Cherbourg, France to Portsmouth, England; from Cherbourg to Poole; from Roscoff to Plymouth; and from Santander, Spain to Plymouth and Portsmouth. Within UK tel: 0870-907 6103; in France tel: 0870-333 1101; in Spain tel: +44 870-536 0360; www.brittany-ferries.co.uk.

P&O Ferries run from Calais, France, to Dover; from Bilbao, Spain to Portsmouth and from Rotterdam and Zeebrugge, Holland, over the North Sea to Hull on England's east coast. From France tel: 0825-120 156; Holland tel: 020-200 8333; Spain tel: 902-020 461; UK tel: 08716-645 645; www.poferries.com.

Stena Line sail from Hook of Holland to Harwich, England. Tel: 0870-570 7070 or +44 870-570 7070 from outside the UK; www. stenaline.co.uk.

Children's Fares
Airlines Infants (under 2 years) either travel free or for about 10 percent of adult fare. Ages 2–12 years qualify for a child's fare, usually 80 percent of adult fare. **Trains** Under 5s free on your knee, aged 5–15 half-price most tickets. **Coaches** Under-2s free on your knee, 3–15s about half-price.

Norfolkline operates between Dover and Dunkerque (approx 1 hour 45 minutes). In the UK, tel: 0844-847 5042; www.norfolkline.com.

If you plan to bring a vehicle over by ferry it is advisable to book, particularly during peak holiday periods. If travelling by night on a long journey it is also recommended that you book a sleeping cabin.

From the US you could arrive in style on Cunard's *Queen Mary 2* in Southampton. Operating between April and December, it takes six nights to cross the Atlantic. For information in the UK, tel: 0845-678 0013; from the US call 1-800-223 0764; www. cunard.com.

GETTING AROUND

Driving
In Britain you must drive on the left-hand side of the road and observe speed limits. It is illegal to use a mobile phone when driving. Penalties for drink driving are severe. Drivers and passengers, in both front and back seats, must wear seat belts where fitted; failure to do so can result in a fine. For further information, consult a copy of the *Highway Code* published by the

BELOW: take to the open road in the Lake District.

TRANSPORT

ACCOMMODATION

ACTIVITIES

A – Z

LANGUAGE

Department for Transport, and widely available in bookshops. Prepare in advance by visiting www.direct.gov.uk.

If you are bringing your own car into Britain you will need a valid driving licence or International Driving Permit, plus insurance coverage and documents proving the vehicle is licensed and registered in your country and that you are resident outside the UK.

Speed Limits

Unless otherwise stated on signs,
- **30mph (50kph)** in built-up areas
- **60mph (100kph)** on normal roads away from built-up areas.
- **70mph (112kph)** on motorways and dual carriageways (divided highways).
- **Camping vans** or **cars towing a caravan** are restricted to 50mph, (80kph) on normal roads and 60mph (100kph) on dual carriageways.

Parking

Road congestion is a problem in most town and city centres, and parking is generally restricted. Never leave your car parked on a double yellow or red line, in a place marked for *permit holders only*, within a white zig-zag line close to a pedestrian crossing, or in a control zone. Also, don't park on a single yellow line when restrictions are in force, usually 8.30am–6.30pm Mon–Fri (consult signs on the kerb; if no days are shown, restrictions are in force daily). These are offences for which you can face a fine. Either use a meter or a car park (distinguished by a white P on a blue background).

Pay particular attention if leaving your car in central London. In many areas illegal parking may result in wheel clamping. This means your car is immobilised with a clamp until you pay (£70) to have it released – a process that can take several hours. Alternatively, your vehicle may be towed away to a car pound. Either way, retrieving your car will cost more than £200, plus a £40 parking fine. To ascertain whether your car has been towed, tel: 020-7747 4747.

Breakdown

The following motoring organisations operate 24-hour breakdown assistance. They have reciprocal arrangements with other national motoring clubs. All calls to these numbers are free.
AA tel: 0800-887 766, or visit www. theaa.com

Britannia Rescue tel: 0800-591 563, or visit www.britanniarescue.com
Green Flag tel: 0800-051 0636, or visit www.greenflag.co.uk
RAC tel: 0800-828 282, or visit www. rac.co.uk

Car hire/Rental

To hire a car in Britain you must be over 21 years old (over 23 for most companies) and have held a valid full driving licence for more than one year. The cost of hiring a car usually includes third-party insurance, mileage and road tax. Depending on the company, it might also incorporate insurance cover for accidental damage to the car's interior, wheels and tyres. However, it does not include insurance for other drivers without prior arrangement.

Some companies offer special weekend and holiday rates, so shop around. International companies (such as those listed below) are keen to encourage visitors to book in advance before they leave home and may offer holiday packages with discounts of up to 40 percent on advance bookings through travel agents or branches in your own country. Many hire firms provide child seats and luggage racks for a small charge.
Avis tel: 0844-581 8181
Hertz tel: 0870-844 8844
Budget tel: 0844-581 2231
Europcar tel: 0870-607 5000

Public Transport

Domestic Flights

From the major international airports there are frequent shuttle services to Britain's many domestic airports. These give quick and easy access to many cities and offshore islands. Airlines providing domestic services include:
British Airways (the country's largest airline), reservations and general enquiries, tel: 0844-493 0787 (from the UK); flight arrival and departure information, tel: 0844-493 0777 (from the UK, daily 6am–8pm); from US tel: 1-800-AIRWAYS; www.british airways.com.
BMI, British Midland International, tel: 0870-607 0555 (within UK) or +44 1332-648 181 (outside UK); www. flybmi.com
Easyjet, tel: 0871-244 2366; www. easyjet.com
Ryanair, tel: 0871-246 0000 (from within UK only); www.ryanair.com

Major Domestic Airports

Bristol tel: 0871-334 4444

East Midlands tel: 0871-919 9000
Leeds-Bradford tel: 0871-288 2288
Liverpool John Lennon tel: 0871-521 8484
Newcastle upon Tyne tel: 0871-882 1121
Norwich tel: 01603-411 923
Southampton tel: 0870-040 0009

Trains

Railways are run by various private regional operating companies. They are not known for punctuality, so if your arrival time is critical allow for possible delays. Avoid rush-hour travel in and out of big cities.

There are many money-saving deals, such as cheap-day returns, available. It can be difficult to find out about special offers, so if in doubt, ask again. Generally, tickets bought at least two weeks in advance are vastly cheaper than standard rates, but they sell out fast. Some saver tickets are available only if purchased abroad before arriving.

It is not usually necessary to buy tickets until the day you travel (except to get these special offers), or to make seat reservations, except over the Christmas and summer holiday period when InterCity trains are fully booked well in advance.

Many trains have first-class carriages with tickets up to twice the price of standard seats. It is sometimes possible to upgrade to first-class at weekends for an extra payment once you board.

On long distances overnight, it may be worth having a sleeping compartment. Available on InterCity trains, these have basic but comfortable sleeping arrangements and must be booked in advance. Information available by calling 08457-484 950; or +44 (0) 20-7278 5240 from abroad; National Rail Enquiries can then give you the phone number to book with the relevant train operator. Tickets can also be booked online at www.thetrainline.com.

Train Enquiries

National Rail Enquiry Service For train times, cancellations and advance bookings by credit card, tel: 08457-484 950 or visit www.nationalrail. co.uk.
Rail Europe For services from Britain, tel: 08448-484 064; www.raileurope.co. uk.

Coaches and Local Buses

National Express operates a large network of long-distance bus services with comfortable coaches running on long journeys, equipped with washrooms and disabled facilities. Fares are (usually) considerably cheaper than the equivalent journey by train, although you must book your seat in advance. For enquiries and bookings, tel: 08717-818 181; www.nationalexpress.com.

National Express provides scheduled day trips to cities of interest such as Bath and Stratford-upon-Avon, as well as transport to music festivals and Wembley and Twickenham stadiums. **Green Line**, tel: 0844-801 7261; www.greenline.co.uk), runs to Legoland and Windsor, among other destinations.

Towns are generally well-served by buses, often owned by private companies; rural communities often have very inadequate services.

Ferries

To reach the Isles of Scilly from Penzance, visitors can travel by the Scillonian ferry or by the Skybus small aircraft (www.islesofscilly-travel.co.uk) tel: 0845-710 5555. There are also helicopter services from Penzance, which are quicker but more expensive www.islesofscilly helicopter.com, tel: 01736-363 871.

Ferries to the Isle of Wight operate from Portsmouth and Lymington, www.wightlink.co.uk, tel: 0871-376 1000. Red Funnel Ferries (www.redfunnel.co.uk) tel: 0844-844 9988, also run ferries to the island, starting from Southampton.

Taxis

Outside London and large cities and away from taxi ranks at stations, ports and airports you will usually have to telephone for a cab rather than expect to hail one in the street. By law cabs must be licensed and display charges on a meter. Add at least 10 percent for a tip.

London "black cab" drivers are famous for their extensive knowledge of the city's streets: they aren't cheap, especially at night, but are generally worth the extra. Minicabs (unlicensed taxis, which look like private cars) are not allowed to compete with black cabs on the street and have to be hired by telephone or from a kiosk. If hiring a minicab, agree to a fee beforehand and don't expect drivers to know precise destinations. Never pick up an unsolicited minicab in the street.

If you have a complaint, make a note of the driver's licence number and contact the Public Carriage Office, tel: 0845-300 7000.

Travelling Around London

If you are staying in London for a while it is worth investing in an *A–Z* street guide which gives detailed information of the capital's confusing complex of streets and post codes.

The Underground (Tube) is the quickest way to get across London. Although one of the most comprehensive systems of its kind in the world, it's also the oldest. Apart from some central stations which

London Travel Passes

● **The Off-Peak One Day Travelcard** is a one-day pass that allows unlimited travel on the Tube, buses, Docklands Light Railway and rail services in Greater London. The card also allows a third off the cost of travel on scheduled Riverboat services. It can be used after 10am on a weekday or all day on a Saturday, Sunday or bank holiday, but not after 4.30am the following day, and is available from all Underground and some mainline stations.
● **Other Travelcards** are valid for 3 days, a week or a month and can be used at any time of day. To buy a pass you will need to supply a passport-sized photograph.
● For details of all available travelcards, visit www.tfl.gov.uk.

have been revamped recently, and the East London line redevelopment work in preparation for 2012, many remain largely unchanged since the 1930s.

The Tube service starts at 5.30am and runs until around midnight. It gets packed in the rush hours (7–9.30am and 4–7pm). Make sure that you have a valid ticket as it is illegal to travel without one and you may be fined. Smoking is prohibited. Fares are based on a zone system with a flat fare in the central zone.

A ride on the Docklands Light Railway is an excellent way to see the re-development of London's old dock area. This fully automated system has two branches connecting up with the Underground network. It operates in the same way as the Tube, with similar fares.

London buses provide a comprehensive service throughout Greater London and have their route and number clearly displayed on the front. Some buses run hourly throughout the night, with services to many parts of London departing from Trafalgar Square. Smoking is prohibited on buses.

Either pay for single journeys on London Transport (expensive, *see page 354*) or buy a one-day or three-day Travelcard *(see panel)* or Pre-pay Oyster Card. The Oyster Card is a format for organising and pre-paying for single trips. Simply touch the card on the reader in tube stations and buses. Visitor Oyster cards cost £2 and are valid for £10 or £15 worth of travel (so total cost of £12 or £17) on a pay-as-you-go basis. They can be topped up with additional credit at

BELOW: arriving at Fenchurch Street station, London.

Rover Tickets

Coach

National Express, tel: 08717-818 181, offers a Brit Xplorer pass, which entitles you to unlimited travel on their coaches for specified periods.

Train

For UK residents there are several passes, including a Family, Senior Citizen's and Young Person's Railcard, valid for one year. They cost a fraction of a long-distance InterCity trip and allow you a third off the full journey fare on off-peak trains. The BritRail ticket (from European travel agents and online in US at www.britrail.com) gives you unlimited travel in Great Britain for specified periods.

Tube stations, London Overground stations, Oyster Ticket Stops and London Travel Information Centres. Buy online at www.tfl.gov.uk. Paying cash for a single journey on the tube within zones 1 and 6 costs a daunting £4. A journey excluding zone 1 costs £3.

There is a flat fare of £1.20 for any bus journey but it is cheaper if you use Oyster Pre-Pay. Buy tickets before boarding from machines at bus stops (a few stops do not yet have machines).

A bus pass (valid in all zones) will cost £3.80 for one day. Travelcards may be used on tube, bus, DLR and National Rail services. Prices vary according to zones covered and duration. Family Travelcards also available.

Call Transport for London on 020-7222 1234 or visit: www.tfl.gov.uk.

Driving in London

If you're staying only for a short time in the Greater London area, and are unfamiliar with the geography of the capital, don't hire a car. Central London is more than ever a nightmare to drive in, with its web of one-way streets, bad signposting, congestion charge and impatient drivers.

Parking is also a major problem in congested central London. Meters are slightly cheaper than NCP car parks, but usually allow parking for a maximum of two or four hours. If parking at a meter, do not leave your car a moment longer than your time allows or insert more money once your time has run out. For either infringement you can be fined up to £80. Some meter parking is free after 6.30pm and all day Sunday, but check the details on the meter.

You are liable to an £8 daily congestion charge if you drive in the central area between 7am and 6pm Mon–Fri. You can pay by ringing 0845-900 1234, visiting www.tfl.gov.uk/roadusers/congestioncharging, or at many small shops.

River Travel and Tours

London

Riverboats are an excellent way to see many major London sights whose history is intertwined with the river. During the summer these are plentiful, but there are limited winter services. Some of London Transport's travel passes allow a third off the cost of travel on scheduled Riverboat services. Boats can be boarded at: Richmond, Kew, Waterloo, Westminster, Embankment, London Bridge, the Tower of London and Greenwich piers.

Circular cruises between St Katharine's and Westminster Pier are available from: **Crown River Cruises**, Blackfriars Pier, tel: 020-7936 2033; www.crownriver.com.

Scheduled services are run by: **Thames River Services**, Westminster Pier to Thames Barrier (Jun-Aug)and Greenwich (year round), tel: 020-7930 4097; www.westminsterpier.co.uk.

City Cruises Departures from Westminster, Waterloo, Tower and Greenwich Piers, tel: 020-7740 0400; www.citycruises.com.

Steam Railways

Many steam rail lines have been restored by enthusiasts UK Heritage Railways (www.ukhrail.uel.ac.uk). Among the most notable are:
Bluebell Railway, Sheffield Park Station, Nr Uckfield, E. Sussex TN22 3QL, tel: 01825-720 800, www.bluebell-railway.co.uk. Britain's most famous line.
Watercress Line, Alresford, Hampshire SO24 9JG, tel: 01962-733 810, www.watercressline.co.uk. Runs through beautiful country over steeply graded track.
Severn Valley Railway, Bewdley, Worcestershire DY12 1BG, tel: 01299-403 816, www.svr.co.uk. Spectacular views.
Great Central Railway, Loughborough, Leics LE11 1RW, tel: 01509-230 726, www.gcrailway. co.uk. One of the most evocative restorations of the steam age.

London Duck Tours Guided tour of Westminster by road and river in amphibious vehicles used in the D-Day landings during World War II. Depart from Waterloo, tel: 020-7928 3132; www.londonducktours.co.uk.

British Waterways

Britain has over 2,000 miles (3,200km) of rivers and canals, the latter a legacy of the Industrial Revolution and now extensively restored. There is a wide choice of vessels to hire. Possibilities include exploring the canals, from the Grand Union in the Midlands to the Caledonian, which stretches from coast to coast in Scotland, or taking a pleasure cruiser along major rivers such as the Thames, Avon or the Severn, or around the Norfolk Broads.

For information, contact:
Waterscape (part of British Waterways), 64 Clarendon Road, Watford, Hertfordshire WD17 1DA, tel: 01923-201 120 (Mon–Fri 9am–5.30pm); fax: 01923-201 300; www.waterscape.com.
The Inland Waterways Association is a voluntary body that fights for the restoration and maintenance of Britain's waterway network. It has saved many waterways that would otherwise have disappeared. Contact the association at: PO Box 114, Rickmansworth, Hertfordshire, WD3 1ZY, tel: 01494-783 453, www.waterways.org.uk.

Lakeside and Haverthwaite Railway, Nr Ulverston, Cumbria LA12 8AL, tel: 01539-531 594, www.lakesiderailway.co.uk. Steep ride, with connections to boats on the lake.
North Yorkshire Moors Railway, Pickering Station. YO18 7AJ, tel: 01751-472 508, www.nymr.co.uk. An 18-mile (30km) line through picturesque moorland.
Paignton and Dartmouth Steam Railway, Queen's Park Station, Torbay Road, Paignton, Devon TQ4 6AF, tel: 01803-555 872, www.paignton-steamrailway.co.uk. Beautiful coastal line, with superb views.
Gloucestershire–Warwickshire Railway, Toddington, Glos GL54 5DT, tel: 01242-621 405, www.gwsr.com. A 20-mile (32km) round trip through the Cotswolds from Toddington to Cheltenham Racecourse.

A CCOMMODATION

HOTELS, YOUTH HOSTELS, BED & BREAKFAST

Choosing a Hotel

A variety of accommodation exists in Britain, from smart luxury hotels in stately homes and castles, to bed-and-breakfast (B&B) accommodation in private family homes or country farmhouses.

By international standards, hotels in Britain are expensive, so if you are holidaying on a tight budget you should consider staying in bed-and-breakfast accommodation. Alternatively there are plenty of youth hostels, which take people of all ages. Wherever you go, always be sure to look at a room before accepting it.

Not all hotels include breakfast in their rates and they may add a service

BELOW: the facade of The Grand Hotel on Brighton's seafront.

charge of 10–15 percent. However, all charges should be clearly displayed on the tariff.

It is advisable to book in advance, particularly at Christmas, Easter and throughout the summer. During the rest of the year there is generally little difficulty in finding somewhere to stay. You can book a room through a travel agent, directly with a hotel or via the Tourist Board.

The Britain and London Visitor Centre at 1 Regent Street, London W1, www.visitbritain.com, provides general information.

Hotel awards The Enjoy England Quality Rose is the mark of England's nationwide quality assessment scheme, whose ratings (1–5 stars) assess accommodation standards in different categories (eg hotels are in a separate category to B&Bs which come under Guest Accommodation), informing you what each category has to offer.

The AA (Automobile Association) provides a simple scheme awarding between one star (basic) to five stars (luxury). See www.theaa.co.uk.

A Michelin award is the accolade for which the most notable of hoteliers strive.

Visit Britain (www.visitbritain.com) produces a series of useful annual *Official Tourist Board* guides dealing with every type of accommodation in Britain, from farms, B&Bs and pet-friendly accommodation to camping and self-catering boating holidays. To be listed, an establishment first has to pay to be inspected and then pay to be given an enhanced listing – so the guides are not totally impartial.

Stately homes Britain has many grand stately homes and castles that have been converted into country-

house hotels. This growing trend in luxury accommodation has saved many historic buildings from dereliction. Most provide an extremely high standard of traditional accommodation and service.

Hotel Listings

Many hotels offer special weekend and low-season breaks between October and April. Details can be obtained from individual hotels, chains of hotels or from Enjoy England whose website lists accommodation discounts and deals.

The suggestions in this book are for hotels in places that will serve as good bases for exploring the regions covered in the guide. Unless otherwise stated, all the rooms have private bathroom facilities.

Hotel Chains

Hotels belonging to big chains such as Holiday Inn, Marriott and Hilton tend to offer a reliable, if at times impersonal, standard of service. In addition there are a host of private hotels. The business traveller on an expense account is increasingly well catered for, in both urban and country areas, where there are many hotels offering large conference rooms and health and leisure facilities in addition to internet and secretarial services. The following groups have hotels in most parts of the country:

Premier Travel Inn tel: 0870-242 8000 in the UK; +44 1582-567 890 outside the UK; www.premierinn.com. It's the budget leader.

Hilton International tel: 0870-590 9090; www.hilton.co.uk.

Accor Hotels tel: 0871-702 9469; www.accorhotels.com.

University Lodgings

Many universities have accommodation to let during the long summer holidays. This can be an inexpensive option (not confined to students), particularly in the capital. Some offer full board. For further information, contact the university in the town of your destination (the local tourist office will advise).

Self-catering Agencies

Blakes Country Cottages
Tel: 0845-268 0756 (UK only); +44 1282-847 883 (overseas)
www.blakes-cottages.co.uk
Over 2,000 cottages in pleasant areas and villages.
Cornish Traditional Cottages
Tel: 01208-821 666
www.corncott.com
About 400 cottages in Cornwall.
English Country Cottages
Tel: 0845-268 0785 (UK only)
www.english-country-cottages.co.uk
Wide variety of country properties including oast houses, barns, castles and manor houses.
Farm Stay UK
Tel: 024-7669 6909
www.farmstayuk.co.uk
Produces the annual Farm Stay UK guide, covering over 1,200 rural retreats.
Forest Holidays
Tel: 0845-130 8225/8226
www.forestholidays.co.uk
Rustic cabins and campsites owned by the Forestry Commission, in Yorkshire, Cornwall and Scotland.

Stepping Back in History

It is possible to stay in restored old buildings, from a medieval castle to a lighthouse. Many such properties have been beautifully restored and are maintained by the Landmark Trust and the National Trust.

The Landmark Trust is a private charity, set up in 1965 to rescue historic buildings. It now has more than 180 properties to let, ranging from castles and manor houses to mills, lighthouses, forts and follies, all restored and furnished in keeping with the original character. Detailed information in a handbook available by post. The book's price is refunded against bookings. Tel: 01628-825 925; www.landmarktrust.org.uk.

The National Trust have more than 400 cottages and smaller houses of historical interest to let, from a romantic cabin hideaway overlooking a Cornish creek to an apartment in York with clear views of the Minster. The National Trust, PO Box 536, Melksham, Wiltshire SN12 8SX, tel: 0844-800 2070; www.nationaltrust cottages.co.uk.

Youth Hostels

There are more than 200 youth hostels in England and Wales ranging from town houses to beach chalets. Facilities and accommodation are basic but cheap, usually comprising shared dormitories of bunk beds.

Some provide a full meals service while others have self-catering kitchens but hostels are only for those who don't mind mucking-in, communal living and a shortage of creature comforts. The maximum length of stay is 10–14 days. You must be a national or international member to stay at a hostel, although anyone of any age can join the association, overseas or in the UK.
Youth Hostel Association (YHA)
Trevelyan House, Dimple Road, Matlock, Derbyshire DE4 3YH
Tel: 01629-592 700
www.yha.org.uk

London Hostels
Earl's Court
38 Bolton Gardens, SW5 0AQ
Tel: 0845-371 9114
186 beds.
Kensington
Holland House, Holland Walk, W8 7QU
Tel: 0845-371 9122
200 beds.
St Paul's
36–8 Carter Lane, EC4V 5AB
Tel: 0845-371 9012
190 beds.
Thameside
20 Salter Road, SE16 5PR
Tel: 0845-371 9756
320 beds.

Inns and Pubs

Inns are a great British institution that have become increasingly popular for accommodation. They are cheaper and smaller than hotels and offer the opportunity of meeting local people.

There are many historic taverns, particularly in rural towns and villages. Many are by road sides where travelling pilgrims may have rested in the Middle Ages or stage coaches stopped. Often then they retain an old-world character with open fires, low beams, ale on tap and a warm ambience. Standards and food vary from basic to sophisticated.

In urban areas pubs may have more of an institutional feel.
CAMRA (Campaign for Real Ale), 230 Hatfield Road, St Albans AL1 4LW.
Tel: 01727-867 201; www.camra.org.uk, publishes a guide, *Beer, Bed & Breakfast*, listing the best accommodation.

B&Bs and Guesthouses

B&Bs tend to be good value, and it is always advisable to book in advance during the peak seasons. B&B accommodation is also available in many farmhouses, which provide rural accommodation. Contact local tourist offices for lists of recommended accommodation. Companies that specialise in B&Bs include:
Bed & Breakfast Nationwide
Tel: 01255-831 235
www.bedandbreakfastnationwide.com
London Bed & Breakfast Agency
Tel: 020-7586 2768
www.londonbb.com
Wolsey Lodges
Tel: 01473-822 058
www.wolseylodges.com
The AA publishes an annual guide to more than 4,000 inspected B&Bs, available from most good bookshops. Visit www.theaa.com.

Reserving and Booking a Room

● When you book a hotel room, ensure that the price quoted is inclusive, and isn't going to be bumped up by a mysterious "travellers' charge" or other extras. Service is usually included in hotel bills.
● If you reserve in advance, you may be asked for a deposit. Reservations made, whether in writing or by phone, can be regarded as binding contracts, and you could lose your deposit or be charged a percentage of the cost if you fail to turn up.

● If you have reserved a room, the hotel will usually keep it for you until early evening, unless you agree otherwise. Rooms must usually be vacated by midday on the day of departure.
● Some accommodation does not allow single-night stays over the weekend or at peak season.
● Most hotels offer extremely good rates if you stay for several nights, or opt for dinner, bed and breakfast. It can be worth your while to bargain. You can also save money by booking online.

LONDON

The price of a hotel room in London is as high as any in Europe. However, cost does not always mean quality, so try to view a room before accepting it. In Apr–Sept, it is advisable to book before you arrive as hotels fill up fast. You can book online at visitlondon.com, whilst justcalllondon.co.uk (tel: 0870-471 8411) allows you to book online or call their hotel reservations centre.

Top Class

Athenaeum Hotel
116 Piccadilly, W1J 7BJ
Tel: 020-7499 3464
www.athenaeumhotel.com
Smart hotel (123 rooms) in the heart of smart London, close to shops and with views over Green Park. A very English hotel, full of character of the "gentleman's club" kind. Excellent service. **£££**

The Berkeley
Wilton Place, Knightsbridge, SW1X 7RL
Tel: 020-7235 6000
www.the-berkeley.co.uk
Many rate the Berkeley as the best in London. It's low key, with a country house, not a business atmosphere. Swimming pool. **££££**

Claridge's
Brook Street, Mayfair, W1K 4HR
Tel: 020-7629 8860
www.claridges.co.uk
Has long had a reputation for dignity and graciousness. **££££**

The Connaught
Carlos Place, W1K 2AL
Tel: 020-7499 7070
www.the-connaught.co.uk
One of the best hotels in London. Superb decor, immaculate service, and a Michelin-starred restaurant. **££££**

The Dorchester
Park Lane, W1K 1QA
Tel: 020-7629 8888
www.thedorchester.com
One of the most expensive in London. Views over Hyde Park. **££££**

Durley House
115 Sloane Street, SW1X 9PJ
Tel: 020-7235 5537
www.durleyhouse.com
Seriously luxurious suites, with all mod cons and private gardens. **££££**

The Lanesborough
Hyde Park Corner, SW1X 7TA
Tel: 020-7259 5599
www.lanesborough.com
Deluxe hotel overlooking Hyde Park. The stately neo-classical facade of the former St George's hospital complements the opulent Regency-style interior. Fitness centre. **££££**

Metropolitan
Old Park Lane, W1K 1LB
Tel: 020-7447 1000
www.metropolitan.london.como.bz
Modern, minimalist and very chic. Home to the Michelin-starred Nobu restaurant. **££££**

The Sanderson
50 Berners Street, W1T 3NG

BELOW: The Lanesborough Hotel.

Tel: 020-7300 1400
www.sandersonlondon.com
Ultra-stylish hotel behind a plain exterior. Philippe Starck-designed interior. **££££**

The Savoy
Strand, WC2R 0EU
Tel: 020-7836 4343
www.fairmont.com/savoy
One of London's legends, with a reputation for comfort and personal service. Reopens 2010 after a dramatic £100 million renewal and convenient for theatreland and Covent Garden. **££££**

Luxury

Blakes Hotel
33 Roland Gardens, SW7 3PF
Tel: 020-7370 6701
www.blakeshotels.com
Exotically furnished with Victorian splendour but with a cosmopolitan, laid-back style. **£££–££££**

Brown's Hotel
Albemarle/Dover Street, W1S 4BP
Tel: 020-7493 6020
www.brownshotel.com
A distinguished, very British hotel, founded by Lord Byron's valet in 1837. Smart Mayfair location and award-winning afternoon teas. **££££**

Cadogan Hotel
75 Sloane Street, SW1X 9SG
Tel: 020-7235 7141
www.cadogan.com
A 19th-century style hotel. Actress Lily Langtry lived in what is now the bar. Good position in between Chelsea and Knightsbridge. **£££**

The Halkin
5 Halkin Street, Belgravia, SW1X 7DJ
Tel: 020-7333 1000
www.halkin.como.bz
Excellent accommodation in a Georgian townhouse. Sleek design, first Michelin-starred Thai restaurant in Europe. **££££**

Pelham Hotel
15 Cromwell Place, SW7 2LA

London

Tel: 020-7589 8288
www.pelhamhotel.co.uk
Elegant Victorian townhouse, with wood-panelled drawing rooms. **££££**

The Ritz
150 Piccadilly, W1J 9BR
Tel: 020-7493 8181
www.theritzlondon.com
World-famous hotel. Not what it was, despite refurbishment. Jackets and ties required in the restaurant. Tea at the Ritz is one of the best. **££££**

The Tower Hotel
St Katharine's Way, E1W 1LD
Tel: 0871-376 9036
www.guoman.com/the-tower
Big, modern hotel in the docklands. Breathtaking locale, with views of Tower Bridge and the river. Near the City. Brisk five-minute walk to nearest Tube station. **£££**

22 Jermyn Street
22 Jermyn Street, SW1Y 6HL
Tel: 020-7734 2353
www.22jermyn.com
Right by Piccadilly, a peaceful townhouse excellent for business trips. Concierge can secure restaurant bookings. **£££–££££**

PRICE CATEGORIES

Price categories are for a double room including breakfast and VAT (value added tax) at high season:
£ = under £100
££ = £100–170
£££ = £170–270
££££ = over £270

Moderate

Academy Town House
17–21 Gower Street, WC1E 6HG
Tel: 020-7631 4115
www.theetoncollection.com
A small, welcoming hotel.
Licensed bar; evening meal
available.. **£££**

Elizabeth Hotel
37 Eccleston Square, Victoria,
SW1V 1PB
Tel: 020-7828 6812
www.elizabethhotel.com
Friendly hotel in elegant
period square, two minutes'
walk from Victoria station.
££

The Rubens at the Palace
39 Buckingham Palace Road,
Victoria, SW1W 0PS
Tel: 020-7834 6600
www.rubenshotel.com
Large traditional hotel with
a smart location opposite
Royal Mews. **£££**

Tophams
24-32 Ebury Street, SW1W 0LU
Tel: 020-7730 3313
www.tophamshotellondon.co.uk
This luxury boutique hotel in
Belgravia occupies five
period houses and is very
popular. Friendly and
welcoming. **£££**

Inexpensive

Airways Hotel
29 St George's Drive, SW1V 4DG
Tel: 020-7834 0205
www.airways-hotel.com
Pleasant budget hotel close
to Buckingham Place,
Westminster Abbey, and
Harrods. Friendly service. **£**

Clearlake Hotel
19 Prince of Wales Terrace, W8 5PQ
Tel: 020-7937 3274
www.clearlakehotel.co.uk
Comfortable. 20 self-
catering rooms and
apartments in a quiet
location with views of Hyde
Park. Good value. **£**

County Hall Premier Inn
Belvedere Road, SE1 7PB
Tel: 0870-238 3300
www.premierinn.com
In the old County Hall by the
river; listed building
opposite Houses of
Parliament. Advance
booking essential. **££**

Curzon House Hotel
58 Courtfield Gardens, SW5 0NF
Tel: 020-7581 2116
www.curzonhousehotel.co.uk
Economical but comfortable
small hotel close to
Gloucester Road
Underground station. **£**

Garden Court Hotel
30–31 Kensington Gardens Square,
W2 4BG
Tel: 020-7229 2553
www.gardencourthotel.co.uk
Friendly, family-run bed-and-
breakfast set in a traditional
English garden square. **££**

THE THAMES VALLEY

Aylesbury

Hartwell House
Oxford Road, nr Aylesbury,
HP17 8NR
Tel: 01296-747 444
www.hartwell-house.com
Country house hotel in large
grounds. Antique-furnished
bedrooms; excellent leisure
facilities. 33 rooms and
suites. **£££**

Henley-on-Thames

Hotel du Vin
New Street, RG9 2BP
Tel: 01491-848 400
www.hotelduvin.com
Located in a converted
brewery close to the river in
this Oxfordshire market
town, this luxury boutique
hotel has a good bistro.
Stylish rooms. **£££**

Red Lion
Hart Street, RG9 2AR
Tel: 01491-572 161
www.redlionhenley.co.uk
Just right for the annual
regatta in early July, this
comfortable, family-owned
hotel overlooks the finishing
post on the River Thames.
Three rooms with four
poster beds. **£££**

Taplow

Cliveden
Taplow, Berkshire, SL6 0JF
Tel: 01628-668 561
www.clivedenhouse.co.uk
Majestic, luxurious hotel.
Once the home of the Prince
of Wales, several dukes and
the Astors, it is surrounded
by acres of National Trust
parkland. **££££**

Windsor

Oakley Court
Windsor Road, Water Oakley,
SL4 5UR
Tel: 01753-609 988
www.principal-hayley.com
Victorian house with
extensive grounds running
down to the Thames. **£££**

OXFORD

Oxford

Bath Place Hotel
4–5 Bath Place, OX1 3SU
Tel: 01865-791 812
www.bathplace.co.uk
Family-run 15-room hotel in
the heart of Oxford
occupying a group of
restored 17th-century
cottages. **££**

Cotswold Lodge Hotel
66a Banbury Road, OX2 6JP
Tel: 01865-512 121
www.cotswoldlodgehotel.co.uk
Beautiful Victorian building
in a quiet conservation area
10 minutes walk from city
centre; 49 rooms. **££**

Eastgate Hotel
73 High Street, OX1 4BE
Tel: 01865-248 332
www.mercure.com
Traditional hotel in central
location, adjacent to the site
of Oxford's old East Gate,
opposite the Examination
Schools. **£££**

Old Parsonage Hotel
1 Banbury Road, OX2 6NN
Tel: 01865-310 210
www.oldparsonage-hotel.co.uk
A fine hotel in a renovated
old parsonage with 30
luxuriously appointed
en-suite bedrooms. The
restaurant is open to non-
residents. **£££**

Randolph Hotel
Beaumont Street, OX1 2LN
Tel: 0844-879 9132
www.macdonaldhotels.co.uk
Grand Victorian 151-room
hotel in central Oxford
offering traditional service
with all the trimmings. **£££**

Great Milton, nr Oxford

Le Manoir aux Quat'Saisons
Church Road
Tel: 01844-278 881
www.manoir.com
Raymond Blanc's renowned
2-Michelin starred

restaurant and hotel.
Stunning gardens, including
a Japanese tea garden.
Luxurious, individually
decorated rooms, some with
their own terrace. **££££**

THE COTSWOLDS

Ampney Crucis

Crown of Crucis
Ampney Crucis, nr Cirencester,
GL7 5RS
Tel: 01285-851 806
www.thecrownofcrucis.co.uk
A 16th-century inn
overlooking the village
cricket green. Good food. **£**

Bibury

Bibury Court
Cirencester, GL7 5NT
Tel: 01285-740 337
www.biburycourt.co.uk
This glorious Jacobean
house fulfils everyone's idea
of a Cotswold manor. Rarely
does such a sense of history
come with so low a price
tag. **£££**
The Swan
Gloucestershire, GL7 5NW
Tel: 01285-740 695
www.cotswold-inns-hotels.co.uk/swan
In a beautiful riverside
setting in its own private
gardens. Antique
furnishings. **££–£££**

Broadway

The Lygon Arms
High Street
Tel: 01386-852 255
www.lygonarms.co.uk
Magnificent 16th-century
coaching inn; antique
furnishings, log fires.
££–£££

Buckland

Buckland Manor
Nr Broadway, WR12 7LY
Tel: 01386-852 626
www.bucklandmanor.co.uk
13th-century manor in
extensive 10-acre
(4-hectare) gardens.**££££**

Cheltenham

The Greenway
Shurdington, nr Cheltenham, GL51
4UG
Tel: 01242-862 352
www.thegreenway.co.uk
Peaceful Elizabethan
mansion covered in Virginia
creeper. Recently
refurbished rooms offer a
luxurious country house
feel. **£££**
Hotel On the Park
Evesham Road, GL52 2AH
Tel: 01242-518 898
www.hotelonthepark.co.uk
Pretty townhouse opposite
Pittville Park with tasteful,
individually decorated
bedrooms and luxurious
bathrooms. No facilities for
young children. **£££**

Lower Slaughter

Lower Slaughter Manor
Nr Bourton-on-the-Water,
Gloucestershire, GL54 2HP
Tel: 01451-820 456
www.lowerslaughter.co.uk
Luxurious 17th-century
manor in own grounds, with
panelled private dining
room and galleried landing.
Superb breakfast.
£££–££££

Stow-on-the-Wold

Grapevine Hotel
Sheep Street, GL54 1AU
Tel: 01451-830 344
www.vines.co.uk
Welcoming hotel in a 17th-
century stone building,
named after the old vine
that shades the
conservatory restaurant. A
good base for touring the
Cotswolds. **££**

Tetbury

The Snooty Fox
Market Place, GL8 8DD
Tel: 01666-502 436
www.snooty-fox.co.uk

An old Cotswold stone
coaching inn on the market
square of this historic town.
Oak panelling, log fires,
antique furniture. Fine
restaurant. Some rooms
with four-poster beds. **££**

Upper Slaughter

Lords of the Manor
Nr Bourton-on-the-Water, GL54
2JD
Tel: 01451-820 243
www.lordsofthemanor.com
A 16th-century former
rectory with Victorian
additions set in the rolling
Cotswold countryside. Many
rooms have parkland and
lake views. Baronial
atmosphere with chintzy
fabrics, Oriental rugs and
antiques. **£££–££££**

SHAKESPEARE COUNTRY

Birmingham

Jurys Inn Birmingham
245 Broad Street, B1 2HQ
Tel: 0121-606 9000
www.birminghamhotels.jurysinns.com
In the heart of the city, this
445-room hotel offers a
superior standard of budget
accommodation.
Comfortable rooms fine for
an overnight stay. **£**

Stratford-upon-Avon

The Howard Arms
Lower Green, Ilmington, CV36 4LT
Tel: 01608-682 226
www.howardarms.com
Characterful inn with eight
bedrooms, all en-suite. A
good mix of antique and
modern. Excellent
gastropub menu. Peaceful
village setting. **££**
Shakespeare Hotel
Chapel Street, CV37 6ER
Tel: 01789-294 997
www.mercure.com
This 17th-century, half-
timbered building, one of
Stratford's most beautiful, is
the best hotel in town.
Centrally located with open
fires, low beams and a good
restaurant. **£££**
Woodstock House
30 Grove Road, CV37 6PB
Tel: 01789-299 881
www.woodstock-house.co.uk
This comfortable B&B is just
ten minutes from the city
centre. 5 en-suite rooms.
Full English breakfast. No
credit cards. **£**

Dudley

Copthorne Hotel
The Waterfront, Level Street,
Brierley Hill, Dudley DY5 1UR
Tel: 01384-482 882
www.millenniumhotels.co.uk
Comfortable modern hotel a
few miles from Birmingham,
located beside a canal. **£**

Edgbaston

Simpsons
20 Highfield Road, Edgbaston,
Birmingham B15 3DX
Tel: 0121-454 3434
www.simpsonsrestaurant.co.uk
Victorian villa with stylish,
themed bedrooms, an
excellent restaurant and a
cookery school. Relaxed
atmosphere. **££–£££**

PRICE CATEGORIES

Price categories are for a
double room including
breakfast and VAT (value
added tax) at high season:
£ = under £100
££ = £100–170
£££ = £170–270
££££ = over £270

CAMBRIDGE AND EAST ANGLIA

Burnham Market

The Hoste Arms
The Green, PE31 8HD
Tel: 01328-738 777
www.hostearms.co.uk
Characterful 17th-century inn on the green of the village near where Admiral Nelson was born and close to Sandringham's royal estate. Restaurant. **££**

Cambridge

Arundel House Hotel
53 Chesterton Road, CB4 3AN
Tel: 01223-367 701
www.arundelhousehotels.co.uk
Privately owned terraced hotel overlooking the River Cam near the centre of town. Restaurant. **£**
Cambridge Garden House
Granta Place, Mill Lane, CB2 1RT
Tel: 01223-259 988
www.doubletree.hilton.co.uk
Modern hotel by river which provides offers on hiring

punts and rowing boats. Central location and fitness centre. **££**

Ely

Lamb Hotel
2 Lynn Road, CB7 4EJ
Tel: 01353-663 574
www.thelamb-ely.com
Former coaching house whose history can be traced to 1416. Located in the town centre and sitting in the shadow of Ely's magnificent cathedral. Includes a four-poster suite. **£–££**

Lavenham

The Angel
Market Place, Suffolk, CO10 9QZ
Tel: 01787-247 388
www.maypolehotels.com/angelhotel
A 15th-century inn overlooking this old wool town's market place. The recommended restaurant

uses fresh local ingredients. Only 8 rooms. **£–££**

Morston, nr Holt

Morston Hall
NR25 7AA
Tel: 01263-741 041
www.morstonhall.com
Comfortable rooms in a flint manor house on the Norfolk coast. Michelin-starred chef. **££–£££**

Southwold

The Crown
High Street, Suffolk, IP18 6DP
Tel: 01502-722 186
www.adnams.co.uk
Owned by Adnams Brewery so the beer is good. Comfortable rooms and two restaurants, one formal, one brasserie-style. **£**
The Randolph Hotel
Wangford Road, Reydon, near Southwold, Suffolk, IP18 6PZ
Tel: 01502-723 603

www.therandolph.co.uk
A 15-minute walk from Southwold, this is a good base for exploring the Suffolk Heritage Coast. **£–££**

Wells-next-the-sea

The Crown Hotel
The Buttlands, NR23 1EX
Tel: 01328-710 209
www.thecrownhotelwells.co.uk
A fine old coaching inn in a pretty port on the north Norfolk coast. Popular bar and restaurant. **££**

CANTERBURY AND THE SOUTHEAST

Canterbury

Falstaff
8–10 St Dunstan's Street, CT2 8AF
Tel: 0844-600 8707
www.foliohotels.com/falstaff
Coaching inn, within easy reach of cathedral and shops. 46 rooms. **££**

Cranbrook

Cloth Hall Oast
Cranbrook, Kent TN17 3NR
Tel: 01580-712 220
Stunning Kentish oast house, set in 5 acres (2 hectares) of gardens. Just 3 bedrooms. Great location for exploring Kent and Sussex. **£–££**

New Romney

Romney Bay House
Coast Road, Littlestone, TN28 8QY
Tel: 01797-364 747
www.signpost.co.uk/london_south.htm
Right by the sea with stunning views. The 10 rooms are splendidly and

individually decorated. Good food and excellent cream teas. **£–££**

Pluckley

Elvey Farm
Elvey Lane, Pluckley, TN27 0SU
Tel: 01233-840 442
www.elveyfarm.co.uk
Historic farmhouse with contemporary rooms (one with a four-poster and hot tub). Set in the village of Pluckley. **££**

Rye

Durrant House
2 Market Street, TN31 7LA
Tel: 01797-223 182
www.durranthouse.com
An attractive Georgian house. Excellent breakfasts. Only 5 rooms and 2 suites. No smoking. **££**
The George in Rye
98 High Street, TN31 7JT
Tel: 01797-222 114
www.thegeorgeinrye.com
The George is Rye's oldest

coaching inn. 24 individually-designed luxury bedrooms with Frette bedlinen. Excellent dining room and superb breakfast. **££ –£££**
The Mermaid Inn
Mermaid Street, TN31 7EY
Tel: 01797-223 065
www.mermaidinn.com
Popular 15th-century inn in this ancient coastal port. Excellent restaurant. There are 31 rooms (8 with 4-poster beds). **£–££**

Tunbridge Wells

Hotel du Vin and Bistro
Crescent Road, TN1 2LY

BELOW: The Mermaid Inn.

Tel: 01892-526 455
www.hotelduvin.com
Individually decorated rooms, friendly, obliging staff, and great breakfasts are good reasons for staying here, in the centre of town. Good bistro. **££**

PRICE CATEGORIES

Price categories are for a double room including breakfast and VAT (value added tax) at high season:
£ = under £100
££ = £100–170
£££ = £170–270
££££ = over £270

BRIGHTON AND THE DOWNS

Alfriston

The George Inn
High Street, BN26 5SY
Tel: 01323-870 319
www.thegeorge-alfriston.com
This 14th-century pub/hotel is in the middle of a pretty village. It has oak-beamed rooms and local fish is a speciality of the restaurant. **£–££**

Arundel

Amberley Castle
nr Arundel, BN18 9LT
Tel: 01798-831 992
www.amberleycastle.co.uk
Genuine 12th-century castle dripping with atmosphere. Opulently refurbished with antiques. **£££–££££**

Swan Hotel
27–29 High Street, BN18 9AG
Tel: 01903-882 314
www.fullershotels.com
A listed building at the heart of a delightful village. Comfortable and popular. Good restaurant. **££**

Brighton

The Grand
97–99 King's Road, BN1 2FW
Tel: 01273-224 300
www.devere-hotels.com
Victorian grandeur and friendly service. Overlooks the beach; indoor pool, gym and spa. Restaurant serves classic British dishes with a contemporary twist. **££–£££**

Old Ship Hotel
King's Road, BN1 1NR
Tel: 01273-329 001
www.barcelo-hotels.co.uk
One of Brighton's oldest hotels. Elegant, traditional but not too grand. **££**

Hotel Pelirocco
10 Regency Square, BN1 2FG
Tel: 01273-327 055
Fax: 01273-733 845
www.hotelpelirocco.co.uk
All rooms individually designed, with their own playstations, in this chic and risqué hotel in the best-preserved Regency square in town. **££**

Chichester

The Millstream Hotel
Bosham, nr Chichester, PO18 8HL
Tel: 01243-573 234
www.millstream-hotel.co.uk
Quiet country hotel near Bosham harbour. Good food. **££**

Suffolk House Hotel
3 East Row, PO19 1PD
Tel: 01243-778 899
www.suffolkhousehotel.co.uk
Privately-run hotel in a fine Georgian building with restaurant and garden. **£**

Eastbourne

The Grand Hotel
King Edward's Parade, BN21 4EQ
Tel: 01323-412 345

www.grandeastbourne.com
Built in 1875, with comfortable rooms and splendid service. Formal restaurant. **£££**

Midhurst

Angel Hotel
North Street, GU29 9DN
Tel: 01730-812 421
www.theangelmidhurst.co.uk
A 15th-century coaching inn. Original tudor beams, antique furniture and several 4-poster beds. **£–££**

HAMPSHIRE, WILTSHIRE AND DORSET

Brockenhurst

Balmer Lawn Hotel
Lyndhurst Road, SO42 7ZB
Tel: 01590-623 116
www.balmerlawnhotel.com
Former hunting lodge in the heart of the New Forest with superb views. Swimming pools, tennis, squash, sauna and gym. **£££**

Careys Manor
Lyndhurst Road, SO42 7RH
Tel: 01590-623 551
www.careysmanor.com
An environmentally-friendly 1888 mansion complete with Thai spa. Rooms in garden wing have balconies overlooking walled garden. **£–££**

New Park Manor
Lyndhurst Road, SO42 7QH
Tel: 01590-623 467
www.newparkmanorhotel.co.uk
Excellent 24-room retreat, in landscaped grounds in the New Forest. Once the hunting lodge of Charles II. Excellent restaurant, croquet lawn, heated pool, spa. **££**

Evershot

Summer Lodge
Summer Lane, DT2 0JR
Tel: 01935-482 000
www.summerlodgehotel.co.uk
Georgian dower house in 4 acres (1.6 hectares) of mature gardens. Tastefully furnished. **££**

Lyme Regis

The Alexandra
Pound Street, DT7 3HZ
Tel: 01297-442 010
www.hotelalexandra.co.uk
Large 18th-century house set in fine grounds over-looking the bay. Comfortable and welcoming. **££**

Lymington

Stanwell House Hotel
145 High Street, SO41 9AA
Tel: 01590-677 123
www.stanwellhousehotel.co.uk
Stylishly decorated Georgian coaching house. Seafood restaurant and bistro. **££**

Melksham

The Pear Tree Inn
Top Lane, Whitley, Melksham, SN12 8QX
Tel: 01225-709 131
www.thepeartreeinn.com
Cosy country inn with eight chich bedrooms and a popular restaurant. **££**

New Milton

Chewton Glen
Christchurch Road, BH25 6QS
Tel: 01425-275 341
www.chewtonglen.com
One of England's best-known country house hotels, in an elegant 18th-century mansion on the edge of the New Forest National Park. The swimming pool is modelled on the bathhouses of ancient Rome. **££££**

Salisbury

Howard's House
Teffont Evias, Salisbury, SP3 5RJ

Tel: 01722-716 392
www.howardshousehotel.co.uk
Attractive 17th-century house in pretty village outside Salisbury. Stylish rooms and attractive gardens. **££**

Sparsholt

Lainston House Hotel
Nr Winchester, SO21 2LT
Tel: 01962-863 588
www.exclusivehotels.co.uk
Beautiful country house in extensive grounds with a good restaurant. Has 50 rooms. **££**

BATH

The Bath Priory
Weston Road, BA1 2XT
Tel: 01225-331 922
www.thebathpriory.co.uk
Gothic-style 19th-century
house in beautiful gardens.
Michelin-starred restaurant.
£££–££££

Bath Spa Hotel
Sydney Road, BA2 6JF
Tel: 0844-879 9106
www.macdonaldhotels.co.uk/bathspa
Near Sydney Gardens and
set in its own extensive
grounds. Excellent
restaurant. **£££**

Bloomfield House
146 Bloomfield Road, BA2 2AS
Tel: 01225-420 105
www.ecobloomfield.com
Upmarket B&B in large
18th-century neoclassical
house. Some 4-poster beds.
No smoking. **££**

Eagle House
Church Street, Bathford, BA1 7RS
Tel: 01225-859 946
www.eaglehouse.co.uk
B&B in a pretty conservation
village just outside Bath.
Friendly and homely but
smart. **£–££**

Francis Hotel
Queen Square, BA1 2HH
Tel: 01225-424 105
www.mercure.com
Traditional Bath stone
building with comfortable
interior; 95 rooms. **££**

Holly Lodge
8 Upper Oldfield Park, BA2 3JZ
Tel: 01225-424 042
www.hollylodge.co.uk
Large Victorian house on
the south side of Bath.
Emphasis on service and
comfort. Excellent
breakfasts. Frilly

furnishings. **££**

The Queensberry Hotel
Russel Street, BA1 2QF
Tel: 01225-447 928
www.thequeensberry.co.uk
Small boutique hotel
occupying three Georgian
houses knocked together.
Comfortable and
characterful, though some
rooms are on the small side.
The esteemed Olive Tree
restaurant is in the
basement. **££–£££**

Royal Crescent Hotel
16 Royal Crescent, BA1 2LS
Tel: 01225-823 333
www.royalcrescent.co.uk
The ultimate address in
Bath, with a central location.
Antiques, paintings,
individually decorated
rooms, a noted restaurant
and a beautiful, secluded

garden at the back. With 45
rooms. **£££–££££**

Villa Magdala Hotel
Henrietta Road, BA2 6LX
Tel: 01225-466 329
www.villamagdala.co.uk
Overlooking Henrietta Park.
Private car park, which is
unusual in the centre of
Bath. Five minutes from the
city centre. **££**

THE WEST COUNTRY

Barwick

Little Barwick House
Barwick, nr Yeovil, BA22 9TD
Tel: 01935-423 902
www.litttlebarwick.co.uk
Unpretentious Georgian
house with gardens. Great
place to escape to. **£**

Bigbury-on-Sea

Burgh Island Hotel
South Devon, TQ7 4BG
Tel: 01548-810 514
www.burghisland.com
Unusual Art Deco hotel on
an island first inhabited in
AD 900 by monks; access
by sea tractor. Agatha
Christie wrote two books
here. The 25 rooms, many
named for past famous
guests, ooze romantic
charm. Price includes
dinner. **££££**

Bradford-on-Avon

Bradford Old Windmill
4 Masons Lane, BA15 1QN
Tel: 01225-866 842
www.bradfordoldmill.co.uk
Hidden-away converted
windmill. No smoking. Three
rooms **££**

Old Manor Hotel
Trowle Common,
nr Bradford-on-Avon, BA14 9BL
Tel: 01225-777 393
www.oldmanorhotel.com
A 16th-century manor
house, newly redecorated.
Restaurant. **££**

Castle Combe

Manor House Hotel
Castle Combe, nr Bath, SN14 7HR
Tel: 01249-782 206
www.manorhouse.co.uk
Parts of this manor house
are 14th-century. Best
rooms have beams,
exposed stone walls and
quality furnishings. Golf
break packages include
unlimited access to the
championship green. **£££**

Chagford, Devon

Gidleigh Park
TQ13 8HH
Tel: 01647-432 367
www.gidleigh.com
Quintessentially English, a
huge, half-timbered house
in 45 acres (18 hectares) of
grounds within Dartmoor
National Park; babbling
brook, log fires and

impeccable service.
Excellent restaurant, with
two Michelin stars. **££££**

Mill End Hotel
Dartmoor National Park, TQ13 8JN
Tel: 01647-432 282
www.millendhotel.com
Pretty old mill, complete
with wheel, in peaceful
setting on River Teign.
Excellent for families; local
produce served in
restaurant. **££**

Colerne, nr Bath

Lucknam Park
SN14 8AZ
Tel: 01225-742 777
www.lucknampark.co.uk
Luxurious manor, all rooms
with marble bathrooms.
Equestrian centre and spa.
££££

Dartmouth

The Royal Castle
11 The Quay, TQ6 9PS
Tel: 01803-833 033
www.royalcastle.co.uk
On Dartmouth's quayside,
this 17th-century coaching
inn serves good Devon
cuisine. 25 rooms, some
with river views. **££–£££**

Fowey

Fowey Hall
Hanson Drive, PL23 1ET
Tel: 01726-833 866
www.foweyhallhotel.co.uk
Imposing turrets outside,
sumptuous decor inside,
but relaxed atmosphere and
children are well catered for.
££

Old Quay House
28 Fore Street, PL23 1AQ

PRICE CATEGORIES

Price categories are for a
double room including
breakfast and VAT (value
added tax) at high season:
£ = under £100
££ = £100–170
£££ = £170–270
££££ = over £270

Tel: 01726-833 302
www.theoldquayhouse.com
Right on the quayside, a traditional exterior conceals sleek modern decor. The views are stupendous and the Q Restaurant is highly recommended. **££–£££**

Marazion/ St Michael's Mount

Mount Haven Hotel
Turnpike Road, Penzance, TR17 0DQ
Tel: 01736-710 249
www.mounthaven.co.uk
A pretty hotel with light, airy rooms, some with balconies and private terraces, overlooking St Michael's Mount. Near Land's End. **££**

Mawgan Porth

Bedruthan Steps Hotel
Mawgan Porth, nr Newquay, TR8 4BU
Tel: 01637-860 860
www.bedruthanstepshotel.co.uk

Family friendly hotel on north Cornish coast. Local produce served in the restaurant. **££–£££**

Monkton Combe

Combe Grove Manor Hotel
Brassknocker Hill, BA2 7HS
Tel: 01225-834 644
www.barcelo-hotels.co.uk
Luxurious 18th-century house and garden lodge. Pools, gym, tennis, golf and driving range. **£££**

Penzance

Abbey Hotel
Abbey Street, TR18 4AR
Tel: 01736-366 906
http://theabbeyonline.co.uk/home.html
Delightful stuccoed building overlooking the harbour. Rooms have period features. **££**
The Queen's Hotel
The Promenade, TR18 4HG
Tel: 01736-362 371

www.queens-hotel.com
Traditional English seaside hotel with wonderful views over Mounts Bay to St Michael's Mount in the distance; dog friendly. **££**
The Summer House
Cornwall Terrace, TR18 4HL
Tel: 01736-363 744
www.summerhouse-cornwall.com
In a blue-painted Regency building just off the seafront. Light, bright decor and a small walled garden. Open Apr–Oct; restaurant open Fri–Sun. **£–££**

St Ives

Carbis Bay Hotel
Carbis Bay, TR26 2NP
Tel: 01736-795 311
www.carbisbayhotel.co.uk
Good restaurant, splendid views of one of Britain's most beautiful bays, private beach. **££**

Ston Easton

Ston Easton Park
Nr Bath, BA3 4DF
Tel: 01761-241 631
www.stoneaston.co.uk
Most notable for its Humphrey Repton gardens, with grotto, bridges over River Norr and 18th-century ice house, this fine Palladian manor provides country house splendour in the Mendip Hills. Restaurant's organic produce comes from the Victorian kitchen garden. **£££–££££**

Tintagel

Michael House
Trelake Lane, Treknow, Cornwall, PL34 0EW
Tel: 01840-770 592
www.michael-house.co.uk
Vegetarian and vegan guest-house with sea-views, in scenic coastal resort. **£**

ISLES OF SCILLY

St Martin's

St Martin's on the Isle
Tel: 01720-422 090
Fax: 01720-422 298
www.stmartinshotel.co.uk
Nestling in a cove, with own quay, this hotel, looking like a cluster of granite cottages, blends with its natural surroundings. Indoor heated pool. **££**

St Mary's

St Mary's Hall Hotel
Church Street, TR21 0JR
Tel: 01720-422 316
Fax: 01720-422 252
www.stmaryshallhotel.co.uk
On the edge of Hugh Town close to the beaches, this hotel has a long-standing reputation for good food. Price includes dinner. **££**

Tresco

Island Hotel
Tel: 01720-422 883
Fax: 01720-423 883
www.tresco.co.uk
Fine hotel with great location in sub-tropical gardens near Old Grimsby. Pool and tennis court. 51 rooms. Price includes dinner. **£££**

HEREFORD AND THE WELSH BORDERS

Chester

Best Western Queen Hotel
63 City Road, CH1 3AH
Tel: 01244-305 000
www.bw-queenhotel.co.uk
Handy for the station, this smart hotel has two restaurants and an Italian garden. **££**

Hay on Wye

Kilverts Hotel
The Bullring, HR3 5AG
Tel: 01497-821 042

www.kilverts.co.uk
Centrally located inn with 12 rooms and a cosy bar. **£–££**

Hereford

Castle House
Castle Street, HR1 2NW
Tel: 01432-356 321
www.castlehse.co.uk
Former home of the Bishop of Hereford. Close to the cathedral, this 15-room hotel provides an excellent base. Renowned for its restaurant. **£££**

Ludlow

Mr Underhills
Dinham Weir SY8 1EH
Tel: 01584-874 431
www.mr-underhills.co.uk
Glorious location beside the weir. Michelin-starred restaurant with rooms. **££**

Shrewsbury

The Lion
Wyle Cop, SY1 1UY
Tel: 01743-353 107
www.thelionhotelshrewsbury.co.uk

Beamed 16th-century inn in centre of this medieval town. 59 rooms. **£**

TRANSPORT

ACCOMMODATION

EATING OUT

ACTIVITIES

A – Z

DERBY TO THE EAST COAST

Belton

Belton Woods Hotel
Nr Grantham, NG32 2LN
Tel: 01476-593 200
Fax: 01476-574 547
www.devere-hotels.com
Lakeside hotel with two
championship-standard
18-hole golf courses and
one 9-hole course. 136
rooms, plus 2 or 3 bedroom
luxury lodges in grounds
with fully equipped kitchens.
££

Derby

Cathedral Quarter Hotel
16 St Mary's Gate, DE1 3JR
Tel: 0115-852 3207
www.cathedralquarterhotel.com
Stylish boutique hotel in
Derby, with 38 rooms. The
19th-century building was
once a police museum. **££**

Grantham

Allington Manor
Allington, nr Grantham, NG32 2DH

Tel: 01400-282 574
www.allingtonmanor.com
Jacobean manor house with
3 sumptuous rooms,
furnished in romantic style.
££

Nottingham

Lace Market Hotel
29-31 High Pavement, NG1 1HE
Tel: 0115-852 3232
www.lacemarkethotel.co.uk
Stylish boutique hotel in the
heart of Nottingham.

Brasserie, cocktail bar and
gastro pub. **££**

THE PEAK DISTRICT

Ashford in the Water

Riverside House Hotel
Bakewell, DE45 1QF
Tel: 01629-814 275
www.riversidehousehotel.co.uk
Small 18th-century house
on the Wye with some
4-poster beds, log fires and
antiques; 15 rooms. **££**

Bakewell

Rutland Arms Hotel
The Square, DE45 1BT
Tel: 01629-812 812
www.rutlandarmsbakewell.com
Jane Austen is said to have
stayed here while working
on *Pride and Prejudice*. Its
54 antique clocks in public
areas hint at its traditional
flavour. **££**

Buxton

Buckingham Hotel
1–2 Burlington Road, SK17 9AS
Tel: 01298-70481
www.buckinghamhotel.co.uk
Old and sometimes creaky
building but welcoming,
informal atmosphere. Bar is
known for its range of real
ales. 37 rooms. **££**
Old Hall Hotel
The Square, SK17 6BD
Tel: 01298-22841
www.oldhallhotelbuxton.co.uk
A landmark since the 16th
century, this dignified hotel
on the square overlooks
Pavilion Gardens with the
Opera House nearby. **£**

Dovedale

Izaak Walton Hotel
Nr Ashbourne, DE6 2AY
Tel: 01335-350 555
www.izaakwaltonhotel.com
One of the Peak's most
stylish and picturesque
hotels, named after the
17th-century author of *The
Compleat Angler* who
fished in the area. In the
jaws of Dovedale beneath
Thorpe Cloud; 35 rooms.
££

Hassop

Hassop Hall Hotel
Nr Bakewell, DE45 1NS
Tel: 01629-640 488
www.hassophallhotel.co.uk
A classical Georgian house
set in spacious parkland
just 2½ miles (4km) from
Bakewell; 13 elegant rooms.
£–££

Hathersage

George Hotel
Main Road, S32 1BB
Tel: 01433-650 436
www.george-hotel.net
Former 16th-century
coaching inn; lovely
courtyard and a fine
restaurant. **££**
Millstone Country Inn
Sheffield Road, S32 1DA
Tel: 01433-650 258
www.millstoneinn.co.uk
Above the village with fine
views down the Hope Valley
to Kinder Scout. **£**

Matlock

Riber Hall Hotel
DE4 5JU
Tel: 01629-582 795
www.riber-hall.co.uk
14-room Tudor mansion
high above town with
wonderful views. **££**

Matlock Bath

Temple Hotel
Temple Walk, DE4 3PG
Tel: 01629-583 911
www.templehotel.co.uk
On a hilltop with splendid
views, this 14-room hotel, in
a gorgeous Georgian
building, is central and has
a bar serving real ale by an
open fire. **£**

Rowsley

**East Lodge Country House
Hotel**
Matlock, DE4 2EF
Tel: 01629-734 474
www.eastlodge.com
Pretty, tastefully furnished
country house in 10 acres
(4 hectares) of grounds, just
off the A6. The restaurant
has a fine reputation.
££–£££
Peacock Hotel
DE4 2EB
Tel: 01629-733 518
www.thepeacockatrowsley.com
Small hotel, recently
acquired by the owner of
Haddon Hall. Stylish,
interior-designed rooms
and a restaurant headed by

Daniel Smith, who has
worked with well-known
chef Tom Aitkins. Famous
in the world of angling for
the quality of fly fishing in
the nearby River Wye.
££

BELOW: The Peacock Hotel.

THE NORTHWEST

Liverpool

Britannia Adelphi Hotel
Ranelagh Place, L3 5UL
Tel: 0871-222 0029
www.britanniahotels.com
The grand classical stone facade provides a major landmark, next to Lime Street station. With 402 rooms, plus health club facilities. **££**

Crowne Plaza Liverpool
St Nicholas Place, L3 1QW
Tel: 0151-243 8000
www.cpliverpool.com
Good location, next to the Royal Liver Building and overlooking the Mersey. Built in 1998, it has a gym and indoor swimming pool. 159 rooms. **£££**

Hope Street Hotel
40 Hope Street, L1 9DA
Tel: 0151-709 3000
www.hopestreethotel.co.uk
Boutique hotel with large, light rooms, wood floors, king-sized beds, friendly staff and the excellent

London Carriage Works restaurant. Central but quiet. **££–£££**

Manchester

Malmaison Manchester
1–3 Piccadilly, M1 1LS
Tel: 0161-278 1000
www.malmaison-manchester.com
Located in a former warehouse, its theatrical red-and-black decor tries to echo the Moulin Rouge. Although it has 167 rooms, it aims for a boutique feel. Bar and brasserie. **£££**

THE LAKE DISTRICT

Ambleside

Rothay Manor
Rothay Bridge, LA22 0EH
Tel: 01539-433 605
www.rothaymanor.co.uk
Quintessential English country house hotel with gardens. Warm and friendly. **££**

Wateredge Inn
Borrans Road, Waterhead, LA22 0EP
Tel: 01539-432 332
Fax: 01539-431 878
www.wateredgeinn.co.uk
Family-run hotel with views over Lake Windermere from most rooms. Lakeshore garden. Restaurant. **£**

Cartmel, nr Grange-over-Sands

Aynsome Manor Hotel
Aynsome Lane, LA11 6HH
Tel: 01539-536 653
www.aynsomemanorhotel.co.uk
16th-century main house and cottage in a picturesque lakeland village, off the tourist track. Rates include dinner. **£**

Easedale

Lancrigg Vegetarian Country House Hotel
Grasmere, Cumbria, LA22 9QN
Tel: 01539-435 317
www.lancrigg.co.uk
Beautiful country house with a separate cottage. Organic, vegetarian food. **£**

Kendal District

Heaves Hotel
Heaves, LA8 8EF
Tel: 01539-560 396
www.heaveshotel.com
Well-preserved Georgian mansion with large bedrooms, a library and fine views. **£**

Keswick District

The Anchorage
14 Ambleside Road, CA12 4DL
Tel: 01768-772 813
www.anchoragekeswick.co.uk
Near lake and town centre. Good views. 7 rooms. Private parking. **£**

Armathwaite Hall Country House
Bassenthwaite Lake, CA12 4RE
Tel: 01768-776 551
www.armathwaite-hall.com
Gym, pool, clay shooting, jogging tracks, quad biking, archery. New spa. Set in 400 acres of ground. **££**

The Borrowdale Gates
Grange-in-Borrowdale, CA12 5UQ
Tel: 01768-777 204
www.borrowdale-gates.com
Large Victorian lakeland house with sweeping views and good food. **££**

The Cottage in the Wood
Whinlatter Forest, Braithwaite, CA12 5TW
Tel: 01768-778 409
www.thecottageinthewood.co.uk
Former coaching house, with contemporary rooms. **£–££**

The Lodore Falls Hotel
Lodore Falls, Borrowdale, CA12 5UX
Tel: 01768-777 285
www.lakedistricthotels.net
Luxury hotel in 40 acres (16 hectares) with excellent facilities. Some rooms overlook Derwent Water. **£–££**

The Mill Inn
Mungrisdale, Penrith, CA11 0XR
Tel: 01768-779 632
www.the-millinn.co.uk
Sixteenth century coaching inn, with six rooms. Good food. **£**

The Pheasant
Bassenthwaite Lake, nr Cockermouth, CA13 9YE
Tel: 01768-776 234
www.the-pheasant.co.uk
This heavily beamed former coaching inn lies in a beautifully peaceful setting. Great bar. **££**

Ullswater District

Netherdene Country House B&B
Troutbeck, CA11 0SJ
Tel: 01768-483 475
www.netherdene.co.uk
Small, comfortable country house set in landscaped gardens. **£**

Sharrow Bay
Sharrow Bay, Lake Ullswater, CA10 2LZ
Tel: 01768-486 301
www.sharrowbay.co.uk
This Italianate luxury hotel is set in formal gardens overlooking Ullswater. The food is exquisite. **££–£££**

Windermere

Miller Howe Hotel
Rayrigg Road LA23 1EY
Tel: 01539-442 536
www.millerhowe.com
Prestigious luxury hotel with stunning views across Lake Windermere towards the Langdale Pikes and beyond. Excellent restaurant. Rates include dinner and breakfast. **£££**

The Samling
Ambleside Road, LA23 1LRTel: 01539-431 922
www.thesamlinghotel.co.uk
Prestigious luxury hotel set in its own 67-acre estate. Woodlands, fields and landscaped gardens. Award-winning restaurant. **£££**

PRICE CATEGORIES

Price categories are for a double room including breakfast and VAT (value added tax) at high season:
£ = under £100
££ = £100–170
£££ = £170–270
££££ = over £270

TRANSPORT

ACCOMMODATION

EATING OUT

ACTIVITIES

A – Z

YORK AND YORKSHIRE

Bolton Abbey

Devonshire Arms Country House Hotel
Skipton, BD23 6AJ
Tel: 01756-718 111
www.thedevonshirearms.co.uk
Open fires, and lounges furnished with antiques from Chatsworth, home of the Duke and Duchess of Devonshire. Michelin starred restaurant. **££**

Harrogate

The Boar's Head
Ripley Castle Estate, nr Harrogate, HG3 3AY
Tel: 01423-771 888
www.boarsheadripley.co.uk
Ten minutes from Ripley. Antiques and comfy chairs. Good, plentiful, inexpensive food; 25 rooms. **££**

The Ruskin Hotel
1 Swan Road, HG1 2SS
Tel: 01423-502 045
www.ruskinhotel.co.uk
Small hotel in centre. Good service and food ; beautiful gardens. **££**

Helmsley

Black Swan Hotel
Market Place, YO62 5BJ

Tel: 01439-770 466
www.blackswan-helmsley.co.uk
Comfortable hotel in the centre of town at the foot of the North York Moors. 45 rooms. Restaurant, tearoom and patisserie. **££**

Pickering

The White Swan Inn
Market Place, YO18 7AA
Tel: 01751-472 288
www.white-swan.co.uk
Former coaching inn, with traditional rooms in main hotel, and contemporary rooms in old stables. Good restaurant. **££**

Settle

The Austwick Traddock
Austwick, Settle, LA2 8BY
Tel: 01524-251 224
www.austwicktraddock.co.uk
Family run hotel in Yorkshire Dales National Park. Just 12 rooms, individually designed. Restaurant. **££**

Staithes

The Endeavour
1 High Street, TS13 5BH
Tel: 01947-840 825
www.endeavour-restaurant.co.uk

Just 4 rooms at this seaside restaurant with rooms. Fish is a speciality. **££**

Wensleydale

The Wheatsheaf
Carperby, nr Leyburn, DL8 4DF
Tel: 01969-663 216
www.wheatsheafinwensleydale.co.uk
Where the author James Herriot and his wife spent their honeymoon. 13 rooms, some with four posters. **£**

York

Dean Court
Duncombe Place, YO1 7EF
Tel: 01904-625 082
www.deancourt-york.co.uk
Comfortable 37-room traditional hotel close to the Minster. **££**

Elmbank
The Mount, YO24 1GE
Tel: 01904-610 653
www.elmbankhotel.com
A city hotel with a country-house atmosphere. **££**

The Groves
15 St Peter's Grove, YO30 6AQ
Tel: 01904-559 777
www.thegroveshotelyork.co.uk
Victorian townhouse within easy walking distance of the city centre. **£**

Ibis York Centre
77 The Mount, YO24 1BN
Tel: 01904-658 301
www.ibishotel.com
Modern, functional 91-bedroom hotel within five minutes' walk of the city walls. **£**

Middlethorpe Hall
Bishopthorpe Road, YO23 2GB
Tel: 01904-641 241
www.middlethorpe.com
Elegant country hotel, run with style in a 17th-century house; 29 rooms. **££–£££**

Minster Hotel
60 Bootham
Tel: 01904-621 267
www.yorkminsterhotel.co.uk
Skilful conversion of two Victorian houses, four minutes from the Minster; rooftop garden with superb views. **££**

NORTHUMBRIA

Durham

Farnley Tower Hotel
The Avenue, DH1 4DX
Tel: 0191-375 0011
www.farnley-tower.co.uk
Renovated Victorian house with guest-house feel situated in a quiet residential street within walking distance of the city centre. Cathedral and castle views. 13 rooms. **££**

Three Tuns Hotel
New Elvet, DH1 3AQ
Tel: 0191-386 4326
www.swallow-hotels.com
Pleasant place to stay in this lovely cathedral town. Traditional atmosphere. Guests have complimentary access to leisure club in hotel lying opposite. **££**

Hexham, Priestpopple

County Hotel
NE46 1PS
Tel: 01434-603 601
www.thecountyhexham.co.uk
Excellent hospitality in a market town. Handy for exploring the Pennines and Hadrian's Wall. Restaurant serves British food using local produce. 8 rooms. **£**

Slaley Hall
Slaley, nr Hexham NE47 0BX
Tel: 01434-673 350
www.devere-hotels.com
Edwardian mansion, set in 1,000 acres (400 hectares). Most rooms in adjacent modern buildings. Spa and golf facilities. **££**

Kielder Water

The Pheasant Inn
Stannersburn, Kielder Water, NE48 1DD
Tel: 01434-240 382
www.thepheasantinn.com
Traditional inn with eight cosy bedrooms, just one mile from Kielder Water. Game pies and local lamb served in the restaurant. **£**

Morpeth

Eshott Hall
NE65 9EN
Tel: 01670-787 777
www.eshott.com
Boutique-style hotel in gracious 17th-century country house, set in its own grounds. **££**

PRICE CATEGORIES

Price categories are for a double room including breakfast and VAT (value added tax) at high season:
£ = under £100
££ = £100–170
£££ = £170–270
££££ = over £270

E ATING OUT

RECOMMENDED RESTAURANTS, CAFES AND BARS

What to Eat

A generation of talented modern British chefs has injected new life into traditional recipes, combining them with French and international influences, to produce lighter, more delicately flavoured meals using the finest ingredients grown on British soil. These days in England it is not difficult to find Michelin starred restaurants, fashionable gastropubs and cool cafés wherever you travel. The sheer range of ethnic food available is extraordinary – especially in London, where it is possible to sample the world's cuisine in one city. England is one of the best places for vegetarian diners too, with many places offering increasingly imaginative choices on their menus.

Meat and fish Look out for fresh local produce, such as salt marsh lamb on Romney Marshes; fresh oysters in Whitstable (eaten only during months with an r in them); fish in coastal regions like Cornwall and beef in Hereford. Many pubs and restaurants make a point of featuring seasonal local produce on their menus, so look out for these.

Sunday lunch is a solid English tradition and is always worth sampling. Traditional weekly feasts are roast beef and Yorkshire pudding with horseradish sauce, and roast pork with stuffing and apple sauce and vegetables. Many pubs serve hearty, good-value roasts.

Pies are an English staple. Among the nation's favourite savouries are steak and kidney, and Melton Mowbray pork pies. Cornish pasties, a mix of meat, potato and vegetables in a pastry packet, are well worth sampling in Cornwall – they were the traditional food of the tin miners. Look out too for traditional sausages (bangers), usually served with mashed potatoes.

Fish and chips is the most characteristic of British dishes, and is best enjoyed on a sunny seafront. However curry is probably the nation's favourite dish today, with particularly good restaurants in London and the area around Birmingham. The following is a selection of Britain's finest restaurants. A much fuller list of the capital's top restaurants can be found in the *Insight Guide: London*.

R E S T A U R A N T   L I S T I N G S

LONDON

Top Notch

Alain Ducasse, The Dorchester
Park Lane
Tel: 020-7629 8866
www.alainducasse-dorchester.com
Two Michelin stars, rising three, at this elegant hotel restaurant. **£££**

L'Atelier de Joel Robuchon
13-15 West Stree, WC2
Tel: 020-7010 8600
www.joel-robuchon.com
French food with Spanish influences at this 2 Michelin-starred restaurant.

Diners sit at a counter, surrounding the kitchen. **£££**

Le Gavroche
43 Upper Brook Street, W1
Tel: 020-7499 1826
www.le-gavroche.co.uk
One of England's top restaurants for years where elegantly balanced French haute cuisine is given a lighter touch by chef Michel Roux. **£££**

Locanda Locatelli
Churchill Intercontinental,
8 Seymour St, W1
Tel: 020-7935 9088

www.locandalocatelli.com
Italian classics from Giorgio Locatelli. **£££**

Traditional

Cockney's Pie and Mash
314 Portobello Rd, W10
Tel: 020-8960 9409
One of the few Victorian pie and mash shops that's not yet fallen victim to London's gentrification epidemic. A no-frills plate of grub for less than a fiver. **£**

J Sheekey
28-32 St Martin Court, WC2

Tel: 020-7240 2565
www.the-ivy.co.uk
Long established fish restaurant, with a new oyster bar. A London favourite. **££-£££**

The Ivy
1 West Street, W1

PRICE CATEGORIES

Price categories are per person for three courses, with half a bottle of wine:
£ = under £30
££ = £30–55
£££ = £55–100
££££ = more than £100

ABOVE: the Oxo Tower restaurant has stunning river views.

Tel: 020-7836 4751
www.the-ivy.co.uk
One of London's most famous haunts; remains surprisingly unaffected. A favourite with theatre and media people. Advance booking essential. **£££**

The Wolseley
160 Piccadilly Wl
Tel: 020-7499 6996
www.thewolseley.com
One of the coolest places to dine in London: grand interiors and great for celebrity spotting, especially at breakfast. **££**

Simpsons-in-the-Strand
100 Strand, WC2
Tel: 020-7836 9112
www.simpsonsinthestrand.co.uk
The Grand Divan is an Edwardian dining room renowned for serving the best roast beef in London. Staunchly traditional. Informal dress not acceptable. **££**

Smiths of Smithfield
67–77 Charterhouse Street, EC1
Tel: 020-7251 7950
www.smithsofsmithfield.co.uk
A lively post-industrial complex in the buzzy Clerkenwell area, by Smithfield meat market. Brunch on a weekend is great fun. **££**

Tate Britain Restaurant
Tate Britain, Millbank, SW1
Tel: 020-7887 8825
Beautiful decor, including a mural by Rex Whistler. Good for lunch. **££–£££**

Contemporary

Kensington Place
201 Kensington Church Street, W8
Tel: 020-7727 3184
www.kensingtonplace-restaurant.co.uk
Good value set lunches and a loyal following at this stylish restaurant. **££–£££**

Hard Rock Café
150 Old Park Lane, W1
Tel: 020-7629 0382
A shrine to rock music. Great hamburgers, long queues, high decibel level. **££**

Joe Allen
13 Exeter Street, WC2
Tel: 020-7836 0651
www.joeallenrestaurant.com
One of London's best-loved American restaurants. **££**

Zinc Bar and Grill
21 Heddon Street, W1
Tel: 020-7255 8899
Classic steak and fish from Conran's chain. **££**

Continental

Alastair Little (French)
49 Frith Street, W1
Tel: 020-7734 5183
Inventive food with an Italian twist. High quality, seasonal ingredients. **££**

The River Café (Italian)
Thames Wharf, Rainville Road, W6
Tel: 020-7386 4200
www.rivercafe.co.uk
Delightful northern Italian food and riverside tables. Menu reflects the seasons. Book well ahead. **£££**

Mesón Don Felipe (Spanish)
53 The Cut, SE1
Tel: 020-7928 3237
Long-established eatery, with a loyal clientele who flock here for the feel-good ambience and tasty tapas. **££**

Mon Plaisir (French)
21 Monmouth Street, WC2
Tel: 020-7836 7243
www.monplaisir.co.uk

Cosy Parisian atmosphere and quality ingredients. Good pre-theatre menu. **££**

Orso (Italian)
27 Wellington Street, WC2
Tel: 020-7240 5269
www.orsorestaurant.co.uk
Basement Italian restaurant popular with theatre and media crowd. **££**

Rebato's (Spanish)
169 South Lambeth Road, SW8
Tel: 020-7735 6388
www.rebatos.com
Worth a detour. Authentic tapas. **££**

Modern European

Oxo Tower
Barge House Street, SE1
Tel: 020-7803 3888
Brasserie and restaurant run by Harvey Nichols. Stunning river view. **££££**

Quaglino's
16 Bury St, SW1
Tel: 020-7930 6767
www.quaglinos.co.uk
The buzz of 1930s London, Conran-style, with a wide menu. **£££**

St John
26 St John Street, EC1
Tel: 020-7251 0848
www.stjohnrestaurant.co.uk
Fergus Henderson transforms offal and odd-cuts into eminently edible dishes. **££**

THE THAMES VALLEY

Bray

The Fat Duck
1 High Street
Tel: 01628-580 333
www.fatduck.co.uk
Heston Blumenthal creates complex dishes such as snail porridge and nitro-scrambled egg-and-bacon ice cream. His quest for new taste sensations earned him three Michelin stars. **££££**

The Waterside Inn
Ferry Road
Tel: 01628-620 691
www.waterside-inn.co.uk
In an idyllic spot overlooking the Thames, this is one of England's most exceptional restaurants. Three Michelin stars. **£££–££££**

Epsom Downs

Le Raj
211 Fir Tree Road
Tel: 01737-371 371
www.lerajrestaurant.co.uk
Stylish innovative Bangladeshi cuisine with a good reputation. **£**

Goring-on-Thames

The Leatherne Bottel
On the B4009 north of Goring
Tel: 01491-872 667
www.leathernebottel.co.uk
An old riverside inn. Excellent food, imaginatively produced, fresh ingredients. Head chef, Julia Storey serves modern European dishes with Pacific Rim influences. **££**

Henley-on-Thames

La Bodega
38 Hart Street
Tel: 01491-578 611
www.labodega-tapas.co.uk
Spacious tapas bar and restaurant with comprehensive menu and good choice of Spanish wines. **££**

Shinfield

L'Ortolan
The Old Vicarage,
Church Lane
Tel: 01189-888 500
www.lortolan.com
Innovative Anglo-French cuisine. Stunning flavours and a feast for the eye as well as the tastebuds. **£–££**

Sonning Eye

The Mill at Sonning
Sonning Eye, Reading
Tel: 0118-969 8000
www.millatsonning.com
Theatre/restaurant in old mill. Combined price for lunch and matinee or dinner and evening show. Nice setting, average food. **££**

Windsor

Browns
The Promenade,
Barry Avenue
Tel: 01753-831 976
www.browns-restaurants.co.uk
Although part of a chain, this bar and brasserie is reliable. Many cocktails. **££**

OXFORD

Great Milton

Le Manoir aux Quat'Saisons
Church Road
Tel: 01844-278 881
www.manoir.com
Raymond Blanc's award-garlanded French restaurant sources 90 types of vegetable and over 70 varieties of herb from its own kitchen garden. Sated guests can stay overnight in deluxe rooms or suites. **££££**

Oxford

Browns
5–11 Woodstock Road
Tel: 01865-511 995
Breakfast, light lunches and three-course meals in a relaxed atmosphere (11am–11.30pm). Bookings only taken for parties of 8 plus, Mon–Thur, so expect queues. **££**
Gee's Brasserie
61a Banbury Road
Tel: 01865-553 540

www.gees-restaurant.co.uk
Well-established restaurant in the Raymond Blanc tradition in a beautiful, airy conservatory. **££**
Brasserie Blanc
71–2 Walton Street
Tel: 01865-510 999
www.brasserieblanc.com
Raymond Blanc's latest venture in Oxford. Light but traditional French dishes in an airy atmosphere – open all day, including for breakfast. **££**

Pizzeria Mama Mia
8 South Parade, Summertown
Tel: 01865-514 141
www.mammamiapizzeria.co.uk
Pleasant and long-established restaurant with excellent pizza. **£**

Thame

The Old Trout
29–30 Lower High Street
Tel: 01844-212 146
Brasserie-style restaurant, especially good for fish. **££**

THE COTSWOLDS

Barnsley

The Village Pub
Tel: 01285-740 421
www.thevillagepub.co.uk
An upmarket gastropub decorated in country-house style, and serving European cuisine using top-quality local organic ingredients, including vegetables grown in Barnsley House Garden across the road. **££**

Bibury

The Swan
Tel: 01285-740 695
www.cotswold-inns-hotels.co.uk
In a stunning location by the bridge over the River Coln, this charming stone hotel puts a stylish European twist on modern British dishes. **£**

Broadway

The Lygon Arms
High Street
Tel: 01386-852 255
www.barcelo-hotels.co.uk
Committed foodies will not begrudge the cost of a meal in the barrel-vaulted Great Hall of The Lygon Arms. Attention to every detail ensures that even straightforward sounding dishes are given gourmet appeal. **££**

Cheltenham

Le Champignon Sauvage
24–26 Suffolk Road
Tel: 01242-573 449
www.lechampignonsauvage.co.uk
Interesting menu including, yes, wild mushrooms, the food has a touch of class,

and chef David Everitt-Matthias has won awards for his desserts. Two Michelin stars. **£££**

Chipping Campden

Red Lion
High Street
Tel: 01386-840 760
www.theredlioninn.org
The emphasis at this popular old coaching inn is on fresh local produce. Daily specials may include chicken and mushroom crêpes or Gloucestershire Old Spot loin of pork. **£–££**

Frampton Mansell

The White Horse
Tel: 01285-760 960
First-rate gastro-pub in a rural setting between

Cirencester and Stroud. **£–££**

Northleach

Old Wool House
Market Place
Tel: 01451-860 366
Authentic French cuisine in the heart of the Cotswolds. Game is a speciality in season. Dinner only (lunch by special arrangement). **££–£££**

Tetbury

Calcot Manor
Tel: 01666-890 391
www.calcotmanor.co.uk
Choose between the romantic candle-lit restaurant, or the unpretentious, friendly Gumstool Inn. **££–£££**

SHAKESPEARE COUNTRY

Birmingham

Rajnagar International
256 Lyndon Road, Olton, Solihull
Tel: 0121-742 8140
www.rajnagar.com
Said to be the best Bangladeshi restaurant in the country with pleasant decor and service and authentic food, especially fish. **££**
V2 Chinatown Eating Place
73–75 Pershore Street
Tel: 0121-666 6683

Laid-back café serving authentic Cantonese food to a studenty crowd. Tasty one-pot meals and fresh roasts daily. East Asian TV and a small library of Manga comic books provide diversion between courses. **£**

Leamington Spa

Queans Restaurant
15 Dormer Place
Tel: 01926-315 522
www.queans-restaurant.co.uk

Simple but accomplished cooking from chef Laura Hamilton. Vegetarian friendly. Attentive service. **££**

Stratford-upon-Avon

Bensons
4 Bards Walk
Tel: 01789-261 116
Bensons is a café/restaurant which is ideal for lunch or an indulgent afternoon tea. **£**

The College Arms
Lower Quinton
Tel: 01789-720 342
Historic country pub, dating back to the 16th century. Good restaurant. **£**

PRICE CATEGORIES

Price categories are per person for three courses, with half a bottle of wine:
£ = under £30
££ = £30–55
£££ = £55–100
££££ = more than £100

CAMBRIDGE AND EAST ANGLIA

Aldeburgh

The Golden Galleon Fish and Chip Shop
137 High Street
Tel: 01728-454 685
If you can stand the queue you will be amply rewarded. Take your fish and chips down to the pebbly beach across the road, or sit upstairs in the restaurant. **£**

The Lighthouse
77 High Street
Tel: 01728-453 377
Fish features heavily on the menu, potted Norfolk shrimps and fish soup are popular dishes. Sara Fox and Peter Hill also run the cookery school nearby (www.aldeburghcookeryschool.com). **££**

Cambridge

Alimentum
152–154 Hills Road
Tel: 0223-413 000
www.restaurantalimentum.co.uk
Skilfully prepared yet unfussy Modern European

dishes. **££**

Midsummer House
Midsummer Common
Tel: 01223-369 299
www.midsummerhouse.co.uk
Walled Victorian house on the banks of the Cam. Elegant modern European cuisine in stylish surroundings. Closed Sunday and Monday. **£££**

Three Horseshoes
Madingley, nr Cambridge
Tel: 01954-210 221
www.threehorseshoesmadingley.co.uk
Stunningly presented Mediterranean-style food served in the airy conservatory-cum-dining-room; lovely puddings, all well priced. **££**

Hintlesham, nr Ipswich

Hintlesham Hall
Tel: 01473-652 334
www.hintleshamhall.co.uk
Country-house hotel serving British food in award-winning restaurant. **££–£££**

Lavenham

Angel Hotel
Market Place
Tel: 01787-247 388
Grilled sea bass fillet with creamed spinach and spiced pork cutlet with braised endive are just two of the mains at Lavenham's oldest inn. **££**

Morston, nr Blakeney

Morston Hall
Morston, Holt
Tel: 01263-741 041
www.morstonhall.com
Michelin-starred chef, Galton Blackiston, features local produce, such as Blakeney lobster and Morston mussels, on the menu. **££–£££**

Norwich

Adlard's
79 Upper St Giles
Tel: 01603-633 522

www.adlards.co.uk
Stylish, welcoming restaurant serving modern British food with a French twist. Their dedication to fresh seasonal produce is apparent in all dishes. **££**

Stanton

Leaping Hare Vineyard Restaurant
Wyken Vineyards
Tel: 01359-250 287
Elegant café-restaurant at one of Britain's most respected vineyards. Californian-style cooking. Set on the edge of a country estate. **£–££**

Swaffham

Strattons
Stratton House, 4 Ash Close
Tel: 01760-723 845
www.strattons-hotel.co.uk
Family-run hotel with a passion for local ingredients, excellent home-grown vegetables. **££**

CANTERBURY AND THE SOUTHEAST

Canterbury

The Goods Shed
Station Road West
Tel: 01227-459 153
www.thegoodsshed.net
A disused Victorian railway building now serves as a farmers' market and restaurant, with excellent fresh (often organic) food. **££**

Rye

Landgate Bistro
5–6 Landgate
Tel: 01797-222 829
www.landgatebistro.co.uk
Food here is a great blend of British and Mediterranean styles. The menu features local seafood, but that is just part of an extensive repertoire. **££**

Tunbridge Wells

Carluccio's Caffé
32 Mount Pleasant Road
Tel: 01892-614 968
www.carluccios.com
Carluccio brings his excellent Italian cooking and flair to Tunbridge Wells. The restaurant is light and airy and there's a deli attached. **£–££**

Whitstable

Whitstable Oyster Fishery Restaurant
Horsebridge
Tel: 01227-276 856
www.oysterfishery.co.uk
Good seafood and fish served in a busy, bistro by the pebbly beach. Can get very busy at lunchtime, booking advisable **££**

BRIGHTON AND THE DOWNS

Amberley, nr Arundel

Amberley Castle
On the B2139 between Storrington and Bury Hill
Tel: 01798-831 992
www.amberleycastle.co.uk
Evocatively restored 12th-century castle. Dine in splendour in the Queen's Room Restaurant . Classic

cuisine is cooked and served with some panache. **££**

Brighton

Gingerman
21a Norfolk Square
Tel: 01273-326 688
www.gingermanrestaurants.com
Modern European cooking with imaginative touches served in a pleasant dining

space. Set menus. **£–££**

Pintxo People
95 Western Road
Tel: 01273-732 323
www.pintxopeople.co.uk
Tapas cantina on the ground floor, restaurant and cocktail bar upstairs. **££**

Terre à Terre
71 East Street
Tel: 01273-729 051
www.terreaterre.co.uk

Popular restaurant offering a brilliantly innovative vegetarian menu. **£–££**

Midhurst

Loch Fyne
Rothermere, North Street
Tel: 01730-716 280
www.lochfyne.com
Seafood is served in a restored listed building. **££**

HAMPSHIRE, WILTSHIRE AND DORSET

Beaulieu

Montagu Arms Hotel
Palace Lane
Tel: 01590-612 324
www.montaguarmshotel.co.uk
Hotel and restaurant serving excellent English food. Ideal base for New Forest. **£££**

Brockenhurst

Simply Poussin
The Courtyard,
49–55 Brookley Road
Tel: 01590-623 063
www.simplypoussin.com

First-rate French cuisine using organic local ingredients. In picturesque New Forest village, near coast. **£–££**

Hordle, nr Lymington

The Mill at Gordleton
Silver Street
Tel: 01590-682 219
www.themillatgordleton.co.uk
Good-value home cooking and a good wine list make this ivy-clad mill-cum-hotel a popular venue. **££**

Portsmouth

Lemon Sole
123 High Street, Old Portsmouth
Tel: 02392-811 303
www.lemonsole.co.uk
You make your selection of fresh seafood from a display and tell the staff how you would like it cooked. **££**

Southampton

P.O.S.H.
1 Queensway
Tel: 08707-426 282

www.posh-restaurant.com
Indian restaurant decked out as an ocean liner, hence the Posh – "Port Out, Starboard Home" – reference. **£**

Winchester

Hotel du Vin & Bistro
14 Southgate Street
Tel: 01962-841 414
www.hotelduvin.com
This is a wine lover's heaven, complete with an attractive menu of top-notch modern British food. **££**

BATH

Bath

The Hole in the Wall
16 George Street
Tel: 01225-425 242
www.theholeinthewall.co.uk
Long-established restaurant, revived to great acclaim. Highly imaginative haute cuisine. **££**
Jamie's Italian
10 Milsom Place
Tel: 01225-510 051

www.jamieoliver.com
Rustic Italian food overseen by celebrity chef Jamie Oliver. **££**
The Moon and Sixpence
6A Broad Street
Tel: 01225-320 088
www.moonandsixpence.co.uk
Modern British food, plus foreign imports. Old favourites with an imaginative twist. Attractive setting. **££**

The Olive Tree
4–7 Queensbury Hotel, Russell Street
Tel: 01225-447 928
www.thequeensberry.co.uk
"Foodie" favourite. Modern British cooking with French, Italian and Spanish influences. **£££**
The Royal Crescent Hotel
16 Royal Crescent
Tel: 01225-823 333
www.royalcrescent.co.uk
Within the walled gardens of

the hotel. Fine food, elegant setting. **£££**

Midsomer Norton

The Moody Goose
The Old Priory Hotel, Church Square
Tel: 01761-416 784
www.moodygoose.co.uk
Exquisite modern English menu including locally-sourced poultry, meat and game. **£££**

THE WEST COUNTRY

Bristol

Bell's Diner
1–3 York Road, Montpelier
Tel: 0117-924 0357
www.bellsdiner.com
Contemporary takes on classic European dishes. A short way out of the centre, but worth the journey.
££–£££
Bordeaux Quay
V-Shed, Canons Way
Tel: 0117-943 1200
www.bordeaux-quay.co.uk
European cuisine, with stress on locally-sourced, organic ingredients. **££**
Culinaria
1 Chandos Road
Tel: 0117-973 7999
www.culinariabristol.co.uk
Trendy little bistro in Bristol suburbs, with an excellent reputation for its trend-

setting Anglo-Provençal cooking. Run by former proprietor of Markwicks.
£–££

Chagford

22 Mill Street
Tel: 01647-432 244
www.22millst.com
Sleek restaurant with rooms, in the Dartmoor National Park. Plenty of seasonal, local produce on the menu. **££**

Colerne

Lucknam Park
(near Bath)
Tel: 01225-742 777
www.lucknampark.co.uk
Sophisticated classic British cuisine by award winning chef Hywel Jones, with a

serious, expensive wine list in the spacious, chandelier-lit dining room of this Georgian manor. **£££**

Dartmouth

The New Angel
2 South Embankment
Tel: 01803-839 425
www.thenewangel.co.uk
John Burton Race's accomplished modern British and European cuisine, in a picturesque setting overlooking Dartmouth harbour and the Dart estuary. **£££**

Fowey

Q
28 Fore Street
Tel: 01726-833 302
www.theoldquayhouse.com

In the Old Quay House hotel, right on the waterfront. Imaginative dishes, superb views. Traditional bistro style. Booking advisable. **££**

Exeter

The Conservatory
18 North Street
Tel: 01392-273 858
Excellent British and Mediterranean menu which changes daily. Relaxed, intimate and romantic setting. **££**

PRICE CATEGORIES

Price categories are per person for three courses, with half a bottle of wine:
£ = under £30
££ = £30–55
£££ = £55–100
££££ = more than £100

TRANSPORT

ACCOMMODATION

EATING OUT

ACTIVITIES

A – Z

Ilfracombe

11 The Quay
Tel: 01271-868 090
www.11thequay.co.uk
Damien Hirst's restaurant
and art gallery, aiming to do
for Ilfracombe. The
imaginative menu is strong
on local seafood and West
Country cheeses, as well as
international dishes.
££–£££

Instow

**The Boathouse
Restaurant**
Marine Parade
Tel: 01271-861 292
www.instow.net/boathouse
Beachfront restaurant and
bar in quiet seaside town in
North Devon. Good seafood
and fish. **£**

Kingsbridge

The Sloop Inn
Bantham, nr Kingsbridge

Tel: 01548-560 489
www.thesloop.co.uk
A 16th-century Inn five
minutes' walk from sandy
Bantham beach and dunes.
Excellent for fish and other
seafood. **£**
Mousehole
2 Fore Street, Mousehole Harbour
Tel: 01736-731 164
www.2forestreet.co.uk
Lovely little French style
bistro with a regularly
changing menu that
features lots of local
produce. Secluded
courtyard garden. **£–££**

Newquay

Fifteen
Watergate Bay
Tel: 01637-861 000
www.fifteencornwall.co.uk
Jamie Oliver's Fifteen
concept restaurant in
Cornwall, helping
disadvantaged young
people train as chefs.
Cornish produce. **£££**

Padstow

The Seafood Restaurant
Riverside
Tel: 01841-532 700
www.rickstein.com
One of the best seafood
restaurants in Britain using
only the freshest ingredients.
Simple dishes cooked with
minimum fuss. Booking
essential. On the pricey side.
Children 3 years and above.
£££

Plymouth

Tanners Restaurant
Prysten House, Finewell Street
Tel: 01752-252 001
www.tannersrestaurant.com
Fine dining in 15th-century
building in the heart of
Plymouth. TV chefs Chris
and James Tanner offer an
inspired range of dishes.
Traditional local produce
predominates, but prepared
with artistic flair. Booking
advisable. **££**

ABOVE: The Seafood
Restaurant in Padstow.

St Ives

Alba
Wharf Road
Tel: 01736-797 222
www.thealba-restaurant.com
Minimalist decor and
harbour views in this
refurbished former lifeboat
building. Set menus (less
expensive at lunch) feature
lots of fish options. **£–££**

HEREFORD AND THE WELSH BORDERS

Chester

**Simon Radley at The
Chester Grosvenor**
Chester Grosvenor Hotel,
Eastgate Street
Tel: 01244-324 024
www.chestergrosvenor.com
This is a thoroughbred
Michelin-starred restaurant
in a grand hotel in central
Chester. Traditional British
food excellently presented
and the bread board is one
of the best around.
Extensive but expensive
wine list. Children over 12.
££–£££

Hay-on-Wye

The Granary
Broad Street (by the Clocktower)
Tel: 01497-820 790
Favourite for light lunches,
teas and early suppers, with
plenty of options for
vegetarians. Low beams, old
pine furniture, a fire in
winter. By the clock tower.
££

Hereford

The Stewing Pot
17 Church Street
Tel: 01432-265 233

www.stewingpot.co.uk
Good modern restaurant not
far from the cathedral. Daily
specials board and great
attention given to local
produce, including English
wine. **££**

Kington

The Stagg Inn
Titley, 3 miles (5km) east of
Kington (B4335), Herefordshire
Tel: 01544-230 221
www.thestagginn.co.uk
Critically acclaimed roadside
inn in north Herefordshire.
Emphasis is on local and

home-grown produce. Great-
value Sunday lunches.
Essential to book. **££–£££**

Ludlow

**The Clive Bar and
Restaurant**
Bromfield
Tel: 01584-856 565
www.theclive.co.uk
Wenlock Edge ham,
Gressingham duck and local
cheeses are just some of
the treats in this restaurant
just outside Ludlow, that
combines elegance with
informality. **££**

DERBY TO THE EAST COAST

Derby

Blenheim House Hotel
Main Street, Etwall
Tel: 01283-732 254
www.blenheimhouseetwall.co.uk
Former farmhouse, that is
now an hotel and
restaurant. Come for bar

meals (there's an open fire
in winter) or Italian inspired
food in the restaurant. **££**
Donington Manor Bistro
High Street, Castle Donington
Tel: 01332-810 253
Elegant surroundings at this
hotel restaurant that serves
modern British food. **££**

Leicester

Café Bruxelles
90–92 High Street
Tel: 0116-224 3013
A trendy bar popular with
most age groups. No food
on Sunday. A range of more
than 30 Belgian beers. **£**

Lincoln

Fourteen Restaurant
14 Bailgate
Tel: 01522-576 556
www.fourteenrestaurant.co.uk
Youthful, modern British
cooking and plenty of
choices for vegetarians. **££**

PEAK DISTRICT

Ashford in the Water

Riverside Country House Hotel
Fennel Street, nr Bakewell
Tel: 0845-012 1760
www.riversidehousehotel.co.uk
In a beautiful position overlooking the River Wye, the conservatory restaurant of this Georgian house offers high-class English cuisine, especially game and fish. **££**

Baslow

Fischer's at Baslow Hall
Calver Road
Tel: 01246-583 259
www.fischers-baslowhall.co.uk
Outstanding Michelin-starred restaurant serving

traditional British food. Local produce might include Derbyshire spring lamb and Chatsworth venison. **£££**

Buxton

Columbine
7 Hall Bank
Tel: 01298-78752
www.buxtononline.net/columbine
Small friendly family-run restaurant. The fish soup is excellent and there's always an English cheeseboard. **££**

Dovedale, nr Ashbourne

Izaak Walton Hotel
Tel: 01335-350 555
The Haddon Restaurant in this 17th-century

farmhouse, set against the backdrop of the Derbyshire Peaks, specialises in Anglo-French dishes. **££**

Hassop

Hassop Hall Hotel
Near Bakewell
Tel: 01629-640 488
www.hassophallhotel.co.uk
One of the finest hotel-restaurants in the Peaks, set in the Peak District National Park. Booking essential. **££**

Hathersage

The George Hotel
Main Road
Tel: 01433-650 436
www.george-hotel.net
The menu includes dishes

such as pan-roasted loin of venison and there's a wide selection of cheeses. **££**
Chequers Inn
Froggatt Edge
Tel: 01433-630 231
www.chequers-froggatt.com
Locally sourced meat and produce served in a wood-floored dining room that is rustic without being fussy. **££**

Sheffield

Greenhead House
84 Burncross Road, Sheffield, Chapeltown
Tel: 0114-246 9004
www.greenheadhouse.com
Offers welcoming friendly service and excellent food. Vegetables and herbs come from their own garden. **££**

THE NORTHWEST

Blackpool

Oliver's Restaurant
Lancaster House Hotel,
272 Central Drive
Tel: 01253-341 928
www.oliversbistro.com
No, not Jamie Oliver, but a chef who knows what to do with good fresh ingredients. Morecambe Bay shrimps. **££**

Liverpool

60 Hope Street
60 Hope Street
Tel: 0151-707 6060
www.60hopestreet.com

Regional ingredients, tasteful preparation and smooth service in an airy venue. Typical dishes: roast crown of wood pigeon with herb risotto or sea bass with clam chowder. **££**
The Monro
92 Duke Street
Tel: 0151-707 9933
www.themonro.com
This gastropub has won plaudits for its locally sourced food, which may include Goosenargh duck breasts or leek and asparagus crêpes. Serves a classic Sunday lunch. **££**

Longridge, nr Preston

The Longridge Restaurant
104 Higher Road
Tel: 01772-784 969
www.heathcotes.co.uk
Paul Heathcote puts his own stamp on modern British cuisine while flying the flag for Lancashire with black pudding and excellent potato dishes. **££–£££**

Manchester

Chaophraya Thai Restaurant

15–17 Chapel Walks
Tel: 0161-832 8342
www.chaophraya.co.uk
A big, sometimes noisy restaurant serving very good Thai food. Reasonable prices, friendly service. **£–££**
Grado
New York Street, Piccadilly
Tel: 0161-238 9790
www.heathcotes.co.uk
Contemporary new wave Spanish serving paellas, tapas. grilled fish and clay-baked flatbreads. Good range of Spanish wine. **£–££**

THE LAKE DISTRICT

Ambleside

The Glass House Restaurant
Rydal Road
Tel: 01539-432 137
www.theglasshouserestaurant.co.uk
A 16th-century mill; Mediterranean and modern British food. **£–££**
The Drunken Duck
Barngates
Tel: 01539-36347
www.drunkenduckinn.co.uk

Award-winning gastro pub serving its own ales. **££**

Bassenthwaite

The Pheasant
Bassenthwaite Lake, Nr Cockermouth
Tel: 01768-776 234
www.the-pheasant.co.uk
Attractive old coaching inn offering good, locally sourced food. Traditional afternoon teas served. **£–££**

Carlisle

Garden Restaurant
Tullie House Museum and Art Gallery, Castle Street
Tel: 01228-618 718
Daily specials, a salad bar, home-baked treats. **£**

Cartmel, nr Grange-Over-Sands

L'Enclume
Cavendish Street

Tel: 01539-536 362
www.lenclume.co.uk
Modern French cuisine in a stylishly converted blacksmith's workshop. **£££**

PRICE CATEGORIES

Price categories are per person for three courses, with half a bottle of wine:
£ = under £30
££ = £30–55
£££ = £55–100
££££ = more than £100

Coniston

Jumping Jenny
Brantwood
Tel: 01539-41715
www.jumpingjenny.com
Coffees, teas and lunches at Brantwood, Ruskin's old home, east of Coniston Water. Magnificent views. **£**

Eskdale

The Woolpack Inn
Holmrook
Tel: 019467-23230

www.woolpack.co.uk
This well-known hostelry in the western Lake District serves reliably good food and ales. **£**

Grasmere

The Jumble Room
Langdale Road
Tel: 015394-35188
www.thejumbleroom.co.uk
Attractive, comfortable restaurant offering a selection of dishes from around the world. **£**

Hawkshead

Queen's Head Hotel
Main Street
Tel: 01539-36271
www.queensheadhotel.co.uk
Traditional English cuisine served in a mellow, wood-panelled room. **££**

Keswick

Highfield Hotel Restaurant
The Heads
Tel: 01687-72508
www.highfieldkeswick.co.uk

Imaginative modern European cuisine and wonderful Lakeland views. The menu changes daily. Two AA rosettes. **££**

Windermere

Gilpin Lodge
Crook Road
Tel: 015394-88818
www.gilpinlodge.co.uk
This fine Lakeland country house hotel serves fresh and unfussy dishes using local produce. **££–£££**

YORK AND YORKSHIRE

Bolton Abbey

Devonshire Arms Country House Hotel
Tel: 01756-718 111
www.thedevonshirearms.co.uk
The Yorkshire Restaurant in this former coaching inn serves classic dishes, with a modern touch. Michelin star. **£££**

Helmsley

Crown Hotel
Market Place
Tel: 01439-770 297
www.tchh.co.uk
Comfortable posting house. Wide choice of country-style dishes served in the bar or lounge area. **£**

Harrogate

Drum & Monkey
Montpellier Gardens
Tel: 01423-502 650
www.drumandmonkey.co.uk
Long-standing local favourite

fish restaurant on two floors, with an informal atmosphere. Dover sole, lobster, oysters, halibut and sea bass are delivered daily. **££**

Ilkley

Box Tree
35-37 Church Street
Tel: 01943-608 484
www.theboxtree.co.uk
Young Marco Pierre White cut his culinary teeth in this intimate 18th-century stone farmhouse that serves "modern French classic" dishes. **££**

Leeds

Brasserie Forty 4
44 The Calls
Tel: 0113-234 3232
www.brasserie44.com
Bright, modern brasserie that's always lively, good value for money. Very popular. **££**

Malham

The Buck Inn
Tel: 01729-830 317
www.buckinnmalham.co.uk
Overlooking the village green. Home-cooked traditional fare in the bar, including speciality Malhan and Masham pie; à la carte in the candlelit restaurant. **£–££**

Northallerton

McCoys At The Tontine
Cleveland Tontine, Staddlebridge
Tel: 01609-882 671
www.mccoystontine.co.uk
Lavish, slightly faded period surroundings, in the bistro, conservatory and restaurant. A relaxed atmosphere and some very interesting food. **££–£££**

Whitby

The Magpie Café
14 Pier Road
Tel: 01947-602 058

www.magpiecafe.co.uk
Legendary harbourside restaurant. Best known for superb Whitby fish and chips, but equally satisfies most other tastes. **£–££**

York

Harville's Restaurant
47 Fossgate
Tel: 01904-654 155
www.harvilles.co.uk
This fine 1930s-style restaurant majors in chargrilled Aberdeen Angus and English Longhorn beef steaks. Also a fish restaurant and an art deco cocktail lounge. **££**

PRICE CATEGORIES

Price categories are per person for three courses, with half a bottle of wine:
£ = under £30
££ = £30–55
£££ = £55–100
££££ = more than £100

NORTHUMBRIA

Chester le Street

Black Knight Restaurant
Lumley Castle Hotel
Tel: 0191-389 1111
www.lumleycastle.com
This restaurant, 7 miles (11km) from Durham, is in the 14th-century ancestral home of the Earl of Scarborough. **££–£££**

Durham

Bistro 21
Aykley Heads House, Aykley Heads
Tel: 0191-384 4354
www.bistrotwentyone.co.uk
Robust classic French country cooking in a 16th-century farmhouse on the edge of the city. Friendly and informal. **£**

Newcastle-Upon-Tyne

Blackfriars Restaurant
Friars Street
Tel: 0191-261 2945
www.blackfriarsrestaurant.co.uk
Reputedly the oldest purpose-built restaurant in Britain, with a medieval banqueting hall. **££**

Seaham

Seaham Hall Hotel
Lord Byron's Walk
Tel: 01915-161 4000
www.seaham-hall.co.uk
Award-winning restaurant in a spa hotel 20 minutes from Newcastle. In 1815 Lord Byron was married in the Byron Room. **£££**

A CTIVITIES

CALENDAR OF EVENTS, THE ARTS, NIGHTLIFE, SPORTS AND SHOPPING

CALENDAR OF EVENTS

January

London International Boat Show ExCeL Exhibition Centre.

February

Chinese New Year In London and Manchester Chinatowns.
Crufts Dog Show NEC, Birmingham. Pedigree dogs compete.
Shrove Tuesday Pancake Day.
London Fashion Week.

March

Ideal Home Exhibition Earl's Court, London. Exhibition of new ideas and products for the home.

April

April Fools' Day (1st) People play practical jokes (only until noon).
London Book Fair Earl's Court, London.
London Marathon One of the world's biggest runs, starting at Greenwich Park and ending at Westminster.
Harrogate Spring Flower Show.
Queen's Birthday (21st) Gun salute in Hyde Park and Tower of London.

May

Bath International Music Festival.
Brighton Arts Festival.
Chelsea Flower Show in grounds of Royal Hospital, London.
FA Cup Final Wembley. The final of the nation's main football competition.

Hay-on-Wye Festival of Literature and the Arts. International event.

June

Aldeburgh Festival of Arts & Music.
Beating Retreat Horse Guards Parade, London. Military bands.
Biggin Hill International Air Fair Biggin Hill, Kent.
Bournemouth Music Competitions Festival.
Dickens Festival Rochester, Kent.
Glastonbury Pilgrimage Abbey Ruins, Glastonbury, Somerset.
Royal Academy of Arts Summer Exhibition, London. Large exhibition of work (till Aug). All works for sale.
Royal Ascot Ascot Racecourse. Elegant and dressy race meeting attended by royalty.
Trooping the Colour Horse Guards Parade, London. The Queen's official birthday celebrations.

July

Birmingham International Jazz Festival.
Cambridge Folk Festival.
Cheltenham Music Festival.
Hampton Court Palace Flower Show.
Farnborough International Airshow Hampshire, biannual event.
British Motor Show ExCel, London.
The Proms Royal Albert Hall, London. Series of classical concerts.

August

Notting Hill Carnival (bank holiday weekend), London. Colourful West Indian street carnival with floats, steel bands and reggae music.

September

London Open House Weekend. Visit buildings not normally accessible.
Salisbury Food & Drink Festival.

October

Birmingham Sidewalk Film Festival.
Cheltenham Literature Festival.
London Film Festival BFI Southbank and some West End venues.
Norwich Jazz Festival.

November

Guy Fawkes Day (5th) Firework displays and bonfires.
London to Brighton Veteran Car Run (first Sunday).
Lord Mayor's Show London. Grand procession from the Guildhall in the City to the Royal Courts of Justice, celebrating the annual election of the Lord Mayor.
Military Tattoo NEC, Birmingham.
State Opening of Parliament Westminster, London.

Rock Music Festivals

Cambridge Rock Festival, 4 days in August, tel: 0845-299 0845, www.cambridgerockfestival.co.uk
Download Festival, Donington Park, Derby, June, www. downloadfestival.co.uk
Glastonbury Festival, June, www. glastonburyfestivals.co.uk
Isle of Wight Rock festival, June, www.isleofwightfestival.com
Reading Festival, August, tel: (info only) 020-7009 3001, www. readingfestival.com

Sightseeing Tours

● All British cities of historical interest have special double-decker buses that tour the sites. Some are open-topped and many have a commentary in several languages.

● The Original Tour is the first and biggest London sightseeing operator. Hop-on and hop-off at over 90 different stops. With commentary in wide choice of languages and a Kids' Club for 5–15 year olds. Buy tickets on bus or in advance. Operates year-round. Tel: 020-8877 1722; www. theoriginaltour.com.

● Big Bus Company operates two routes of hop-on hop-off services. Tel: 020-7233 9533; www.bigbustours. com.

● Duck Tours use World War II amphibious vehicles which drive past famous London landmarks before taking to the water. Departure from Chicheley Street, Waterloo. Tel: 020-7928 3132; www. londonducktours.co.uk.

● Golden Tours offer a wide choice of day trips for London and sites and cities all over Britain. Tel: 020-7233 7030, or within USA tel: 1-800-548 7083; www.goldentours.co.uk.

December

London International Horse Show, Olympia. Major international show-jumping championships.

New Year's Eve, by the Thames London. Thousands of people congregate to watch the firework display, hold hands and sing *Auld Lang Syne* at midnight.

THE ARTS

Theatre

Britain's rich dramatic tradition is reflected in the quality of its theatre.

Most towns and cities have at least one theatre that hosts productions from their own company or from touring companies that may include the Royal Shakespeare Company (RSC) and the National Theatre (NT). For comprehensive information, go to www.theatresonline.com.

It is advisable to book tickets in advance, from the box office or through commercial ticket agents in major cities.

London

Around half of London's theatres – including fringe and suburban – are in the West End, centred around Shaftesbury Avenue and Covent Garden.

Tickets West End shows are popular so good tickets can be hard to obtain. If you cannot book a seat through the theatre box office, try Ticketmaster, 173 Arlington Road, NW1, tel: 0870-534 4444 (UK); +44 161-385 3211 (overseas); www. ticketmaster.co.uk.

Avoid ticket touts unless you're prepared to pay several times a

ticket's face value for a sold-out show. The "tkts" booth at Leicester Square has unsold tickets available at bargain prices on the day of the performance. Located in the Clock Tower building and open Mon–Sat 10am–7pm, Sun noon–3pm. Payment is by cash or card and there may be long queues (www.tkts.co.uk). Some theatres, such as the National, keep back some tickets to sell at the box office from 9.30am on the day.

Fringe There is usually no problem buying a ticket on the door. Consult listings in London's weekly *Time Out* magazine, newspapers or check www. theatreguidelondon.co.uk.

Open-air plays On summer afternoons and evenings Shakespeare's plays are performed (weather permitting) at the open-air theatre in Regent's Park. Check www.openairtheatre.org for listings.

Barbican Arts Centre, Silk Street, London EC2Y 8DS, tel: 020-7638 8891. Purpose-built arts complex containing the Barbican Theatre, Concert Hall and The Pit which are well thought-out and comfortable with good acoustics, although somewhat sterile. Not easy to find your way around. Tube: Barbican.

National Theatre, South Bank, SE1, tel: 020-7452 3000; fax: 020-7452 3030. A wide range of modern and classical plays staged in three theatres in this concrete structure beside the Thames: the Olivier, the Lyttelton and the Cottesloe. Tube: Waterloo. www.nationaltheatre.org.uk

Royal Court Theatre, Sloane Square, SW1, tel: 020-7565 5000. Home to the English Stage Company, which produces plays by contemporary playwrights. Tube: Sloane Square (Circle line).

Shakespeare's Globe, 21 New Globe Walk, Bankside SE1, is a

reconstruction of Shakespeare's original open-to-the-elements Elizabethan theatre. It hosts summer seasons of plays, recreating the atmosphere of the 16th-century performances. There is a choice of (recommended) bench seating or standing, actors are encouraged to interact with the audience; amplification and artificial lighting are not used. An engaging and authentic experience. The Globe Exhibition uses touch screens and includes a guided tour of the theatre (tel: 020-7902 1500; www.shakespeares-globe.org; Apr–Oct Mon–Sat 9am–12.30pm and 1–5pm, Sun 9–11.30am and noon–5pm, tours every 15–30 mins.

Stratford Upon Avon

The Royal Shakespeare Theatre, Stratford-upon-Avon. Currently being rebuilt and scheduled to open in 2010. The Royal Shakespeare Company (RSC) is meanwhile performing in the Courtyard Theatre, box office tel: 0844-800 1110. The **Swan Theatre** (an Elizabethan-style playhouse) where works by Shakespeare's contemporaries are performed is closed while the RST is being redeveloped. **The Other Place**, where modern productions are performed, will re-open as the RSC's studio theatre. The RSC season at Stratford runs from April to October. www.rsc.org.uk

Manchester

Manchester has a number of theatres, among them **The Lowry Centre**, Pier 8, Salford Quays, Manchester, tel: 0870-787 5780, www.thelowry.com, where two theatres stage high-quality theatre and musical performances.

Newcastle-Upon-Tyne

Theatre Royal, 100 Grey Street, tel: 08448-112 121; www.theatreroyal.co.uk. Beautiful Edwardian Theatre. Drama, opera and dance. Regional home of the RSC. **Northern Stage**, Barras Bridge, tel: 0191-230 5151; www. northernstage.co.uk. Has three stages after a £9 million refurbishment. Home of Newcastle's Northern Stage company; co-host RSC season.

Liverpool

Liverpool's **Playhouse**, Williamson Square, tel: 0151-709 4776 and the related **Everyman**, Hope Street, tel: 0151-709 4776 both stage excellent and sometimes innovative works. The **Empire**, Lime Street, tel: 0844-847 2525 concentrates on light entertainment and musicals.

Classical Music

Many British cities have their own professional orchestras and promote seasons of concerts. These include the Royal Liverpool Philharmonic, The Hallé in Manchester and the City of Birmingham Symphony. In London there are the London Philharmonic and, at the Barbican Arts Centre, the London Symphony Orchestra.

In the summer in London the BBC sponsors the Proms at the Royal Albert Hall. The BBC also funds several of its own orchestras, including the BBC Symphony.

Chamber music has considerable support in Britain and there are professional string and chamber orchestras such as the English Chamber Orchestra and The Academy of Ancient Music.

London Venues

Barbican Hall, Silk Street, London EC2Y, tel: 020-7638 8891, is home to the London Symphony Orchestra and the BBC Symphony Orchestra.
Royal Festival Hall, Belvedere Road, London SE1, tel: 0871-663 2500, www.southbankcentre.co.uk, is the premier classical music venue. Free Friday lunchtime classical, jazz and folk performances in the foyer. Also in the South Bank complex are the Queen Elizabeth Hall (chamber concerts and solos) and the small Purcell Room.
Wigmore Hall, 36 Wigmore Street, London W1, tel: 020-7935 2141, www.wigmore-hall.org.uk, is an intimate hall renowned for its lunchtime and Sunday morning chamber recitals. There are evening peformances, too.
Royal Albert Hall, Kensington Gore, London SW7, tel: 020-7589 8212, www.royalalberthall.com, comes alive in summer for the BBC-sponsored Promenade Concerts.

Open-air concerts Summer evening concerts are performed at the Kenwood Lakeside Theatre, Kenwood House, Hampstead Lane, NW3 (tel: 0870-333 1181, www.picnic concerts.com).

Outside London

Major venues attracting world-class performers include:
Bridgewater Hall, Manchester, tel: 0161-907 9000.
Birmingham Symphony Hall, NEC, tel: 0121-780 3333.
City Hall, Northumberland Road, Newcastle, tel: 0191-261 2606.
The Sage, Gateshead Quays, tel: 0191-443 4666.
Philharmonic Hall, Hope Street, Liverpool, tel: 0151-210 2895.

Opera

The Royal Opera and the English National Opera perform regular seasons in London.
Royal Opera House, Bow Street, London WC2, tel: 020-7304 4000. Home to the Royal Ballet and the Royal Opera, this is a magnificent theatre with a worldwide reputation for lavish performances in original language. Dress is formal and tickets expensive unless you are prepared to stand or accept a very distant view.
London Coliseum, St Martin's Lane, London WC2N, tel: 0871-911 0200. This elegant Edwardian theatre is where the English National Opera (ENO) stages performances in English; ticket prices are lower than at the Opera House.
Opera North Regional opera companies include Opera North, which is based in Leeds at the Grand Theatre, 46 New Briggate, LS1 6NZ, tel: 0870-121 4901, and tours the north of England.

Glyndebourne

For classical music lovers Glyndebourne is a highlight. Off the beaten track in Sussex, it is not the most obvious site for a major international opera festival. But ever since an ex-Eton schoolmaster inherited a mansion there and built an opera house, it has attracted top artists from around the world and become a major event. Performances are in the evening (bring your own Champagne and picnic hampers) from May until August. Tel: 01273-815 000, www.glyndebourne.com.

Buxton The Opera House, Water Street, SK17 6XN, tel: 0845-127 2190, hosts a major opera, theatre and music festival (3 weeks in July).

Ballet and Dance

Major venues are the Royal Opera House and the London Coliseum, home to the Royal Ballet and English National Ballet respectively.
Sadler's Wells, Rosebery Avenue, EC1R 4TN, tel: 0844-412 4300 is a flexible state-of-the-art venue, with innovative programmes of contemporary and classical dance. Other performances at the Peacock Theatre, Kingsway, WC2 (same phone number for bookings).
Birmingham Royal Ballet, based at the Hippodrome, tel: 0121-245 3500, tours nationwide.
Northern Ballet School Based at the Dancehouse Theatre, 10 Oxford Road, Manchester, tel: 0161-237 9753. Tours whole UK.

NIGHTLIFE

Late Spots

If you're under 30 and believe the hype, London is one of the best places to party in the world. It has built a solid reputation as one of the great international clubbing centres. But not all nightlife is dance-till-dawn. The older generation can enjoy drinking bars, casinos and smart nightclubs.

Despite its reputation, and despite a relaxation of licensing laws in recent years, London is not an especially late city. Most restaurants, pubs and even bars have wound down by 1am, leaving just a few determined establishments to stagger on until the city awakes.

BELOW: last night of the Proms at the Royal Albert Hall.

TRANSPORT
ACCOMMODATION
EATING OUT
ACTIVITIES
A – Z

Jazz Clubs

Jazz Café, 5 Parkway, Camden NW1.
Tel: 0844-847 2514 (tickets)
Intimate jazz club in Camden Town
that attracts some top names.
Jazz@Pizza Express, 10 Dean Street,
W1. Tel: 0845-6027 017.
This Soho branch of the pizza chain
has a high standard of performers.
Ronnie Scott's, 47 Frith Street, W1.
Tel: 020-7439 0747.
Scott, who died in 1996, had eclectic
taste, and this is still reflected in this
legendary Soho venue, which has
hosted some of the biggest names in
jazz since 1959. Very relaxed.

Dance Clubs

Café de Paris, 3–4 Coventry Street,
SW1. Tel: 020-7734 7700.
Posh old dancehall attracts an older
sophisticated crowd. Trendy/smart.
Electric Ballroom, 184 Camden High
Street, NW1. Tel: 020-7485 9006.
This old dancehall has a huge main
dance floor where on Saturday nights
Shake attracts a mixed crowd playing
hits of the 1970s, '80s and '90s.
Upstairs it's R&B and hip-hop.
The Fridge, Town Hall Parade, Brixton
Hill, SW2. Tel: 020-7326 5100.
Spectacular one-nighters. Worth
seeking out. Tube: Brixton.
Heaven, The Arches, Villiers Street,
WC2. Tel: 020-7930 2020.
Submerged beneath the Charing
Cross development is one of the best
dance clubs in town. Gay nights are
Tuesday, Wednesday, Friday and
Saturday. Very casual dress code.
Mass, St Matthew's Peace Garden,
SW2. Tel: 020-7738 7875.
Atmospheric Brixton venue in the
bowels of a converted church. Wide
range of music, with great R&B in the
Friday Nite Mass.
Ministry of Sound, 103 Gaunt Street,
SE1. Tel: 0870-060 0010.
This renowned dance club is London's
top house-music venue.
Soho Lounge, 69–70 Dean Street,
W1. Tel: 020-7734 1231 (10am–
6pm). Tel: 020-7734 4895 (night line).
West End basement club with a
variety of one-nighters – a favourite
with Soho regulars – caters for all
musical tastes, from reggae to heavy
metal. Trendy.

Comedy/Cabaret

Comedy Store, 1a, Oxendon Street,
SW1. Tel: 0870-060 2340.
A night at this well-established venue
for stand-up comedians will remind
you that comedy need not always be

Walking Tours

There are designated, well-marked
walking paths all over Britain:
around the coasts, across the
Pennines, over the South Downs,
along Hadrian's wall, and many
other places. Local tourist offices
will supply information and sell
detailed walkers' maps, many
giving distances, estimated times
and levels of difficulty.

accompanied by canned laughter. On
a good night, the comedians in the
audience are as famous as those on
stage. Avoid sitting in the front row
unless you want to become part of
the show.
Jongleurs, Middle Yard (Camden
Lock), Chalk Farm Road, NW1. Also
at Battersea and Bow. Tel: 0870-787
0707.
Leading stand-up comedy club.
Camden attracts the best acts.
Madame Jo Jo's, 8 Brewer Street,
W1. Tel: 020-7734 3040.
Ultra-camp transvestite revue bar
popular for hen or stag nights.
Lacking in the sleaze and daring
associated with Soho's sometimes
unsavoury past, Madame Jo Jo's still
offers one of the best late-night
outings in London with captivating
cabaret shows from Kitsch Cabaret
with Teri Pace and her male leggy
lovelies in their amazing costumes.
Closes 3am.
Stringfellow's, 16 Upper St Martin's
Lane, WC2. Tel: 020-7240 5534.
This slightly tongue-in-cheek lap-
dancing joint is strong on tacky
glamour, so dress accordingly.

SPORT

Tickets

Tickets for major sporting events can
be purchased from agents such as
Ticketmaster, tel: 0870-534 4444;
www.ticketmaster.co.uk; and Keith Prowse,
tel: 0844-209 0382; www.keithprowse.
com.

Spectator Sports

Football (Soccer)

This is the country's most popular
spectator and participant team
sport. The professional season is
August–May.
   Most Premier League matches can
be watched only on satellite TV. The
climax of the English season is the FA

Cup, played at the new Wembley
Stadium.
   League matches usually start Sat
or Sun at 3pm, midweek 7pm. Results
are aired on Saturday at 4.45pm on
the main terrestrial channels (BBC
and ITV). Radio 5 Live (693 or 909 AM)
and talkSPORT (1053 or 1089 AM)
broadcast matches and discuss the
sport at length with experts and
listeners.
   For details of Premier League
fixtures, check www.premierleague.com for
club contact details; for other English
fixtures, www.football-league.co.uk.

Rugby

Rugby is said to have been invented
when one of the pupils of Rugby
public school picked up the ball and
ran in a game of football early in the
19th century. It is a national
institution today, with two types
(Union, played in Scotland, Wales
and predominantly the South of
England) and League (the north of
England game).
   Rugby Union, formerly for amateurs
only, is now professional. The season
runs from September to May, with
matches played at Twickenham,
Murrayfield and the Millennium
Stadium. One of the highlights of the
season is the Six Nations
Championship, a knock-out between
England, Ireland, Scotland, Wales,
France and Italy.
   Rugby League culminates in the
Super League final at Old Trafford in
September.
   For details of Rugby Union fixtures,
tel: 0871-222 2120; www.rfu.com. For
Rugby League, tel: 0871-226 1313;
www.rfl.uk.com.

Cricket

Quintessentially English, cricket can
be seen on village greens up and
down the country throughout the
summer. Usually a light-hearted
performance, it is played by very
amateurish amateurs, with a visit to
the pub a ritual at the close of play.
   England's professional teams
compete in a national championship,
with 4-day matches taking place all
summer. But one of the most
entertaining ways to be initiated into
the intricacies of the game is to go
along to a pacier, less serious one-day
match or Twenty20 game.
   On an international level, every
season England plays 5-day Test
Matches against one or two touring
teams from Australia, India, New
Zealand, Pakistan, Sri Lanka or the
West Indies. These take place at half
a dozen grounds in Britain including

Lords and the Oval in London, Edgbaston in the Midlands and Headingly in Leeds. Test match tickets are sought-after and sell out well in advance, but there's generally less competition for seats for one-day internationals.

The governing body of the world game is Marylebone Cricket Club (MCC), based at Lord's Cricket Ground, St John's Wood, NW8, tel: 020-7616 8500; www.lords.org. Cricket can also be seen at the Oval, Kennington, SE11, Surrey County Cricket Club, tel: 08712-461 100; www.surreycricket.com. For outside London, see www.play-cricket.com.

Equestrian Sports

Flat racing takes place between March and early November. The most important races are the Derby and Oaks at Epsom, the St Leger at Doncaster and the 1,000 and 2,000 Guineas at Newmarket. The Royal Ascot meeting is a major social event where racegoers dress in their finest.

Steeplechasing and hurdle racing take place from September to early June. The National Hunt Festival meeting at Cheltenham in March is the most important event; the highlight is the Gold Cup. The most famous steeplechase, watched avidly and gambled on by millions in Britain, is the Grand National held at Aintree in Liverpool.

Show jumping is the equestrian sport every young rider aspires to. Major events are the Royal International Horse Show and the British Jumping Derby at Hickstead, West Sussex, the Horse of the Year Show at the NEC, Birmingham, and the Olympia International Horse Show in London.

Polo matches take place at Windsor Great Park or Cowdray Park, Midhurst, West Sussex on summer weekends. The governing body is the Hurlingham Polo Association, tel: 01367-242 828; www.hpa-polo.co.uk).

Horse Trials are held in spring and autumn nationwide. The major 3-day events (cross-country, show jumping and dressage) are held at Badminton, Bramham, Burghley, Chatsworth and Gatcombe.

The main equestrian body in Britain is The British Horse Society, which governs the Pony Club and Riding Club. It also runs the British Equestrian Centre at Stoneleigh in Warwickshire, where it is based. For further information, contact The British Horse Society, Stoneleigh Deer Park, Kenilworth CV8 2XZ, tel: 0844-848 1666; www.bhs.org.uk.

Athletics

Athletics are governed by the Amateur Athletics Association (AAA), with the main national sports centre for athletics at Crystal Palace, south London, tel: 020-8778 0131; www.englandathletics.org.

Golf

The most important national golfing event is the Open Championship, which takes place every July. Other prestigious competitions include the Ryder Cup for professionals and the Walker Cup for amateurs. Both of these are played between Britain and USA every other year. Another prestigious tournament is the World Match Play Championship at Wentworth, Surrey, in September.

For information on dates and venues of tournaments contact the Professional Golfers' Association (PGA), Centenary House, The Belfry, Sutton Coldfield, West Midlands, B76 9PT, tel: 01675-470 333.

The Sporting Calendar

February
Rugby Six Nations Championship.

March
Racing Cheltenham Gold Cup, Cheltenham, Gloucestershire.
University Boat Race Oxford and Cambridge, on the Thames between Putney and Mortlake, London.

April
Horse Racing, Grand National Race Meeting, Aintree, Liverpool.
London Marathon, Greenwich Park, London.
Rugby Union County Championship Final, Twickenham. Six Nations Cup.
Snooker World Championship, Sheffield.

May
Football FA Cup Final, Wembley Stadium.
Golf PGA Championship, Wentworth Club, Surrey.
Horse Trials Badminton, Gloucestershire.
Horse Racing 1,000 and 2,000 Guineas Stakes, Newmarket, Suffolk.
Horse Show Royal Windsor, Home Park, Windsor.
Cricket Test Matches.

June
Cycling London to Brighton bike ride.
Horse Racing Royal Ascot, Ascot, Berkshire. The Derby, Epsom, Surrey. The Oaks, Epsom, Surrey.
Tennis British Tennis Championships, Queen's Club, London. Wimbledon Lawn Tennis Championships, All England Lawn Tennis and Croquet Club: the world's most famous tennis tournament, held in southwest London suburb.
Cricket Test Matches.

July
Show Jumping Royal International Horse Show, Hickstead.
Motor Racing British Grand Prix, Silverstone, Northamptonshire.
Rowing Henley Royal Regatta Week, Henley-on-Thames.
Golf Open Championship, venue varies.
Cricket Test Matches.
Polo Cartier International, Guards Polo Club, Surrey.

August
Horse Racing Glorious Goodwood.
Polo Cheltenham Cup.

Sailing Cowes Week Regatta, Isle of Wight.
Cricket Test Matches.
Rugby League Carnegie Challenge Cup Final.

September
Cycling The Tour of Britain 8-day road race.
British Superbike Championship Silverstone, Northamptonshire.
Golf: World Matchplay, Wentworth, Surrey. British Masters, the Belfry, W. Midlands.

October
Great North Run, Newcastle. The world's largest half-marathon.
Show Jumping Horse of the Year Show, NEC, Birmingham.

November
Lombard RAC Car Rally, Harrogate, North Yorkshire.
RAC London–Brighton Veteran Car Run is a 60-mile (100km) race for 500 cars built before 1905.

December
Olympia, The London International Horse Show, Olympia, London.

Wimbledon Tennis Championship

The Wimbledon fortnight is one of Britain's best-loved sporting highlights, attracting nearly 400,000 spectators in person and millions of television viewers worldwide. It takes place in June/July on the immaculate grass courts at the All England Club in Wimbledon, southwest London.

Most tickets are allocated by public ballot (obtain an application form by sending a stamped SAE to the Ticket Office, AELTC, PO Box 98, Wimbledon, London SW19 5AE by the end of the previous year). For details, tel: 020-8971 2473; www. wimbledon.org. Around 1,500 tickets are kept back for some courts if you are prepared to camp out the night before, and spare seats are always to be had late-afternoon. Expect to pay around 25p per strawberry if you want to try the strawberries and cream.

Motor Racing

The heart of motor racing worldwide, Britain has produced a number of World Champions, from Mike Hawthorn and Jim Clark to James Hunt, Nigel Mansell, Damon Hill and Lewis Hamilton. The British Grand Prix, the highlight of the British motor racing calendar, is traditionally held at Silverstone, however there are plans to hold it at Donington in the near future. But Britain's race tracks (most notably Brands Hatch and Donington) also host a range of race meetings, from touring cars to powerful single seaters. Rallying is also very popular.

Details of races from the Motor Sports Association, tel: 01753-765 000 or visit www.msauk.org. See also www.brdc.co.uk.

Participant Sports

For information on sports and leisure facilities in each area you can contact the local council's leisure services department. Alternatively, get in touch with Sport England, 3rd Floor, Victoria House, Bloomsbury Square, London WC1B 4SE, tel: 020-7273 1551; www. sportengland.org.

The English Federation of Disability Sport promotes and develops sport for people with disabilities. For further information, contact EFDS, Manchester Metropolitan University, Alsager Campus, Hassall Road, Alsager, Stoke on Trent ST7 2HL, tel: 0161-247 5294; www.efds.co.uk.

Angling

Fishing is Britain's top participant sport, attracting 8 million people. A useful website is www.anglingnews.net/bodies.asp, which lists many British angling clubs.

Golf

Even the most famous clubs are open to the public. St Andrew's, however, is so much in demand that games are subject to a lottery. Courses close to London are generally heavily booked. To find a local course, visit www.uk-golf guide.com. You can book a session, often at a discount, at almost 250 clubs around the UK through www. teeofftimes.co.uk.

Horse Riding

There are plenty of public riding stables in rural areas, but most do not let riders out unaccompanied. Pony trekking is particularly popular on Dartmoor, Exmoor, in the New Forest and in Wales.

For further information and a list of approved riding stables, contact The British Horse Society, Stoneleigh Deer Park, Kenilworth CV8 2XZ, tel: 08701-202 244; www.bhs.org.uk).

Tennis

There are tennis courts in some of Britain's public parks that anyone can use free-of-charge. Contact the Lawn Tennis Association for regional offices and information on clubs and facilities: The Lawn Tennis Association, National Tennis Centre, 100 Priory Lane, Roehampton, London SW15 5JQ, tel: 020-8487 7000; www.lta.org.uk.

Watersports

Britain offers plenty of opportunities to those interested in sailing, particularly on the south coast and around Pembrokeshire, southwest Wales, but also on the lakes and lochs of the north of England and Scotland; Kielder Water, situated in northwest Northumberland, is the largest man-made reservoir in northern Europe with a shoreline of more than 27 miles (43km). The lake offers the opportunity to take part in a variety of watersports (www. kielderwatersc.org). There are excellent facilities for canoeing, windsurfing, jet skiing and boating too on Britain's many inland waters. Cornwall is a popular surfing centre.

There is a National Water Sports Centre at Holme Pierrepont, Nottinghamshire (www.national watersportsevents.co.uk).

SHOPPING

What to Buy

If you are looking for something typically British to take back home, there's a remarkably wide choice.

● **Cloth and wool** An important centre for the cloth and wool industry is Bradford, through which 90 percent of the wool trade passed in the 19th century. The area's many mill shops are a bargain-hunter's paradise where lengths of fabric, fine yarns and fleeces from the Yorkshire Dales can be bought. Some mills give guided tours. The Lakeland Sheep and Wool Centre in Cockermouth, Cumbria, hosts excellent daily sheep shows and sells high-quality goods.

● **Suits** The flagship of Britain's bespoke tailoring industry is Savile Row in London where gentlemen come from all over to have their suits crafted. Other outlets for traditional British attire are Burberry's (for raincoats and more), Aquascutum, Austin Reed and Jaeger which have branches in Oxford Street and Regent Street in London and in many department stores in other cities.

● **Fashion** Britain has a thriving fashion market, with its heart in London. Its top designers (including Caroline Charles, Jasper Conran, Katharine Hamnett, Bruce Oldfield, Stella McCartney, Paul Smith and Vivienne Westwood) are the height of haute couture and world-famous. Many top international designers can also be found in London's Knightsbridge and Mayfair, and to a lesser extent in department stores nationwide. For quality everyday clothing Marks & Spencer's stores retain their popularity. Mulberry is famous for its leather accessories, from personal organisers to weekend bags, all embossed with the classic tree logo.

● **China and porcelain** Top-price china, glass and silver items can be found in Regent Street and Mayfair in London at exclusive shops such as Thomas Goode, Asprey and Garrard. Stoke-on-Trent (in "the Potteries", Staffordshire) was the home of the great china and porcelain houses, including Wedgwood and Royal Doulton, Minton, Spode and Royal Stafford (www.thepotteries.org). Wedgwood still exists and has a visitor centre where you can often pick up some real bargains. You can also visit Dartington Crystal at Great Torrington in Devon.

● **Jewellery** The centre for British jewellery production is in Hockley, Birmingham, an industry that developed here in the 18th century along with other forms of metal working such as brass-founding and gun-smithing. Today hundreds of jewellery manufacturers and silversmiths are based here.

● **Perfumes** English flower perfumes make a delightful gift. The most exclusive of these come from Floris in Jermyn Street, and Penhaligons in Covent Garden, London. The Cotswold Perfumery in the picturesque village of Bourton-on-the-Water, Gloucestershire, makes its own perfumes.

● **Antiques** If you are coming to Britain to look for antiques it is worth getting in touch with the London and Provincial Antique Dealers' Association (LAPADA), 535 King's Road, London, SW10, tel: 020-7823 3511. It runs a computer information service on the antiques situation throughout the country. A number of antiques fairs are held nationwide throughout the year and many towns such as Bath, Harrogate and Brighton have antique centres and markets.

● **Consumables** British delights that are easy to take home include Twinings or Jacksons tea and numerous brands of chocolate.

Bendicks is famous for its after-dinner mints, Thornton's produces fine confectionery made from fresh ingredients while, on a more popular level, Cadbury's is a national favourite.

Britain is particularly proud of its conserves, jams, honeys, pickles and mustards (not least the famous anchovy spread, Gentleman's Relish). Local delicatessens and farm shops nationwide are often worth exploring for edible gifts. Some regional specialities to look out for include: Cornish pasties and saffron buns, Bakewell tarts (correctly termed puddings), Eccles cakes, Kendal mint cake and Yorkshire parkin, a type of gingerbread.

For Britain's food at its finest, visit Fortnum & Mason, 181 Piccadilly, London W1, an Aladdin's cave of mouthwatering goodies.

● **Crafts** Almost every town has a weekly street market where cheap clothes and domestic ware can be bought and there may also be a good presence of local crafts. There are many workshops in rural areas of Britain where potters, woodturners, leatherworkers, candlemakers and other craftspeople can be seen producing their wares. A free map can be obtained from the Crafts Council, 44a Pentonville Road, London N1, tel: 020-7806 2500.

● **Books** London's Charing Cross Road has long been the centre for

ABOVE: designer shoes for sale.

secondhand and specialist bookshops, though there are fewer these days than there used to be. Waterstones branches nationwide are popular, and Foyles in London has five crammed floors.

Outside London, university towns are the best source of books. Blackwells in Oxford and Cambridge is equally good for publications in English and most prominent foreign languages. Serious book lovers should head for Hay-on-Wye, on the border of England and Wales (see page 253); it has more than 30 bookshops and also hosts a lively literary festival, with top-notch guests, in late May (www.hayfestival.com).

● **Gifts** Some of the best places to seek out tasteful presents to take home are museum gift shops (especially the ones at London's British Museum and the Victoria and Albert Museum) and the shops on National Trust properties.

Markets and Boot Sales

Many towns have regular open-air farmers' markets. Some in the south have French markets when French traders cross the Channel to sell their fresh produce.

London has several traditional markets which have become tourist attractions over the years:

● **Camden Market**, NW1. Hugely popular at the weekends, this sprawling market near Camden Lock sells clothes, jewellery, arts and crafts, food and antiques.

● **Columbia Road Flower Market**, E2. Cut flowers and houseplants are sold here at wholesale prices on Sundays, 8am–2pm. Other specialist shops on Columbia Road open to coincide with the market.

● **Petticoat Lane**, Middlesex Street, E1. London's oldest market is so-named for the undergarments and lace once sold here by French Huguenots. Cheap clothes, fabrics and leather goods are still sold here on some of the 1,000 stalls.

● **Portobello Road**, W11. Renowned for its antiques, this is also a good place to pick up fashionable and vintage clothing, art and general bric-a-brac. It gets very crowded on Saturdays, but has a buzzing atmosphere.

● **Spitalfields**, Commercial Street, E1. This historic covered market has been gentrified with cafés and boutiques, but remains a great place to spot new talent, as many young fashion and jewellery designers sell their wares here. Music, vintage clothing, organic food and childrenswear are sold too.

A phenomenon all over Britain is the weekend **boot sale**, held in out-of-town fields or disused airfields. Participants sell all kinds of household goods – and junk – from the boot (trunk) of their car. In America, it would be known as a massive tag sale, and has the same friendly atmosphere. Some venues have hundreds of pitches.

Export Procedures

VAT (value added tax) is a sales tax of 17.5 percent (reduced to 15 percent during 2009) that is added to nearly all goods except food (excluding that in restaurants), books and children's clothes. It is generally included in the price marked on the item. Most large department stores and smaller gift shops operate a scheme to refund this tax to non-European visitors (Retail Export Scheme), but often require that more than a minimum amount (usually £50) is spent.

For a refund you need to fill in a form from the store, have it stamped by Customs on leaving the country and post it back to the store or hand it in to a cash refund booth at the airport. If you leave the country with the goods within three months of purchase you will be refunded the tax minus an administration fee.

A – Z

A HANDY SUMMARY OF PRACTICAL INFORMATION, ARRANGED ALPHABETICALLY

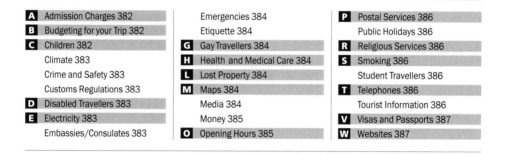

A dmission Charges

The major national museums and galleries, such as the British Museum, National Gallery, Imperial War Museum and the various Tate galleries, are free, but if there is a special exhibition you will have to pay a charge. Some municipal museums are free; others make a charge. A comprehensive website is www.24hourmuseum.org.uk.

The Great British Heritage Pass (www.britishheritagepass.com), which can be bought only outside the UK, gives entry to nearly 600 attractions; the cost of a 15-day pass would work out at less than £4 a day. This includes stately homes and gardens run by the National Trust and English Heritage. Passes to cover only the properties of one of these bodies can be bought through www.visitbritaindirect.com.

If you're planning to visit a lot of attractions in the capital, it's worth looking at www.londonpass.com; prices start at £70 (adult) or £40 (child) for one day, but six-day passes are better value. Note that they don't cover some pricey attractions such as Madame Tussauds and the London Dungeon.

B udgeting for Your Trip

Due to changes in exchange rates, England is currently offering better value for those visitors coming from the euro-zone and North America. However, it can still be an expensive destination to visit: not just accommodation (which is particularly pricey in London), but also food, drink, transport and entry to attractions. Even after you have paid for your accommodation you should probably allow around £60 per day if you're eating out and visiting attractions. However, you can save substantial sums of money by purchasing passes from English Heritage/the National Trust, if you're touring and intend to visit historic sights. And London also has many free attractions that are well worth seeking out: the tourist board will have information.

C hildren

For ideas on museums and other attractions suitable for children of various ages, see *Top Attractions for Families, page 8.*

Accommodation. Some hotels do not accept children under a certain age, so be sure to check when you book. Most restaurants accept well-behaved children, but only those that want to encourage families have children's menus and nappy-changing facilities. Only pubs with a Children's Certificate can admit children, and even these will usually restrict the hours and areas open to them. Publicans, like restaurateurs, reserve the right to refuse entry.

Public transport. Up to four children aged 11 or under can travel free on London's Underground if accompanied by a ticket-holding adult. Eleven–13-year-olds can get unlimited off-peak travel for £1 per day or "Kids for a Quid" single fares if travelling with an electronic Oyster card-holding adult, as can 14–15-year-olds providing they have a photo Oyster card (this can take up to two weeks to obtain and you need to be an EU national).

Buses are free for all children under 16, but 14–15-year-olds will need a 14–15 Oyster photocard. Buses can take up to two unfolded pushchairs (buggies) at one time (they

CLIMATE CHART

London

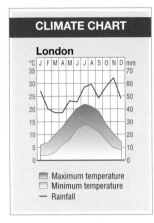

■ Maximum temperature
□ Minimum temperature
— Rainfall

must be parked in a special area halfway down the bus). Any further pushchairs must be folded.

Supplies. Infant formula and nappies (diapers) can be found in chemists (pharmacies) and supermarkets.

Hospitals. In a medical emergency, take your child to the Accident & Emergency department of the nearest hospital. If you require over-the-counter medications such as Calpol (liquid paracetamol) late at night in London, Bliss Pharmacy (5 Marble Arch; tel: 7723 6116) is open until midnight every day.

Climate

In a word, unpredictable. In a few words, temperate and generally mild. It is unusual for any area in the British Isles to have a dry spell for more than three weeks, even in the summer months from June to September. However, it rains most frequently in the mountainous areas of north and west Britain where temperatures are also cooler than in the south.

In summer, the average maximum temperature in the South of England is in the 70s Fahrenheit (23–25°C), although over 80°F (27°C) is not unusual, especially in London. During the winter (November to February) the majority of Britain, with the exception of mountainous regions in the North, tends to be cold and damp rather than snowy.

For recorded weather information, tel: 0871-200 3985 or visit www.metoffice.org.

What to Wear

Temperatures can fluctuate considerably from day to day so come prepared with suitable warm- and wet-weather clothing whatever the

season. Generally, short sleeves and a jacket are fine for summer but a warm coat and woollens are recommended for winter.

On the whole the British tend to dress casually and with a few exceptions formal dress is not essential, although a jacket and tie is required by smart hotels, restaurants and clubs.

The young are particularly style-conscious and as a consequence there is a strong presence of trendy street fashion in Britain's cities. At the other end of the scale, the British reputation for conservative and traditional clothing such as waxed jackets, tweeds, woollen jumpers, cords and brogues is still evident, especially in rural areas.

Crime and Safety

Serious crime is low, but in big cities the Dickensian tradition of pickpocketing is alive and well. Hold on tightly to purses, do not put wallets in back pockets, and do not place handbags on the ground in busy restaurants. Gangs of professional thieves target the Tube in London.

In a genuine emergency, dial 999 from any telephone (no cash required). Report routine thefts to a police station (address under Police in a telephone directory). The threat of terrorism has led to an increase in police patrols and heightened security at airports and major train stations, so don't hesitate to report any suspicious packages.

Customs Regulations

If you enter the UK directly from another European Union (EU) country, you no longer need to exit Customs through a red or green channel – use the special EU blue channel, as you are not required to declare any goods you have brought in for personal use. However, if you bring in large amounts of goods such as alcohol, tobacco or perfume you may be asked to verify that they are not intended for resale.

Visitors entering the UK from non-EU countries should use the green Customs channel if they do not exceed the following allowances for goods obtained outside the EU, or purchased duty-free in the EU, or on board ship or aircraft:

● **Tobacco** 200 cigarettes or 100 cigarillos or 50 cigars or 250g of tobacco
● **Alcohol** 4 litres still table wine plus 1 litre spirits (over 22 percent by volume) or 2 litres fortified wine, sparkling wine or other liqueurs.

● **Gifts** £340 worth of gifts, souvenirs or other goods, including perfume.

It is illegal to bring animals, certain drugs, firearms, obscene material and anything likely to threaten health or the environment without prior arrangement. Any amount of currency can be brought in.

For further information contact **HM Customs and Excise**, New Kings Beam House, 22 Upper Ground, London, SE1 9PJ; tel: 0845-010 9000; www.hmrc.gov.uk.

D isabled Travellers

Details of transport access for disabled people can be found on a government website, www.dft.gov.uk/transportforyou/access.

www.artsline.org.uk is a disability access website providing searchable information on over 1,000 arts venues across London.

Toilets: Britain has a system of keys to open many of the public toilets available for disabled people. To obtain a key, contact RADAR on 7250 3222, www.radar.org.uk. There is a charge of £3.50 (plus value-added tax – VAT) for the key and £10.25 (including post and packing) for the guidebook detailing their locations.

E mbassies and Consulates

Most countries have diplomatic representation in London (a selection is given below). Others can be found through the Yellow Pages or by calling Directory Enquiries.

Australia, Australia House, Strand, London WC2 4LA, tel: 020-7379 4334; www.australia.org.uk.
Canada, 1 Grosvenor Square, London W1K 4AB, tel: 020-7258 6600; www.dfait-maeci.gc.ca/canadaeuropa.
India, India House, Aldwych, London WC2 4NA, tel: 020-7836 8484; www.hcilondon.org.
New Zealand, 80 Haymarket, London SW1Y 4TQ, tel: 020-7930 8422; www.nzembassy.com.
South Africa, South Africa House, Trafalgar Square, London WC2N 5DP, tel: 020-7451 7299; www.southafrica house.com.
United States, 24 Grosvenor Square, London W1A 1AF, tel: 020-7499 9000; www.usembassy.org.uk.

Electricity

230 volts. Square, three-in plugs are used, and virtually all visitors will need adaptors if planning to plug in their own equipment.

TRANSPORT
ACCOMMODATION
EATING OUT
ACTIVITIES
A – Z

Emergencies

Only in an absolute emergency call 999 for fire, ambulance or police. In the case of a minor accident or illness, take a taxi to the nearest casualty department of a hospital. For non-urgent calls to the police in London, dial 0300 123 1212; outside the capital, ask Directory Enquiries *(see Telecommunications entry below)* for the number of the nearest police station. They will also be able to give you the telephone number of your country's embassy or consulate if needed.

Etiquette

England is far less formal and stuffy than many people imagine – you will not, for example, see people shaking hands all the time or wearing bowler hats, and hardly any men wear ties these days. However queue jumping is still frowned upon (it goes against the innate English sense of "waiting your turn") and people appreciate the use of "please" and "thank you", whether you're purchasing items in a shop or asking for directions. Many travellers loathe having to listen to the noise of someone else's music leaking through earphones (so turn the sound down) or sitting next to people consuming smelly food. Make sure you always stand on the right when on the escalators on the tube in London, the left side is for those who are in a hurry and are walking. Casual dress is accepted in most places, but a few restaurants still expect men to wear a jacket, so check if you're booking somewhere upmarket.

G ay and Lesbian Travellers

With Europe's largest gay and lesbian population, London has an abundance of bars, restaurants and clubs to cater for most tastes. Many of them will make space for one or more of London's free gay weekly magazines, *Boyz*, the *Pink Paper*, and *QX*. Monthly magazines on sale at newsstands include *Gay Times*, *Diva* and *Attitude*.

Two established websites for meeting other gay people in London are www.gaydar.co.uk and the female version, www.gaydargirls.com. Other websites reflecting Britain's gay scene include www.rainbownetwork.com and www.outuk.com.

Useful telephone contacts for advice and counselling include **London Lesbian and Gay Switchboard** (tel: 020-7837 7324)

and **London Friend** (7.30–10pm, tel: 020-7837 3337). Support and advice about legal issues concerning HIV and Aids is available from the **National Aids Helpline** (tel: 0800-567 123).

H ealth and Medical Care

If you fall ill and are a national of the EU, you are entitled to free medical treatment. Many other countries also have reciprocal arrangements for free treatment. Most other visitors have to pay for medical and dental treatment and should ensure they have adequate health insurance.

In the case of minor accidents, your hotel will know the location of the nearest hospital with a casualty department. Self-catering accommodation should have this information, plus the number of the local GP, on a notice in the house. **Treatment:** Seriously ill visitors are eligible for free emergency treatment in the Accident and Emergency departments of National Health Service hospitals. However, if they are admitted to hospital as an in-patient, even from the accident and emergency department, or referred to an out-patient clinic, they will be asked to pay unless they fall into the above exempted categories.

Walk-in clinics: There are many National Health Service walk-in centres across the country, usually open seven days a week from early morning to late evening, 365 days a year. A charge may be made to non-EU nationals.

Chemists (pharmacists): Boots is the largest chain of chemists, with many branches around the country. As well as selling over-the-counter medicines, they make up prescriptions.

Accidents: In the case of a serious accident or emergency, dial **999**.

L ost Property

If you have lost your passport, you must get in touch with your embassy as quickly as possible.

For possessions lost on trains you must contact the station where the train on which you were travelling ended its journey. The same applies if you leave something on a coach. For anything lost on public transport in London, contact the Transport For London Lost Property Office, 200 Baker Street, NW1 5RZ, tel: 020-7486 2496, fax: 020-7918 1028, from 9.30am–2pm, Mon–Fri, or fill in an enquiry form, available from any London Underground station or bus garage. Leave at least three full

working days after the loss before visiting the lost property office.

M aps

Insight Guides' best-selling *FlexiMaps* are laminated for durability and easy folding and contain clear cartography as well as practical information. British titles include *London, Cornwall, the Cotswolds, Edinburgh* and the *Lake District*.

In London, map lovers should head for Stanford's (12–14 Long Acre, in the Covent Garden area), one of the world's top map and guidebook stores.

Media

Newspapers

With more than 100 daily and Sunday newspapers published nationwide, there's no lack of choice in Britain. Although free from state control and financially independent of political parties, many nationals do have pronounced political leanings. Of the quality dailies *The Times* and *The Daily Telegraph* are on the right, *The Guardian* and *The Independent* in the middle. On Sunday *The Observer* leans slightly left of centre, while the *Independent on Sunday* stands in the middle and the *Sunday Times* and *Sunday Telegraph* are on the right.

The Financial Times is renowned for the clearest, most unbiased headlines in its general news pages, plus exhaustive financial coverage.

The mass-market papers are a less formal, easy read. *The Sun, The Star* and *News of the World* (out on Sunday) are on the right and obsessed with the Royal family, soap operas and sex. *The Mirror, Sunday Mirror* and *Sunday People* are slightly left. In the mid-market sector, the *Daily Mail* and *Mail on Sunday* are slightly more upscale equivalents of the *Express* and *Sunday Express*.

Some cities have free newspapers, paid for by advertising and often handed out at railway stations.

Listing Magazines

To find out what's on in London, the long-established weekly *Time Out* (out on Wednesdays) is supreme. But Saturday's *The Guardian* includes a good free supplement previewing the week ahead and there are daily listings in the *Evening Standard*.

For details of events elsewhere, the quality daily newspapers have a limited listings section, but your best port of call is a Tourist Information Centre *(see page 386)*. Many local

ABOVE: roadside wall post boxes are common in rural districts.

papers have a weekly section on Fridays with details of places to visit and things to do in their area. Two websites to try are: www.timeout.com and www.bbc.co.uk.

Foreign Newspapers

These can usually be found in large newsagents and railway stations nationwide. Branches of W.H. Smith, in larger towns, usually have a reasonable selection.

Television

Britain has a somewhat outdated reputation for broadcasting some of the finest television in the world. There are five national terrestial channels: BBC1, BBC2, ITV, Channel 4 (C4) and Five. Both the BBC (British Broadcasting Corporation) and ITV (Independent Television) have regional stations that broadcast local news and varying programme schedules in between links with the national networks based in London (see local newspapers for listings). The BBC is financed by compulsory annual television licence fees and therefore does not rely on advertising for funding. The independent channels, ITV, C4 and Five are funded entirely by commercials.

BBC1, ITV and Five broadcast programmes aimed at mainstream audiences, while BBC2 and C4 cater more for cultural and minority interests. However, the advent of cable and satellite channels has forced terrestrial stations to fight for audiences with a higher incidence of programmes such as soap operas and game shows. Both the BBC and ITV also have satellite channels.

There are hundreds of cable and satellite channels on offer, ranging from sport and films to cartoons and music. Pricier hotel rooms often offer a choice of cable stations, including CNN and BBC News Channel.

Radio Stations

As well as the sample of national services listed below – note that frequencies may vary in different parts of the country – there is a wide range of local radio stations which are useful for traffic reports.

BBC Radio 1 98.8FM
Britain's most popular radio station, which broadcasts mainstream pop.

BBC Radio 2 89.2FM
Easy-listening music and chat shows.

BBC Radio 3 91.3FM
24-hour classical music, plus some drama.

BBC Radio 4 93.5FM
News, current affairs, plays.

BBC Radio Five Live 909MW
Rolling news and sport.

BBC World Service 648kHz
International news.

Classic FM 100.9 FM
24-hour classical and movie music unpompously presented.

Absolute Radio 105.8FM
Middle-of-the-road rock music.

Kiss FM 100FM
24-hour dance.

Money

Most banks open between 9.30am and 4.30pm Monday–Friday, with Saturday morning banking common in shopping areas. The majority of branches have automatic teller machines (ATM) where international credit or cashpoint cards can be used, in conjunction with a personal number, to withdraw cash.

The major banks offer similar exchange rates, so it's worth shopping around only if you have large amounts of money to change. Banks charge no commission on travellers' cheques presented in sterling. If a bank is affiliated to your own bank at home, it will make no charge for cheques in other currencies either. But there is a charge for changing cash into British currency.

Some high-street travel agents, such as Thomas Cook, operate *bureaux de change* at comparable rates. There are also many privately run *bureaux de change* (some of which are open 24 hours a day) where exchange rates can be low but commissions high.

Currency: Pounds, divided into 100 pence. Exchange rates against the US dollar and the euro can fluctuate wildly.

Euros: A few shops, services, attractions and hotels accept euro notes, but give change in sterling. Most will charge a commission.

Credit cards: International credit cards are accepted in most shops, hotels and restaurants.

Tipping

Most hotels and restaurants automatically add a 10–15 percent service charge to your meal bill. It's your right to deduct this amount if you're not happy with the service. Sometimes when service has been added, the final total on a credit card slip is still left blank, the implication being that a further tip is expected: you do not have to pay this. You don't tip in pubs, cinemas or theatres, but it is customary to give hairdressers, sightseeing guides, railway porters and cab drivers an extra amount of around 10 percent.

O pening Hours

Town centre shops generally open 9am–5.30pm Mon–Sat, although a few smaller shops may close for lunch in rural areas. Many small towns and villages have a half-day closing one day in the week and shopping centres in towns and cities are likely to have at least one evening of late-night shopping. Increasing numbers of shops are open on Sunday, usually 10am–4pm.

Supermarkets tend to be open 8 or 8.30am–8 to 10pm Mon–Sat and 10 or 11am–4pm on Sunday, and some branches of the larger stores are experimenting with all-night opening on certain days of the week (often Thursday or Friday night). Some local corner shops and off-licences (shops licensed to sell alcohol to be consumed off the premises) stay open until 10pm. However, there are proposals to ban off-licences and supermarkets selling alcohol to under-21s in an effort to curb binge drinking.

Most offices operate 9am–5.30pm Mon–Fri with an hour for lunch.

British pubs' opening hours vary due to flexible closing times granted by an extended opening hours licence. Some have a 24-hour opening licence. Some may close for periods during the day, while others may just apply for the extended opening hours licence for special events such as New Year's Eve.

P ostal Services

Post offices are open 9am–5.30pm Monday–Friday, and 9am–12.30pm on Saturday. London's main post office is in Trafalgar Square, behind the church of St Martin-in-the-Fields, It is open Monday–Friday until 6.30pm, until 5.30 pm on Saturday.

Stamps are sold at post offices, selected shops and newsagents, some supermarkets and from machines outside larger post offices. There is a two-tier service for mail within the UK: first class should reach its destination the next day, and second class will take a day longer. The rate to Europe for standard letters is the same as first-class post within Britain.

Mail can be forwarded to you at any post office in Britain if it is addressed c/o Poste Restante. More information at www.postoffice.co.uk.

R eligious Services

Although Christians, according to census returns, constitute about 71 percent of the population, half never attend church, so visitors will have no trouble finding a place in a pew. All the major varieties of Christianity

Public Holidays

Compared to most of Europe, the UK has few public holidays:
January New Year's Day (1)
March/April Good Friday, Easter Monday
May May Day (first Monday of the month), Spring Bank Holiday (last Monday)
August Summer Bank Holiday (last Monday)
December Christmas Day (25), Boxing Day (26).

On public holidays, banks and offices are closed, though most shops are open (except on Christmas Day). Roads are often a nightmare as people head for the coast or the countryside or to see relatives.

are represented. Britain is a multi-faith society and other main religions, including Buddhism, Hinduism, Judaism, Islam and Sikhism, are freely practised. About 23 percent of Britons follow no particular religion.

S moking

Smoking is banned in all enclosed public spaces, including pubs, clubs and bars (though not in outside beer gardens).

Student Travellers

International students can obtain various discounts at attractions, on travel services (including Eurostar) and in some shops by showing a valid ISIC card. www.isiccard.com

T elephones

It is usually cheaper to use public phones rather than those in hotel rooms as hotels make high profits out of this service.

British Telecom (BT) is the main telephone operating company and provides public telephone kiosks. Some public phones take coins only, some plastic phone cards and/or credit cards, and some all three. Phone cards can be bought from post offices and newsagents in varying amounts between £1 and £20.

Public telephone boxes are not as ubiquitous as they used to be. Now that so many people have mobile phones, they are not considered essential. Stations and shopping centres in particular are good places to look for them. In country areas, try a pub.

The most expensive time to use the telephone is 8am–6pm weekdays, while the cheapest is after 6pm on weekdays and all weekend. Calls are charged by distance, so a long-distance conversation on a weekday morning can eat up coins or card units in a phone box.

Numbers beginning with the prefixes 0800, 0500, 0321 or 0808 are freephone lines. Those prefixed by 0345, 0645 or 0845 are charged at local rates irrespective of distance. Those starting with 0891, 0839, 0640, 0660 and 0898 are costly.

The Directory Enquiries service, once exclusively a BT money-earner, was opened up to competition from other companies and the result was a confusing variety of expensive numbers such as 118500 or

Time Zone

Greenwich Mean Time (GMT) is 1 hour behind Continental European Time, 5 hours ahead of Eastern Seaboard Time, and 9 hours behind Sydney, Australia. British Summer Time (GMT + one hour) runs from late March to late October.

118118. A better bet is to use British Telecom's online service, www.192.com.
Cellphones: You can buy pay-as-you-go SIM cards from most mobile phone retailers and many electrical stores. If your mobile phone accepts SIM cards from companies other than the one you usually use it with, you should be able to register the SIM and use it during your trip.

Useful Numbers
Emergencies 999
Operator 100
Directory Enquiries (UK) 118 500, 118 888 or 118 811
International Directory Enquiries 118 505, 118 866 or 118 899
International Operator 155

Tourist Information

Visit Britain (formerly The British Tourist Authority) has offices worldwide. Visit www.visitbritain.com or write to request information.
Australia
Level 16, Gateway, 1 Macquarie Place, Sydney, NSW 2000
Tel: 02-9377 4400
Fax: 02-9377 4499
Canada
5915 Airport Road, Suite 120 Mississauga, Ontario, L4V 1T1
Tel: 1888-VISITUK
Fax: 905-405 1835
New Zealand
17th Floor, NZI House, 151 Queen Street, Auckland 1
Tel: 9-303 1446
Fax: 9-377 6965
Singapore
01-00 GMG Building, 108 Robinson Road, Singapore 068900
Tel: 65-6227 5400
Fax: 65-6227 5411
South Africa
PO Box 41896, Lancaster Gate Hyde Park Lane, Hyde Park, 2196
Tel: 11-325 0343
Fax: 2711-325 0344
USA – Chicago
625 N. Michigan Avenue, Suite 1001, Chicago, IL 60611
Tel: 1-800-462 2748

USA – Los Angeles
Office not open to the public
Tel: 310-470-2782
Fax: 310-470-8549
USA – New York
7th Floor, 551 Fifth Avenue, New York, NY 10176-0799
Tel: 1-800-GO 2 BRIT or 212-986 2266

Tourist Information in London

British Travel Centre Britain and London Visitor Centre, 1 Regent Street, Piccadilly Circus, London SW1Y 4NS; www.visitbritain.com.
Lastminute.com offer a booking service for theatre tickets and accommodation throughout Britain. Tickets for rail, air and sea travel and sightseeing tours can be bought from the travel agency desk. The centre also has an internet lounge and a currency exchange bureau. The centre is open 9.30am–6.30pm Mon, 9am–6.30pm Tue–Fri and 10am–4pm weekends (during summer it is open 9am–5pm Sat).
Visit London Britain and London Visitor Centre, 1 Regent Street, Piccadilly Circus, London SW1Y 4NS; www.visitlondon.com.
Transport for London Travel Information (Tfl) publishes various maps and guides for visitors – available from Heathrow underground station, Victoria and Euston mainline stations (main concourse). London Bridge and Hammersmith have bus information centres. For further information, tel: 020-7222 1234.

Information Centres

There are more than 800 Tourist Information Centres (TICs) throughout Britain, which provide free information and advice on local sights, activities and accommodation. Most are open office hours, which are extended to include weekends and evenings in high season or in areas where there is a high volume of visitors all year round. Some close from October to March. TICs are generally well-signposted and denoted by a distinctive *i* symbol.

For general information about the whole of the country, contact (by phone or fax only): **The English Tourist Board/British Tourist Authority**, Thames Tower, Black's Road, London W6 9EL, tel: 020-8846 9000, from US tel: 1-800-GO 2 BRIT; fax: 020-8563 0302; email: travelinfo@visitbritain.org; www.visitbritain.com. This site can be used to access information from regional tourist

boards by clicking on the relevant area of the map.

Alternatively, the following are information offices for different regions. You can write or telephone for information, but they are administrative offices only and cannot be visited in person.
East of England Tourist Board, Toppesfield Hall, Hadleigh, Suffolk IP7 5DN, tel: 01473-822 922; fax: 01473-823 063; www.visiteastofengland. com.
London Tourist Board and Convention Bureau, 6th Floor, Glen House, Stag Place, London SW1E 5LT, tel: 020-7234 5800; fax: 020-7932 0222; www.visitlondon.com.
Tourism Southeast, 40 Chamberlayne Road, Eastleigh, Hants SO50 5JH, tel: 02380-625 400; fax: 02380-620 010; www.visitsoutheast england.com.
Southwest Tourism, Woodwater Park, Exeter EX2 5WT, tel: 01392-360 050; fax: 01392-445 112; www. visitsouthwest.co.uk.
Yorkshire Tourist Board, 312 Tadcaster Road, York YO24 1GS, tel: 01904-707 961; fax: 01904-701 414; www.yorkshire.com.
Northumbria Tourist Board, Aykley Heads, Durham DH1 5UX, tel: 0191-375 3000; fax: 0191-386 0899; www. visitnortheastengland.com.
Cumbria Tourist Board, Ashleigh, Holly Road, Windermere LA23 2AQ, tel: 01539-444 444; www.golakes.co.uk.
Greater Manchester Tourist Board, Churchgate House, 56 Oxford Road, Manchester M1 6EU; tel: 0161-237 1010; www.visitmanchester.com.
The Mersey Partnership, 12 Princes Parade, Liverpool L3 1BG, tel: 0151-227 2727; www.liverpool.com.

Websites

www.insightguides.com includes comprehensive hotel listings.
www.visitbritain.co.uk The official tourism site, covering just about everything. plus a booking service for flights, travel cards and rail passes.
www.visitlondon.com The capital's official tourist board site, with lots of advice, listings, links, special deals.
www.thisislondon.com Run by the *Evening Standard*; has detailed listings of events.
www.streetmap.co.uk locates the address you type in.
www.24hourmuseum.co.uk has up-to-date information of what UK museums are exhibiting.
www.bbc.co.uk is a gigantic site, particularly useful for news and weather forecasts.
www.guardian.co.uk is one of the best

newspaper websites, especially good on cultural events.

Tour Operators and Travel Agents

The Association of Independent Tour Operators and Travel Agents (AITO) represents Britain's main specialist tour operators, who operate to a code of practice. For details of their members and their specialities contact AITO, 133A St Margaret's Road, Twickenham, tel: 020-8744 9280, www.aito.co.uk

V isas and Passports

To enter the UK you need a valid passport (or any form of official identification if you are an EU citizen). Visas are not needed if you are an American, Commonwealth citizen or EU national (or come from most other European or South American countries). Health certificates are not required unless you have arrived from Asia, Africa or South America.

If you wish to stay for a protracted period or apply to work in Great Britain, contact the **Immigration and Nationality Directorate**. First look at the website: www.ind.homeoffice.gov.uk. The postal address is Croydon Public Enquiry Office (PEO), Lunar House, 40 Wellesley Road, Croydon, CR9 2BY, tel: 0870-606 7766.

W eights and Measures

It's a mess, reflecting Britain's ambivalence about whether it prefers its Imperial past or its European present. So you will fill up a car with litres of fuel (which may be as well since an Imperial gallon is confusingly larger than a US gallon) but roadsigns will direct to your destination in miles. You buy beer by the pint in a pub. A supermarket will sell you a pint of milk, but most other drinks are packaged as litres. In a few controversial cases, greengrocers have been fined for selling vegetables by the pound instead of by the kilo.

The main conversions are:
Kilometres and miles
1 mile = 1.609 kilometres
1 kilometre = 0.621 miles
Litres and gallons
1 gallon = 4.546 litres
1 litre = 0.220 gallons
Kilos and pounds
1 pound = 0.453 kilos
1 kilo = 2.204 pounds

FURTHER READING

Good Companions

Artist's London by David Piper, Fascinating images of London over the ages.

Cider with Rosie by Laurie Lee. Memories of an idyllic youth in Gloucestershire.

The Concise Pepys by Samuel Pepys. A first-hand account of the Great Fire of London and daily life in 17th-century England.

The English: A Portrait of a People by Jeremy Paxman. Semi-serious study of English character.

A Guide through the District of the Lakes by William Wordsworth. Lyrical descriptions of the poet's beloved Lake District.

A History of Britain by Simon Schama. Readable three-volume narrative linked to a BBC series.

Hound of the Baskervilles by Sir Arthur Conan Doyle. Sherlock Holmes and mystery on the moors.

In Search Of England by Michael Wood. English identity considered through a series of intelligent yet accessible historical essays.

Jamaica Inn by Daphne du Maurier. A tale of Cornish "wreckers" who loot shipwrecks.

London: A Concise History by Geoffrey Trease. Good illustrated history.

London: The Biography by Peter Ackroyd. Mammoth work on the great city, seen as a living organism.

Lorna Doone by R.D. Blackmore. The story of a tragic heroine and her lawless family on Exmoor.

Mrs Dalloway by Virginia Woolf. A day-in-the-life of an Edwardian matron in London.

Notes from a Small Island by Bill Bryson. Best-selling comic's walking tour of Britain.

Oliver Twist by Charles Dickens. The classic tale of Victorian pick-pockets in London's East End.

Pride and Prejudice by Jane Austen.

Secret London by Andrew Duncan. Uncovers London's hidden landscape from abandoned Tube stations to the gentlemen's club.

The Literary Guide to London by Ed Glinert. A detailed, street-by-street guide to the literary lives of London.

A Shropshire Lad by A.E. Housman. Poems on the themes of Shropshire country life, and the life of a soldier.

England's Thousand Best Houses by Simon Jenkins. An invaluable guide.

Tilly Trotter by Catherine Cookson. Set in Durham, the story of a girl born into a poor family in Victorian times.

Tour Through the Whole Island of Great Britain by Daniel Defoe.

Underground London: Travels Beneath the City Streets by Stephen Smith.

Vanishing Cornwall by Daphne du Maurier. A perceptive view of the changing face of Cornwall.

Westward Ho! by Charles Kingsley. Heroic tale of West Country seafarers.

Tess of the D'Urbervilles by Thomas Hardy. Rural life and tragedy in the Wessex countryside.

Wuthering Heights by Emily Brontë. Passion and repression on the brooding Yorkshire Moors.

Send Us Your Thoughts

We do our best to ensure the information in our books is as accurate and up-to-date as possible. The books are updated on a regular basis using local contacts, who painstakingly add, amend and correct as required. However, some details (such as telephone numbers and opening times) are liable to change, and we are ultimately reliant on our readers to put us in the picture.

We welcome your feedback, especially your experience of using the book "on the road". Maybe we recommended a hotel that you liked (or another that you didn't) or you came across a great bar or new attraction we missed.

We will acknowledge all contributions, and we'll offer an Insight Guide to the best letters received.

Please write to us at:
**Insight Guides
PO Box 7910
London SE1 1WE**
Or email us at:
insight@apaguide.co.uk

Other Insight Guides

The **Insight Guides** series includes books on *Great Britain, Scotland, Ireland, Edinburgh, London* and *Oxford*, as well as *Best Hotels: Great Britain & Ireland*.

Insight Step by Step *London*, written by local experts, has 20 self-guided walks and tours, and includes a useful full-size fold-out map.

For quick reference, **Insight Smart Guide** *London*, with an A–Z format, suggests hundreds of things to see and do, ranging from architecture and theatre to shopping and pubs.

Insight Fleximaps: are designed to complement our guidebooks. Insight Fleximap *Channel Islands, Cornwall, Cotswolds, Edinburgh, Jersey, Lake District* and *London* combine clear, detailed cartography with a durable laminated finish to give ease of use.

ART & PHOTO CREDITS

Alamy 106, 134, 193, 337
Alnwick Castle 344T, 345
Alton Towers Resort 256T
Ben Barden/Cumbria Tourism 7CL,
292/293
Finn Beales 253
Beamish Museum Ltd. 8TR, 340
David Beatty/APA 274T, 275, 276T,
278R, 279, 280T, 281, 297&T, 298,
303
Bridgeman Art Library 74
British Museum 88R
Britainonview 132, 183, 208,
312TR, 315R, 332, 334/335, 341,
382
Burghley House 266
Cabinet War Room 83
**David Chalmers/Historic Royal
Palaces** 96T
Chester Cathedral 256R, 257T
Collections/John D Beldom 117
Collections/McQuillan & Brown
251, 257
Collections/ Nick Oakes 287
Corbis 40, 46, 67L , 120
Steve Cutner/APA 190/191, 195,
197T, 198, 199, 201, 355
Derby Cathedral 261
Chris Donaghue 126
E.T. Archive 53
Lydia Evans/APA 6/7, 6CR&B, 9BR,
59, 138, 140, 141, 143, 144R, 145,
146L&R, 147T, 206/207, 212&T,
214, 215, 218, 219(all), 220, 221,
223&T, 224(all), 225T, 226&T,
228/229, 234T, 235, 238L, 239T,
240&T, 241, 242, 243, 244L&R,
245&T, 372
Mary Evans PL 24C, 25B, 200
Neil Farrin/AWL Images 7TR
fotoLibra 14/15 , 17L, 157 , 171,
176/177, 227, 248/249 , 253T,
255T, 256L, 316/317, 329
Fotomas 24TR
Glyn Genin/APA 47, 75T, 78T, 79T,
81T, 82T&B, 83T, 86&T, 88L&T, 90R,
91&T, 94T, 96, 97&T, 98, 102, 103T,
104T, 105, 115, 118, 119, 120T,
130T, 131T, 133, 135, 139, 141T,
142, 143T, 144L&T, 146T, 147,
154L&R, 155, 169&T, 170L, 174,
175L, 179, 181T, 185(all), 186&T,
187, 189T, 194, 202, 210, 211,
217L, 258/259, 263, 265R, 266T,
267(all), 278L, 288T
Getty Images 37 , 38, 41, 80B,
124/125, 200T
Mike Guy/V.K. Guy Ltd 271

Tony Halliday 127, 129, 132T, 152,
153T, 156&T, 268/269, 270, 281T,
295, 319, 323R, 324, 326, 327L,
338, 339, 343, 344
Blaine Harrington 111T
**Historic Royal Palaces, Crown
copyright** 104
Robert Hollingworth 225
iStockphoto.com 6TL&CL, 20, 27,
153, 197, 254/255, 388
Michael Jenner 150
Lyle Lawson 25T
LCP/APA 76T, 87T, 90T
Lincoln Cathedral 262
Lincolnshire Tourism 263T, 265L
Manchester City Art Galleries 50
Memorial/The Kobal Collection 39
The Mersey Partnership 284/285,
286
Metropolitan/Design Hotels 355T
National Gallery, London 9TR
National Maritime Museum 30, 34
National Portrait Gallery 26, 135T,
301T, 322T
**Newsteam.co.uk/Historical Royal
Palaces** 8TL&B, 111
NTPL/Joe Cornish 16, 58, 336,
346T
NTPL/Penny Tweedie 184
OSF Photo Library 328T&B
Photolibrary.com 44/45, 121
Pictures Colour Library 21L,
62/63, 181, 250, 260, 264, 288
Andrea Pistolesi 17R
Press Association Images 80T, 196
Mark Read/APA 5, 230, 234, 235T,
236, 237T, 238R, 239, 241T, 243T,
244T, 246
William Shaw/APA 7CR, 54,
64/65, 67BR, 272, 273, 274,
276, 277&T, 280, 282, 283&T,
290, 291L&R, 299&T, 300&T, 301,
302&T, 304, 305L&T, 308/309,
310, 314&T, 315L, 321, 322B,
323L, 327R, 332R, 351, 364
Peter Smith/St Paul's Cathedral
92, 93
Tom Smyth/APA 375, 385
**Sir John Soane's Museum/Martin
Charles** 89T
Richard Sowersby/Rex Features
148/149
Starwood 357
Homer Sykes 377
Ray Tang/Rex Features 49
Ming Tang-Evans/APA 3B, 4T&B,
9TL&BL, 21R, 55, 56L&R, 66, 72,
73, 75, 76, 77, 78, 79L&R, 81, 84,

85&T, 87, 89L&R, 90L, 94, 95, 100,
101, 103, 107, 108, 109, 110, 350,
353, 367, 368, 381
Tips Images 7BL
Topham Picturepoint 34, 51, 52,
134T, 182T, 247L&R, 289, 318, 346
Bill Wassman 209, 216
Andrew Wiard/reportphotos.com
105T
Roger Williams 348
Dave Willis/Cumbria Tourism 294
Corrie Wingate/APA 2/3, 7BR,
10/11, 12/13, 18, 19, 57, 60/61,
67TR, 112/113, 114, 119T, 130,
133T, 136/137, 158/159, 164,
165, 170R, 172, 173, 175R, 178,
188, 189, 192, 203, 231, 360
Phil Wood/APA 213, 216T, 217R,
218T, 233, 237, 311, 312B&TL,
313, 325&T, 330, 331&T, 332T,
333L&R
World Pictures/Photoshot 48
Crispin Zeeman 160, 161, 162,
163, 164T, 166, 167, 170T

PICTURE SPREADS

42/43: Blenheim Palace 42/43;
iStockphoto.com 42BL&BR, 43TR,
CL&BR; **Redbrick Communications
Ltd** 43BL
122/123: Country Life 122/123,
123BL&BR; **fotoLibra** 122BL&CR,
123CL&TR; **Pictorial Press** 122C
204/205: Britainonview 204BL,
205CL; **Country Life** 204/205;
fotoLibra 204BR; **Tony Halliday**
205BR; **iStockphoto.com** 205BL
306/307: Mark Cator/Impact
307BR; **Adam Davy/Empics**
306BC; **Ben Edwards/Impact**
306BR; **Mary Evans** 306TL&BL,
307TR; **Michael Jenner** 307BL;
John Marsh/Empics 307CR; **Tony
Page/Impact** 306/307

Maps of London reproduced by permission of
Geographers' A–Z Map Co. Ltd. Licence No. B4642
© Copyright 2009. All rights reserved.
Licence number 100017302

Map Production:
original cartography - Colourmap
Scanning Ltd.

© 2010 Apa Publications GmbH & Co.
Verlag KG (Singapore branch)

Production: Linton Donaldson

INDEX

Numbers in italics refer to photographs

LONDON'S TOP SITES

WESTMINSTER ABBEY

Features: West Door (**A**); South Aisle (**C**); North Aisle (**D**); Choir (**E**); The Sanctuary (**F**); door to cloisters (**S**); Chapter House (**T**); Chamber of the Pyx (**U**); undercroft or crypt (**V**).
Chapels: St Georges's (**B**); Abbot Islip (**H**); St John the Baptist (**I**); St Paul's (**J**); Henry V's chantry chapel (**K**); Henry V (**L**); Henry VII (**M**); St Nicholas's (**N**); St Edmund's (**O**); St Benedict's (**P**); St Faith's (**R**). **Tombs & Monuments:** British statesmen, in the North Transept (**G**). Poets' Corner, in the South Transept (**Q**)

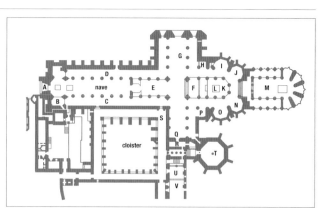

ST PAUL'S CATHEDRAL

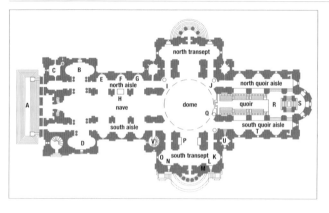

Features: marble steps (**A**); oak pulpit (**Q**); High Altar (**R**); Dean's pulpit and stairs to crypt (**U**); stairs to dome (**V**). **Chapels:** St Dunstan's (**B**); All Souls' (**C**); St Michael & St George's (**D**); American Chapel of Remembrance (**S**). **Tombs & Monuments:** Lord Leighton (**E**); General Gordon (**F**); Viscount Melbourne (**G**); Duke of Wellington (**H**); Joshua Reynolds (**I**); Dr Samuel Johnson (**J**); Admiral Earl Howe (**K**); Admiral Collingwood (**L**); JMW Turner (**M**); Sir John Moore (**N**); General Abercromby (**O**); Lord Nelson (**P**); John Donne (**T**)

TOWER OF LONDON

Entrance (**A**); Lion Tower (**B**); Middle Tower (**C**); Byward Tower (**D**); The Bell Tower (**E**); St Thomas's Tower (**F**); Traitors' Gate (**G**); Bloody Tower (**H**); Wakefield Tower (**I**); King's House (**J**); Gaoler's House (**K**); Tower Green (**L**); Beauchamp Tower (**M**); Royal Chapel of St Peter ad Vincula (**N**); Jewel House (**O**); Regimental Museum (**P**); Hospital (**Q**); New Armouries (**R**); White Tower (**S**); Wardrobe Tower (**T**)

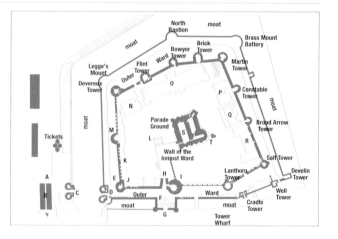

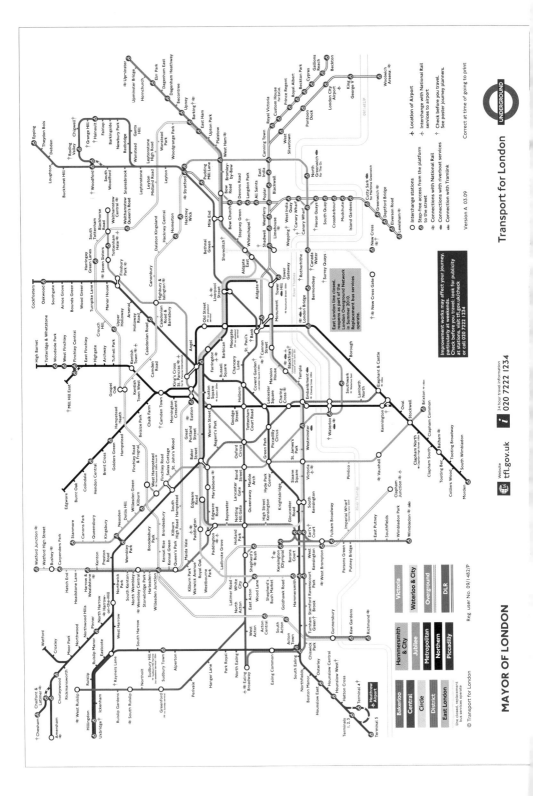

MAYOR OF LONDON

Transport for London

Website tfl.gov.uk

24 hour travel information
020 7222 1234

Reg. user No. 09/1482/P

© Transport for London

UNDERGROUND